MAINE ROADS TO GETTYSBURG

MAINE ROADS
TO GETTYSBURG

How Joshua Chamberlain, Oliver Howard,
and 4,000 Men from the Pine Tree State
Helped Win the Civil War's Bloodiest Battle

TOM HUNTINGTON

STACKPOLE
BOOKS
Guilford, Connecticut

Published by Stackpole Books
An imprint of The Rowman & Littlefield Publishing Group, Inc.
4501 Forbes Boulevard, Suite 200, Lanham, Maryland 20706
www.rowman.com

Distributed by NATIONAL BOOK NETWORK
800-462-6420

British Library Cataloguing in Publication Information Available

Library of Congress Cataloging-in-Publication Data

Names: Huntington, Tom, 1960– author.
Title: Maine roads to Gettysburg : how Joshua Chamberlain, Oliver Howard, and 4,000 men from the Pine Tree State helped win the Civil War's bloodiest battle / Tom Huntington.
Description: Lanham, Maryland : Stackpole Books, an imprint of Globe Pequot, 2018. | Includes bibliographical references and index.
Identifiers: LCCN 2017059147 (print) | LCCN 2017059406 (ebook) | ISBN 9780811767729 | ISBN 9780811718400 (hardcover) | ISBN 9780811767729 (e-book)
Subjects: LCSH: Gettysburg, Battle of, Gettysburg, Pa., 1863. | Maine—History—Civil War, 1861–1865—Regimental histories. | United States—History—Civil War, 1861–1865—Regimental histories. | United States—History—Civil War, 1861–1865—Campaigns. | Chamberlain, Joshua Lawrence, 1828–1914. | Howard, O. O. (Oliver Otis), 1830–1909. | Soldiers—Maine—History—19th century.
Classification: LCC E475.53 (ebook) | LCC E475.53 .H894 2018 (print) | DDC 973.7/349—dc23
LC record available at https://lccn.loc.gov/2017059147

∞™ The paper used in this publication meets the minimum requirements of American National Standard for Information Sciences—Permanence of Paper for Printed Library Materials, ANSI/NISO Z39.48-1992.

Printed in the United States of America

To my parents,
Milton and Lillian Huntington,
for—among many other things—having the
wisdom to make sure I was born and raised
in the great state of Maine.

CONTENTS

List of Maps

ACKNOWLEDGMENTS

I'VE LIVED IN PENNSYLVANIA FOR MORE THAN TWO DECADES NOW, AND my previous books covered soldiers from the commonwealth. For this book, I've symbolically returned to the land of my birth—Maine. If nothing else, the research for *Maine Roads to Gettysburg* provided me with a good excuse to head north and spend some time in the Pine Tree State. Not that I needed an excuse!

During my travels, I made multiple visits to the George J. Mitchell Department of Special Collections & Archives at Bowdoin College's Hawthorne-Longfellow Library, where Marieke Van Der Steenhoven and the rest of the staff were always friendly and helpful. A long, long time ago, when I was a student at Bowdoin, I used to work at the library. Back then, I never dreamed I would be returning to Bowdoin to do research for a book about the Civil War—and a book that included material about one of my fraternity brothers, Joshua Lawrence Chamberlain. (I should point out that Chamberlain and I did not attend Bowdoin at the same time.)

I would also like to thank the people at Bowdoin for the terrific job digitizing the letters of Oliver Otis Howard. Having all that correspondence just a mouse click away made my job a lot easier, even if it did prevent me from spending even more time in Brunswick.

Also in Brunswick, the staff of the Pejepscot Historical Society were welcoming and eager to help. Looking further south, I'd like to thank Leslie L. Rounds of the Dyer Library in Saco and Zoe B. Thomas of the Saco Museum for providing the transcripts for John Haley's unpublished journal notebooks.

Many thanks also to the staff of the Maine State Archives, which has such a great collection of materials. The letters they put up on the web for the Civil War sesquicentennial were a huge help, and I quoted from a lot of them. But that's just the tiniest tip of the iceberg in the files of the Civil War Regimental Correspondence, which includes literally thousands of letters dealing with the creation and maintenance of Maine's Civil War regiments. Before one of my research expeditions to Maine, I neglected to make sure the archives was going to be open during my visit. To my shock and horror, I learned they were closed that week. The staff there has my heartfelt thanks for letting me into the research room nonetheless.

I would like to thank Desiree Butterfield-Nagy in special collections at the Raymond H. Fogler Library at the University of Maine, Orono. I emailed her a list of things I wanted to consult, and when I arrived bright and early on the morning indicated, I found everything sitting on carts waiting for me. It was a great way to start the day.

Thanks to the Fifth Maine Regiment Museum Collection, Peaks Island, Maine, for permission to quote from the John French letters. (The museum, on a scenic island in Casco Bay, is well worth a visit.) Patti Whitten of the Damariscotta Historical Society was also very helpful digging up background about James A. Hall.

Outside of Maine, I remain impressed by the staff and the facility at the Army Heritage Center in Carlisle, Pennsylvania. That's another amazing resource. John Heiser at Gettysburg National Military Park was instrumental in making my visits to the library there productive. In addition, I had fruitful visits to the Hay Library at Brown University (for the Selden Connor letters) and the Sophia Smith Collection at Smith College (the Adelbert Ames papers). The Cumberland County Library System proved invaluable, and my home library in New Cumberland was a great help with interlibrary loans. Support your local library!

I also want to express my appreciation for Andrea Solarz, the great-great-grandaughter of the 6th Maine's Charles Amory Clark, for letting me quote from her ancestor's letters, and to Ron Coddington for helping me get in touch with her.

I would be remiss if I didn't thank everyone at Stackpole Books for all their help and support. Publisher Judith Schnell, another Maine native, gave me the go-ahead for the book, and the crack editorial team—including Dave Reisch and Stephanie Otto—made the whole process flow smoothly. Speaking of smooth, my thanks to copy editor Brett Keener for making my prose less lumpy, saving me from errors, and untangling my thicket of endnotes. I must also thank Charlie Downs for looking over the galleys and saving me from several embarrassing errors. Any that remain are, of course, my responsibility.

On the non-editorial side, thanks most of all to my lovely wife, Beth Ann. Over the past few years, she's seen our summer vacations turn into research expeditions, but she makes sure we have a good time. I could not have written this book without her love and support.

INTRODUCTION

Joshua Chamberlain Returns to Gettysburg

In proportion to the number of her troops in the action, no one of the eighteen states whose regiments flew the stars and stripes on this hard-fought field contributed more than Maine to the victory. At whatever point the battle raged, the sons of the Pine Tree State were in the melee.

— SELDEN CONNOR, OCTOBER 3, 1889

The Maine veterans returned to Pennsylvania in October 1889, 26 years after they had fought at Gettysburg with the Army of the Potomac. For three days in July 1863, the Union troops had withstood the attacks of the Army of Northern Virginia, and they had emerged victorious in what would be the bloodiest battle of the Civil War. When the smoke had cleared, nearly 8,000 soldiers were dead, 27,000 were wounded, and an additional 11,000 were captured or missing. The soldiers who had fought then were now much older, if not always wiser. It was likely that many of them were making their first trip back to the field where they had risked life and limb for the Union cause on a battlefield far from their Maine homes. Unlike so many, they had survived that battle and the war, and now they returned to reminisce, exaggerate, and relive one of the crowning moments of their lives.

The chief reason for this visit was the dedication of monuments to the Maine units that had fought here. The solid stone sentinels, many of them chiseled from Hallowell granite, were intended "to commemorate and perpetuate the conspicuous valor and heroism of Maine soldiers on that decisive battlefield of the war of the rebellion." There were 15 monuments, representing the regiments, batteries, and battalions that had struggled in the epic battle.[1]

The dedication day, October 3, brought perfect autumn weather. The ceremonies began at 9:00 A.M. with a national salute fired from guns on Cemetery Hill, the strategic high ground that Maine native Oliver O. Howard had selected as an ideal defensive position when he arrived there on the first day of battle. After the salute, Governor Edwin C. Burleigh and the state's other Gettysburg commissioners set out to inspect the monuments; accompanying them was Hannibal Hamlin, the Maine Republican who had served as President Abraham Lincoln's first vice president. At each regimental monument, they listened to dedication speeches alongside the men who had fought with that particular unit. "It was the rare pleasure of the company to hear the stories of many exciting scenes of the battle from the lips of narrators, who had also been actors in those scenes," recalled one participant.[2]

That evening a large crowd gathered at the county courthouse for the overall dedicatory ceremonies. Anyone eager to hear the former vice president speak would have been disappointed, because Hamlin's exertions during the day had left the 80-year-old too exhausted to attend. Maj. Greenlief T. Stevens, who had commanded the 5th Maine Battery during the battle—and had the knoll where his battery was posted named after him—called the meeting to order and introduced a speaker who still retained enough energy to talk.

Joshua Lawrence Chamberlain stood to speak. Twenty-six years earlier he had commanded the 20th Maine Volunteer Infantry on the rocky, wooded slopes of Little Round Top, and his soldiers had successfully fought off attack after attack by Confederates from the 15th Alabama Infantry. Later in the war, Chamberlain was severely wounded, shot through both hips during a battle outside Petersburg, Virginia. Chamberlain's wounds were so severe, in fact, that Lt. Gen. Ulysses S. Grant promoted him to brigadier general on the spot, thinking that he couldn't survive. Perhaps they had been mortal wounds—but, if so, they wouldn't kill Chamberlain until more than five decades had passed. In the years after the war, Chamberlain served as governor of Maine and president of his alma mater, Bowdoin College. His Civil War experiences, especially his successful defense of Little Round Top, remained the high point of his life.

Chamberlain was now 61 years old. His hair and drooping mustache had long since turned gray, and his war wounds left him in near-constant discomfort. If anyone had a right to be tired, it was Chamberlain. He had already given a speech that day, when he and other veterans of the 20th Maine had assembled with their wives and others at Little Round Top to dedicate their monument. "You were making history," he told the men who had fought under him. "The centuries to come will share and recognize the victory won here, with growing gratitude. The country has acknowledged your service. Your State is proud of it." After the ceremonies on Little Round Top, the gathering moved west through the woods to pay homage at the spot where the regiment's Company B had been during the fighting, when it had risen up from behind a stone wall at the struggle's climax to pour a volley into the unsuspecting Confederates' flank. Then the group climbed the steep slopes of Big Round Top to dedicate the monument that marked the position the regiment had taken and occupied during the night of July 2. Chamberlain made another short speech there.[3]

Now he had one more speech to make. As he looked out over the faces in the audience, Chamberlain could be excused if he saw ghosts. Not just the spirits of the thousands of Maine men who had died in the war—the victims of shot, shell or, more likely, disease—but also the ghosts of much younger men who had been replaced by the graying veterans staring back at him. After war had broken out in 1861, young men from all over Maine had joined the cause. Many of them felt compelled to do their part to restore the Union. Others felt the stirring of adventure, or the chance to see the world outside their own state. And there were even some who wanted to strike a blow against slavery, the root cause of the war. They came from all walks of life. They were farmers, lumberjacks, fishermen, sailors, students, lawyers, and teachers. For all of them, it's safe to say, their experiences in the war had been transformative. Missing limbs and scars testified to the physical effects, but life as a soldier in the American Civil War left wounds that were harder to see, psychic scars that few people in the nineteenth century understood. Those who were lucky enough to survive returned to their homes and resumed their lives. Now they had come back to this small Pennsylvania town where so much blood had been shed to receive recognition for what they had done and endured.

"The State of Maine stands here to-day for the first time in her own name," Chamberlain told the assembly. For back in 1863, he explained in his usual florid, oratorical style, Maine had fought at Gettysburg as part of a greater whole—the United States of America. "For which great end, in every heroic struggle from the beginning of our history until now—a space of more than two hundred years—she has given her best of heart and brain and poured out her most precious blood." The Union men who fought at Gettysburg, Chamberlain told the gathered veterans, had played a part in a struggle that was much bigger than themselves, greater, even, than their home states. They had fought to preserve their country. That said, Chamberlain couldn't resist extolling the role the Pine Tree State had played during the American Civil War. "[W]herever there was a front, the guns of Maine thundered and her colors stood."

Near the end of his speech, Chamberlain recited a passage that has echoed down through the years, one that is still quoted today. "In great deeds something abides," he said. "On great fields something stays. Forms change and pass; bodies disappear; but spirits linger, to consecrate ground for the vision-place of souls. And reverent men and women from afar, and generations that know us not and that we know not of, heart-drawn to see where and by whom great things were suffered and done for them, shall come to this deathless field, to ponder and dream; and lo! the shadow of a mighty presence shall wrap them in its bosom, and the power of the vision pass into their souls."[4]

One thing that abides at Gettysburg is the reputation of Joshua Lawrence Chamberlain. There's no doubt that he and his men made a courageous and bloody stand on the south flank of Little Round Top on July 2, 1863. When his division commander, Brig. Gen. James Barnes, wrote his official report on the battle, he felt compelled to include a lengthy account of Chamberlain's role. "Colonel Chamberlain, of the Twentieth Maine Volunteers, whose service I have endeavored briefly to describe, deserves especial mention," Barnes wrote. There have been several books written about Chamberlain and his regiment since, including John J. Pullen's *The Twentieth Maine* and Thomas Desjardin's *Stand Firm, Ye Boys From Maine*. Chamberlain told his story quite often, too. Yet there was a time when Chamberlain and his regiment were not widely known, not until novelist Michael Shaara made Chamberlain a centerpiece of his 1974 Pulitzer Prize–winning novel, *The Killer Angels*, which was later adapted as the movie *Gettysburg*. In 1990, documentarian Ken Burns devoted a good deal of time to Chamberlain in his epic documentary *The Civil War*. Suddenly, the Maine colonel was a Civil War celebrity.[5]

Chamberlain's current prominence bothers some historians, who argue over the details of his story or maintain that Little Round Top was not all that vital to the Union victory at Gettysburg. It bothered some of Chamberlain's contemporaries, too. Ellis Spear, who fought on Little Round Top as a major in the 20th Maine, grew tired of the plaudits sent Chamberlain's way, and by Chamberlain's acceptance of them. He called their brigade commander, Strong Vincent, "the true hero of Little Round Top (if any officer is to have that honor)." Writing to the 20th Maine's first commander, Adelbert Ames, in 1913, Spear pointed out that the park road at Little Round Top was not named after Vincent, who was mortally wounded in the fighting. (It was named after Chamberlain.) "'Dead men tell no tales,'" said Spear. "That is left to the living if they desire it, and this thing wears upon my nerves, though I have no personal complaint whatever."[6]

<hr />

Over the years the 20th Maine's fight on Little Round Top has become Gettysburg's *Rashomon*, an event witnessed differently by its various participants. By 1889 Capt. Howard L. Prince, who was acting as the regiment's historian, had to concede that the conflicting accounts made it difficult to determine exactly what had happened during the flurry of action on July 2. "It is not believed to be possible to reconcile all the theories and beliefs of the actors, even in so small a space as the front of a regiment," Prince admitted, "and when we fail, as sometimes we must, we must conclude, that as there is a substantial agreement on the main features of the action, these disputed details were seen from different points, or were viewed at different stages as part of a whole."[7]

None of that dissuades the thousands of people who visit the modest granite monument on Little Round Top. They come to salute Chamberlain and his men, and often leave behind small tributes—notes, pennies, American flags—in honor of the Mainers who fought and died there. Chamberlain's fame even extends out into our solar system. In 2015 he had a rock on Mars named after him. The Red Planet is, of course, named after the Roman god of war.[8]

Chamberlain's fame has also overshadowed the roles other Maine regiments and soldiers played at Gettysburg. You can practically write the story of the three-day battle just by highlighting the roles of Maine units and individuals. Selden Connor, who had been in command of the 7th Maine during the battle and, like Chamberlain, went on to serve as the state's governor, also spoke to the gathered veterans that night in October 1889. "In proportion to the number of her troops in the action, no one of the eighteen states whose regiments flew the stars and stripes on this hard-fought field contributed more than Maine to the victory," he said. "At whatever point the battle raged, the sons of the Pine Tree State were in the melee."[9]

That started with James Hall's 2nd Maine Battery, which fought desperately with the I Corps on July 1, and it continued up to the actions of the 19th Maine Volunteer Infantry on July 3, when it stormed into the "Bloody Angle" on Cemetery Ridge to help repulse Pickett's Charge. The 16th Maine made a valiant stand on the battle's first day; on July 2, the 17th Maine fought in the Wheatfield, the 3rd Maine was in the Peach Orchard, and the 4th Maine made its stand in Devil's Den, at the extreme left of the III Corps' extended line. Later that day, Maine sea captain-turned-artilleryman Freeman McGilvery, from the army's artillery reserve, set up batteries along Cemetery Ridge that kept the attacking Confederates from piercing the Union line. In the words of one artilleryman, McGilvery "was the only field officer who realized and tried to remedy the situation. He was fearless and untiring in keeping the enemy from discovering the widening gap in our line." One of the units McGilvery ordered to hold its position "at all hazards" was Edwin Dow's 6th Maine Battery. Dow later said that McGilvery "was ever present, riding up and down the line in the thickest of the fire, encouraging the men by his words and dashing example, his horse receiving eight wounds, of which he has since died, the gallant major receiving only a few scratches."[10]

Adelbert Ames, the first commander of the 20th Maine and the soldier who taught Joshua Chamberlain the arts of war, led his brigade with the XI Corps on July 1. General Howard, who hailed from Leeds, was at one point the Union's commanding general on the field before being superseded by Winfield Scott Hancock.

After the war, a soldier who had fought with the 19th Maine at Gettysburg heard Chamberlain speak about the 20th Maine's role in the battle. When the talk was over, he went up to Chamberlain. "I see, General, you claim that the 20th Maine saved the day at Gettysburg," he said with some heat.

"Certainly," Chamberlain replied.

"Hitherto," the soldier said, 'I had thought it was the 19th Maine that saved the day there."

"And you thought rightly," Chamberlain told him. "Don't you know that every picket that sticks to the fence may claim the credit of keeping the pigs out of the garden?" The 19th Maine man decided that was "a very simple and sensible explanation."[11]

"We do not claim a monopoly of the glory won on this field," said Charles Hamlin, the son of the former vice president and an assistant adjutant general to Maj. Gen. Andrew Humphreys during the battle, when he addressed his fellow Maine veterans that night at Gettysburg. "But it is with justifiable pride, as we scan the line occupied by the living arch throughout the long three days' contest, we note the pivotal points made memorable by the presence and conspicuous valor of Maine soldiers." While it may be an exaggeration to say that Maine saved the Union at Gettysburg, its soldiers certainly played vital roles in the victory.[12]

"No coward has disgraced the fair name of the Pine Tree State," claimed an early history of Maine's role in the Civil War. Obviously, that's not true. Many brave soldiers from Maine fought in the war, but there were also plenty of men whose courage failed them, as well as shirkers, liars, thieves, and opportunists. There were even two men from Maine, Danville Leadbetter and Zebulon York, who served as generals for the Confederacy. Others born in the Pine Tree State fought as ordinary soldiers for the South.[13]

Abner Small, who wrote two slightly jaundiced accounts of his experiences with the 3rd and 16th Maine regiments, provided one account of the many soldiers to whom "valor" and "glory" were just words. "We had a few—very few—pessimists among us, constitutional growlers, who were, on the opening of every campaign, attacked with a dyspeptic foreboding that defeat and disaster would follow us," Small wrote in his history of the 16th Maine. "With them we always marched too long and marched too fast, but never fast enough to get ahead of their dismal prophecies. They had an ingrained hatred of discipline, cursed red tape by the great gross, and itched with a desire to 'see a live Johnnie and draw a bead on him.' Their desires were never gratified, for the Johnnies seemed to have had an intuitive perception of these ferocious fighters' intentions, and kept out of sight, hence the few casualties in the immediate front of these rascally bummers."[14]

On the other hand, sometimes even the least reputable men found hidden reservoirs of courage on the battlefield, and there were many times when the most steadfast soldiers crumbled under fire. They were human, after all, with all the associated vices and virtues. That's one reason why so many people find the Civil War irresistibly fascinating. Even more than a century and a half later, as we peer back into this chaotic, violent period of our history, we can still see traces of ourselves—the good and the bad—staring back at us.

Whether they enlisted as a lark, to find adventure, see new places, help save their country, or end slavery, the soldiers from Maine—like the soldiers from any state—found that war changed them. Many wrote home to share their experiences, or captured them in memoirs and unit histories after the war. Some of them, such as Joshua Chamberlain, were eloquent. Others could barely spell. But all who wrote about their war felt a need to communicate what they had gone through, whether it was the mind-numbing tedium of winter camp, or the adrenaline-surged rush of battle. People fought the Civil War, and people can be strange, complex, and fascinating creatures.

Take, for example, the experience of Freeman McGilvery on July 2. The story of how this former sea captain threw together an improvised artillery line that helped save the battle has been told before, but who knows about the resentments, recriminations, and accusations that had been swirling about through Maine's artillery units—much of it due to McGilvery's intense desire for promotion? When McGilvery found Edwin Dow and the 6th Maine Battery in the late afternoon of July 2, it must have been an interesting encounter. McGilvery had been actively trying to prevent Dow from getting permanent command of the battery, and had accused him of public drunkenness. Dow had responded by demanding a court-martial for McGilvery. That's what happens when you place ambitious people in high-pressure situations. They rub up against each other and interesting things happen.

The Maine soldiers' roads to Gettysburg had already been long and difficult by the time they reached Pennsylvania in the summer of '63. The nation had been at war for more than two years. Many of the Maine soldiers who fought at Gettysburg had already experienced plenty of combat, as well as weeks and months of tedious camp life between the fights. They carried regimental flags emblazoned with the names of their battles—Gaines' Mill, Glendale, Malvern Hill, Antietam, Fredericksburg, Chancellorsville, and more. Farm boys who had never ventured farther than a few miles from their homes found themselves in Virginia, slogging their way up the Peninsula toward Richmond—and then heading the other way. Many had entered the war thinking it was going to be over fairly quickly, before realizing it was going to be long and bloody, and that the country was going to be transformed before it was over.

Maine owed its very statehood to the sectional tensions that eventually blew up into civil war. The region had belonged to Massachusetts until it entered the Union in 1820 as part of the Missouri Compromise, with Maine becoming a free state and Missouri a slaveholding one. The compromise maintained an uneasy balance between slave and free states, but cracks that would turn into fissures were already starting to break up the nation. In 1855, Maine elected Anson P. Morrill as its governor, the first chief executive from the new Republican Party. That was also the party of an Illinois politician named Abraham Lincoln, and in 1860 Maine's Hannibal Hamlin became Lincoln's running mate and then his vice president. (Had Andrew Johnson not replaced Hamlin for the 1864 election, Maine might have had its first president following Lincoln's assassination.) South Carolina responded to the election of Lincoln, a man "whose opinions and purposes are hostile to Slavery," by announcing its secession from the Union.

When the Confederate attack on Fort Sumter in Charleston Harbor started the war in April 1861, Maine citizens rallied to the Union. "In the glorious uprising that took place no State was in advance of Maine in showing its devotion to the national cause," wrote the authors of the 1865 history *Maine in the War of the Union*. That might not be a completely objective assessment, as the war's passions still burned brightly when the authors published their book in 1865, but it's true that Maine remained largely pro-Union—with some exceptions, of course. For example, in the town of Freedom, a man named Robert Elliot began recruiting his own militia units. State authorities suspected that Elliot planned to use them to resist the Union cause, not support it; they had Elliot arrested and sent to Fort Lafayette, a prison in New York Harbor where the government sent those suspected of disloyalty. Elliot saw the light, swore his allegiance to the United States, and was released on November 7, 1861. In 1863, citizens of the Democratic-leaning town of Kingfield, nestled among the state's western mountains, mounted an attempt to resist the draft. The state sent a company of soldiers to put down the "rebellion," but all ended peaceably.[15]

Those with a more patriotic spirit responded rapidly to President Lincoln's April 1861 call for 75,000 volunteers. Some of them came from Bowdoin College, a small institution in the town of Brunswick. The college had opened in 1802 with only a president, a professor, and eight members of its first freshman class. Although the school grew slowly at first, by the time the war broke out it had established a solid reputation. Future president Franklin Pierce and poet Henry Wadsworth Longfellow had both graduated from Bowdoin in 1825, and the college became known as an "eastern seat of learning." It also furnished a surprising number of soldiers for the Civil War. By the end of the war, "Bowdoin College could claim that a larger percentage of its alumni participated in the war than any other college in the North," wrote historian David K. Thomson.[16]

The most famous Bowdoin alumnus of the Civil War was Joshua Lawrence Chamberlain, but around 290 other graduates became soldiers—and not only for the Union. John Cummings Merrill, class of 1847, was born in Portland but joined the Confederacy as an army surgeon. His brother, Charles (class of 1851), fought for the Union and commanded the 17th Maine at Gettysburg. Arthur McArthur (class of 1850) was another Bowdoin graduate who threw in his lot with the South. He had been Oliver Otis Howard's roommate when they both attended North Yarmouth Academy, where McArthur earned a reputation for his hard drinking. Travels through the South gave him an appreciation for slavery, which he believed was "mutually beneficial to the master & slave." McArthur ended up in Louisiana, and joined one of that state's regiments as a captain. He was killed by a sharpshooter in Winchester, Virginia, in 1864.[17]

Bowdoin influenced the war beyond the battlefield. Harriet Beecher Stowe, the wife of Bowdoin professor Calvin Stowe, wrote *Uncle Tom's Cabin* while living in Brunswick. The hugely popular book helped fan the flames of abolitionist sentiment throughout the North. Otis Howard's mathematics professor, William Smyth, was also the editor of the *Advocate of Freedom*. Published in Hallowell since 1838, it was the state's first antislavery paper.[18]

In response to Lincoln's call for troops, the state initially raised two regiments, the 1st and 2nd Maine Volunteers. The state legislature, called into a special session later in April, passed an act calling for a loan of $1 million for the war effort and summoned 10,000 volunteers to man 10 regiments. Per capita, by the end of the war Maine contributed more soldiers to the Union effort than any other state, with some 73,000 serving. Eighteen thousand of them became casualties.

Some 4,000 of those Maine men fought at Gettysburg over the three bloody days in July 1863. For many who survived, the battle remained the high point of their lives. Some talked about it until the day they died; others buried it deeply into the unconscious and tried to forget its horrific events. None of them emerged unchanged from the killing fields of Gettysburg. Whether they liked it or not, they had become a band of brothers. As Joshua Chamberlain told some of the survivors in October 1889, "Those who fell here—those who have fallen before or since—those who linger, yet a little longer, soon to follow; all are mustered in one great company on the shining heights of life, with that star of Maine's armorial ensign upon their foreheads forever—like the ranks of the galaxy."

CHAPTER I

Maine Goes to War

I shall endeavor to do my duty and if I am unfortunate why so mite it be the cause is just, and if my humble life can help drive out those traitors from the soil it may freely go.

—JOHN FRENCH, 5TH MAINE

In November 1860 Abraham Lincoln was elected president of the United States. His victory tore the nation apart. Southern states, seeing Lincoln as an imminent threat to the institution of slavery, reacted quickly. South Carolina announced its secession in December and other states prepared to follow suit. War appeared inevitable, but Maine—like the rest of the nation—remained woefully unprepared for conflict. "There are at present only thirty-six organized military companies in the State," Davis Tillson, the state's adjutant general, reported in December. "And but very few of them, at all, answer the purposes for which they were designed and chartered. Most of them have but a fitful and uncertain life, resulting in nothing but vexation and annoyance to their members."[1]

Israel Washburn was inaugurated for his first one-year term as Maine's governor on January 3, 1861. Born in the town of Livermore, he had practiced law in Orono and served in the Maine legislature and the U.S. Congress. He was a strong antislavery man and had helped found the Republican Party. Washburn was small of stature—no more than five feet six inches tall—and clean shaven, with short hair and light blue eyes that gleamed from behind wire spectacles. He was the oldest of seven brothers and three sisters. One of the brothers, Elihu Washburne (who had attached an "e" to his name because it looked more English), moved to Illinois, where he became a Republican congressman and the political patron of a still-obscure soldier named Ulysses S. Grant. Another brother, Cadwallader Colden Washburn, ended up in Wisconsin, became a U.S. congressman two years after his brother, and took command of the 2nd Wisconsin Cavalry after war broke out. He eventually became a major general and commanded a corps. It was a distinguished family indeed. On one occasion, the brothers got together and began arguing about who had the most impressive record. They put the question to a vote and the result was a tie—every brother had voted for himself. Cadwallader, the general, won on the second ballot.[2]

In his inaugural address, Washburn downplayed the danger to the republic. "We are told that the slave States, or a portion of them, will withdraw from the Union," he said. "No, they will not. They cannot go, and in the end will not want to go. They would know that their strength and happiness lay in the Union."[3]

Washburn, of course, was overly optimistic. Hannibal Hamlin, Lincoln's Maine-born vice president–elect, nursed no such illusions. James Dunning, a friend from Bangor, spoke to Hamlin just before his inauguration and asked him if he thought there would be a war. "Dunning, there's going to be a war, and a terrible one, just as sure as the sun will rise tomorrow," Hamlin replied.[4]

—◆—

Thomas W. Hyde had a frontline perspective on the nation's political divisions. Hyde, born in Italy to parents from Bath, Maine, was studying at Bowdoin College when he received an offer to spend a year at the new University of Chicago. He and two other students jumped at the chance, even though far-off Chicago seemed to be "almost the Western wilds." Hyde arrived just in time for the Republican convention in May 1860. The entire city seemed to buzz with excitement. "One could hardly walk a block without encountering a band or music or witnessing a knot of people telling each other what they had seen or speculating on the probable action of the convention," noted one visitor. At night, thousands of "Wide Awakes," a paramilitary wing of the Republican Party, marched through the streets. Inside a huge wooden structure called the Wigwam, politicians thundered and promoted their candidates, while behind the scenes they cut backroom deals in the quintessential smoke-filled rooms. New York's William Seward seemed the odds-on favorite for the presidential nomination, but Salmon P. Chase of Ohio, Pennsylvania's Simon Cameron, and Missouri's Edward Bates all nursed hopes that they would become the party's choice. Abraham Lincoln remained home in Springfield, Illinois, but he had capable men in Chicago to back his candidacy.[5]

Hyde visited the Wigwam and heard Owen Lovejoy transfix the crowd. Lovejoy had been born in the Maine town of Albion in 1811. He was another Bowdoin graduate, an ardent antislavery man, and an early member of the Republican Party. His older brother Elijah had been a staunch abolitionist and the editor of an antislavery journal in Alton, Illinois. Owen had followed his brother west and was present in 1837 when Elijah was murdered as he tried to protect his printing presses from a mob of anti-abolitionists. Watching Owen transfix the crowd in the Wigwam, Hyde believed him "the greatest stump orator I ever heard. He would hold spellbound for two hours at a time nine thousand people in this vast hall, tearing his coat off and then his vest and cravat in the excitement of his invective against slavery, though never alluding to the fact that but a short time before his brother had been shot by a pro-slavery mob."[6]

Hyde and his fellow students nourished hopes that William Pitt Fessenden, the U.S. senator from Maine, would get the nomination. Fessenden's youngest son, Sam, was one of Hyde's friends at Bowdoin. In the end, of course, the convention picked Lincoln. Maine went strongly for the Republican in the November general election, giving him all eight of its votes in the electoral college as well as 62.2 percent of the popular vote. Nationally, Lincoln won less than 40 percent of the popular vote, with the Southern states leaning strongly against him. Around 30 percent of Maine's voters went for Northern Democrat Stephen Douglas; Southern Democrat John Breckinridge won 6 percent, and John Bell of the Constitution Union Party received only 2 percent.[7]

Hyde sometimes saw the president-elect in Chicago. The first encounter was at the home of attorney and Lincoln supporter Norman B. Judd. "Mr. Lincoln looks pale and worn by anxiety and the foreshadowed cares of office," Hyde wrote home to Annie Hayden of Bath, the young women he would later marry. "He is raising a beard which will materially improve his appearance." Hyde described another party where he watched Lincoln regale the men around him with stories. "I found it very hard to realize that I was standing before the president elect and was not listening to the jovial autocrat of some country town," he said.[8]

In his memoirs, Hyde claimed he was present for Lincoln's first meeting with Hannibal Hamlin. Born in Paris Hill, Maine, in 1809, Hamlin had entered politics as a Democrat and won election to the state legislature in 1835 and then, in 1843, to the U.S. House of Representatives. He was "tall, and gracious in figure, with black, piercing eyes, a skin almost olive-colored, hair smooth, thick and jetty" and he possessed "a manner always courteous and affable." Courteous and affable he may have been, but his complexion and his abolitionist politics led enemies to suggest he was a mulatto. One of his antagonists was Kentucky congressman Garrett Davis; the two men clashed so vehemently in Washington that Hamlin began carrying a pistol for protection.

Hamlin was still a Democrat when won a special election to the Senate in 1848. Encouraged by Maine newspaper editor and nascent politician James G. Blaine, in 1856 Hamlin won election to the Maine governorship as a Republican, but resigned almost immediately so he could return to the Senate. He wanted to stay there, and the news that he had been nominated as Lincoln's running mate came as a complete surprise. "I neither expected nor desired it," he wrote to his wife. "But it has been made and as a faithful man to the cause, it leaves me no alternative but to accept it."[9]

Hamlin and Lincoln met for the first time in Chicago on November 21. Historians place the meeting at the Tremont House hotel, but Hyde remembered it taking place at the home of Jonathan Young Scammon, where he was lodging. (Hyde must have been milking his Maine connections for all they were worth, for Scammon was Maine-born and had moved to Illinois in 1835. He eventually became Norman Judd's law partner.) In his memoirs, Hyde recalled seeing Lincoln and Hamlin regard the other "with a deep look of interest" before moving off for a private conversation. According to Hyde, once the vice president departed, Lincoln turned to Scammon and said, in reference to the rumors about his vice president's background, "Well, Hamlin isn't half so black as he is painted, is he Scammon?"[10]

Hyde said Scammon even took him on a visit to Lincoln in Springfield, where Hyde attended a party at Lincoln's house and pitched in to help the president-elect's secretaries, John Hay and John Nicolay, sort through Lincoln's voluminous mail. Passions were running so high that the young men soaked especially suspicious packages in water before opening them.

While in Springfield, Hyde met Ephraim Elmer Ellsworth, a young military enthusiast and founder of the U.S. Zouave Cadets of Chicago. Ellsworth's Zouaves dressed in colorful uniforms patterned on those worn by French soldiers in Algeria, and they enthralled audiences with intricate drill routines. "Capt. ELLSWORTH is a young man, but a wonderful tactician, who has his company under the most perfect control, not only in camp, but while scaling walls over inclined planes formed by the backs of their stooping comrades, lighting as skirmishers, executing the Cashing bayonet exercise, or while on parade," wrote the *New York Times* in July 1860. Ellsworth later studied law at Lincoln's law office and became almost a surrogate son to the president.[11]

─✦─

The smoldering embers of sectional difference burst into the flames of war early on the morning of April 12, 1861, when Confederate guns began bombarding Fort Sumter in Charleston Harbor. The fort's commander, Maj. Robert Anderson—who had once headed the Kennebec Arsenal in Augusta—surrendered the next afternoon. President Lincoln responded with a call for 75,000 volunteers to put down the rebellion.

Maine now had a new adjutant general. In January, the state legislature elected John Hodsdon to the post. Born in Hallowell as John Littlefield—he changed his name after he was adopted following his father's death—Hodsdon had gained military experience as a militiaman when he joined the Bangor Light Infantry at the age of 16. He had spent time on Maine's disputed boundary with Canada in 1839 when tensions there threatened to flare into war. He remained with the militia and rose to the rank of brigadier general. His head of dark, unruly hair gave him an air of a harried administrator, but Hodsdon proved supremely capable throughout the war years as his office raised and supplied the state's military units and dealt with the myriad issues they brought with them. Each year he compiled an official report, and the six volumes totaled around 8,000 pages by the time he resigned his post in 1867. According to one contemporary history, "It is universally conceded among military men, that Maine had, in the person of John L. Hodsdon, the most efficient Adjutant General to be found in the North."[12]

Hodsdon's appraisal of the military situation was even bleaker than his predecessor's. "The bombardment of Fort Sumter at Charleston, on the twelfth of April last, by those who should have been its defenders, found Maine as little prepared to furnish troops for maintaining the integrity of the Union as it is possible to conceive," he reported. On paper, the state's militia numbered some 60,000 men but at best only 1,200 were ready for any kind of duty, and even they were woefully unequipped for the field.[13]

Such unpreparedness did not dampen Maine's ardor for war as news of Sumter spread across the state. Some women in Skowhegan found a cannon and fired a 34-shot salute. Lewiston, Auburn, and Portland raised militia companies, and the Lewiston Light Artillery became the first unit that Governor Washburn accepted into service. Fifty men volunteered in Cherryfield; China raised a company of men; and one Henry Humphrey of Thomaston said he would donate $15,000 to supply an artillery battery.

In Waterville, Joshua Nye opened a recruiting office on the day after Lincoln's call for volunteers. Nye, the treasurer of the Androscoggin and Kennebec Railroad Company, began recruiting from his office at the corner of Main and Elm Streets. The first man to sign up was Charles A. Henrickson, a student at Waterville (later Colby) College. Henrickson's "patriotic zeal and exaltation" about enlisting proved so distracting to his fellow students that the college closed temporarily.[14]

Not to be outdone, brothers William and Francis Heath and their friend James H. Plaisted opened their own recruiting office in Waterville.

6

William Heath had already led an exciting life since his birth in Belfast in 1834. "In his early youth Col. Heath exhibited that precocity of which indicates, not infrequently, the man of genius," read one obituary. "During the hours usually occupied in boyish sports, Heath was at home finding a keener enjoyment in the companionship of the historian and poet." The gold rush lured this prodigy to California and from there he continued west to the Sandwich Islands and all the way to China. By the time he was 16, Heath had traveled around the world. He studied at Yale, but graduated from Waterville College and began practicing law. Heath moved to Minnesota, served as U.S. Consul for the British Provinces in Montreal, and returned to Maine in time for the war. His younger brother Francis, who served under William in a company of the 3rd Maine at the start of the conflict, would later perform sterling service as the colonel of the 19th Maine at Gettysburg.[15]

Washburn called a special session of the legislature on April 22, during which the lawmakers authorized raising $1 million and enlisting 10,000 men to fill 10 regiments. The initial enlistment period was three months. The 1st Regiment was organized 16 days after Sumter's surrender. Nathaniel Jackson, who had been the captain of the Lewiston Light Infantry, was elected colonel. He soon put his military experience to good use, writing Hodsdon to point out that Lincoln's call for troops had made no provisions for providing each regiment with a quartermaster, the officer responsible for making sure the men were fed and equipped. Jackson requested that Hodsdon wire Secretary of War Simon Cameron and rectify the issue, which he apparently did.[16]

By the end of April, the citizens of Bangor had set up seven recruiting offices. Those unable or unwilling to enlist contributed money to help support the families of men going off to war. The town's women volunteered to make clothing for the soldiers, using sewing machines at Fenno & Hale's store at 24 Main Street. "Think of it!" marveled the authors of *Eastern Maine in the War of the Rebellion*. "Delicate women sat there, day after day, gradually forming from the shapeless mass of cloth, garments for loved ones; garments soon to be rent by the bullet or the bayonet, and drenched, may be, with the life current of him so dear to the maker. No wonder the men of the land were fighters! How could they be otherwise when the women set them such an example of heroism?" All throughout the state men made speeches, towns raised new flagpoles, government bodies passed resolutions, and private citizens donated money to help put down the rebellion.[17]

John French, a 21-year-old carpenter living in Lewiston, was one of the many young men swept up by the patriotic fervor. French decided to enlist in the 5th Maine regiment. Although old enough to sign up without parental permission, he felt obligated to explain himself to his family. "Dear Parents, Brothers & Sisters," he wrote on April 30. "Perhaps you will condemn my actions, but I feel that I am but doing my duty to my country. I have enlisted and when you get this letter I shall probaly be in Fort Preble at Portland. think not that this is a hasty step, for it is not so. I did not act in a moment of excitement but concidered it calmly. . . . I tell you by gosh I feel as though I could fight like a hero and if I could get Jef Davis's hide I think my fortune would be made."

French's major concern was that he might not get a chance to fight. "I shall endeavor to do my duty and if I am unfortunate why so mite it be the cause is just, and if my humble life can help drive out those traitors from the soil it may freely go," he wrote. "I should not have hesitated in the first place if I had been alone but the thoughts that it might cause you sorrow held me back, but the strong desire in my bosom grew stronger and at last I thought I must go and go I did and I wouldn't back out now on no terms."[18]

Charles Amory Clark was a student at Foxcroft Academy in Piscataquis County, preparing for college, when war broke out. As soon as they heard the news of Fort Sumter, Clark and his fellow students went to some nearby woods, chopped down two pine trees, and used them to make a liberty pole. At dawn, the students raised the American flag and woke nearby townspeople with their cheering. Clark and his roommate, Sewall C. Gray, tossed a coin to see who would get to be the first man to enlist from Piscataquis County. Clark won. Both young men ended up in the 6th Maine, a regiment that seemed divided about evenly between men from the coast and those from inland. Clark though it "a happy combination of the sailor, the lumberman, the student, the farmer, the merchant, and the laborer."[19]

The Southern states had left the Union because they felt Lincoln's election threatened slavery, a vital component of the Southern social fabric and the region's economic life. Slavery, said Alexander Stephens, the new Confederacy's vice president, "was the immediate cause of the late rupture and present revolution." Yet, while slavery had caused the conflict, it's safe to say that few Maine men enlisted to end that institution. They were fighting to save the Union. The census of 1860 counted only 1,140 black people living in the state, and many of the lumbermen from the inland forests or the fishermen from Downeast regions had never seen an African American. The plight of enslaved Southern blacks had little impact on their lives. One Maine soldier recalled "that at this time the public sentiment was for the '*Union as it was*,' which meant as far as slavery was concerned that each state should mind its own business. In our anxiety for the Union, we of the North lost sight of what appeared a secondary matter. The slavery question was crowded aside the better to put down the rebellion!"[20]

There were even some people who blamed Northern abolitionists for starting the war. "There is far more danger to the peace of the country, in my opinion, from the bad, bitter, unscriptural temper with which the institution of slavery has been assailed, than from slavery itself," preached a Congregationalist minister from Bath in January 1861. Pascal Gilmore was a 16-year-old from the Bangor area when he enlisted, and he had no love for abolitionists either. He later wrote, "The extravagant statements of these men, and the sharp invective goaded the Southerners to desperation, causing them to believe that a majority at the North were rank abolitionists restively biding their time to free the slaves and humiliate the South," he believed. "In this way, as it seems to me, the free states were largely responsible for precipitating hostilities."[21]

John Mead Gould was a bank teller in Portland when war broke out. At first he hoped the government would give up Sumter to the Confederacy and end the fighting. On April 22 he admonished himself in his journal. "John M. Gould! you shall defend that liberty and your life shall not be valued equal to a worms till treason has perished and right is triumphant!!" The next day he went to the Portland armory to sign what he called his "death warrant" by enlisting in the Portland Light Guards, which became Company C of the 1st Maine. On May 3 Gould joined the rest of his company at city hall to be officially mustered in. Colonel Jackson, Capt. J. W. T. Gardiner of the 1st U.S. Dragoons, and the regimental surgeon studied each man ("or pretended to," said Gould), after which roll was called. Each man shouted "Here!" and marched past the officers, slapping the strap of his musket sharply with his left hand as he passed. Five men didn't pass muster and weren't allowed to enlist.[22]

Governor Washburn visited the regiment at Westbrook, in a camp named after him. The governor inspected the troops, received a 14-gun salute, watched some drill, and addressed the men "at length in a very appropriate manner." Not long afterwards, measles broke out in the regiment, forcing the 1st Maine to remain in Portland until June 1. The regiment then made a leisurely trip south, with stops for celebrations in Newburyport, Massachusetts (the birthplace of its colonel), and Boston. In New York the son of a former Maine governor presented them with a flag. Another Maine native had written a poem for them, titled "To the First Regiment of Maine." It began:

> Ye Sons of Freedom and of Maine,
> On to the glorious fight,
> When thus your country calls you forth,
> To battle for the right.
> Go where the traitor sword is drawn,
> Raise there your banner high,
> And let the war song ever be
> "We conquer or we die![23]

War was serious business, but that didn't mean there wasn't time for levity, or that soldiers wouldn't find ways to tweak authority figures. Gould later wrote a very droll account of what he called Colonel Jackson's "famous speech" in New York, an address "which no man who heard will ever forget."

"It was entirely extempore and had the merit of brevity, and it made, not the orator, but the one addressed famous ever afterward," Gould wrote. "The Adjutant was hastening toward the opposite side of the square when the Colonel called him. The Adjutant did not hear—the only man in the regiment that did not, by the way. He called again and still no attention except from the 700 men and seven times 700 spectators who were all attention. Therefore he roused himself for his effort, and delivered the speech, which was taken down in short hand or some other way, and is recorded as follows:

SPEECH OF 'OLD JACKS',
SUNDAY, JUNE 2, 1861, IN FRONT OF CITY HALL, NEW YORK.
'JIM!—Ho! JIM!!'

"Moved by his eloquence the great assemblage of soldiers and citizens burst into one grand responsive echo—'JIM!' 'JIM!' 'JIM!' 'JIM!' 'JIM!' &c., which they kept up for a long time, and indeed, as far as the soldiers were concerned, they haven't quite quit it yet."[24]

The soldiers, whom the *New York Times* described as "a stalwart and sturdy class of men [who] look as if they could stand some of the rough usage which many of our volunteers have been obliged to undergo," went to a barracks, while the officers headed to the Astor House to enjoy "a sumptuous dinner."[25]

Then it was off to Philadelphia, and later a much tenser trip through Baltimore. A hotbed of secessionism, the Maryland city had erupted into violence on April 19 when the 6th Massachusetts marched through town while changing trains on its way to Washington. The resulting riot killed 4 Union soldiers and wounded 39, and at least a dozen citizens of Baltimore died during the melee. Two of the regiment's dead were Maine natives—Addison O. Whitney of Bethel and Sumner H. Needham of Belmont. Worried that the same thing might happen again, Colonel Jackson ordered his men to load their muskets and fix bayonets, but the citizenry remained quiet. The regiment reached Washington without further incident.[26]

The 1st Maine did not participate in the battle of Bull Run on July 21, and when the three-month enlistments expired in August, the regiment returned to Portland to be mustered out. Despite the fact that the regiment had not fired a shot in anger, Portland's mayor asserted that their "moral power" had been "formidable."[27]

Thanks to the measles that had infected the 1st Maine, the 2nd Maine was the first regiment to leave the state. The regiment was organized in Bangor, a city inflamed by war fever almost as soon as word of the Fort Sumter attack arrived late on April 12. Levi Emerson, formerly of the police force, immediately began planning to raise a company of militia. On April 18, he opened a recruiting office over a market, found a drummer to "drum up" volunteers, and began adding names to his roster. Two days later, his newly formed company marched past cheering crowds to city hall, where the men listened to patriotic speeches and basked in the applause of their neighbors and friends.[28]

Emerson's company became part of the 2nd Maine, which elected Charles Jameson, a lumberman and businessman from Old Town, as its colonel. Jameson was active in Democratic politics, and in 1862 would run for governor against Washburn as a War Democrat. Despite his lack of military experience, he proved to be both talented and courageous on the battlefield. "He is one of the *best* men I ever knew—as brave as a lion, and still as tender hearted as a child," wrote one of the soldiers who served under him.[29]

The regiment's camp became a popular place to visit, and crowds showed up each day to watch the soldiers drill in their fine new uniforms. It was going to be such a glorious war, and a short one, too. But when they were issued their uniforms, the men also received something that must have provided a sobering dose of reality—packets of bandages.

The regiment departed Bangor by train on May 14. It was a cloudy day, with rain threatening. The Bangor Cornet Band led the regiment out of its camp and down to the city's First Parish Church. Vice President Hamlin waited there to address them. "It matters little when one throws off this mortal coil—but how and where it is important—and at no time and in no place can man better die, than when and where he dies for his country and his race," he said. The rain started to fall, and the regiment finished its march to the railroad station, where the soldiers had 15 minutes to say goodbye to loved ones. "It was the first hard lesson which war teaches, and many a light hearted lad grew sad as he thought of the possibilities of the future," noted *Eastern Maine in the Rebellion*. Then the soldiers piled aboard the 16 cars of their train, which pulled out of the station at 10:45 A.M. Cannons roared, whistles shrieked, and the citizens of Bangor cheered.[30]

The governor addressed the regiment in Augusta, and then the train journey continued to Portland and Boston. In Boston the regiment boarded the steamer *State of Maine*, and continued toward New York. While on Long Island, the 2nd Maine nearly suffered its first casualty, when the accidental discharge of a revolver sent a bullet into the breast of Pvt. George K. Ingalls of Company B. Fortunately, Private Ingalls carried a Bible in his breast pocket, and the good book saved his life.[31]

Before the regiment could embark for Washington, though, measles made an appearance, and the troops were quarantined in a camp on the East River. Once given a clean bill of health, the regiment continued its journey south. Like the 1st Maine, the 2nd marched through Baltimore with guns loaded and bayonets fixed. When the unit reached the nation's capital, it made camp on Meridian Hill. And then it waited for its first taste of war.

———

At the United States Military Academy above the Hudson River in West Point, New York, mathematics instructor Oliver Otis Howard followed events as the country fractured. He heard the reports about the attack on the 6th Massachusetts in Baltimore. More bad news arrived from Alexandria, Virginia, on May 24. Elmer Ellsworth, Thomas Hyde's acquaintance from Springfield, had been killed by a Rebel sympathizer. Ellsworth had been in command of the 11th New York when he spied a Confederate flag flying atop the Marshall House hotel in Alexandria. He went inside to remove it. As Ellsworth came back downstairs with the flag, the building's proprietor, James Jackson, shot him dead. Ellsworth was the first Union officer to die in the war. His body lay in state in the White House, and President Lincoln mourned the death of his young friend. Hearing all this news, Howard knew he had to do something.

Howard had been born on November 8, 1830, in a large, multi-chimneyed house built by his grandfather, Seth Howard, in the tiny

Androscoggin County town of Leeds, in the southwestern part of the state. The boy was named after his other grandfather, Oliver Otis. His father, Rowland Bailey Howard, had brought his young wife, Eliza, to Leeds in 1830 to help Seth rescue the farm from debt. The Howards raised cattle and fowl and grew apples on their 80 acres, but the real money came from horses. The future general's father developed a knack for horse trading. Oliver, whom everyone called Otis, was the oldest of three children. Rowland followed four years later, and Charles four after that.

Howard credited a business trip his father made to New York State with having some long-term repercussions on his life, because Rowland returned to Maine with Edward Johnson, a young African American boy who lived with the family for four years. He and young Otis worked and played together. "I have always believed it was a providential circumstance that I had that early experience with a negro lad," recalled Howard, who would lead the Freedmen's Bureau after the Civil War, "for it relieved me from that feeling of prejudice which would have hindered me from doing the work for the freedmen which, years afterwards, was committed to my charge."[32]

Howard's father died on April 30, 1840. Eliza married John Gilmore when Otis was 11, and the family went to live with their stepfather some six miles away from the Howard farm. Otis later went to Hallowell, on the Kennebec River near Augusta, to live at the home of his uncle, John Otis. There he worked to earn his board and attended a local school, where he learned to deal with local bullies. After one incident, when he and a local tough tangled in his uncle's yard, John Otis took him aside. "I glory in your spunk," he said. He also told his nephew something that the young man adopted as a personal motto. "Be sure you are right and then go ahead."[33]

When Howard was 15 years old—after spending weeks rising at 4:00 A.M. and studying until midnight to prepare for the entrance exam—he was accepted at Bowdoin College. Howard wanted to be a schoolteacher, but when his cousin William Otis failed to get into West Point, John Otis suggested that Oliver might want to try instead. "This was the turning point in my career," he recalled years later. After graduating from Bowdoin, Howard left for West Point in August 1850.

On his way to the military academy, Howard met Edmund Kirby Smith, an alumnus who had fought in the Mexican War. Howard and Smith traveled together, and Smith explained some of West Point's traditions to the new plebe. "Indeed, I think that Captain Smith's kind warnings saved me from a good deal of annoyance and from some laughable mistakes that a candidate is almost sure to make unless he is thus befriended," Howard wrote. Howard arrived at West Point and reported to Seth Williams, the academy's adjutant. Williams also happened to be from Augusta.

Howard's experiences at West Point were not always pleasant. Even a decade before the outbreak of the Civil War, he noticed how the issue of slavery was already creating discord among the cadets. And for reasons that Howard doesn't fully explain in his memoirs, he was "cut" by some other cadets, who refused to speak to him or even acknowledge his existence. One leader of the hostile clique was G. W. C. "Custis" Lee, whose father, Robert E. Lee, was the military academy's superintendent. In his autobiography, Howard recalled being visited by the elder Lee in the hospital after suffering a severe fall in the gymnasium that required a lengthy period of recovery. (An unsigned article in the *Newark Sunday Call* on February 6, 1910, claimed a different reason for Howard's injury. According to this account, at dinner one night a Southern cadet said, "We treat niggers like cattle, and kill 'em when we like." Retorted Howard, "Colored people have a right to live, sir." Outraged, the Southerner brained him with a heavy glass, sending Howard to the hospital.)[34]

Howard graduated fourth in his class of 1854, and he chose to serve in the army's ordnance department. He knew the arsenals where ordnance personnel were assigned had houses for married officers—and Howard intended to get married. He had met Elizabeth Ann Waite, a cousin of his freshman roommate, when he was still at Bowdoin. Even though army general-in-chief Winfield Scott advised the recent graduate that young officers should remain single, Howard had his sights fixed on matrimony. He and Lizzie married on February 14, 1855, in Portland. A theater in town burned down that night, and Howard rushed from his wedding to take his turn at the fire engine.

After a stint at the Watervliet Arsenal in Troy, New York, Howard received temporary command of the Kennebec Arsenal in Augusta. There he met James G. Blaine, then the editor of the *Kennebec Journal*. Blaine was a Pennsylvania native, but he had moved to Augusta to take over the paper. Howard remembered him as a slightly disheveled man with a perpetually unbuttoned coat and disordered hair "due to sundry thrusts of his fingers." "But the distinguishing feature of his face was that pair of dark-gray eyes, very full and bright. He wore no beard, had a slight lisp in speech with a clear, penetrating nasal tone."[35]

During another stint at Watervliet, Howard noticed that sectional divisions were creating tensions among the base's formerly tight-knit military family. The commander's wife, in particular, had become increasingly intolerant of any talk of abolition. It probably did not help that Howard's brother Rowland, an "ardent" member of the new antislavery Republican Party, was beginning to influence Otis's political leanings.

And then, like a "clap of thunder from a clear sky," orders came for Howard to report to Florida, then in an unsettled condition due to ongoing conflict with the Seminole tribe. The assignment meant separation from his family, including his one-year-old son, Guy, and a long journey to a country where "the mosquitoes were more abundant and of a larger size than any I had ever seen before." Howard battled insects in Florida, but did not get an opportunity to tangle with the Seminoles, and his one attempt at leading a peace mission apparently ended without success.

Howard did have a life-changing experience in Florida—his "conversion." Once again, it was brother Rowland who influenced him. Otis had not been particularly religious while growing up. Rowland had become such a devout Christian he gave up his law studies to join the ministry, and he had been writing to Otis about his experiences and sending him books to read. On May 31, 1857, in Florida, Otis had his own "awakening," a religious conversion sparked by his attendance at Methodist revival meetings. "I had the feeling of sudden relief from the depression that had been long upon me," he wrote. "The joy of that night was so great that it would be difficult to attempt in any way to describe it. The next morning everything appeared to me to be changed—the sky was brighter, the trees more beautiful, and the songs of the birds were never before so sweet to my ears." Howard was now "a different man, with different hopes and different purposes in life." From that point on, Oliver Otis Howard became known for his piety. Some later called him "the Christian Soldier." His men, perhaps less admiringly, referred to him as "Old Prayer Book."[36]

Unlike many officers in the often hard-drinking army, Howard also became a teetotaler. When forced to drink a toast, he did it with water, "the only beverage fit for a soldier." Like Thomas Jackson, the Confederate soldier who would become the legendary Stonewall, Howard had reservations about fighting on the Sabbath. "Whether this be the superstition or the religion of a people, wise men will respect it," he wrote. "To violate the Sabbath weakens the soldiers who come from our churches and Sunday schools."[37]

In any event, when the born-again Howard received orders to leave Florida and return to West Point as an instructor in mathematics, he was a changed man. He considered leaving the army to join the ministry, but satisfied himself with hosting social prayer meetings at the military academy and becoming superintendent of the campus's Sunday school.

All the prayer in the world could not prevent the rupture that was about to tear the country apart. At West Point the growing divide meant increasing unpleasantness. The academy was especially shocked when William Hardee, who had written an influential work on infantry tactics and had served as commandant of cadets, resigned his army commission in January 1861. By then, Lincoln had been elected president, and South Carolina had announced its secession from the Union. "As we men from the North and South, at our post on the Hudson, looked anxiously into each other's faces, such indeed was the situation that we knew that civil war with its unknown horrors was at hand," Howard said.[38]

When Howard wrote to Israel Washburn and offered his services to the state, the governor declined. The men in each regiment elected their own officers, he explained. But others heard of Howard's offer, and in May he received a letter from old acquaintance James G. Blaine, now Maine's speaker of the house. Blaine had arranged to get Howard the command of a regiment. Howard worried he wasn't experienced enough to accept the colonelship, and thought it might be better if he started as a major. He asked another officer at West Point—a Pennsylvanian named John Fulton Reynolds, who was the academy's commandant of cadets—what he should do. Reynolds was blunt. "You'll accept, of course, Howard," he said. Howard did.[39]

On May 29, Howard reached Augusta and learned that he had been elected colonel of the 3rd Maine. He resigned his commission with the regular army to join the volunteers, and established himself at the Augusta House on State Street. He used the establishment's large porch and balcony to meet with some of his officers. At the statehouse, Howard also met Governor Washburn. "He had a large, strong face, full of resolute purpose, and habitually covered his eyes with glasses for near-sightedness, so that he did not prepossess a stranger on first approach; but the instant the introduction had passed a wonderful animation seized him and changed the whole man," Howard recalled. "He was at that time replete with patriotic enthusiasm and energy, and soon held a foremost place among the war governors of his time."[40]

Howard also renewed his acquaintance with Blaine, a man whose energy and ambition had already made him a political force at the age of 30. "He excelled even the nervous Washburn in rapid utterance," Howard wrote. "Nobody in the Maine House of Representatives, where he had been for two years and of which he was now the Speaker, could match him in debate."[41]

Accompanied by Blaine and Washburn, Howard walked over to a nearby park to meet his new command. He found his men milling about in some disorder. Washburn hopped up on a half hogshead and made an impromptu address to introduce the new colonel to the men who had elected him. Howard, already feeling insecure about his youth and inexperience, felt his reception was decidedly lackluster, and thought the men probably thought he looked too young and soft to inspire much confidence. He may have had reason for his misgivings. Abner R. Small, a corporal in Company G from Waterville, recalled being unimpressed. "We saw a pale young man, taller than the governor, and slender, with earnest eyes, a high forehead, and a profusion of flowing moustache and beard," remembered Small. He thought Howard talked more like a preacher than a soldier. "He told us all about himself and his little family and the Ten Commandments."[42]

Howard was further disappointed when the regiment elected another candidate over his brother Rowland for chaplain. But he was pleased that his brother Charles joined as a regimental clerk. Like his older brothers, Charles had graduated from Bowdoin College (class of 1855), after which he studied at Bangor Theological Seminary, as his brother Rowland had, with his eye on the ministry. Charles was as devoutly religious as his brothers, his conversion having come four years before Otis's. Charles would prove invaluable to Otis, providing the kind of spiritual support his older brother needed. Lizzie came to believe that, in the field, Charles was better than a wife, and Otis agreed. "Charlie is a dear good brother, bold & fearless in the saddle, kind and gentle in quarters," he said. "We always move on in perfect harmony."[43]

The new colonel had little time to get used to his new command, or for his regiment to get used to him. He received word that Washington expected the 3rd Maine to depart Augusta on June 5.

Howard remembered the morning his regiment marched off to war as a particularly beautiful one. The sky was free of clouds, the trees were green with leaves, and a large crowd had turned out to say its farewells as a troop train waited on the tracks by the Kennebec River. The locomotive blew its whistle and rang its bell, the signal for the soldiers to begin streaming from their camp to the railroad. Parents hugged their sons, tears were shed, and prayers for safe returns were lifted to the sunny skies. The soldiers climbed aboard the train, some of them clambering onto the roofs of the cars. Howard climbed up with them and brandished his sword for the crowd. As the regimental band struck up a patriotic air, the train slowly pulled out of Augusta, heading south along the Kennebec. Throngs of well-wishers waved goodbye, worried that they would never see their sons or husbands again. The green soldiers, no doubt, wondered if they would return home alive.

"Who can forget his last look at that multitude on the hillside—the swift motion of waving handkerchiefs, flags, and outstretched hands!" wrote Howard in his memoirs. "A curve in the track shut off the view; and thus departed this precious, typical freight of war."[44]

CHAPTER 2

Maine Spills Blood

*Our men fought well and stood fire like heroes but it was of no use.
All the other troops had left, and the Rebels were coming upon us
in overpowering numbers so the order to retreat was given and we
turned our back to the enemy. I don't wish to say anything of what I
saw on the field. God grant that I may never see the same again. Our
retreat was all confusion and turmoil.*

— George Rollins, 3rd Maine

Hiram Berry seemed a somewhat unlikely general. When war broke out,
he was already 37 years old and had a wife and daughter. He had been
a carpenter, builder, businessman, bank president, state legislator, and
mayor, but his only military experience had been with local militia. Yet
Berry performed so well with the Army of the Potomac, some people
even thought he might command it one day.

Berry was born on August 27, 1824, on the family farm in what is
now Rockland. He grew up with a love of reading and of horses. When
he was 21, Berry and another local man named Elijah Walker began
working together as carpenters. Berry soon expanded his carpentry work
into contracting and building and eventually became one of Rockland's
most prominent businessmen. He married Almira M. Brown in 1845 and
the couple had one daughter, Lucy.

Young Berry had wanted to attend West Point, an interest that
may have been sparked by his family lineage. His grandfather had been

an officer in the American Revolution, and his father had volunteered to fight in the War of 1812, but had gone no farther than Eastport, Maine, where he served as an orderly sergeant. Berry's mother, however, objected to his West Point plan, so he joined a local artillery company instead. Later he organized the Rockland City Guards, a militia unit that wore flashy blue-and-gold uniforms with high bearskin hats. On August 31, 1858, the Guards served as an escort for Senator Jefferson Davis of Mississippi when the former secretary of war and the future president of the Confederate States of America visited Belfast. "With such troops as are now before me, we may defy the combined forces of the world and shout the song of freedom forever," said Davis. (On the same trip to Maine, Davis also received an honorary degree from Bowdoin College.)[1]

Berry was a Democrat, not a Lincoln Republican, but he traveled to Augusta to volunteer his services as soon as the war started. He returned home with the approval to raise a regiment, the 4th Maine. At a public meeting in Rockland on April 23, someone tossed a $20 gold coin on the floor and said it would go to the first man who volunteered. Stephen H. Chapman, a strapping six-foot plus, picked up the coin. He later became Berry's sergeant major. The 4th Maine ended up with four companies from Rockland, two from Belfast, and additional ones from Damariscotta, Winterport, and Wiscasset. The soldiers of the new regiment elected Berry as its colonel.[2]

Elijah Walker, Berry's business partner and the foreman of the town's Dirigo Engine Company, remained uncertain about enlisting. As a married man with seven children, the youngest a baby of seven months, he had pressing family obligations. Yet Walker, too, decided to answer the call to preserve the Union. Not only did he volunteer the 25 men of his engine company, he also opened a recruiting office and signed up 80 more. He became the captain for Company B.[3]

When the 4th Maine left Rockland on Monday, June 17, 1861, enthusiastic throngs of citizens cheered the soldiers as they marched down to the town wharf in their new gray uniforms to board the steamer *Daniel Webster* for a cruise to Portland. More cheering crowds greeted them when their train reached Boston, and still more when they reached

New York. The "strong and sturdy specimens of Maine's true nobility" marched up Broadway in oppressive heat (Berry noted that the temperature reached 95), and the Sons and Daughters of Maine, natives of the state now residing in New York, provided a reception and presented flags.

"Shall this flag ever trail in the dust?" Berry asked his men.

"No!" they shouted.

"Will you defend it so long as you have a right arm?" Berry asked.

"We will, we will!" the men replied, to cheers and applause from the gathered New Yorkers.

In Philadelphia, the men found a hot meal—and bathing facilities—waiting for them. "The pretty waiting maids were very attentive to the wants of the boys from Maine, who were ready to affirm that the girls of Philadelphia could not be excelled except by those of the Pine Tree State," wrote Berry's biographer.

Baltimore, that hotbed of secessionism, offered a cooler reception. Berry distributed ammunition to his men as a precaution. The 4th Maine made it peacefully through the city, but Berry noted that the men in the crowds lining the streets looked "dark and sullen" as the regiment marched across town to board a train for Washington.[4]

Otis Howard had a reasonably uneventful trip to Washington with the 3rd Maine. Almost as soon as his train left Augusta, it slowed for a brief stop in neighboring Hallowell, where his mother waited to bid goodbye to her son. The regiment received a warm welcome in Brunswick, home to Howard's first alma mater, and another in Portland. Militia escorted the men through Boston, where they listened to a speech by Governor John A. Andrew, a fellow Bowdoin graduate.

From Boston, the regiment took the steamer *Bay State* to New York, where the soldiers disembarked in pouring rain. Members of the Sons of Maine waited at the dock to escort them up Broadway to the armory on White Street, and presented the regiment with a flag. Howard received his first war wound during the ceremony when the surging crowd jostled him off the gun carriage he had been using as a speaking platform and his heavy saber crushed his big toenail when he hit the ground. The injury troubled him for the rest of his life. On a happier note, Lizzie Howard brought the children down from West Point to say goodbye to their father.

George Rollins was a good-natured student from Vassalboro who had enlisted in Company G as a private when he was only 17, and he was having a grand adventure so far. "I had the best time in Boston," he wrote to his father. "I never saw so many people before. From the depot to the Common the streets were so crowded that the policemen could hardly make way for us....it was a vast sea of faces." In New York, though, Rollins experienced the differences between the officers and the enlisted men. The officers were taken to dinner at the Astor House, while the enlisted men were left to fend for themselves. "We made ourselves as merry as possible but there were some sour looks," Rollins said. He concluded, "I do not regret the step I have taken yet."[5]

Like other regimental commanders who had come before him, Howard had his men load their weapons when they reached Baltimore. He was surprised to find that the people there seemed cheerful as they watched his men march by, although he did notice there were no United States flags flying from any of the public buildings.[6]

In Washington, Howard picked up the tab (50 cents apiece) for breakfast for his men at Willard's Hotel. He then reported to Joseph Mansfield, who commanded the Department of Washington, and spent a miserable night in the rain on Meridian Hill. That night, Howard remembered, one soldier badly injured himself when his own musket discharged, a sign that these green soldiers might not be prepared for what faced them.[7]

Cpl. Abner Small remembered the incident differently. He said Howard had forgotten to have the regiment unload its weapons after Baltimore, and one soldier accidentally shot the man in front of him. When Howard then had his men discharge their weapons into the air, a number of their bullets riddled tents of the nearby 2nd Maine, fortunately without injury.[8]

Small was aptly named, standing only about 5 feet 4 inches tall. He was born in Augusta but was living in West Waterville when the war broke out. His Civil War carte de visite reveals a balding young man with a big mustache and a sardonic cast about his eyes. The accounts he wrote about his war experiences have a sardonic cast about them, too, though it took long years of war, including a spell in a Confederate prison, to infect him with cynicism. In the early days of the conflict Small, as was the case with many young soldiers, was simply having a good time. "My health is first-rate & I am in excellent spirits—I have gained wonderfully in both since I came into camp—don't mind sleeping on the ground nor getting wet," he wrote to friends back in Maine on July 7.[9]

Private Rollins was enjoying himself, too. He marveled at the view from Meridian Hill. He could look out over the whole city—"literally crammed to overflowing every hill and nook fit for camps is occupied"—and into Virginia, "where for seven miles there is one continuous encampment." Army life suited him just fine. "We have corned beef and potatos, sometimes in hash, and sometimes separate, fresh beef two or three times a week, beans the same, coffee in the morning and tea at night," he informed his parents. "Each man has a plate, knife and fork, spoon and dipper." Unlike many soldiers who were disappointed by Washington's squalor and its muddy avenues, Rollins said Washington was "a splendid place I tell you. It is situated on a level tract of land, and the streets are very wide being shaded by trees so that one feels delighted in passing through them." He got a chance to explore the Navy Yard and, in an excited letter home, wrote, "I could cover a dozen sheets in describing all I saw but I haven't time to say any more."[10]

Like many other commanders, Howard's first big hurdle was getting his soldiers to submit to military discipline. Bowing to authority—especially authority they had elected themselves—did not come naturally to independent-minded lumbermen, fishermen, and sailors. "One moment we were free men to go and come as we pleased, and the next saw us amenable to all the arbitrary and despotic rules of the war department," remembered Small. In a typical example from a little later in the war, a quartermaster sergeant in the 6th Maine refused to remove his cap when he delivered a message to a lieutenant colonel. "I stood upon my rights as a free American citizen to wear my cap when I was out of doors, and undertook to explain that I had made the regulation salute, which was all that could be required of me," the sergeant explained. He was court-martialed, reduced to private, fined, and had his sergeant's chevrons torn off in front of the regiment.[11]

After learning that some of his free-spirited men had violated their furloughs, Howard stopped issuing passes altogether. "The regiment must be drilled, disciplined and made ready for war," he reasoned. "Ours was not a holiday excursion."[12]

Indeed, it wasn't, and Rebels weren't the only enemy these new soldiers had to combat. Disease, especially in the crowded, unsanitary army camps, was an ever-present danger, especially for men from isolated rural areas who had grown up with limited exposure to germs and viruses. Fortunately for the 3rd Maine, one of the people traveling with the regiment was Sarah Sampson of Bath, the wife of Charles A. L. Sampson, the captain of Company D. Mrs. Sampson, one history said, "had the unexampled benevolence to devote herself to the welfare of the sick without any assurance of recompense." She had plenty to keep her busy, too. People noted that soldiers from Maine, big and vigorous as they appeared, were often the first to become ill. George Rollins fell sick with the mumps, but he was lucky, for he quickly recovered. "We have a grand doctor, grand because he tells the men not to take medicine if they can help it, and if they can not help it to doctor themselves at any rate to keep out of the hospital," Rollins told his parents. Howard was not so fortunate. At the end of June, he fell seriously ill with cholera and for a time lay at death's door, with Sarah Sampson caring for him.[13]

Once he recovered, Howard learned that he would not be personally leading the 3rd Maine into combat after all. Instead, he would be commanding a brigade, comprising four New England regiments: the 3rd, 4th, and 5th Maine and the 2nd Vermont. Maj. Henry Staples of Augusta took command of the regiment.

Howard's brigade belonged to the division commanded by Samuel P. Heintzelman. A Pennsylvanian, Heintzelman had graduated from West Point in 1826 and served in the Mexican War and in the American Southwest. He was somewhat odd looking. One artilleryman said that "ugly as his pictures are, they flatter him: a little man, almost black, with short coarse grey hair and beard, his face one mass of wrinkles, he wears the most uncouth dress and gets into the most awkward positions possible." Howard described him as "a hardy, fearless, energetic character." Heintzelman also had "a frank way of expressing the truth, whether it hurt or not," something the new brigade commander soon learned. On July 6, Howard took his brigade via steamer down the Potomac to Alexandria. As Howard marched his men through town, he noticed Heintzelman watching them critically. "Colonel, you have a fine regiment," the general said. "They march well and give promise for the future, but you are not well drilled—poor officers, but good-looking men!" Howard was embarrassed.[14]

Howard's soldiers were certainly not the only ones unprepared for combat, as Brig. Gen. Irvin McDowell knew only too well. McDowell was the general who would lead the new Union army—christened the Army of Northeastern Virginia—in the first major battle of the war. The Ohio native had graduated from West Point in 1838 and served in Mexico. When war began, Major McDowell was manning a desk in the adjutant general's office in Washington. With the backing of fellow Ohioan Salmon P. Chase, Lincoln's secretary of the treasury, McDowell was promoted to brigadier general. Although General-in-Chief Winfield Scott offered only somewhat reluctant backing, McDowell received command of the Union forces in Washington.

McDowell was not the most charismatic of generals, and he demonstrated a marked inability to remember his subordinates' names, not the greatest way to inspire loyalty. He also came across as stiff and humorless. "Personally he was something of an enigma," wrote William C. Davis in *Battle at Bull Run.* "A bad listener, he frequently lost himself in thought while others were speaking." Even Chase, his political patron, admitted that McDowell's demeanor made it "difficult for his officers to feel any very warm personal sentiments toward him."[15]

The most charismatic general in the world would have struggled with the hand fate had dealt McDowell. Before the war he had never commanded more than eight soldiers in the field; now he had to handle an army of 35,000. Most of those soldiers were untrained and untested. In addition, McDowell lacked the necessary equipment and transportation to get his army into the field in a condition necessary for combat. Yet there was a growing popular clamor for the Federal army to take the field and put an end to the crisis. "Forward to Richmond!" demanded a headline in Horace Greeley's influential *New York Tribune* on June 26, and Greeley kept repeating that battle cry in his paper for the next three weeks.[16]

"I wanted very much a little time, an opportunity to test my machinery, to move it around and see whether it worked smoothly or not," McDowell later said. He did not get it. Under increasing pressure from press and public to do something—anything—Lincoln ordered McDowell to move against the Confederates in Virginia. When McDowell protested that his men were not ready, Lincoln famously replied, "It is true that they are green. So are the Confederates. You are all green alike."[17]

Second Sergeant William Higgins of the 3rd Maine had his own concerns. The sergeant, who hailed from the coastal town of Georgetown, near Bath, felt that the smoothbore musket he had been issued was not what he needed to fight the enemy. So on July 10 he sat down and wrote a letter to the governor. "I have asked many times for a <u>pistol</u> but can't have any," Higgins told Washburn. His officers told him the government furnished pistols to first sergeants only. To get around that bureaucratic obstacle, Higgins suggested the governor go to the state arsenal, procure a navy revolver, and send it to him as a gift. He promised he would use it faithfully to defend his country. "I will wait patiently for your answer <u>for one week</u>, and if I ever was to return to Maine I will call and tell you whether you <u>send me one or not</u>."[18]

Less than a week after Higgins wrote his letter, on July 16, the reluctant McDowell began moving forward. That day George Rollins found time to compose a letter to his parents in Vassalboro. "I am about to go off on a march, and have a few moments time to write," he said. "Our Div. (the second) is getting together and are going on to Richmond, that is eventually—but have got to clear the way first."[19]

Blocking the road to Richmond was a force called the Army of the Potomac, under the command of Gen. Pierre Gustave Toutant Beauregard. Its 22,000 men held positions near the important rail junction of Manassas, about 22 miles from Washington and behind a wandering creek called Bull Run. McDowell's army set out to confront the Confederates in four separate columns. Daniel Tyler's division was to the north, where it would pass through Vienna; David Hunter was south of Tyler, aiming straight toward Fairfax Court House; Dixon Miles's division turned farther south to follow the Braddock Road towards Centreville. Heintzelman, the farthest south, followed a road that roughly paralleled the Orange & Alexandria Railroad.

Howard soon learned how ill-prepared his men were for the campaign when two of them shot themselves with their own guns. One of them was mortally wounded when he grasped his loaded musket by the muzzle so he could knock an apple from a tree.[20]

That wasn't the only thing that bothered the Christian General, though; his soldiers swore too much. "I wish we had men who had more respect for the Lord," he wrote to his wife on July 18. "We might then expect his blessing." He had other problems with his men, too. Unused to long marches in the hot sun with all their heavy equipment, they began to fall out of the ranks and straggle. Some left their formations to pillage the homes they passed. Howard was irritated to learn that entire brigades in front of him slowed progress to a crawl by crossing a narrow stream one by one on a single log, or halting to carefully remove shoes and socks. The Union forces also had to clear obstructions the retreating Rebels had left in the roads, further slowing things, while the untried commanders feared ambushes and moved "as timidly as old maids eating shad in the dark," as Abner Small put it. The result was a slow, disorganized approach towards Bull Run that gave Beauregard plenty of time to prepare.[21]

On July 18 portions of Tyler's division engaged in some fighting along Bull Run by Blackburn's Ford. In a hint of things to come, a portion of the 12th New York broke and ran to the rear. Tyler admitted that the fire the regiment faced was "severe," but said there was "no excuse for the disorganization it produced."[22]

In the meantime, Gen. Robert Patterson was supposed to prevent Confederates in the Shenandoah Valley under Joseph Johnston from reinforcing Beauregard. However, Johnston managed to slip away from Patterson, and his men began arriving in Manassas by railroad on July 20. McDowell's plans were already starting to unravel.

Hiram Berry, commanding the 4th Maine in Howard's division, scratched out a letter home on July 18. "We are now only eight miles from Manassas Gap, and bound thither, enemy in front all the way, trees across the roads, bridges all burned, etc. Hard labor to clear the way."[23]

———

On Saturday night, July 20, McDowell gathered his commanders at his headquarters in Centreville. Using a map spread on the ground inside his tent, McDowell outlined his plan. He wanted Tyler's division to make a diversionary attack at a stone bridge where the Warrenton Turnpike crossed Bull Run. While the Confederates were dealing with this threat on their right, the divisions under Hunter and Heintzelman would move north along the Bull Run, cross the stream at Sudley and Poplar Fords, and turn south to surprise the enemy with an attack on its left.

It was a good plan, on paper at least, but perhaps too complex for this green army. "It is now generally admitted that it was one of the best-planned battles of the war, but one of the worst-fought," wrote William T. Sherman, who commanded a brigade in McDowell's army. "We had good organization, good men, but no cohesion, no real discipline, no respect for authority, no real knowledge of war."[24]

After the meeting in McDowell's tent, Howard assembled his brigade for a short prayer session. "Every soldier of my command seemed thoughtful and reverent that night," he recalled. Elijah Walker of the 4th Maine recalled how the general called his men together and told them that "before the setting of the sun some of us will be in eternity." Said Walker, "Many of us thought it poor tactics to instruct us in at that time."[25]

It was still dark the next morning when the Union forces broke camp for their offensive. The divisions began to get into each other's way almost immediately, creating gridlock on the roads. Howard's brigade, in the rear of Heintzelman's division, did not lurch into motion until long past daybreak. Before long, men were falling out of the ranks to sit down by the side of the road and rest. Later that morning, Heintzelman selected Howard's men to serve as a reserve force. Waiting behind the lines for their first taste of combat, they could hear the sounds of battle growing in volume out of sight in front of them. "I cannot forget how I was affected by the sounds of the musketry and the roar of the cannon as I stood near my horse ready to mount at the first call from McDowell; for a few moments weakness seemed to overcome me and I felt a sense of shame on account of it," Howard recalled. "Then I lifted my soul and my heart and cried: 'O God! enable me to do my duty.' From that time the singular feeling left me and never returned."[26]

God may have assuaged Howard's nervousness, but He did not do much for the Union cause as a whole. Things did proceed well at first. Tyler created his diversion to the south, and Hunter and Heintzelman's divisions made slow progress on a narrow trail through brush and dust toward the Confederate left. The Union soldiers crossed Bull Run, but an alert Confederate officer, E. Porter Alexander, spotted their approach from a signal station and sent out alerts. Rebel forces, recognizing Tyler's sound and fury around the stone bridge for the diversion it was, began moving reinforcements to the threatened left. Fighting erupted on Matthews Hill, the slope behind a stone house, a prominent landmark that stood alongside the Warrenton Turnpike. It became a bloody and confusing introduction to war for soldiers on both sides. Bullets shattered limbs, cannonballs removed heads, and canister turned men into bloody shreds. Confusion and chaos reigned for Federals and Rebels alike, but the Union forces got the better of these first encounters. They pushed forward, down to the turnpike and back up toward the strategic high ground of Henry Hill, a flat-topped rise where an 84-year-old widow named Judith Carter Henry had a little house. It was on this hill that Confederate general Thomas Jackson received the nickname that helped turn him into a legend—Stonewall.

Down by the stone bridge on the Warrenton Turnpike, Tyler began to turn his diversion into a real attack and ordered his men forward. At first the enemy fell back before them, but then artillery and infantry on Henry Hill began laying down a hail of shot and shell that stopped the advance in its tracks. Col. Erasmus Keyes—a Massachusetts native who had moved to Maine when young and attended West Point from that state—led one of Tyler's brigades. He ordered the 2nd Maine and the 3rd Connecticut forward to sweep the enemy off the hill. "The gallantry with which the Second Maine and Third Connecticut Regiments charged up

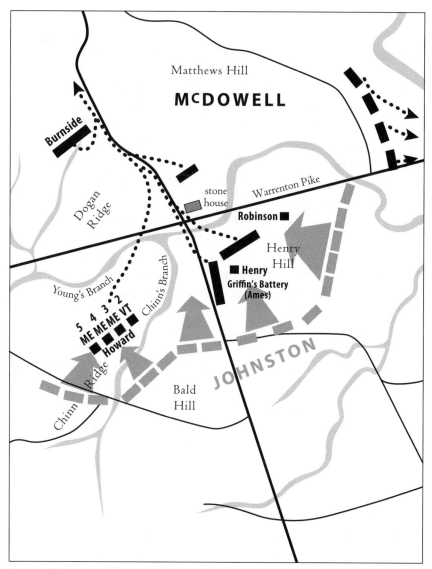

First Bull Run

the hill upon the enemy's artillery and infantry was never, in my opinion, surpassed," Keyes wrote.[27]

William Lawrence was a sergeant in Company G of the 2nd Maine. In a letter home, he described how his brigade waited a half mile from the battlefield for about an hour before receiving the order to move forward at double-quick. As the regiment trotted into battle, Rebels suddenly opened fire from behind a fence. The Maine soldiers returned fire, forcing the enemy to retreat behind some haystacks. The Union soldiers prepared to flush them out, but then a Confederate battery opened on them. "We stood it without flinching until we were ordered by Col. Keyes to flank into the woods," Lawrence remembered. The company's captain did not hear the order, though, and Company G remained by itself in the field, "and I guess the enemy will remember us, for just as sure as one of them showed his head he was sure not to need his rations the next day," said Lawrence. Finally, the company fell back and joined the rest of the regiment in the woods. They did not, Lawrence added, show their backs to the enemy. "I think if we had had another regiment to back us, we would have taken that battery in spite of all the devils in the Southern Army."

Still, despite his bluster, Lawrence admitted, "It was an awful day for us." He saw a friend, Henry Holden, fall with a bullet through a leg. Lawrence encountered another, William Deane, as he was being led off the field after being shot through the throat. Deane had been carrying a flag that Maine women living in San Francisco had made especially for the first regiment from their home state to take the field. Lawrence joined the party helping Deane to safety. Enemy cavalry intercepted the group, but Lawrence managed to slip away. "Capt Jones and one of the lieutenants of Company C, Brewer Artillery, were killed," he wrote home. "Lieutenant Richardson, of Capt. Emerson's company, had his leg taken off by a cannon ball. Sergeant Staples, of Company H, Gymnasium Company, tells me that Fuller Orff was shot in the abdomen and bled internally, and that he was dying when he last saw him. I don't know half —but it is said that one-half of our regiment is killed, wounded and missing."

Martin Jose of Hampden had both legs blown off as he charged an enemy battery. "Have you carried the battery?" he asked as he lay dying. "Tell mother I fell fighting for my country." One lucky survivor was a young soldier who had been hit in the cheek by a bullet that miraculously exited through his open mouth, leaving him with just a minor wound.[28]

Colonel Charles D. Jameson of the 2nd Maine also received praise for his bravery, once leading six of his men "into the very jaws of death" to recover the wounded. "Little can you imagine how our hearts swell towards our brave boys, for their heroic conduct in this great fight," wrote one of his men. "Our State has not been disgraced, whatever may have been the conduct of the officers of some other States. All honor to the Second Maine and its brave officers. The State owes them a debt of gratitude she can never repay."[29]

Keyes reported that "the fire became so hot that an exposure to it of five minutes would have annihilated my whole line." Despite the bravery the Maine and Connecticut soldiers demonstrated, the brigade fell back toward the stone bridge. Keyes was contemplating another attempt to take Henry Hill when he received word that the Union army was withdrawing. He and his brigade fell in with "the retreating mass" and crossed back over Bull Run. "Half an hour earlier I had supposed the victory to be ours," the disappointed general observed.[30]

Capt. Charles Griffin reached the battlefield sometime around 11:30 A.M. Griffin, the commander of Company D of the 5th United States Artillery, had piercing eyes, a thick, bristling mustache, and an explosive temperament. "He had a contentious disposition and a volatile temper and was given to profuse criticisms of colleagues and superiors he considered slow witted, obtuse, or incompetent," wrote historian Edward G. Longacre. One of his officers was Adelbert Ames, a young lieutenant about to have his first taste of combat.[31]

It would appear that Adelbert Ames was destined for a life at sea. On his mother's side he was related to Oliver Hazard Perry, the hero of Lake Erie, and Matthew Calbraith Perry, a naval officer who had worked to curtail the African slave trade. His father, Jesse, was a sea captain, and his mother, Martha, sometimes accompanied her husband on his global voyages. Adelbert, known as Del, was born in Rockland on October 31, 1835, and grew up among the wharves and docks of Rockland harbor. In the fall he went hunting for ducks and geese with his father and John, his older brother. On a few occasions, young Del went to sea with his father as cabin boy on long trading voyages aboard the family's schooner. He had sailed around Cape Horn and through the Straits of Magellan and had visited Europe, Africa, and Asia.

He grew up in a staunchly antislavery household. "Adelbert's attitude towards slavery was ingrained," his daughter, Blanche, wrote. "He had absorbed intense dislike for it, not only from his parents but from his whole environment. Slavery was repugnant to the moral feelings of the majority of the people he met." Harriet Beecher Stowe's *Uncle Tom's Cabin* became a strong influence.

Ames's uncle was friendly with Maine politicians and he used his influence to procure an appointment to West Point for his nephew. Ames entered the military academy in 1856 and thrived there, even as growing sectional conflict increased tensions among the cadets. He graduated in 1861 as a first lieutenant and received an assignment to Charles Griffin's battery. He was also elected colonel of the 4th Maine, Hiram Berry's regiment, but the regular army would not let him accept a commission in the volunteers.

"Adelbert Ames was every inch a dashing young officer who barked his orders in a deep voice," wrote his only biographer—who may have been biased, because it was his daughter. There was something of the eagle in Ames's piercing eyes. He kept his hair fairly short but had a soup-strainer mustache and a long goatee. "He stood six feet in height, very erect, broad shouldered and athletic. He had an impressive head; his photographs taken as a cadet show a wide forehead and even features. His hair was dark brown; his eyes a hazel brown, under level black eyebrows, could be piercing and imperative. But they were more often twinkling with humor, for he had a zest for life and confidence in the inherent goodness of human beings."[32]

The war tested that confidence, starting at Bull Run, where Griffin's battery played a crucial role. As the battle seemed to be tilting in the Union army's favor, McDowell ordered the batteries of Griffin and James Ricketts forward to Henry Hill, where they endured deadly fire from nearby Confederate infantry and artillery. Rebel sharpshooters holed up in the Henry house turned their attention to Ricketts's men, so the battery shelled the house, not knowing that the poor widow Henry was still inside. She had been too ill to abandon her home as the contending armies approached, and she was mortally wounded during the barrage.

Griffin, who had expressed his displeasure with his exposed position—no doubt in strong language—observed a line of men approaching from his right. He prepared to fire upon them, but chief of artillery William F. Barry insisted they were Union soldiers coming to support the battery. In fact, they were Confederates of Jackson's brigade. By the time the Union artillerymen realized their error, the enemy were close enough to fire a volley in which "every cannoneer was cut down and a large number of horses killed," Griffin reported.[33]

Ames was already a casualty with a serious thigh wound, but the young lieutenant refused to leave his guns. Unable to stand or ride a horse, he directed the battery's fire while sitting on the ground, and his soldiers helped him to his feet and placed him on a caisson whenever the guns shifted position. Finally, they put Ames in an ammunition wagon and began to retreat. Ames later received the Medal of Honor for his actions at Bull Run.

The fighting continued to rage back and forth on Henry Hill, but the loss of Griffin's and Ricketts's batteries indicated that tide was beginning to turn, slowly but inexorably, in the Rebels' favor.

Howard's brigade remained in reserve. After what seemed an endless wait, an aide from McDowell arrived with orders for Howard to move forward. Ahead the soldiers heard the rattle of muskets and the roar of cannon. They moved out at double-quick on the hot afternoon, and the hard pace and brutal heat soon took their toll. "The blankets began to fall, and everything impeding the progress of the men was cast aside as worthless," remembered George Rollins. More and more soldiers collapsed, exhausted. "Men seemed to fall in squads by the roadside, some sun-struck, some bleeding at nose, mouth, ears; others wind-broken, while others were exhausted to such a degree, that the threatening muzzle of the officers' pistol, failed to induce them a step further," wrote a soldier in the 5th Maine. Those that remained began passing the debris of battle—ambulances filled with wounded, men with bullet wounds, and bloody limbs. "I was sorry, indeed, that those left of my men had to pass that ordeal," said Howard.[34]

"We kept hearing that our men were gaining the day and we would be there just in time to give the Rebels a farewell shot but as we neared the field different words were being brought us and as we came upon the field we met our men in retreat," wrote Rollins. "All this didn't stop us, but on we went. Shells began to burst about us and cannonballs served to make us dodge a little but not to stop our progress for we hadn't had a shot at the enemy yet."[35]

At the far right of the Union lines, on a rise called Chinn Ridge, Howard formed his brigade into two lines: the Vermont regiment and the 4th Maine in front, the 3rd and 5th Maine following. Howard, on horseback, watched his men as they went into battle. "Most were pale and thoughtful," he recalled. "Many looked up into my face and smiled."[36]

It was around 2:00 when Hiram Berry received Howard's order to move the 4th Maine forward. The men who remained in the ranks after the punishing double-quick march formed a line of battle and were immediately raked by enemy fire. The first man to fall was Sgt. Maj. Steven H. Chapman, the tall soldier who had picked up the gold coin at the meeting in Rockland. He approached Berry to ask for orders, warned the colonel to avoid unnecessary exposure, and then returned to his colors, where he fell less than a minute later. "Tell my wife I am shot—God bless her," he murmured. Then he died, leaving five fatherless children. One by one more soldiers fell, dead or dismembered. A shell killed Asahel Towne; B. W. Fletcher lost an arm; Lt. William H. Clark of Wiscasset was killed by another shell; a cannonball tore the legs off P. Henry Tillson of Thomaston.[37]

Berry felt surprisingly calm during his first experience of combat. He did not believe he would be hit, and didn't worry about it. Even as men fell to his left and right, he remained focused on his command responsibilities. When Chapman dropped, Berry took up the flag and held it. Bullets tore his clothing and one hit his horse.

Howard then brought up his second line. "The next thing we knew, we were in the field on the hill and facing the enemy," wrote Small of the 3rd Maine. "I can only recall that we stood there and blazed away. There was a wild uproar of shouting and firing. The faces near me were inhuman." Small saw a piece of solid shot kill one of his close friends, David Bates. The 5th Maine suffered its first casualty when a cannonball struck Sgt. Alonzo Stinson, a baby-faced sergeant in Company H. His brother Harry, a private in the same company, remained with the dying Alonzo and was later taken prisoner. Decimated by an artillery piece on its right and swept up by retreating cavalry, half the 5th Maine quickly broke. "It was a hot place," Howard wrote. "Every hostile battery shot produced confusion, and as a rule our enemy could not be seen." Remaining on Chinn Ridge was obviously futile, and Howard ordered a retreat. [38]

"We made a stand and fought the best we could with that battery raking us on the right and musketry playing upon us in front," George Rollins told his parents. "Our men fought well and stood fire like heroes but it was of no use. All the other troops had left, and the Rebels were coming upon us in overpowering numbers so the order to retreat was given and we turned our back to the enemy. I don't wish to say anything of what I saw on the field. God grant that I may never see the same again. Our retreat was all confusion and turmoil."[39]

In fact, the retreat turned into something just short of a rout. The soldiers didn't move "at first in a panicky manner, but steadily, each according to his own sweet will," Howard said. Some flank fire from Confederate troops commanded by Gen. E. Kirby Smith, the helpful captain who had advised Howard upon his arrival at West Point, generated a contagious panic. "Confusion, disorder seized us at once," wrote the 5th Maine's George Bicknell. "How we traveled! Nobody tired now. Every one for himself, and having a due regard for individuality, each gave special attention to the rapid momentum of his legs. We reached the road, and here all discipline was at an end. Our regiment, like every other, was entirely broken up. Strike for the camp of last night the best you can, was the last direction any one heard."[40]

Abner Small observed his fellow soldiers, their eyes red and their faces black with powder or shiny with sweat, as they left the battlefield.

"They were dirty and weary and angry," he wrote. "So was I." He couldn't remember where they recrossed Bull Run, but recalled how the retreating soldiers lost all sense of organization when they entered the woods on the other side. Some men smashed their muskets to pieces against the trees.[41]

Capt. William S. Heath of Waterville, the former child prodigy who was now captain of the 3rd Maine's Company H, walked alongside Howard's horse crying with frustration because his men would not obey his orders. At some point Heintzelman rode by, wearing a sling for a wounded arm, and swore at Howard for not keeping control of his men; Heintzelman must have sworn at many officers that day. Howard, of course, did not swear, but it would not have done any good anyway. In the end he simply tried to spread word that the brigade should fall back to its old campsite at Centreville. From there they made their way back to Alexandria.[42]

The battle had been a disaster for McDowell's army, but Hiram Berry emerged from his first experience of combat with renewed confidence in his abilities as a soldier. He was also pleased with the way his men had performed. Unlike the 5th Maine, the 4th Maine had not broken and run. "My regiment fought bravely and stood their ground manfully," he told his wife. He was not so pleased with their weapons, which had become so overheated they couldn't be fired. "Had they been properly armed, the result of Sunday's loss would have been somewhat different," he wrote in his official report. He was saddened that so many men had fallen in what turned out to be a defeat, but he also seemed to have gained a sense of his own impunity. "I shall come out all right I have no doubt," he assured his wife; "shall do my whole duty, and I never again, probably, shall be placed in such a position should the war last for years as that at Bull Run." He was wrong about that.[43]

❦

George Dyer of Calais was in Washington, working as assistant quartermaster general for Maine. After Bull Run, he wrote to Governor Washburn with his impressions of how the Maine regiments had done in the battle. It was a varied report card. "The 2nd was pretty badly cut up on Sunday, is represented as having lost 150 men," he reported. "The

3rd has lost about as many. The 4th as many or more. The 5th still worse. The 2nd, 3rd and 4th behaved well in battle. The 5th it is said broke and ran badly. Scattered and many are prisoners. In fact as regards the whole of Howard's Brigade, they were panic stricken, and lost about everything except muskets, and a large part of these. We picked up 100 fugitives from our reg'ts in the City yesterday & put them in quarters and provided for them." He concluded, "Matters here in most horrible confusion."[44]

The commander of the 5th Maine was Mark H. Dunnell of Portland, a lawyer and a one-time legislator. When the war began Dunnell was the U.S. consul in Veracruz, Mexico. His patriotism aroused, he received permission to return home, where he helped raise the regiment and was elected colonel. As Dyer noted, Dunnell's soldiers did not perform well at Bull Run. After the battle, Dunnell wrote to Governor Washburn, informing him of the "terrible and complete" defeat. The Rebels captured the regiment's equipment, he said, leaving the men of the 5th Maine "in a forlorn condition." Furthermore, Dunnell wanted the state to reimburse him for money he had spent to buy food for the men when they first reached Washington—a total of $211.50—as well as an additional $36.00 for various other expenses. "I don't want one dollar which belongs to Maine but I am too poor and have lost too much for me to give the state anything," Dunnell wrote.[45]

John French, the Lewiston carpenter who had joined the 5th Maine, was not feeling quite as pessimistic as Dyer and Dunnell. He wrote home, "although we had a terable fight was obliged to retreat we was not whiped & our loss is not near as large as it is reppresented in the papers."[46]

There was one Maine paper that took delight in the Confederate victory at Bull Run, and that was Marcellus Emery's *Bangor Democrat*. In an editorial on July 30, Emery gloated over the battle's results and predicted what the Union armies could expect in the future. "Onward the shouting myriads will pour, until again met by the unequalled and invincible genius of Davis, Beauregard, Johnston and Lee, and the iron nerves of these noble men, who are defending their firesides and their homes, from the ruthless assaults of fanaticism and fury," he wrote. "Victory may again perch upon their banners for a short time, but long ere they will have reached Richmond, disaster will again have overtaken them, and, defeated and routed they will once more fly back to the Potomac in wild confusion, leaving the battle-field, and the wayside stained with the blood of thousands."[47]

This was all too much for some citizens of Bangor, whose sons, husbands, neighbors, and friends had stained the battlefield with their blood. On the afternoon of Monday, August 12, while Emery was out to lunch, a crowd of men forced their way into the newspaper's offices. John Tabor, a local blacksmith, smashed the presses with a sledgehammer, and others began tossing everything they could get their hands on—type, presses, furniture, fixtures—out of an upper-story window into the street. A growing mob set fire to everything that would burn. They added furniture from the nearby barbershop owned by Joseph Jones, who had voiced pro-South opinions. When Emery returned from his meal, he was greeted with cries of "Lynch him!" and "Give him some tar and feathers!" The mob gave chase, but Emery managed to escape by dashing into a drugstore and out the back door.[48]

Back on July 12, Private Rollins of the 3rd Maine had written to his parents that he was "going to visit Jeff D. at his residence" and give the Rebels "a stern rebuke." Instead, the fighting at Bull Run had provided Rollins and his fellow soldiers a cold dose of reality. "I don't hope to get home now til the three years are up," Rollins wrote to his parents afterwards. "I have yet to see many more battles and endure many hardships before this war is brought to a close."[49]

CHAPTER 3

McClellan Makes His Move

I saw my first man killed that day—a shell cut him in two. I think he was the first man killed in the Army of the Potomac, Joe Pepper, of Bath. He used to work for us at home, and when I went out to help bury him that night and took his wife's picture from his bloody pocket, for a moment I would have given all I had in the world to get out of the army; the horror of it was so cruel.

—THOMAS HYDE, 7TH MAINE

On Friday, March 7, 1862, Hiram Berry went up in a balloon. It was not a pleasure jaunt. Reports had indicated heavier-than-usual smoke from Confederate positions in Virginia near the Occoquan River and around Fairfax Station. That might have been a sign that the Rebels were burning supplies in preparation for a retreat. To learn more, General Heintzelman had asked aeronaut Thaddeus Lowe to bring one of his observation balloons to little Pohick Church. George Washington had once worshipped and served as a vestryman at the church, but the neat brick building had become just one more victim in war-ravaged northern Virginia. "Windows were all broken out, doors gone, pews nearly gone, being used for fire wood by our pickets," observed a Union soldier. Souvenir seekers had removed half the pulpit and rain fell through the roof and down the smoke-blackened walls.[1]

The church was not the focus of attention today. All eyes were directed up toward the huge silk envelope of Lowe's balloon. The New

Hampshire–born Lowe was a pioneer in the use of hydrogen balloons as a means of observing the enemy in wartime. He had impressed Lincoln with a demonstration from the White House lawn, where he had used a telegraph to transmit his observations to the ground 500 feet below. After the disaster at Bull Run, Lincoln had appointed Lowe as the chief aeronaut in the Union's nascent balloon corps.

Balloons obviously offered a great way to watch the enemy from a distance. Heintzelman had made a few ascents himself on March 5, but poor weather had limited his observations. Berry hoped for better visibility. With soldiers on the ground firmly grasping the tethers so the balloon didn't escape and drift over to the Confederate lines, Berry ascended to 2,000 feet above the battered church. From his perch in the basket, he had a sweeping view of the contested territory along the Occoquan River—a view that included no Rebels. Joseph Johnston's Confederate army had already abandoned its forward positions along the Occoquan. As soon as he got back on the ground, Berry communicated his findings to Heintzelman. His information added to other reports coming in from Virginia, and together they rendered obsolete all of Maj. Gen. George McClellan's long-gestating plans.

Many things had changed for the Union army outside Washington since Bull Run. It had a new commander—George McClellan—and a new name—the Army of the Potomac (not to be confused with Beauregard's force). What had not changed was its position. The army remained essentially where it had ended up after the panicked retreat from Bull Run, in and around the defenses of Washington. As spring approached, the public and the Lincoln administration impatiently waited for the army to spring into motion. Unlike Irvin McDowell, though, the new army commander proved resistant to outside prodding. He was not going to move his army until he was ready—no matter how long that took.

They called McClellan the Young Napoleon. Born in 1826, the son of prominent Philadelphians, McClellan graduated second in West Point's class of 1846. One of his classmates was the future Stonewall Jackson.

McClellan fought in the Mexican War, at times under Capt. Robert E. Lee. Despite a military career that looked as promising as it could be in the slow-moving antebellum army, McClellan resigned his commission in 1857 and embarked on a successful career in railroads. He left railroads behind when war broke out and he received an offer from the governor of Ohio to take charge of the state's soldiers as a major general of volunteers. Soon he had command of the Department of the Ohio and was the second-ranking officer in the army, behind only general-in-chief Winfield Scott. At a mere 34 years of age, McClellan became a Union hero after scoring some victories in the mountainous regions of Virginia (largely pro-Union sections that would later split off and become West Virginia). For a nation looking for any light in the darkness, McClellan's victories provided a bright spot. The *New York Herald* called him "the Napoleon of the Present War."[2]

The dust had hardly settled from Bull Run before McClellan received a summons from Washington to take command of the army there. "[B]y some strange operation of magic I seem to have become *the* power of the land," he wrote to his wife on July 27. In Washington, McClellan launched into a flurry of organizing, training, drilling, and supplying as he readied his new command—which he named the Army of the Potomac on August 20—for a renewed campaign against Johnston and Beauregard. He was helped in his labors by his efficient and well-liked assistant adjutant general, Seth Williams of Augusta. Another Maine native who proved to be efficient and essential for the Army of the Potomac was Rufus Ingalls, who served as its quartermaster. It was Ingalls's responsibility to keep the army fed and equipped, and he did that job well. Born in Denmark, Maine, in 1818, Ingalls had been Ulysses S. Grant's roommate when they were both plebes at West Point, and he had ably performed quartermaster duties from coast to coast in the years since. He was "perhaps the only officer in a position of great responsibility who gave satisfaction to every commander of the Army of the Potomac from first to last," wrote historian Ezra J. Warner. With his new command gaining in strength and organization, McClellan scored his first major victory by the start of November, when he successfully maneuvered the aging, overweight Winfield Scott into retirement. Now he was not only the commander of the Army of the Potomac, he was also the general-in-chief of the Union armies.[3]

Adelbert Ames was also in Washington, recovering from his Bull Run wound. When Charles Griffin was promoted, Ames received command of the battery. "It was given unsolicited," Ames wrote proudly to his parents in October. "As I received this position as a free gift from my superiors I shall exert myself more strenuously if possible than if it had come by force. 'Ames' Battery' will make a noise if I have my way."[4]

Otis Howard received a temporary demotion after Bull Run, when his brigade was broken up. He returned to the 3rd Maine, in a brigade commanded by John Sedgwick. For the often-sensitive Howard, the demotion stung. Back in Maine, word reached Rowland Howard that his older brother was being overzealous when it came to proselytizing to his soldiers, and he worried that it would cost Otis the respect of his men and officers. "I cannot think it much use in the whole for you to 'preach' to the men," Rowland, a minister himself, cautioned. "Let the chaplain do that. A few words from you in favor of Religion at the proper time backed up by a devout life will do more than <u>arguments</u> or <u>appeals</u> from you. . . . O that God would give you <u>wisdom</u> & discretion as well as faith & zeal." He advised Otis to talk to their brother Charles, who was serving on the general's staff, about the matter.[5]

Perhaps the sense that people were talking about him in Maine, his lack of promotion to brigadier general, and the general sense of discouragement after Bull Run had Howard feeling a bit defensive. When a woman signing herself "one who knows" wrote to chastise him for neglecting his men and allowing them to eat "moldy wormy hard bread and tainted meats," Howard determined her identity and fired off "a few simple facts" in a four-page letter. "You have made accusations against me which would not only destroy my reputation at home if true but when complained of any officer he could be court martialed and dishonorably discharged from the service," he wrote. Howard appears to have been especially stung by her charge that he was "one who pretends to do your duty to God." "My religion consists in striving to do my duty," he wrote.

Howard must have felt vindicated when she wrote back and begged his forgiveness for misjudging him.[6]

Howard's family now included son Guy, daughter Grace, and baby Jamie, and his separation from them added to his funk. When he could find the time, he sent his children neatly printed letters about life in camp, often illustrated with little drawings. He worried that they would not remember their "Papa." Lizzie, who had moved from West Point back to Maine, where she had to deal with establishing a home, raising the children, and handling the finances, did her best to keep Otis informed about the state of affairs in Leeds. Howard was still feeling blue on September 23 when he wrote his wife a long letter. "I have been waiting two or three days for assignment to duty," he told her. "I can't help feeling restless & a little homesick because I have nothing in the way of duty to do; but doubtless before this reaches you everything will be settled." Howard wrote about how he went to visit McClellan but the general would not see him. He felt as though he was "in disgrace at head quarters."

"I hesitate about sending you this letter for fear of touching your loving heart with pain, but it is perhaps better that I should open my own," he wrote Lizzie. "I find that my Heavenly Father doeth all things well. I was a little disappointed to return to my regiment—now I see clearly how much better for it & for me. I am impatient at waiting for assignment & get a little offended at slights." All the setbacks, he told Lizzie, just brought him closer to Jesus. "He can raise me up or bring me down."[7]

Howard's dark night of the soul soon ended, but it revealed how he often labored under a fundamental sense of insecurity. His mood improved when he received command of a brigade under Gen. Silas Casey, consisting of the 45th and 61st New York, 5th New Hampshire, 81st Pennsylvania, and the 4th Rhode Island. Howard was pleased that the officers of all his regiments except the 5th New Hampshire were "strictly opposed to drinking," but at least the Granite Staters had "expelled" all the "drunkards." Like Heintzelman before him, Casey was initially disappointed by the performance of Howard's men. During a review in Washington, the general moaned, "Oh, oh, what a fizzle!" as he watched Howard's brigade march by in some disorder. Fortunately, there would be plenty of time to put things right.[8]

Abner Small later claimed he was glad to see Howard move on from the 3rd Maine so Henry Staples could return to command. "Howard had set us a brave example in battle and otherwise had led us ably enough, but his vanity and cold piety had wearied and repelled us," Small wrote. At least that's what he said after the war. Small didn't feel so negative in 1861 when he told friends, "Col. Howard made a splendid 'colonel' & we were fast becoming well disciplined, a crack regiment he left us & the result is a serious trouble in the 4 Maine Reg."[9]

The problems in the 4th Maine that Small mentioned stemmed from the confusion over terms of enlistment. Once Bull Run demonstrated that soldiering was not such a grand adventure after all, some soldiers decided they had done enough. They insisted they had enlisted for only three months and they wanted to go home. Hiram Berry was at a loss over how to handle the problem. "He was too tender-hearted," said Elijah Walker. "He would not punish a man nor allow others to do so to any extent, and when men became homesick they took advantage of his kindness." Unwilling to punish his soldiers, Berry had the malcontents transferred to the 38th New York and their company broken up.[10]

Other regiments had gone through similar experiences. In a letter to his parents, Stephen W. Dawson of the 2nd Maine complained, "They are trying to humbug us in for three years but they can't do it." George Rollins of the 3rd Maine wrote home about the "great deal of excitement" among some of his fellow soldiers, who believed they didn't have to serve more than three months out of state. Rollins doubted that was the case, but he asked his father to send him a copy of the enlistment law. "I want the law to refute others," he wrote.[11]

The spirit of unrest infected the 5th Maine, too. Colonel Dunnell resigned at the end of August, and Col. Nathaniel Jackson, the "Old Jacks" who had previously led the 1st Maine, took over. Jackson had a reputation as a strict disciplinarian, and his arrival nearly led to mutiny. Cries of "send Jackson home!" rang out through the camp. Some soldiers filled canteens and bottles with black powder and tossed them on campfires so they would explode. The protests became so disruptive that brigade commander Henry Slocum sent an aide to threaten troublemakers with imprisonment. This was enough to convince the officers that they had better settle things down, and they did. "So ended the mutiny in the Fifth Maine, nor was a second ever attempted," wrote regimental historian George Bicknell. "Under Colonel Jackson the regiment grew; a strict discipline was inaugurated, special care was given to the comfort and welfare of the troops, and but a few weeks rolled by before we were as proud of our battalion as we were ashamed before." It might also have helped that around this time the men received their first pay since they had enlisted, the sum of $26.24 paid out in gold.[12]

For the ordinary soldiers, life in their winter camps was woefully short of adventure and glory. "Father I regret having enlisted for camp life is something that is not suited to my mind yet while I stay I shall try to do my whole duty," wrote the 3rd Maine's John L. Little, who was recuperating from illness in a Washington hospital that October.[13]

There were some rude comforts. Pvt. Charles Doak of the 6th Maine wrote home to describe his holiday. "The day before Christmas we had to clean up our things then we spent the evening in merriment," he said. "At nine oclock we went to bed and had a pleasant nap till morning then it was turn out to roll call then it was a wish you mery Christmas all over the Regt then after that came breckfast what do you suppose it was that we had well I will tell you we had baked beans and hot biscuit and coffee then we had turkey for diner it was nice baked beef and potatoes then for supper we had fried donuts and hot tea. We had the day to our selfs to go any whare we wanted to but that has pased and now comes New Years and thare is considerable excitement in getting ready to day for it." Doak was content with his lot in this new life. "We have a plenty of cloths to ware and have a good log house to sleep in and have a fire-place in it and it looks a good deal like an old farmers house with the fire place in it to make it look comfitable and plesant."[14]

"I am well, but have no news of importance to write," noted John S. French of the 5th Maine in a letter home on January 28, 1862. "[T]he weather is still morderate, and muddy, and, about all we have to do is to eat, smoke, sleep, read the papers, tell stories, sing songs, and—but I guess I shall make out that we do conciderable if I keep on, but then, it ain't likely that we do all of these things at once oh! No of cource not." French assured his family back in Lewiston that he was keeping clear of the usual camp vices of drinking, gambling, and stealing, and he had even been selected by his captain to serve as his company's drill master.[15]

George Rollins decided to try his hand at writing for a temperance journal called the *Fountain*. He started with a vignette of life in winter camp, describing the variety of jury-rigged stoves the soldiers used to keep their tents warm. They were made of tin, stone, and brick, while a lucky few men managed to purchase real stoves. "Between the tents, may be seen numerous chimneys, usually of barrels and mud; but occasionally a confiscated stone pipe, puffs its satisfaction at being once more in the service of the friends of the Union," Rollins wrote. "He who says that this randomeness of living is altogether an unpleasant one, is not of our number; for I assure you that a soldiers life is not devoid of its charms, tho' it is not a life I would prefer."[16]

Adelbert Ames, his wound now healed, wrote home to his parents on New Year's Eve. "With a stove in my tent and a buffalo robe as a blanket I manage to live comfortably," he said. He remained busy keeping the affairs of his battery in order. "No one is more anxious for an advance than I, when our leaders see fit to order the movement," Ames told his parents. "In fact I am very anxious to go into battle and whip our enemies, yet I have sufficient confidence in our commanders to wait without murmuring."[17]

Only three days before his balloon adventure, Berry had traveled to Washington to answer a summons from Hannibal Hamlin. The vice president wanted to personally deliver some good news. Berry had been promoted to brigadier general and would receive command of a brigade. "What pleased me most and what will be the most joyful news to you," Berry wrote to his wife, "is that I was informed that I had earned my promotion by faithful duty, and good conduct at Bull Run, and that I was not under any obligation to any one, having been the builder of my promotion." Berry knew how politics often greased the wheels of advancement in the Army of the Potomac. "I came here friendless as far as influence goes, having been a Democrat, and of course not especially in favor," he noted. If that weren't enough, Hamlin had told Berry that the 4th Maine was considered the army's best regiment.[18]

It must have been heady stuff for the former mayor of Rockland. The regiment's sergeants all chipped in to purchase a sword for him, and the officers bought him a silver service. Capt. James D. Earle remembered when Berry rode up to his new brigade headquarters in Charles S. Hamilton's division of the newly formed III Corps. "Is this the headquarters of the 3rd Brigade?" Berry asked. Earle confirmed it, then queried. "Is this not General Berry?"

"Yes, I suppose so," Berry said. "*Colonel* sounds more natural to me, but I believe I *am* General, now."[19]

His brigade consisted of the 2nd, 3rd, and 5th Michigan and the 37th New York. Although he had no regiments from his native state in his new command, Berry did request "one or two of his Maine boys" for his staff. One of them was Edwin Smith of Wiscasset, the son of former Maine governor Samuel E. Smith. Yet another Bowdoin College alumnus, Smith had taken time after his graduation to make a "grand tour" of Europe. He had only recently returned home when war broke out, and he joined the 4th Maine, the first person from Wiscasset to enlist. At Bull Run, it was said, Smith was one of the last of the regiment's officers to leave the field, and he had been forced to use his revolver to hold the enemy back long enough to escape.[20]

❧

Despite increasing impatience from the president, McClellan's army had remained motionless before Washington, and McClellan stubbornly refused to share his plans. Finally, reluctantly, McClellan unveiled his strategy. He wanted to take his army on transports to the town of Urbanna, Virginia, just upstream from where the Rappahannock River flowed into Chesapeake Bay. From there he would march on Richmond. But once Hiram Berry's balloon observations confirmed that Johnston was retreating—past Centreville, beyond Manassas, and all the way to a new line behind the Rappahannock—McClellan's Urbanna plan became obsolete. He had to go back to the drawing board. He now decided to ship his army all the way to Fort Monroe, a Union-held strongpoint at the tip of the Peninsula between the York and James Rivers, and launch his campaign against Richmond from there.

———

One day in the spring of 1862, as the Army of the Potomac was making its slow, laborious slog up the Peninsula from Fort Monroe toward the capital of the Confederacy, Thomas Hyde noticed two directional signs nailed to a tree. One was weather-beaten and had obviously been in place for a long time. "21 miles to Richmond," it read. The other one looked much newer, and it pointed north. It read, "647 miles to Gorham, Maine."[21]

Once again, Hyde was a long way from home.

Hyde had been in Illinois when the war began, so he joined Ephraim Ellsworth's Chicago Zouaves amid the patriotic fervor that followed Lincoln's call for troops. His company was not selected to head east with the rest of the regiment. Eager to get into the fray, he then enlisted in a regiment raised by abolitionist firebrand Owen Lovejoy that later became the 39th Illinois. However, when Hyde heard news that the 3rd Maine was leaving for war, he decided to return home and join a Maine regiment. Instead, he ended up back at Bowdoin, where he taught drill and worried that he would never get a chance to fight. Bull Run showed Hyde that his fears were groundless, because the United States certainly needed more troops to put down the rebellion. He found three like-minded friends, Sam Fessenden, George O. McLellan, and George Morse, and they tracked down a lawyer named Frederick Sewall—a Bowdoin graduate who would later serve on Otis Howard's staff and then command the 19th Maine—to swear them into the service of the United States. Then they went to Augusta to get the papers necessary to raise a company.

Sam Fessenden was the youngest son of Maine senator William Pitt Fessenden, and he had already gained some experience with sectional conflict. Back in June 1856, at the tender age of 15, Sam had run away from home to throw his weight behind the Free-Soilers in Kansas, when the territory was being torn apart by conflict between proslavery and antislavery factions. If he found adventure, so much the better. He headed to Kansas, determined, he said, "to rush into exploits of some kind, the more dangerous the better I thought, and looked around for an opportunity of acting on my resolution." Senator Fessenden feared for his son's life, but Sam had been lucky. His band of Free-Soilers had hardly arrived in Kansas when they were surrounded by a mob of proslavery "border ruffians" and forced back on a steamer and out of the territory. His father didn't learn of Sam's whereabouts until that fall.[22]

In Bath, Hyde, Fessenden, and McLellan opened a recruiting station and printed out handbills. They read:

> *ONE CHANCE MORE.*
> *A few good men wanted for the Bath Company of the 7th Regiment.*
> *Pay and sustenance to commence immediately.*
> *$15.00 A MONTH.*
> *$22.00 bounty and $100.00 when mustered out of service. Apply at*
> *their recruiting office, opposite J. M. Gookin's store, Front Street.*
> *Bath, Maine, Aug. 6, '61.*

They called their new company the Harding Zouaves after Col. E. K. Harding, a Bath native who served as the state's quartermaster general. As the volunteers came in, Hyde signed them up and sent them to Augusta. He was eager to follow and "taste the sweets of command." Before long he joined the rest of the regiment in the capital on the long lawn in front of the statehouse, where he had "a supper that no one can appreciate who has not eaten beans baked in a hole in the ground." Later that night it began to rain, so Hyde decided to put the men of his company up in a local hotel at his own expense, while he and his officers slept in tents and experienced the rigors of army life.[23]

The regiment's first colonel, Edwin C. Mason, could not get released from the regular army, so Thomas H. Marshall, formerly from the 4th Maine, received command. Ill health had forced Marshall to leave Bowdoin College when he was a sophomore, but he had done all right for himself, and he had served as a state senator from Waldo County before the war. By some accident, Selden Connor and Hyde had both been elected major. Governor Washburn solved the dilemma by appointing the 23-year-old Connor as lieutenant colonel.[24]

Connor hailed from Fairfield, Maine. He graduated in 1859 from Tufts College in Massachusetts, and moved to Woodstock, Vermont, to study law shortly after Lincoln's election. He didn't take the threat of war too seriously, but the attack on Fort Sumter changed all that. War became the "all-engrossing" topic of conversation in Woodstock—"people talk, think and care for nothing else," Connor said. His own thoughts were full of "bristling bayonets" and "ensanguined fields." Motivated by a love of Union, Connor followed the senior member of his firm into the Woodstock Light Infantry. "Like most of my comrades I was not an Abolitionist, but a Lincoln Republican, opposed to the extension of slavery but not advocating a crusade against it," he said later.[25]

"War is a dreadful thing to contemplate, but is by no means the worst thing that can befal [sic] a nation," he wrote to his sister. "Government protects us, and when she is threatened it is our duty to protect her." The Woodstock Light Infantry became part of the 1st Vermont, a three-month regiment that spent time in Virginia without seeing combat. Connor was mustered out in early August 1861 after an uneventful three months. Within a couple of weeks he received a telegram informing him that he had been elected major of the 7th Maine.[26]

Hyde recalled being "appalled" by his own "ignorance and inefficiency," but he did know a little bit about drill. "Fresh from my Zouave training, I soon had Company D in shape, and I loved every man in it," he wrote. "The delight of a first command was on me, and even now I can see the faces of all, from the tall man on the right to little Charlie Price, the shortest, on the left. I see them just as they looked then, enthusiastic and boyish, but of those eighty most are now with the silent majority. Four years in the 7th Maine did not prove favorable to longevity."[27]

Sam Fessenden's older brother, James, became involved in the war effort when Governor Washburn asked him to raise a company of United States Sharpshooters. The sharpshooters were the brainchild of Col. Hiram Berdan, a mechanical engineer and a crack shot who had made a name for himself in amateur shooting events. (During the war, Berdan gained a reputation as an unscrupulous liar who was more concerned with his patents and his business interests than with the war effort. Historian Wiley Sword noted Berdan's "excessive vanity, petty actions, conniving manner, and want of personal courage on the battlefield.") Berdan proposed creating two regiments of skirmishers and snipers comprising top marksmen from throughout the country. Candidates had to pass a shooting test in which they fired from either 100 yards (holding their weapons) or 200 (with their weapons supported) and had to place 10 shots at a combined distance of no more than 50 inches from the bull's-eye, an average of five inches per shot. Fessenden soon learned how difficult it was to meet Berdan's exacting requirements. Writing to the governor on September 21, 1861, Fessenden confessed that he could not find a single man who could qualify. "I have not felt at liberty to enlist any who are not now up to the mark and consequently have made no enlistments," Fessenden said. His lieutenant, a Rockland stonecutter named Jacob McClure, had better luck in his part of the state, and by the time the company left Maine on November 13, 93 men had joined.[28]

In Washington, the officers began to grumble about the way they were being treated and they wrote to Governor Washburn with their complaints. "We are getting humbugged and we have heard nothing but humbug since we came here," Lt. Silas Barker told the governor.

"We have been grossly deceived regarding the nature and purpose of our organization," Fessenden complained. "Our men were enlisted under the promise that we were to act as a special corps, to be armed with superior rifles (Sharps) and to be detailed especially for a particular service and not to be placed . . . on the same footing as an ordinary infantry regiment." The Sharps rifle was a breech-loading weapon that was markedly superior to ordinary muzzleloaders and let the shooter fire much faster. Where a soldier with a muzzleloader generally had to stand to load his weapon, a man equipped with a breech-loading Sharps could reload while lying down or hiding in a tree.

Jacob McClure told Washburn that rumors in camp said the sharpshooters were going to receive ordinary rifled muskets. "The men will not consent to take a musket for an hour, for as soon as that is done we are on a level with the infantry," wrote McClure. "The men are a fine body of whole souled Maine boys reddy and willing to do their duty if they are used for what they was enlisted for . . . if they will give us the Rifle that was promised to us and a chance to see the enimy there is no doubt but the Maine boys will drop in the lead and show where they come from."[29]

—◦—

The 7th Maine left the state on August 23 and had a prolonged stay in Baltimore. While there, Colonel Marshall fell sick; he died of typhoid fever just before the regiment was supposed to depart for Washington. Responsibility for the move fell on Connor's shoulders. He assumed the burden with mixed feelings as he waited to see if he would receive permanent command. "I am very young: but I think I am about ten years older in experience than I was six months ago," he wrote his father. He told his sister, "I had rather take the office to myself than to play second fiddle to some political nincompoop (good word isn't it?)."[30]

Connor managed to get the regiment to Washington. Major Hyde was not impressed by the nation's capital, which he thought was a "shambling, straggling, dirty and forlorn place." Once established at Camp Griffin, the regiment became part of the third brigade in William F. "Baldy" Smith's division of the VI Corps. Life became a succession of drilling and picket duty, as fall turned into winter, and winter slowly gave ground to the approaching spring. Edwin Mason returned to the regiment to replace Marshall, removing the burden of command from young Connor's shoulders.

On March 11, the 7th Maine broke camp and began marching toward Manassas, now that Johnston had abandoned the town and moved his army behind the Rappahannock. "We expect to be in Richmond in a fortnight," Hyde wrote home. Much later he noted, "We got there in a little over four years, but our hopefulness was pleasant just the same."[31]

Finding Manassas empty of Rebels, the regiment marched back to Alexandria in pouring rain. On March 23, the men boarded the steamer *Long Branch* and began the journey to Fort Monroe. "I am in my element now; it begins to look like soldiering in earnest," Connor wrote home.[32]

The 7th Maine was one of seven Maine units that took part in McClellan's grand campaign. Over the next week or so, these regiments and all the other pieces of the army began coming ashore in Virginia. Thomas Hyde found time to ride over to the deserted Chesapeake Female College in Hampton—which his sweetheart, Annie Haydon, had been attending just a year earlier before making a hurried departure back to New England after the attack on Fort Sumter. During this extended buildup to combat, Hyde realized that "the real business was about to begin." He remembered watching some of his men shooting at birds, "little thinking how the same men would soon be bringing down human game."[33]

McClellan finally got his cumbersome war machine creaking into motion on April 4. Its first target was the town of Yorktown, where George Washington's troops and their French allies had defeated the British 81 years earlier. The Rebels there, a small force of only about 8,000 men under "Prince" John Magruder, were using some of the trenches that Washington's army had dug. Heintzelman's III Corps followed a route directly towards the town, with elements of Erasmus Keyes's IV Corps (with the 7th Maine at the forefront) on Heintzelman's left, moving down the Peninsula's center. It soon became readily apparent that McClellan's army was relying on inadequate maps and unreliable information about the quality of the roads, which proved to be poor, especially when it rained and the pathways turned into quagmires.

Hyde encountered his first Rebels on the way to Yorktown. The 7th Maine, acting as skirmishers, had emerged from some woods and spied cavalry led by an officer on a white horse. The horseman fired his revolver, and then disappeared with the rest of the Confederates down the road. Pressing on, the Maine soldiers reached the Warwick River, which flowed from Yorktown across the Peninsula to the James River. Rebel fortifications stood on the other side. Believing he had received an order to "draw the enemy's fire" (when in fact it had been to cease firing), Hyde advanced all the way to the creek. Enemy soldiers on the far side started shooting at him, but Hyde managed to duck into some bushes before they could find his range.

"I saw my first man killed that day—a shell cut him in two," Hyde recalled. "I think he was the first man killed in the Army of the Potomac, Joe Pepper, of Bath. He used to work for us at home, and when I went out to help bury him that night and took his wife's picture from his bloody pocket, for a moment I would have given all I had in the world to get out of the army; the horror of it was so cruel."[34]

Otis Howard and his brigade remained near their place of embarkation. He was now part of the II Corps under veteran soldier Edwin "Bull" Sumner. "No one in the Union army was more admired as a leader of men in the heat of battle," wrote historian Stephen W. Sears about Sumner; "no one had risen in rank further beyond his capacity." Howard's brigade belonged to the division commanded by Vermont native Israel Richardson, known as "Fighting Dick." He was a big man, and somewhat sloppy in appearance. "I think he is a good man, but I wish he got up earlier in the morning & was a little more active," said Howard. Otis was wondering when he would get a chance to see battle again, having become increasingly impatient at the army's slow pace. He became even more alarmed on April 9 when McClellan visited the division and Howard overheard him tell another officer that he could not take Yorktown without a "partial siege." That meant a time-consuming operation of digging trenches, building fortifications and batteries, and transporting heavy siege cannons within range of the enemy positions. McClellan's promising start was grinding to a halt.[35]

"We are having a pretty good taste of soldiers life now, but the boys have faith in McClellan so they don't growl much," said George Redlon, a soldier in the 4th Maine. "They are rather impatient to commence operation upon Yorktown."[36]

❦

The Union army remained stalled in front of Yorktown. Many of its soldiers lay down their muskets and took up picks and shovels. Hiram Berry, now happily in command of "one of the largest and best brigades in the army," put his civilian experience to good work by overseeing the repair of two Confederate sawmills and using them to produce lumber for the siege fortifications. "I have a fine command and am pleased with the officers," Berry wrote home on April 12. "My way of living here is not that which any one would court; sometimes we eat, and some days we eat not at all. We sleep on the ground, but all are cheerful. It has rained three days at a time, during which we were all drenched to the skin, but all feel willing to go through anything to assist in closing this cursed war." He optimistically estimated the conflict would be all but over by July 1.[37]

One day, George Redlon watched as Berry rode by and spotted one of his men in soaking-wet clothes. The general stopped and asked the soldier if he had anything dry to wear. The man said he did. Berry told him to change as soon as possible so he wouldn't catch cold. Then he rode on. "What kind of general is that?" the soldier asked a member of the 4th Maine. "I never had a general speak to me in that kind of way." That was just Berry's style, the Mainer replied—"always looking out for his men."[38]

CHAPTER 4

Howard Loses His Arm

I trust when Richmond falls the war closes. I shall then be with you. I have accomplished my object, and shall feel ready, willing, yes, anxious to retire at the earliest moment. I want nothing; no place, no position that takes me from home.
—HIRAM BERRY, THIRD BRIGADE, THIRD DIVISION, III CORPS

Thomas Hyde was about to see some real fighting. After his taste of combat on the banks of the Warwick, the young major had settled into the often-dreary routine in front of Yorktown. He had worked on a detail that felled trees to corduroy a road, and noticed the way soldiers marveled at how the "hardy lumbermen from Northern Maine" could cut a swathe through the forest. There were moments of excitement, too, such as a sharp skirmish that killed his Bowdoin friend George O. McLellan. "He was only a sergeant in the 7th Maine but to the end of the war I thought that a proud position," Hyde wrote. On another occasion, Hyde went out with three companies to probe the enemy's position. A bullet hit the man in front of him, making a noise "like a sledge on wood." Afterwards, Hyde reported to General Sumner and gave him a map he had drawn. Sumner seemed astonished that such a young man could be a major. "My God! Sir you will command the armies of the United States at my age, sir," said Old Bull, who was 65 years old at the time.[1]

At this point, Hiram Berry had a new division commander. His old one, Charles Hamilton, had been too vocal in his criticisms of

McClellan, so the commanding general replaced him with Brig. Gen. Philip Kearny, one of the war's more colorful characters. Kearny was a native New Yorker who had been born into wealth in 1815 and became even wealthier when his grandfather died and left him a million dollars. Now that he was independently wealthy, Kearney could do whatever he wanted. He wanted to join the army, so he enlisted and received a commission in the 1st U.S. Dragoons. Sent to France to study cavalry tactics, Kearny fought as an observer with the French Chasseurs d'Afrique in Algiers. While serving under Gen. Winfield Scott in 1847, he was wounded and lost his left arm during the fighting at the gates of Mexico City. The missing limb didn't slow him down, though. Kearny learned to grasp his horse's reins in his teeth while he waved his saber with his right hand. After Mexico, Kearny returned to Europe and fought for Emperor Napoleon III in Italy. It was also in Europe that the 38-year-old Kearny fell in love with a 20-year-old American named Agnes Maxwell. Kearny's wife refused him a divorce, but Agnes moved into his estate with him anyway. Eventually, Kearny's wife relented and he married his new young bride. When war broke out, Kearny received command of the New Jersey Brigade. "His abrupt speech and his imperious manner denoted a proud disposition, and a character incapable of flattery or of dissimulation," wrote the Comte de Paris, who served as an aide to McClellan during the war. Brusque, ill-tempered, and impatient, Kearny had a reputation as a fierce fighter. And he learned to loathe George McClellan.[2]

As McClellan's preparations to blast Yorktown into submission inched forward, his soldiers weren't entirely lacking in excitement. On April 22, Selden Connor wrote to his father about one incident. "I was trotting along a few yards in rear of the line as coolly as you please," Connor wrote, "when suddenly 'crack' sounded a rifle from the bushes in front and down dropped a man directly in front of me: in a moment—'zip' went a ball close by me; one touch of the spur and I was in the bushes in an instant and off my horse. We went a few rods further, driving their pickets before us, and came to an opening where we halted in accordance with the orders of the General. I went to Lieut. Johnson to speak with him about the position and 'whiz' went a ball just between us. It was amusing to see the alacrity with which Johnson supported a tree on the right and I another on the left."[3]

McClellan planned to open his attack on Yorktown with an overwhelming barrage of artillery on May 5, a month after his arrival on the Peninsula. Joseph Johnston never gave him a chance. In the pre-dawn hours of May 4, following an artillery bombardment of their own, the Confederates began quietly slipping away from Yorktown under the cover of darkness, moving up the Peninsula toward Williamsburg. McClellan had gained a nearly bloodless victory, but Johnston had bought 30 valuable days.

McClellan sent Brig. Gen. George Stoneman's cavalry off to nip at the heels of the retreating Rebels. Following the cavalry were the infantry divisions of Joseph Hooker and William F. "Baldy" Smith, Hooker on the left, Smith on the right. On a road near the Warwick River Col. Edwin Mason of the 7th Maine had a close brush with death when he stepped on a "torpedo," one of the explosive devices the retreating Rebels buried in the roads or used to booby-trap their Yorktown fortifications. Fortunately, only the percussion cap exploded. Mason had some of his men crawl on their hands and knees to uncover more mines in the roadway. Selden Connor almost stepped on one, coming "within two inches of certain death." Other commanders, enraged by the Rebels' unsportsmanlike conduct, had Confederate prisoners move ahead and disarm any hidden devices.[4]

On May 4 it began to rain. The steady downpour turned roads into creeks, creeks into swamps, and swamps into impassable obstacles. The muck bogged down the heavy artillery and made marching a chore for wet and filthy soldiers, who sank ankle-deep. Joe Hooker, an ambitious Massachusetts soldier who liked to fight and to connive against his superiors, found that "the roads were frightful, the night intensely dark and rainy, and many of my men exhausted from loss of sleep and labor from the night before in the trenches." Late that night, he called for a halt and waited for morning.[5]

Hooker resumed his march early on May 5 but found the way to Williamsburg blocked by a formidable earthen fort that John Magruder had named after himself. Fort Magruder was the centerpiece of a network of redans, rifle pits, and fortifications that stretched across the Peninsula. The Confederates had cut down trees in front of the fort to give themselves a clear field of fire. Hooker had not yet earned the nickname "Fighting Joe," but he was already living up to it. "Being in pursuit of a retreating army, I deemed it my duty to lose no time in making the disposition of my forces to attack, regardless of their number and position, except to accomplish the result with the least possible sacrifice of life," Hooker wrote. He sent forward the brigade of Maine native Cuvier Grover, supported by artillery.[6]

It was the start of a day of "violence and slaughter," as Hooker described it, of attacks and counterattacks through the rain, mist, fog, and smoke. As the day wore on, James Longstreet's division of Confederates reinforced the enemy, and Hooker's outnumbered men began running low on ammunition. The Rebels had captured several of their cannon, which had become stuck in the mire. The situation looked critical. Heintzelman reached Hooker's front and, realizing the demoralizing state of affairs, found a regimental band and ordered them to start playing. "Play!" he shouted, "play, it's all your good for. Play, d—n it. Play some marching tune! Play Yankee Doodle, or any doodle you can think of; only play something." He also sent orders to Kearny to move up in support of Hooker. Kearny did so, with Hiram Berry's brigade in the lead.[7]

The first obstacle Berry encountered was a division from Sumner's II Corps, slowed by the mud and rain and blocking the road. Berry found an alternate route toward the sounds of battle. When that road began veering in the wrong direction, Berry had his men throw their knapsacks on the ground and embark on a difficult cross-country trek through woods and gullies in Hooker's direction. "General Berry is entitled to great credit for the energy he displayed in passing the obstructions on the road, and for the gallant manner in which he brought his brigade into action at the turning point of the battle," wrote Heintzelman, who reportedly nearly burst into tears of joy when he saw the reinforcements arrive.[8]

With Kearny's help, Berry placed his regiments in position and ordered his men forward. Capt. Edwin Smith of his staff led the advance personally, and had two hats shot off his head and several bullets pierce his clothing. "His conduct was, indeed, most gallant and noble," Berry

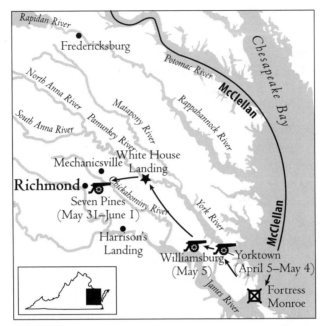

The Peninsula

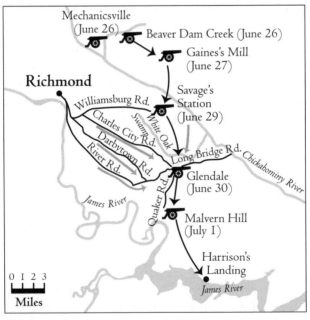

The Seven Days

noted. The hottest fighting took place on the left, where Confederates tried and failed at a flanking movement.[9]

The situation on Hooker's front had stabilized by the time evening fell. The exhausted, cold, and wet soldiers settled in for the night. "Berry's timely arrival had saved General Hooker from being overwhelmed by superior numbers, and from this time General Hooker conceived the strongest admiration for General Berry and was ever after his constant and steadfast friend," wrote Berry's biographer. Kearny, who could be scathingly critical about officers he didn't respect (including McClellan and Heintzelman), had nothing but positive things to say about the former mayor of Rockland. Later that month, Kearny took time to write to Governor Washburn about the contributions of Maine soldiers in his command. In particular, Kearny praised Berry, whom he said demonstrated "a genius for war, and a pertinacity in the fight that proved him fit for high command." He also had good things to say about Brig. Gen. Charles Jameson, who had started the war in command of the 2nd Maine, became Maine's first general, and now commanded Kearny's First Brigade.[10]

The other part of the battle of Williamsburg took place about a mile away from Hooker, separated by swamps and forests. It was fought under Winfield Scott Hancock, who commanded a brigade in the II Corps. Hancock was a consummate warrior. The Pennsylvania native had graduated from West Point in 1844 and had served in Mexico and on the Western frontier. He had been army quartermaster in Los Angeles when the war began. Hancock "was tall and well proportioned, had a ruddy complexion, brown hair, and he wore a mustache and a tuft of hair upon his chin," recalled one Maine soldier, who thought the general was "the best looking officer in the army." He also had a reputation as one of the army's most fluent swearers.[11]

Hancock's brigade was in the division commanded by Baldy Smith, who received word about some unmanned Confederate redoubts to the rear of Fort Magruder. With Sumner's reluctant approval, Smith sent Hancock forward with his brigade, reinforced by the 7th Maine and the 33rd New York. The expedition followed a road that crossed Cub Creek Dam and led to the abandoned Rebel position. There was another deserted redoubt in the marshland just beyond it. Hancock positioned his artillery and infantry, including both the 6th and 7th Maine, and drove away some Confederate skirmishers. He then waited for reinforcements before attacking. Instead, he received a message from Sumner ordering him to fall back. Not wishing to retreat, Hancock stalled, sending his own message to Sumner explaining the situation. He opened up an artillery barrage, and then had his infantry begin to fall back to a more defensible line near the first fortification. As the men began moving, the Confederates sent out an attacking force. It was just the excuse Hancock needed to remain and fight.

As Hancock was delaying, Thomas Hyde had gone forward as a skirmisher. He found the whole experience of working cautiously through the tangled woods, always expecting to see an enemy soldier hiding behind a tree, to be "rather gruesome." He returned safely to his own lines—despite drawing fire from his own men on the approach—just before the Rebels launched their attack on Hancock's position. They were commanded by Jubal Early, Robert E. Lee's profane "bad old man." Seeing Hancock's men moving back toward the first redoubt, the Confederates thought the Federals were retreating. Their "exultation knew no bounds," said Hiram Burnham, the bear-like old lumberman who commanded the 6th Maine. "They poured out from the cover of the woods and rushed toward us, crying out 'Bull Run,' 'Ball's Bluff,' &c. It was with difficulty that I restrained my men from facing about and taking vengeance for these taunts upon the spot."[12]

The time for vengeance came soon enough. When the advancing Rebels reached a rail fence, Burnham sensed they felt flush with victory. "But it was our turn now," he wrote. "Every man was in his place, and we poured a volley into them which thinned their ranks terribly." The Rebels recovered and resumed the advance, and the Maine soldiers fired another destructive volley. "They wavered, they faltered, they halted," said Burnham. Then they broke and fled.[13]

The 7th Maine was to the right and rear of Hancock's position. Like Burnham, Colonel Mason had difficulty restraining his men as they fell back toward the redoubt. Once Hancock gave the order to attack, Mason told his men to fix bayonets and charge. "From my place on the left of the regiment, I saw General Hancock galloping toward us, bareheaded, alone, a magnificent figure; and with a voice hoarse with shouting he gave us the order, 'Forward! charge!'" Hyde recalled. "The papers had it that he said, 'Charge, gentlemen, charge,' but he was more emphatic than that: the air was blue all around him." Thus inspired, the regiment charged. Selden Connor said the 7th Maine's fire had the Rebels "dropping like tenpins, one after another: they could not endure it—so turned and fled in wild confusion followed by our deadly fire."[14]

Charles Amory Clark, the Foxcroft Academy student who had enlisted in the 6th Maine, was now a second lieutenant with the regiment's Company A. He was badly bruised by a spent bullet while trying to rally his men during the fighting, but emerged otherwise unharmed. After the battle he was struck by the toll the fighting had taken on the Rebels. "Everywhere the ground was strewn with Confederate dead and dying," Clark remembered. "The loss which the enemy had sustained was something marvelous. I doubt if at any time during the entire war our forces inflicted such amazing destruction with such little loss to themselves." Once the fighting was over, Clark's main concern became constructing a comfortable bed. He found two fence rails, placed them on the ground, and threw his rubber blanket over them. He then fell into a deep slumber. "It made no difference that the rain poured in torrents, and the victims of the battlefield lay thickly around us. Only those who have slept upon a battlefield can know the deep and dreamless sleep which comes, when the conflict is ended which has tried mind and body alike to their utmost."[15]

The next day's dawn revealed that the Confederates had broken off contact and resumed their march up the Peninsula toward Richmond. The Federal regiments that had fought in the battle emerged with a renewed sense of pride in their abilities. Connor was especially pleased when McClellan rode up to the regiment and made a spontaneous speech congratulating them on their "bravery and gallant conduct." "As I listened my heart swelled with pride and gratification: I felt a few inches taller, and all the blood in me seemed to rush to my face," Connor wrote to his sister. "The 7th would follow him to the death."[16]

Thomas Hyde seconded that feeling. Writing to his mother he said, "It was the proudest event of our lives and we feel now more than ever, that whoever slanders George B. McClellan, *our second Washington*, does himself shame and his country harm."[17]

———

Otis Howard's time on the Peninsula had been relatively uneventful, but that would change soon enough. As he had feared when he overheard McClellan talk about his plans, Howard had experienced "a long and peaceful sojourn near Yorktown" during the monthlong siege, not exactly what he had wanted or expected. On the morning of May 4, he had just finished hosting a breakfast Bible reading and discussion in his tent ("We read that chapter of Daniel which tells the story of Shadrach, Meshach, and Abednego passing through the fiery furnace") when he received word that the Confederates had abandoned their fortifications. Howard assembled his brigade and sent it in pursuit of the retreating enemy, but he was stuck in the rear of Sumner's division and made frustratingly slow progress, hobbled by the rain and the mud, and also by the fear of Confederate "torpedoes." Howard gave up his horse to a sick officer, but the roads were so muddy that he had to walk alongside and keep a firm grip on the halter to keep from falling into the mire. His brigade didn't even make it past Yorktown until darkness fell on May 5, and then he received orders to backtrack and board transports to go up the York River. He did ride up to the Williamsburg battlefield after the fighting was over, and he saw dead soldiers lying in the mud. "I stopped, dismounted and looked at them in the face. I could not help feeling the same towards friend & foe then," he wrote his wife.

Howard had mixed feelings about the Yorktown campaign, writing to Lizzie that he believed McClellan should have attacked immediately rather than laying siege. "But I do not believe he lacks genius for his profession, but I think he inclines too much to <u>engineering</u>," he judged.[18]

When the fighting that became known as the battle of Fair Oaks or Seven Pines started on May 31, Howard and the rest of Israel Richardson's division were on the opposite side of the Chickahominy River, the swampy waterway that flowed east of Richmond and down to the James.

The river divided McClellan's army, which had elements posted on each bank. Union engineers had built two bridges across the Chickahominy, one called the Grapevine Bridge, and the other the more prosaically titled Long Bridge. Usually the Chickahominy was slow and placid as it wound lazily through the Virginia swampland, but another epic downpour had turned it into a roiling cauldron that threatened to tear the bridges apart. That would have stranded the three corps under Sumner, Fitz John Porter, and William Franklin on the north side of the Chickahominy.

That's exactly what Joseph Johnston was hoping when he planned to deliver a knockout blow against the Union forces on the waterway's south side. But disorganization among his various commanders turned Johnston's sledgehammer attack into a series of flailing punches. Dissipated as it was, the force of the blow was still enough to drive back green frontline troops in Silas Casey's division and threaten a Confederate victory.

Hiram Berry began pushing his Michigan regiments forward through swampy and wooded ground toward the sounds of the battle, moving against a tide of retreating Federals. Col. Stephen G. Champlin of the 3rd Michigan ordered a bayonet charge, but soon fell wounded. Berry ordered in the 5th Michigan and then the 37th New York. By sundown, his men had run low on ammunition and were raiding the cartridge boxes of the dead and wounded, but the Union line had stabilized. It was a bloody day for Berry's men. One of the casualties was his aide Edwin Smith, shot through the head while leading men into battle. Another member of the staff reported how Berry's eyes filled with tears when he learned of Smith's death. Berry arranged to recover the body, and soldiers placed the corpse in a blanket and hauled it three miles out of the swampy woods where Smith had fallen.[19]

On the north side of the Chickahominy, Sumner had been waiting impatiently for orders to join the fighting. Stung by criticisms of his performance at Williamsburg, Sumner had his men march forward to the bridges and wait in formation, ready to cross at a moment's notice. John Sedgwick took his division to the Grapevine Bridge, and Richardson marched downstream to Long Bridge. The surging current eventually swept away Long Bridge, but Sedgwick and later Richardson made it across the Grapevine Bridge, with only the weight of their marching troops keeping the waters from tearing the span apart. Sedgwick reached the fighting in time to stabilize the Union lines, and then night fell.

Howard arrived too late to participate in the fighting on May 31. "As we approached the front a thick mist was setting in and a dark, cloudy sky was over our heads, so that it was not easy at twenty yards to distinguish a man from a horse," he recalled. Nelson Miles, one of his aides, suggested that Howard dismount and lead his horse to keep from trampling the dead and wounded who lay underfoot.[20]

June 1 was a Sunday, not a day on which the pious Howard preferred to fight. Still, he had no choice. The Confederates renewed the battle around 5:00 A.M., and before long the fighting "was as severe as any in the war." Howard's horse was shot, and he saw some of his men wavering. Riding forward on a replacement mount, he led the 64th New York ahead, while his brother Charles rode in advance of the adjacent 61st. A bullet hit Howard in the right forearm. After his brother rode over and bound up the wound, Howard continued his advance. Another volley crackled through the woods. This time a bullet shattered Howard's right elbow. A lieutenant from the 64th New York helped the general to the ground. Growing faint, Howard summoned Col. Francis Barlow of the 61st New York and told him to take command of this part of the line. Then Howard was helped to the rear, where he found Gabriel Grant, the surgeon for William French's brigade. Grant bound up the wounded arm. Charles Howard was back here too, badly wounded in the thigh.

Still able to walk, Howard made his way to the rear. At one point a soldier whose fingers had been shattered by a bullet helped support him. A half mile or so further Howard found the house where his brigade surgeon, Gideon S. Palmer of Gardiner, had set up shop for his gory business. Palmer examined the arm, and told Howard it would have to come off. "All right, go ahead," the general said. "Happy to lose only my arm."

After a long wait, Howard was placed on a stretcher. The surgeon tightened a tourniquet around his upper arm, and then had the wounded general brought into the amputation room. Howard found the place to be "a little grewsome withal from arms, legs, and hands not yet all carried off, and poor fellows with anxious eyes waiting their turn." After being placed on the operating table, Howard received chloroform and fell into a deep sleep. The surgeon then sawed off Howard's right arm, which joined the growing pile of discarded limbs on the blood-soaked floor.

The next morning, on his way to Fair Oaks Station, Howard ran into Phil Kearny. The one-armed Kearny eyed Howard's empty sleeve. "General, I am sorry for you; but you must not mind it; the ladies will not think the less of you!" he said.

Howard laughed, perhaps a bit ruefully. "There is one thing that we can do general," he replied, "we can buy our gloves together!" Then Howard climbed aboard the train for a jarring and painful three-hour rail journey to White House Landing. There he encountered Sarah Sampson, the Maine woman who had nursed him back to health earlier in the war. Her husband, Charles, was now in command of the 3rd Maine and she had come with him to the Peninsula. The two wounded Howard brothers asked her to accompany them to Fort Monroe. Once there she found them a surgeon who could better dress their wounds, and then she bid farewell to them as they embarked on the first leg of their trip home to Maine.[21]

Hiram Berry had emerged physically unscathed from the fighting so far, but the war was taking its toll nonetheless. On June 14, he wrote home that he was "pretty well, but greatly careworn." He added, "One thing is certain, I never in all my eventful life endured so many sufferings and privations as I have the past ten months." Three days later he wrote to his wife and expressed his desire to return home by August for his daughter's sixteenth birthday. He still believed the end of the war was near. "I trust when Richmond falls the war closes," he wrote. "I shall then be with you. I have accomplished my object, and shall feel ready, willing, yes, anxious to retire at the earliest moment. I want nothing; no place, no position that takes me from home."[22]

It had been a long, slow, cautious campaign. Some of McClellan's generals began referring to their commander as the "Virginia Creeper," but no one could deny that the Army of the Potomac had come promisingly close to the gates of Richmond. Its soldiers could see the city's church steeples off in the distance, and hear their bells ringing. It seemed inevitable that the Confederate capital would fall, bringing an end to the war. "*Richmond was to be* ours," wrote Charles Bicknell of the 5th Maine, summing up the optimistic feelings. "No one doubted it. Our triumph was soon to be heralded in every part of the world."[23]

Robert E. Lee felt differently. Lee, who had been serving as an advisor to Confederate president Jefferson Davis, became commander of the force he named the Army of Northern Virginia after Joseph E. Johnston had been wounded during the battle of Seven Pines. A much more aggressive general than Johnston, Lee hoped to send McClellan reeling back from Richmond. He aimed to strike while the Union army was still divided by the unpredictable Chickahominy, with Fitz John Porter's V Corps still on the north side. The resulting week of warfare became known as the Seven Days' Battles.

Surprisingly, it was McClellan who attacked first, in a tentative offensive on June 25 that unfolded around the site of the fighting at Seven Pines. In the battle of Oak Grove, McClellan gained about 600 yards, at the cost of 626 casualties. North of the Chickahominy, Lee launched his own offensive on June 26, but stumbled into a poorly coordinated attack at Beaver Dam Creek near the shantytown of Mechanicsville. The Union soldiers of the V Corps successfully beat back the Confederates, but Porter ordered a retreat to what he felt was a better defensive position closer to the bridges across the Chickahominy. It was near a mill owned by a secessionist named William Gaines. "The enemy, pursuing our rear guard from Mechanicsville with very little loss to our troops, soon notified us that we could not cross the Chickahominy without making a stand," noted Col. Charles Roberts of the 2nd Maine. Porter's sole corps of about 34,000 men was badly outnumbered by Lee's 57,000, now that an unusually sluggish Stonewall Jackson had finally arrived from the Shenandoah Valley to add his weight to Lee's army.[24]

The fighting at Gaines' Mill began around 12:30 p.m. on June 27, when Lee threw A. P. Hill's division at Porter's line, arrayed on a bluff above Boatswain's Swamp. "For nearly two hours the battle raged, extending more or less along the whole line to our extreme right," wrote Porter. "The fierce firing of artillery and infantry, the crash of the shot, the bursting of shells, and the whizzing of bullets, heard above the roar of artillery and the volleys of musketry, all combined was something fearful."[25]

As the fighting raged on the north side of the Chickahominy, the 5th Maine on the south side received orders to break camp, cross the creek, and reinforce Porter. Their brigade, under the command of Col. Joseph J. Bartlett, approached the battlefield around 4 P.M. and encountered a violent and chaotic scene. "The infantry moving steadily to the front, cavalry galloping here and there, artillery wheeling and counterwheeling, couriers dashing hither and thither, cannon roaring, musketry rattling, clouds of smoke rising from the fields, or rolling through the woods; it was indeed an awful scene, yet grand and sublime," remembered George Bicknell. "Take away the thought of death and suffering, and it was one upon which no one could look with other emotions than those of awe and admiration. But we were not there to admire scenes and landscapes. We may have been needed to complete the picture."[26]

Bartlett first threw the 16th New York into the fray to support regulars under George Sykes, whose line was bending and about to break. Then he sent in the 96th Pennsylvania, which wilted under the fire. Bartlett had no choice but to send in "Old Jacks" and the 5th Maine. "This regiment also changed its front in the most soldierly manner, and under the sweeping storm of iron and leaden ball sent up their battle-shout and rushed upon the enemy forcing back his lines and holding the crest of the hill in our front," Bartlett reported. The roar of battle was deafening, so loud the soldiers could hardly hear their own shouts. Bullets filled the air and thudded into human flesh. Colonel Jackson fell wounded and William S. Heath assumed command. It wasn't long before Heath, the young man who had circled the globe by the age of 16, was dead, shot in the head. "Comrade after comrade fell upon either side, yet there was no faltering," wrote Bicknell. "About sunset the fire came too hot; it was more than flesh and blood could resist, and backward the men began to fall." Brigade commander Bartlett noticed that the colors of one of his regiments lay on the ground. "Boys, don't leave your colors—about face!" he ordered, and the men turned back, charged, and recovered the flag.[27]

Bicknell described the battle as a "terrific slaughter, accompanied with terrible scenes." Porter's outnumbered men beat back charge after charge, but the lines, bent time and again, were beginning to break, with men streaming to the rear. An ill-advised cavalry charge late in the evening accelerated the unraveling. Sent reeling back through the lines after a bloody repulse, the Union horsemen sowed disorder and confusion. As his lines began to crumble under the pressure, Porter ordered his men to fall back. By early the next morning, they had crossed the Chickahominy.

After the 5th Maine had retreated, officers announced that McClellan, on the other side of the Chickahominy, had entered Richmond. The Maine soldiers cheered loudly, only to learn later the story had been a ruse, intended to raise cheers that the enemy might interpret as a sign that reinforcements had arrived. "Suffice it to say, there was but very little cheering, no matter what the nature of the news may have been, in the Fifth Maine Regiment after that," Bicknell wrote.[28]

McClellan had no intention of attacking Richmond. Instead, unnerved by the fighting north of the Chickahominy, he decided to order something that seemed suspiciously like a retreat. McClellan called it a "change of base." He made preparations to move his base of supply from White House Landing on the York River to Harrison's Landing on the James, clear across the Peninsula. According to Maj. H. L. Thayer, Hiram Berry's provost marshal, when Kearny and Hooker learned of McClellan's plans, they rode to the general's headquarters to protest. Berry went with them. So did Heintzelman. Kearny did most of the talking, urging McClellan to let him move on Richmond and, at the very least, liberate the Union captives from Libby Prison. When McClellan refused, "General Kearny denounced him in language so strong, that all who heard it expected he would be placed under arrest until a general court-martial could be held, or at least he would be relieved from his command."[29]

Kearny remained unpunished, and McClellan began moving his army toward the James, where it could rely on protection from navy gunboats on the river. But first came an orgy of destruction, as the Union soldiers wrecked all the supplies they could not take with them. Trains were set ablaze and run off bridges, which were then destroyed. Huge piles of food were set alight. Ammunition went up in huge explosions. "Here an immense pile of hard bread in boxes, enough to feed a province of starving Russians for days, was blazing; there a long line of whiskey barrels was being destroyed; farther on was a huge holocaust of hospital stores, and new clothing was at the will of every chance comer," noted Hyde. "The stragglers got drunk on the remnant of whiskey, and decked themselves out in new army raiment, but they were few in number. Generally the regiments were well closed up and in great spirits for a fight." When the Confederates attacked the Union rear guard at Savage's Station, even the sick and wounded in the Union hospital there, some 2,500 of them, were left behind.[30]

The rest of the Union army began moving along the narrow roads and tracks through the bogs and woods of White Oak Swamp toward Harrison's Landing. The 5th Maine acted as a rear guard while the rest of the army streamed south. At around 2:00 A.M. on June 29, it finally received orders to fall back and join the retreat. "Such sights as met our vision!" remembered Bicknell, "the vast bodies of troops upon the move, the immense trains of baggage-wagons, ambulances, and artillery, a mighty mass, yet all moving like clock-work, were seldom seen even by the soldier. Slowly we marched forward, suffering intensely from the hot sun." In the 7th Maine, Hyde remembered chewing on twigs as a means to keep his thirst down during the day, and falling asleep while his horse continued to plod its way through White Oak Swamp in the pitch dark of night. Stonewall Jackson, offering a lukewarm pursuit, set up his artillery on the far edge of the swamp and commenced shelling the retreating Federals.[31]

McClellan's strung-out army provided a tempting target for Lee, who aimed to slice through the columns near the crossroads hamlet of Glendale. Here the Union army turned down the Quaker City Road to head toward the James. Lee sent his army down from Richmond on several roads that converged at Glendale.

Henry Slocum's division, and with it the 5th Maine, made camp at the Charles City Cross Roads, still serving as a rear guard for the retreating army. Kearny's division, including Hiram Berry's brigade, was on their right. McClellan rode through camp on the morning of June 30. He still displayed that mysterious magnetism that made his soldiers love him, even when he was retreating. "It certainly gave great cheer to the boys to see their beloved commander," wrote Bicknell. "No one can question the place which he held in their affections at that period." The soldiers had just finished a hurried dinner when word came that Rebels were approaching in force. Growing fire—the crackle of muskets and the boom of artillery—announced their arrival. "Never was the nerve of our regiment more severely tested than at this fight, and never did it behave with greater credit to itself and all concerned, than under the terrible cannonading of Charles City Cross Roads," Bicknell wrote. Shot and shell swept through the air. The solid shot tore off tree branches that fell onto the soldiers, while shell fragments took a more direct toll. Then the roar of the guns gradually died, and in the sudden silence the Union soldiers could see the Rebel infantry approaching. "Like an irresistible mass, on they came," Bicknell wrote. Now it was time for the Union artillerymen to try their hands, and their loads of grape and canister began taking a bloody revenge on the Rebels. Soldiers fell, but others replaced them in the ranks. "The roar of the cannon, the terrific yell of the charging columns, is deafening," wrote Bicknell. Smoke filled the air; the ground shook. The surviving attackers tramped on, coming closer and closer. The cannon fired again. "The form of the enemy's column reels and trembles. It had accomplished all that human power could do. Back, back, it falls, and the guns of Slocum's division, handled and supported by brave men, were victorious."[32]

With Kearny sick, Hiram Berry was in temporary command of his division. The Pennsylvania Reserves were in Berry's front when the Rebels attacked, and they were driven back. "I immediately put my Brigade into the gap made in our lines, and sent for reinforcements," Berry reported. "The battle raged fearfully; we were losing heavily, and it cost us many men to retake the position lost by the Pennsylvania troops." As the sun set, Berry was in the same position where he had begun, but he had lost, in killed and wounded, nearly 400 men.[33]

In the predawn hours the next day, the 5th Maine prepared to quietly slip away from its exposed position. Officers whispered their commands and soldiers made sure their muskets or canteens wouldn't rattle and betray their movement. The Union soldiers made a hushed retreat away from the enemy and toward the security of numbers. At one point Philip Kearny, back in the saddle, rode by. "Move on steady, boys," he whispered, "but if the hounds tread on your heels, kick." Dawn began to brighten the sky, but by then Slocum's division was within Union lines on a rise of land called Malvern Hill.[34]

Here, on July 1, the two armies played out the last act of the Seven Days. On the Union side, the battle was fought mostly by the artillery, which wreaked havoc on Lee's disorganized attacks. One Maine soldier who got his licks in at Malvern Hill was Adelbert Ames. For a young soldier seeking the glory of combat, the Peninsula Campaign had initially been a frustrating experience. "I am quite disgusted with my own ill luck," he wrote on June 15 to his parents, who had moved to Minnesota. "I might as well be in St. Paul as here, so far as fighting goes." Ames did not get a taste of combat until Gaines' Mill on June 27. Assigned to support Baldy Smith's division and posted near a house belonging to James Garnett on the north side of the Chickahominy River, his Battery A "was subjected to a terrific cannonade." In his official report, Ames wrote that his guns silenced the enemy's after about an hour and a half. "Their loss is supposed to have been considerable."[35]

Ames and his battery slogged its way across the Peninsula toward the James as part of McClellan's change of base until it reached the commanding slope of Malvern Hill and waited for the enemy there. Ames's battery was posted on the left of the Union lines with the brigade of Charles Griffin, his former commander. When Confederate general Rans Wright sent his brigade—four regiments from Georgia and one from Louisiana—forward up the sloping wheat fields toward the Union lines, Ames and the other Union batteries unleashed a killing fire. In his report, Ames noted that his six guns fired a total of 1,392 rounds during the battle. The commander of his brigade of the artillery reserve, George L. Getty, reported, "The battery remained on the field during the entire day, and was handled with great skill," and he added, "First Lieutenant Adelbert Ames, commanding Battery A, Fifth Artillery, deserves particular mention for gallantry and skill at the battles of Chickahominy [Gaines' Mills] and Malvern Hill." For his actions that day, Ames received a brevet promotion to lieutenant colonel.[36]

There was no question about who won the field. McClellan's army did, fending off Lee's disorganized attacks so bloodily that Confederate general D. H. Hill declared the battle was not war, "it was murder." McClellan also had the support of the navy gunboats on the James. Onboard the USS *Galena*, Sam Washburn—one more of the Washburn brothers from Livermore—wrote his brother Elihu and said, "we shelled the sons of bitches for four hours yesterday afternoon & are all ready to give it to them again." Washburn saw McClellan come aboard the vessel (when, critics charge, he should have been on dry land directing his retreating army). Like McClellan, Washburn believed the Union army was greatly outnumbered, by five to one, in his estimation.[37]

Once it became obvious that the Union defenders had bloodily repulsed the Rebel attacks on Malvern Hill, Fitz John Porter, who had overseen the fighting, sent a message to McClellan suggesting an attack, but the Young Napoleon had already issued orders for the army to make the final leg of the retreat to the James. He had snatched defeat from the jaws of victory.

After bidding farewell to the Howards at Fort Monroe, Sarah Sampson had returned to White House Landing to continue her work for the wounded and sick. "Such suffering and confusion I never before witnessed," she said. The doctors were so overwhelmed that even relatively minor wounds became infected due to inattention. She cared for George Gordon of the 3rd Maine's Company I, who had been shot through both legs. Sampson asked him if he was willing to lose them. "Yes, rather than my life," he replied, "and rather my life than not to have been there." In the end he lost both legs and life. She also treated General Jameson, who had fallen seriously ill and would die on his way back to Maine, one of the many thousands of soldiers struck down by disease instead of bullets. Sampson had been at Savage's Station on June 25, taking down the names of wounded Maine soldiers, but had to return to White House Landing when it was evacuated. She lost her lists and all of her possessions in the ensuing "skedaddle." Shortly afterward, her husband fell ill and resigned his commission, and Sarah returned with him to Bath. "It is with great reluctance that I leave at a time when my services are so much, ever so much needed; and when my opportunities and facilities for affording relief to the suffering are daily extending," she wrote to Adjutant General Hodsdon. But she said her first duty was to her husband. "He has lost none of his patriotism, though I think his confidence in some of the commanders somewhat shaken at least."[38]

Not everyone had lost confidence in McClellan. Selden Connor, who had taken command of the 7th Maine during the retreat when Colonel Mason fell sick, told his father that McClellan had done "all that a general could do with the means at his disposal." Furthermore, he added, "The whole retreat was conducted orderly and systematically and when we turned at bay upon the enemy it was always for their discomfiture." But Connor also had the mistaken belief, as McClellan did, that the Army of the Potomac had been greatly outnumbered, by more than two to one. He also realized that the Union needed more men if it wanted to defeat the Confederacy. "If Maine does her full share as of course she will in answer to the call, she must raise several new regiments in addition to filling those already in the field," he said. Connor worried that might mean seeing unqualified men being promoted over him, and he did not want to see that happen. "I confess to being proud, and I don't want to see men sporting the eagle who have been taking Richmond in bar-rooms all winter while we have been wallowing in Virginia mud."[39]

While waiting with his battery at Harrison's Landing, Adelbert Ames decided to write to Israel Washburn. "Now, I am very anxious to command a Regiment of Maine troops," he told the governor. "And it is with many misgivings that I offer myself as a candidate for so high and important a position." If Ames really had any misgivings, they were overcome by his ambition. Promotions were few and far between in the artillery. A young man of promise, like Ames, would do better in the infantry.[40]

CHAPTER 5

Ames Gets a Regiment

I feel that we are fighting for our country—for our flag—not as so many stars & stripes but as the emblem of a great & good & powerful nation—fighting to settle the question whether we are a nation, or only a basket of chips—*whether we shall leave to our children the country we have inherited—or leave them without a country—without a name, without a citizenship among the great powers of the earth.*

—JOSHUA LAWRENCE CHAMBERLAIN, 20TH MAINE

On July 4, 1862, John P. Lancaster found it difficult to keep his mind on work as he helped his father with the chores on the family farm in Richmond. He was trying to muster up the courage to raise a difficult topic. Chores finished, father and son were about to enter the house when John stopped. "Father," he said, "President Lincoln has called for 300,000 more soldiers. It is my turn now."

Lancaster remembered how a brief look of anguish flashed across his father's face before he spoke. "John," he said, "I have told you for the past year that there would be time enough for you to enlist, and you see I was right, but I agree with you now, though God knows how it pains me to say it, I think it is your turn now." John remained outside while his father went into the house to break the news to the rest of the family.

Lancaster joined Company A of the newly formed 19th Maine and was soon with the regiment in Bath. He was young and naïve and had a great deal to learn about war. "How many times I have laughed since when I think of the presentation of swords to the Lieutenants of company A, and the speeches they made," he remembered many years later, long after war had taken his innocence. "They said those swords should never be stained except by traitor's blood. Poor fellows, how little they knew what they were talking about. Yet we cheered them, not because of their eloquence, nor soldierly bearing, for they stammered and looked terribly awkward, but because we thought the sentiment good."[1]

McClellan's misfortunes on the Peninsula had provided another stark demonstration that the war would be neither quick nor easy, and that the country needed more Union soldiers to win it. In May, the Maine legislature authorized the governor to add a sixteenth regiment to the troops it had already raised. On July 2, President Lincoln put out a call for 300,000 more three-year volunteers. Governor Washburn responded with a statement "to the people of Maine" two days later. "An additional number of troops is required by the exigency of the public service, and if raised immediately, it is believed by those who have the best means of knowledge, that the war will be brought to a speedy and glorious issue. ... Of this number the President of the United States desires and expects that Maine should furnish her proportion or quota." The state offered to raise four more infantry regiments, plus a cavalry regiment, a sharpshooter company, and six batteries of light artillery.[2]

In August Adelbert Ames received orders to take a leave of absence, return to Maine, and assume command of one of the new infantry regiments. The regiment was the 20th Maine. Unlike the state's other units, which had distinctly regional origins, the 20th Maine was cobbled together from all over the state. The colonel was from Rockland, the lieutenant colonel from Brunswick, the major from Bangor, and the adjutant from Portland. It had 10 companies, and men from at least 10 different counties manned them.[3]

Samuel Keene was 29 when he enlisted in the 20th Maine, making him somewhat older than the average recruit. Born in the coastal town of Bremen, Keene had attended college in Waterville for two years before finishing his education at Union College in Schenectady, New York. He served as the principal of an academy for two years and then decided to take up the law. He had been lawyering in Rockland when war broke out, and had been married for less than four months, to Sarah Prince of Thomaston, when he enlisted. "His prospects were brilliant, his hopes high, his profession promised him honor and ample remuneration," read an obituary. "But other aims and duties were before him. His country was in trouble, he sympathized with her in her distress and he flew to her relief." Keene enlisted as a lieutenant in Company I but was soon promoted to captain of Company F. He began keeping a meticulous diary with succinct entries of each day's events, noting the weather, his activities, the letters he sent and received, and the people he saw. He often complained of being "blue" and of longing for home.[4]

Bowdoin graduate Ellis Spear was teaching in Wiscasset and growing increasingly discouraged by the Union reverses during the first year of the war. When he heard Lincoln's call, Spear decided to raise a company. Even with a $100 bounty as bait, he found recruiting slow going until he teamed up with two other men. Working together, they signed up 87 volunteers, "almost wholly of the original New England stock, all sturdy, reliable characters, self-respecting and as good as any that had been organized into regiments." The recruits formed Company G of the 20th Maine, and Spear became its captain.[5]

When Spear reported to the new colonel's tent at Portland's Camp Mason, he found Ames in conversation with the regiment's lieutenant colonel. Spear quickly received the impression that Ames was not very happy with his new command; in fact, he felt it was "highly unsatisfactory." Discipline was nonexistent. Men didn't even know how to salute properly. The band was terrible. It was, in the colonel's own words, "a hell of a regiment."[6]

Spear was already acquainted with Ames's lieutenant colonel, for that officer had been one of his professors at Bowdoin. He was born Lawrence Joshua Chamberlain on September 8, 1828, in Brewer, on the opposite shore of the Penobscot River from the bustling port town of Bangor. Chamberlain later reversed the order of his first and middle names, but his family still called him Lawrence. The oldest of four sons and one daughter, Lawrence grew up on his family's farm, where he learned the virtues of hard work and self-reliance. In one oft-told tale, the wheel of a hay wagon became wedged between two stumps and he could think of no way to move it. "Do it, that's how," his stern father told him, and Lawrence eventually found a way. As a young man he suffered from a stammer that he had to conquer through his "power of will." It was, perhaps, another application of his father's lesson of self-reliance.[7]

Probably due to his mother's influence, young Chamberlain developed a love of music and learning. His father had been a Maine militiaman, and he gave his son an appreciation for military matters. Lawrence even spent a term at a military school in Ellsworth until his family's financial difficulties forced him to withdraw. Instead of the army, the pious young man aimed for a career in the ministry. After teaching some school in the Brewer area, he entered Bowdoin College in 1848, where he displayed a remarkable talent for language, eventually becoming able to read in seven, not counting English. He also spent some evenings at the home of one of his professors, whose wife, Harriet Beecher Stowe, sometimes read to students portions of a novel she was writing. The novel was *Uncle Tom's Cabin*.[8]

At Bowdoin Chamberlain fell in love with his pastor's adopted daughter, Frances Caroline Adams. He and "Fanny" became engaged in 1852 but didn't marry for more than three years. In the meantime, Lawrence, his eye still on a life in the ministry, returned north for further study at the Bangor Theological Seminary. The couple finally married on December 7, 1855, but it appeared to be a relationship in which Fanny did not reciprocate Lawrence's ardor and one that suffered strains, especially after the war. The couple settled in Brunswick, and Lawrence began teaching at Bowdoin. He was still there as professor of modern languages when war broke out in 1861, and he watched as more and more of his pupils took up arms. Chamberlain was scheduled to go on a sabbatical in Europe, but he decided to join the army instead.

On July 14, 1862, Chamberlain wrote a letter to Governor Washburn and asked for a commission. "I have always been interested in military matters, and what I do not know in that line, I know how to learn," he wrote. After seven years at Bowdoin, Chamberlain told the governor, he understood the importance of education and his role at the school. "But, I fear, this war, so costly of blood and treasure, will not cease until the men of the North are willing to leave good positions, and sacrifice the dearest personal interests, to rescue our country from Desolation, and defend the National Existence against treachery at home and jealousy abroad. This war must be ended, with a swift and strong hand; and every man ought to come forward and ask to be placed at his proper post."[9]

If Stowe's novel about the evils of slavery had stirred something in Chamberlain's soul, he didn't show it. He never displayed any abolitionist tendencies. He joined the army to save the Union. "I feel that we are fighting for our country—for our flag," he said, "not as so many stars & stripes but as the emblem of a great & good & powerful nation—fighting to settle the question whether we are a nation, or only a *basket of chips*— whether we shall leave to our children the country we have inherited—or leave them without a country—without a name, without a citizenship among the great powers of the earth."[10]

Chamberlain enlisted despite the disapproval of his father, who told his son the conflict was "not our war." (It's worth pointing out that the elder Chamberlain named one of his sons after John C. Calhoun, the proslavery South Carolina politician who espoused the doctrine that states could nullify federal laws.) The Bowdoin faculty opposed his decision as well; Chamberlain was surprised by the "unexpected degree of opposition" he received. Professor William Smyth told him he would probably return from war "shattered" and "good-for-nothing." One letter that made its way to Governor Washburn in Augusta said that Chamberlain "is nothing at all; that is the universal expression of those who know him." Nevertheless, Washburn granted Chamberlain's request and appointed him lieutenant colonel of the 20th Maine.[11]

Chamberlain's brother Tom also joined the regiment. The youngest of the four brothers, Tom seemed to lack the restless ambition that propelled Lawrence. He was the only one of the brothers who had not attended Bowdoin, and he had been working as a clerk in a Bangor store when he joined the 20th Maine. His older brother tried, but failed, to get him the appointment of quartermaster sergeant. "He is abundantly competent for the place having been for some time chief clerk in F. M. Sabine's store, and I would like him to receive the appointment," Chamberlain wrote the governor's aide-de-camp. Tom did not get the post, but he joined as a private and was later promoted to sergeant. Like Charles Howard did for his older brother, Tom Chamberlain provided familial support for Lawrence in the field.[12]

Joshua Lawrence Chamberlain was no longer a professor. He was a student again, and he began diligently applying himself to learning the art of war.

In answer to Lincoln's call, recruiters began to fan out across the state to find young men willing to leave their homes and take up arms to restore the Union. One of the recruiters was Abner Small, who had moved up in the world since fighting with the 3rd Maine at Bull Run. After enduring the winter encampment, Small learned that his regiment needed recruiters back home. He jumped at the chance. Once in Augusta, he received a summons to Israel Washburn's office. The governor asked him to recruit soldiers for the new 16th Maine regiment. If he signed up enough, Small would become a company captain. Small set out to find volunteers. By his own admission, he was terrible at it, managing to recruit only two. The low point came in the town of Readfield Corner, when Small signed up a boy who turned out to be a minor. The young man's father threatened to turn Small into a "dead hero" if he didn't leave town immediately. It was discouraging work. Fortunately, the new regiment's colonel, Asa Wildes of Skowhegan, realized Small was better suited to be the adjutant, the officer responsible for the regiment's paper trail, and he offered him the position. Small accepted.[13]

George D. Bisbee was a young law student in the village of Dixfield on June 17 when a tall man in a soldier's uniform drove into town on a wagon. Sitting beside him was a man playing a fife; in the back was a boy with a drum. The duo started to play and a crowd gathered. When enough people had assembled, the tall man introduced himself. He was Capt. Daniel Marston, he hailed from Phillips, and he had come to recruit soldiers for Company C of the 16th Maine Volunteer Infantry.

Bisbee not only signed up, he volunteered to help Marston recruit, and he soon had his own office in Farmington.[14]

Mustered in with 960 men on August 14, 1862, the 16th Maine reached Washington a week later and marched out onto the "sacred soil" of Virginia the next day. There the new soldiers received their first experience of war's real glory, by digging rifle pits. "It was not to our liking, as infantry, to be turned into gunners and ditch diggers, but in the exigencies of war our preferences were not consulted," wrote Small. On Friday, August 29, the regiment heard the distant sounds of battle from somewhere out in Virginia. It was Second Bull Run. Three days later the raw Maine soldiers watched the battered remnants of John Pope's Army of Virginia stagger back to the safety of the fortifications around Washington. The Union had suffered another demoralizing defeat.[15]

John Pope was supposed to be the answer to George McClellan. Lincoln's little remaining confidence in the Young Napoleon rapidly dissipated after the disappointments on the Peninsula, and the president sought a general who could win victories in Virginia. Pope had scored some success along the Mississippi in Missouri, so Lincoln summoned him east to assume command of a cobbled-together force called the Army of Virginia. Pope immediately created rancor within the Army of the Potomac by issuing a bombastic proclamation stating that he planned on always seeing the backs of his enemies and would fight on the offensive, not the defensive. McClellan railed to his wife about this "paltry young man who wanted to teach me the art of war." Lincoln added insult to injury when he ordered another Western general to Washington. This was Henry Halleck, nicknamed "Old Brains" for his supposed intellectual capability. Lincoln named him general-in-chief of all the Union armies, the job he had taken away from McClellan so the Young Napoleon could focus on the Army of the Potomac. McClellan interpreted Halleck's appointment as "a slap in the face."[16]

Robert E. Lee had a pretty good sense of McClellan's limitations as well. After he sent the Union army back to Harrison's Landing on the James, Lee realized that his opponent lacked the initiative to stir from his sanctuary and attack Richmond. He decided to gamble by sending Stonewall Jackson north across the Rapidan River to attack Pope's army. At the battle of Cedar Mountain on August 9, Jackson tangled with Maj. Gen. Nathaniel Banks, who commanded a corps under Pope. Like the Bull Run battle a year earlier, the fight at Cedar Mountain began well for the Union side. With temperatures on a sweltering afternoon approaching 100 degrees, Banks aggressively pushed his men into battle and forced the Rebels back. One Confederate casualty early in the fighting was Brig. Gen. Charles S. Winder, the man Jackson had personally selected to replace him at the head of his Stonewall Brigade. Now in command of a division, Winder was mortally wounded by a shell fragment during a two-hour artillery duel between the contending forces.

The fatal shell had been fired by the 2nd Maine Battery, commanded by a young Damariscotta native named James Hall. Mustered in November 1861, the battery had seen little combat but lots of travel, as it journeyed from Washington to Manassas; to Front Royal, Virginia; back to Manassas; to Warrenton, Virginia; and eventually to Cedar Mountain, with various stops in between. (One of its original lieutenants had been Sam Fessenden, the senator's son and Thomas Hyde's friend from Bowdoin. By the time the battery reached Cedar Mountain Fessenden had moved to a staff position with Gen. Zealous Tower.) As part of the 2nd division of Irvin McDowell's III Corps in Pope's army, Hall's battery served under Maj. Davis Tillson, the division's chief of artillery and Maine's former adjutant general. Tillson complimented Hall on his performance at Cedar Mountain, saying his battery "poured in upon the enemy a fire that for precision and rapidity could not have been surpassed."[17]

The Union's initial infantry attacks had been equally successful, and for a time it appeared that they would break Jackson's lines. But the tide began to shift after Stonewall himself arrived to rally his troops. Reinforcements from A. P. Hill provided the tipping point, and the Union soldiers began retreating.

One of the regiments in the battle was the 10th Maine, which traced its ancestry back to the state's first regiment. In the confusing early days of the war, the men who volunteered for the 1st Maine had officially enlisted for two years, but they received assurances they would not have to serve for more than three months. They returned to Maine without fighting at First Bull Run. Governor Washburn considered calling the regiment back to serve its full two years, but instead sent 200 of its soldiers to the 10th, a new two-year regiment. At Cedar Mountain it formed part of Samuel Crawford's brigade of Banks's corps. Crawford was a Pennsylvanian who had been serving as an army surgeon at Fort Sumter when the war started, and he had given up medicine for the infantry. As a result, some of his soldiers called Crawford "Old Pills," much to his displeasure.

This was the 10th Maine's first combat experience—even the veterans from the 1st Maine who had mustered in some 15 months earlier had never fired their guns in anger. That included the regiment's colonel, George L. Beal of Norway. Beal had worked as an express messenger before the war and had been captain of the Norway Light Infantry, a militia unit. He became the first man from Oxford County to enlist once Governor Washburn made his appeal for soldiers, and his militia company became part of the 1st Maine, with Beal serving as its captain.[18]

Beal and his new command would see their first action at Cedar Mountain. Crawford received orders to push his four regiments forward. The soldiers fixed their bayonets, crossed a fence, and with a cheer charged into a wide-open field. There they met "a fatal and murderous fire from the masses of the enemy's infantry, who lay concealed in the bushes and woods on our front and flank," Crawford reported. Fighting was hand-to-hand at some places, Crawford said, but it was hopeless, "and my gallant men, broken, decimated by that fearful fire, that unequal contest, fell back again across the space, leaving most of their number upon the field."[19]

The 10th Maine advanced into battle late in the day, having spent the afternoon in support of a battery. The soldiers passed through a wood, and then crossed a wheat field, growing increasingly worried as they saw men to their right slowly retreating under fire. "Give them three down-east cheers!" shouted Colonel Beal. It wasn't long before Beal, too, recognized the wisdom of falling back, and he found a low ridge that provided a slight bit of shelter. Maj. Louis H. Pelouze, one of Banks's staff officers, arrived and demanded that Beal move forward again. John Mead Gould, who had been promoted to lieutenant since his time with the 1st Maine and now served as the regimental adjutant, watched Pelouze engage Beal in a lively discussion. "The staff officer grew furious and appeared to be having a fist-fight with the Colonel, so animated were the gesticulations of the two officers," Gould recalled. More and more enemy soldiers were darting into view in the woods to the front and the inexperienced Maine soldiers began to fall under their fire. It was growing dark and the flames shooting from the enemy's muskets were clearly visible in the increasing gloom. Finally, the 10th Maine got the chance to fire its first volley of the war. "We who were in line can never forget the tremendous crash and echo it made," said Gould, who thought that a bayonet charge might have driven the Rebels from the woods. Instead, the enemy fire continued taking a toll, "and our line began to wilt in a way none of us ever knew before or since."[20]

It was a deadly serious business, but Gould later recalled how ludicrous the scene must have appeared, as soldiers frantically loaded and fired from all conceivable positions—lying down, crouching, standing— or rammed charge after charge into their guns. The men who had been hit by enemy fire jumped and kicked and flailed about, like a "crowd of whirling dervishes." Gould also noticed the variety of sounds that bullets made, from the zip of a minié ball to the "singing" of the slower-moving buck-and-ball fired from smoothbores.

Beal finally gave the order to retreat. Crawford's brigade fell back, with the 10th Maine serving as rear guard. "There was no skedaddle, according to the strict meaning of that word," said Gould, "though our organization was broken, the officers had no great trouble keeping us together." A full moon had risen, providing enough visibility for the exhausted men to see where they were going. The next morning Crawford was talking with Colonel Beal. "Where is my splendid Brigade?" he asked. "Where are all my brave fellows?" Gould said the general "cried like a child."[21]

Two of the regiment's soldiers were Horace and Lyman Wright, a father and son from Auburn. Lyman was only 16 years old. Five days after the fighting his father took pen in hand to write an anguished letter home to his wife. "I will try to compose myself to write you a few lines to let you know how we are but you must prepare yourself for the worst," he cautioned. "Lyman had his right arm shot off and a flesh wound through the thigh." The badly wounded young man had nearly become a prisoner, but he managed to hobble away and get help. "[I]t near about breaks my heart to see my poor boy with but one arm and to be a cripple for life," his father wrote, "but it is so and I will write you as often as I can and let you know how he is getting along."[22]

After beating back Banks's attack, Jackson remained in place for two days. When Pope did not offer battle again, Jackson slipped back across the Rapidan. The battle had been a Confederate victory, "but in the exhibition of pluck and hard fighting our army was altogether first," Gould averred, "and we were fought by Jackson and his best troops, two to one, and three to one, but never even-handed. Let the future historian remember that." Pope's first encounter with the Army of Northern Virginia had left him with a bloody nose. Worse was to follow.[23]

❦

Back on Harrison's Landing, McClellan was supposed to hurry the Army of the Potomac north to support Pope. McClellan took his time, acting either out of spite or from his innate inability to do anything quickly. He was more than willing to leave Pope "to get out of his scrape" on his own.[24]

Elijah Walker, Hiram Berry's old business partner, now commanded the 4th Maine. A grizzled 44-year-old with a short dark beard and quizzical blue eyes, Walker was an independent Maine man who didn't hesitate to speak his mind. The regiment didn't leave its camp until Friday, August 15, and didn't reach Yorktown until late Tuesday, August 19. There the 4th and three other regiments from its brigade crammed themselves aboard the steamer *Merrimac* for a miserable two-day voyage to Alexandria. Once disembarked, they piled aboard railroad cars the next morning for a trip down the Orange and Alexandria Railroad to Warrenton Junction, and marched five miles more to take up a position as the brigade's advance regiment.[25]

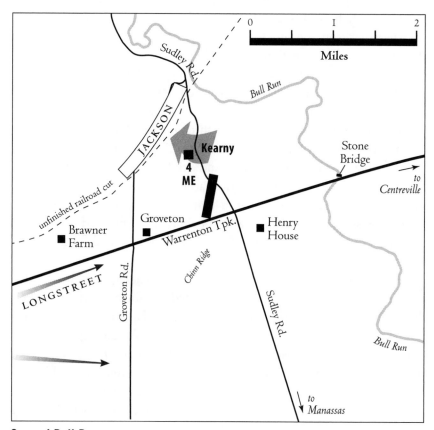

Second Bull Run

On August 27, the regiment set out on another "toilsome march," this time down the railroad to Catlett's Station and onward to Manassas Junction. When they finally reached their destination around noon, it was readily apparent that the Rebels had already been there. The junction was a mass of smoldering wreckage, with track torn up, locomotives destroyed, and Union supply stores looted. Walker said it "was a scene that an artist would eagerly have sketched for a typical picture of the horrors of war." Stonewall Jackson and his "foot cavalry" had made an appearance, done their business of destruction, and then vanished somewhere in Virginia, leaving John Pope mystified about where they had gone.[26]

Robert E. Lee, satisfied that McClellan posed no threat to Richmond, had gone on the offensive. Lee had sent Jackson on a long, swooping movement around Pope's army, through the Bull Run Mountains at Thoroughfare Gap and on to Manassas. After destroying the Union supplies there, with his men eating and drinking as much as they could, Jackson had marched on, toward the battlefield where he had gained his nickname just a little more than a year earlier. There Jackson found a good defensive position in the woods behind an unfinished railroad cut near the crossroads hamlet called Groveton, and he waited for the rest of Lee's army to join him.

When Pope finally got word of Jackson's whereabouts, he decided the Rebels were retreating, and he directed his forces to head in their direction and "bag the whole crowd." The 4th Maine received its orders on August 29 and moved north to find Jackson. According to Walker's reports, the regiment reached the battlefield at about 9:30 A.M., just in time to take part in a joint attack by the divisions of Kearny and Hooker. Kearny's men were on the right, and Pope intended them to provide more of a diversion for the Rebels while Brig. Gen. Curvier Grover of Hooker's division made the main attack.

Grover was another Maine man, who hailed from Bethel. (His brother La Fayette was an Oregon congressman and future governor of that state.) He had graduated fourth in his class from West Point in 1850 and had fought well under Hooker on the Peninsula. Grover's attack at Groveton initially succeeded beyond his wildest dreams. He took advantage of cover offered by some woods and approached a gap in the Confederate defenses. After firing one volley, his men charged the railroad cut with bayonets lowered and routed the surprised Confederates. But the further Grover's men pushed into the breach the stiffer the resistance became. "Men dropped in scores, writhing and trying to crawl back, or lying immovable and stone-dead where they fell," recalled one soldier. "The Union line now began to waver. It had no artillery and no supports." Grover had his horse shot out from under him. His soldiers, fighting alone within Jackson's lines, were beaten back.[27]

Kearny's division was on Grover's right, and by the time it began to move Grover's men were being driven out of the woods. Walker had the 4th Maine advance at double-quick to the position assigned to them, so the men were already tired and disorganized by the time they got there. They hadn't long to wait before the Confederates pursuing Grover's men reached their flank and poured "so hot an enfilading fire down my line that I caused my men to fall back a short distance," Walker reported. Again Walker found himself outflanked; once again he fell back. This time he received some support from the 40th and 1st New York regiments and moved forward again, only to retreat one last time as darkness fell. The Union soldiers had almost broken Jackson's lines, but not quite.[28]

August 29 had offered opportunity to John Pope; August 30 brought disaster. While he was occupied with Jackson, Pope had been ignoring evidence that James Longstreet had arrived on the field with his 28,000 men. Pope had expected Fitz John Porter to launch an attack from the Union left on the 29th, but Porter had not moved because he discovered Longstreet on his front. (Pope had Porter court-martialed after the battle. Years later, Longstreet testified that he was, in fact, on the field, evidence that eventually led to Porter's exoneration.) On August 30, after carefully placing his men and assuring himself that everything was in readiness, Longstreet finally moved forward, swinging his men around the Union left like a great bear trap snapping closed on his foe. Pope's illusions about a Confederate retreat were finally shattered, and he could no longer doubt Longstreet's presence. All he could do, if he were lucky, was save his army.

He did, but only barely. Stuck in the middle of a savage contest on Chinn Ridge—just south of Pope's route to safety along the Warrenton Turnpike—stood the guns of the 5th Maine Battery. Governor Washburn had taken a personal interest in the battery's creation back in 1861, and he had lobbied Washington for the assignment of a skilled artilleryman to command it. Somewhat reluctantly, McClellan's chief of artillery, William F. Barry (the man who had so disastrously assured Charles Griffin that the soldiers approaching his battery at First Bull Run were Union men), recommended George Leppien, a Pennsylvania native with German parents who had received a military education in Germany. "Though a Pennsylvanian by birth and educated abroad, his fame belongs to Maine," said the *Augusta Kennebec Journal*. "He was particularly proud of identifying himself with our State. He was proud of his connection with us, proud of the reputation of the Maine troops, and especially proud of his own Battery."[29]

Leppien was away sick for Second Bull Run, so Lt. William Twitchell commanded the battery. As Pope's army collapsed on the afternoon of August 30, Gen. Zealous Tower ordered the 5th and the 2nd Maine Batteries forward with his own brigades to defend Chinn Ridge and keep the Rebels from cutting the Warrenton Turnpike. Late that afternoon Maj. Davis Tillson galloped up to the 5th Maine Battery. He was now in command of the artillery in the III Corps' 2nd division. "Limber up and follow me!" Tillson ordered. The battery had barely managed to get into the position when the Confederates overwhelmed it, shooting down its men and horses. Twitchell was one of the officers killed, and his men were forced to leave his body on the field, along with all but one of the battery's guns.[30]

Another casualty that afternoon was Sam Fessenden, the senator's once-wayward son and Thomas Hyde's friend from Bowdoin. He fell mortally wounded while leading Tower's men into battle. Of the four patriotic Bowdoin students who had banded together to raise men for the 7th Maine, only Hyde and Morse still lived.

Things looked desperate on August 30, but Pope managed to extricate his army from the closing jaws of Lee's trap. Thanks were due in large part to John Reynolds and his division of Pennsylvanians, who provided a stubborn defense on Henry Hill—where Adelbert Ames had been wounded the year before—and gave Pope's army the opening it needed to retreat in relative good order in the direction of Centreville.

⸺

Since losing his arm at Seven Pines, Otis Howard had spent much of his time back in Maine recruiting more soldiers for the Union cause. "Our fathers, with their blood, procured for us this beautiful heritage," he told his audiences. "Men now seek to destroy it. Come, fellow citizens, regardless of party, go back with me and fight for its preservation." Recruiting was important work, but Howard was eager to contribute in a more direct way. Less than three months after the loss of his limb, Howard returned south to rejoin the army. At the time, Pope was trying in vain to determine what Lee and Jackson were up to, and McClellan was fuming about the upstart interloper from the West as he reluctantly sent pieces of his army to support the Army of Virginia.[31]

Howard reentered the war amid these changing and confusing circumstances. When he reached Washington he received a "frigid" reception from Halleck, but his bruised feelings were salved when he learned that the general-in-chief treated other generals with the same lack of cordiality. Heintzelman, on the other hand, treated him "like a son," and Bull Sumner "not only received me with affection, but has kept me here at his head quarters & entertained me," he told Lizzie. The bad news was that Howard would not get his old brigade back. It was now commanded by Brig. Gen. John Caldwell, a Vermont native who had been teaching in the Maine town of East Machias when the war began. Caldwell had entered the conflict as colonel of the 11th Maine and fought with the regiment on the Peninsula before rising to brigade command.[32]

Sumner offered Howard the "California Brigade," formerly under Oregon senator Edward Baker, who had died at Ball's Bluff in October 1861. Howard had hardly assumed his new command when Sumner received orders to send his corps to Alexandria, and then to push out toward Chain Bridge on the Potomac to protect Washington against a rumored raid by Jeb Stuart's Confederate cavalry. Stuart failed to show, so Sumner returned the corps to Alexandria, only to send it out again to

Centreville. The confused maneuvering reflected Halleck's mindset as he attempted to decipher Lee's movements. By the time Howard reached Centreville it was too late to do anything for John Pope. The beaten Army of Virginia was already streaming back from the battlefield. Howard received orders to perform reconnaissance and determine the position of Lee's army.

In the meantime, Lee had sent Stonewall Jackson on a course around the retreating Union army's left flank in an attempt to cut it off. But Pope was better prepared this time, and he had troops waiting for Jackson at Chantilly. During a battle that unfolded in a savage thunderstorm on September 1, the hot-tempered and impetuous Phil Kearny met his end. While performing some personal reconnaissance in the storm and darkness, Kearny accidentally rode into enemy lines. He tried to bluff his way back to safety, but Confederate soldiers opened fire and shot him off his horse. The one-armed general died instantly. Kearny and Otis Howard would not get the opportunity to buy their gloves together.

Howard commanded the rear guard as the dejected army retreated to the safety of Washington. "Who will forget the straggling, the mud, the rain, the terrible panic and loss of life from random firing, and the hopeless feeling almost despair of that dreadful night march!" he recalled.[33]

Outside the capital, Abner Small and the 16th Maine watched Pope's battered army trudge back to the welcoming defenses of Washington. "Raw and inexperienced as we were, the contemplation of the column passing with its ragged banners; the long ambulance train, with its terrible freight of torn and crushed humanity; the wounded limping painfully in the rear, and all the evidences of war, carried home to our hearts a crushing sense of the business we were engaged in," Small recalled. "And yet grim jokes and criticisms were indulged in at the expense of poor Pope and the authors of the go-to-Richmond policy." If there was any reason for cheer, it was when word came that Lincoln had restored McClellan to command of a reunited Army of the Potomac. The old McClellan magic worked its spell on the soldiers who loved him. "No one, except envious rivals, then held his failures against him," said Small. "A glory of great expectations encompassed him with a superficial brilliancy. Troops cheered themselves hoarse at sight of him. Our regiment, like many others, hailed him extravagantly as a savior."[34]

For McClellan, the defeat of Pope was something of a personal triumph. He relished the opportunity to bask in the love of his soldiers as he rode out from Washington to greet them. "I leave it to others who were present the description of what then occurred," he wrote, "the frantic cheers of welcome that extended for miles along the column; the breaking of ranks and the wild appeals of the men that I should then and there take them back on the line of retreat and let them snatch victory out of defeat." McClellan did not do that, of course, but he did launch into a whirl of activity as he regained control of his army and got it organized. He had no time to dawdle, for Lee was once again taking the offensive.[35]

CHAPTER 6

The 7th Maine Makes a Charge

*It was, indeed, a sad sight to walk over the sides of that mountain, and
see the strong men who had fallen in support of what we could only feel
to be an unrighteous cause. While, of course, we rejoiced in our brilliant
victory, we could not repress a sigh as we thought of the fate of our noble
comrades, who were either killed, or suffering from wounds and pains.*
—CHARLES BICKNELL, 5TH MAINE

Joshua Chamberlain received a gift from the citizens of Brunswick on
September 1. It was a beautiful gray-and-white stallion. He named it
Prince. Two days later the 20th Maine left Portland's Camp Mason for
the rail journey to Boston, and from there on to war. Despite Adelbert
Ames's best efforts, the regiment was "scarcely organized, partially armed,
substantially undrilled and uninstructed." One of those uninstructed
soldiers was Holman Melcher, a farm boy from Topsham, a small town
across the Androscoggin River from Brunswick. Holman did not attend
nearby Bowdoin College; he went to the Maine State Seminary (later
Bates College) in Lewiston instead. When he was mustered into the 20th
Maine as a corporal, he had just turned 21 and was working as a teacher.
He was six feet tall, had hazel eyes, auburn hair, and a long, oval face.
Melcher marched out of Camp Mason with his blanket strapped to the
top of his knapsack; a haversack with his food hanging on his left side; a
pouch for the caps that ignited the ammunition in his musket; a sheath
for his bayonet; and his Enfield musket.[1]

On the streets of Boston, the regiment's Theodore Gerrish, a private from Aroostook County, saw an old sailor watching the regiment march through town. "Where are you from?" the sailor called. "From the land of spruce gum and buckwheat cakes," one of the soldiers yelled back. The regiment boarded the steamer *Merrimac* for the sea voyage to Alexandria. During the passage, the soldiers heard about the recent misfortunes of McClellan's army on the Peninsula and John Pope's at Second Bull Run. Ames took advantage of the time at sea to teach his officers as much as he could about military tactics.[2]

The 20th Maine didn't have much time to sightsee in Alexandria, although a few soldiers found an opportunity to visit the Marshall House, where Elmer Ellsworth had been gunned down in 1861. "We climbed to the roof from which the flag had been torn, and stood on the stairs where the blood of the brave patriotic colonel had mingled with that of the disloyal Jackson," Gerrish remembered. Some of the soldiers hacked off pieces of the stairs as souvenirs.[3]

When the regiment marched through Washington, they found the capital city filled with the detritus of a defeated, demoralized army, and spent an uncomfortable night camped out in an empty lot "on a downy bed of dead cats, bricks and broken bottles." The next morning they crossed the Long Bridge back into Virginia. Unused to marching with heavy weapons and full knapsacks and suffering in the Virginia heat, the newly minted soldiers made a forlorn appearance. Ames was visibly and audibly annoyed. When the regiment finally staggered into its campsite, Ames exploded and castigated his men, saying if that was the best they could do they should just desert.[4]

Maj. Ellis Spear bristled over Ames's high-handed treatment. "The men, every one of them, sore, chaffed, heated & exhausted, by a march which they knew had been made unnecessarily hard, & who had done their best, listened in an angry mood to this angry lecture from a man who had ridden all the way on horseback," he said.[5]

———

McClellan divided his army into three wings—the right under Ambrose Burnside, comprising the I and IX Corps; the center, commanded by Bull

Sumner, which included the II and XII Corps; and the left under William Franklin, who had the V and the VI Corps. The army left Washington on September 7 and began moving north into Maryland in pursuit of Lee, who had already reached Frederick, Maryland. There Lee divided his army. He sent one force under Stonewall Jackson on a long expedition to capture a small garrison at Martinsburg, Virginia, after which it was to swing around to capture the much larger Union force at Harpers Ferry. James Longstreet and D. H. Hill moved west to cross over South Mountain, the long ridge that ran like a spine through Virginia and Maryland and into Pennsylvania. He stopped in Boonsboro, where he could keep McClellan from pushing through the passes and attacking Lee's divided forces.

McClellan knew about this, because a Confederate courier had dropped a copy of Lee's orders in a field outside Frederick, and the fortuitous discovery had made its way up the chain of command to the Young Napoleon. Now aware of what Lee intended, McClellan devised a multipronged approach to the problem of defeating him. He dispatched Franklin's wing to force its way through the southernmost passage on South Mountain, Crampton's Gap, and then proceed down the other side into Pleasant Valley. From there Franklin could move south and relieve the threat against Harpers Ferry. The other two wings would move west from Frederick and cross South Mountain via passes to the north.

The 5th Maine belonged to Joseph Bartlett's brigade in Henry Slocum's division of the VI Corps, part of the force that Franklin planned to push through Crampton's Gap. Like every regiment that had campaigned on the Peninsula and beyond, the 5th Maine had been greatly reduced by war and disease. "Our own regiment now numbered but three hundred and ninety men who were able to carry a musket; but those three hundred and ninety were *strong* men, and were *determined* men," wrote George Bicknell.[6]

During the push toward the gap on September 14, Slocum placed the 5th Maine and the 16th New York in the advance. The regiments marched toward Confederate artillery and its supporting infantry that waited at the base of the green hump of South Mountain. The Rebels were posted across the road that led up to the gap, with a stone wall in front of them. Around 4:00 P.M. the enemy artillery began to hurl iron in the direction of the Union troops, who had to march about three-quarters of a mile, climb over fences, and pass through a cornfield—all while keeping their formation while under fire. Once the Federals had closed to within about 350 yards of the enemy line, they raised their muskets and fired. "For over an hour we poured volley after volley into the enemy's ranks," Bicknell wrote. "Never did men work harder than did the noble soldiery of those two regiments. Almost every man seemed angry because he could not load and fire more rapidly."[7]

Eventually, ammunition began to run low, and the Maine soldiers noticed the arrival of enemy reinforcements. There were signs that the Rebels were preparing to charge. "It was a sight which caused our blood to run cold," Bicknell wrote. The men of the 5th Maine began casting worried looks to the rear, wondering whether they would get reinforcements, or, at the very least, more ammunition. Finally they received orders to fall back and take cover on the opposite side of a slight rise. As they passed over the rise, the beleaguered soldiers were relieved to see the rest of Slocum's division waiting there, lined up in battle formation and ready to advance. The 5th Maine fell back behind the first line. "Forward!" came the order, and the long blue lines lurched into motion. "The earth almost trembled beneath the tread of mighty men," Bicknell recalled. Now it was the Rebels' turn to feel apprehensive. The enemy soldiers fired a single volley and fled up the mountain, the Union troops following. "The men swept forward with a cheer, over the stone-wall, dislodging the enemy, and pursuing him up the mountain-side to the crest of the hill and down the opposite slope," Franklin reported.[8]

Standing on top of South Mountain, Bicknell had mixed feelings about the victory. "It was, indeed, a sad sight to walk over the sides of that mountain, and see the strong men who had fallen in support of what we could only feel to be an unrighteous cause," he said. "While, of course, we rejoiced in our brilliant victory, we could not repress a sigh as we thought of the fate of our noble comrades, who were either killed, or suffering from wounds and pains."[9]

Franklin had managed to force a passage through Crampton's Gap, but he moved too slowly to save Harpers Ferry and its 12,000 troops, which surrendered to Jackson on September 15. The 5th Maine remained at Crampton's Gap for two days, during which time its soldiers could hear the sounds of fighting to the north and west. On September 17, they received their orders to move toward the din of the battle.

After its brutal march, the 20th Maine finally caught up to its brigade. Under the command of Daniel Butterfield, it belonged to George Morell's division of Porter's V Corps and also included the 12th, 17th, and 44th New York—also known as the Ellsworth Avengers—and the 83rd Pennsylvania and the 16th Michigan. The regiment headed out on another difficult march with its brigade in pursuit of the Rebels on September 12. As the long line of men in new blue uniforms moved north, more and more of them fell out of formation, exhausted, footsore, sunburnt, thirsty, and demoralized.

By the time the regiment reached Frederick, the city was filling with wounded from the fighting for South Mountain to the west. Outside of town, the Maine men passed a band of Confederate prisoners being escorted to captivity. These were the first Rebels most of the soldiers had ever seen. Gerrish remembered them as "tall, lank, slouching looking fellows, clad in dirty gray uniforms." More wounded awaited when they reached South Mountain, where they could also see the destructive effect of shot and shell on the buildings and terrain. Corporal Melcher recoiled from the stench of dead horses and saw cattle that the Rebels had killed but hadn't had time to eat before being driven away.[10]

It was September 16, and from the other side of the mountain came the faint rumble of combat. The two enemy armies had encountered each other late that day near the banks of Antietam Creek. The fighting would renew with an unprecedented fury the next morning. In the meantime, the 20th Maine bedded down for the night. "The stars twinkled down sorrowfully through the gloom, and the mists came in gentle showers from the skies, as if the angels were weeping over those who were to be slain upon the morrow," Gerrish recalled.[11]

The fighting started early the next morning outside the little town of Sharpsburg, near the Potomac River and Antietam Creek. Joe Hooker's I Corps had skirmished with the enemy the evening before, and

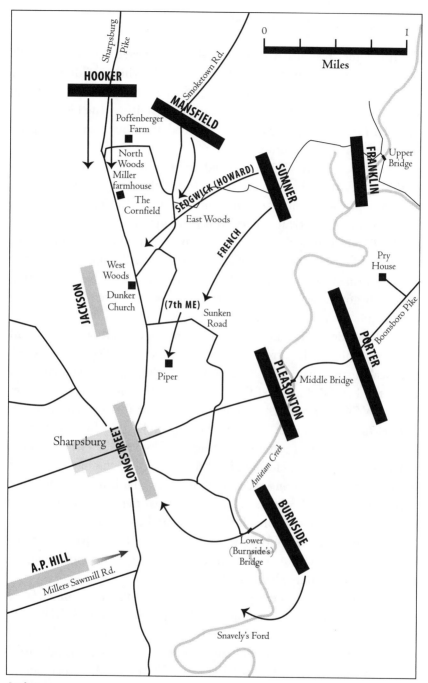

Antietam

"Fighting Joe" resumed the action when he started his troops south through a cornfield in the direction of a little white building known as the Dunker Church. Soldiers from Stonewall Jackson's command, some newly arrived from Harpers Ferry, were waiting. The bloody fight between Hooker's and Jackson's men ebbed and flowed over the cornfield throughout the morning.

Samuel Crawford's brigade, including the 10th Maine, now belonged to the XII Corps, which had become part of the Army of the Potomac after Second Bull Run. The commander of the XII Corps was Joseph Mansfield, a Connecticut native, West Point graduate, and Mexican War veteran. Mansfield, a dignified 58-year-old with white hair and beard that gave him the appearance of an Old Testament prophet, had headed the Department of Washington but chafed to receive a field command. He finally got the assignment to the XII Corps on September 12, just in time to join his new command in Frederick.

Colonel Beal was still leading the 10th Maine, although Crawford had placed him under arrest on September 2 after a dispute over some hay. Beal's men, exhausted after a hard march through mud and rain, had taken the hay from a Rebel farm so they could make beds on the wet ground. When Crawford heard about it, he sent for Beal and told the colonel to order his men to return the hay under guard and then post sentries to prevent any more pilfering. Beal protested. His men were wet and tired, he said. He would tell them to return the hay, but would not insult them by forcing them to do it under guard, and he would not have any of his tired soldiers act as sentries that night. Crawford placed him under arrest, but restored him to command a few days later. Actions like that did not endear Crawford to the men of the 10th Maine. "If this were not a military mob we would turn out and give him a ducking in the river," fumed John Mead Gould.[12]

Such resentments were pushed aside now that the regiment faced combat. As Hooker's corps attacked through the cornfield, Mansfield held his corps in reserve north of a forested area called the East Woods. It was a tense wait. Enemy shells soared over the soldiers' heads and buried themselves in the earth behind. The roar of battle on the other side of the trees increased in volume, and more and more Union soldiers began pouring through the woods in retreat. "All of us did not notice these changes, and many did not even get up to look to the front, but we all saw Gen. Mansfield riding about the field in his new, untarnished uniform, with his long, silvery hair flowing out behind, and we loved him," remembered John Mead Gould. "It never fell to our lot to have such a commander as he. Very few of us had ever seen him till three days before this, but he found a way to our hearts at once."[13]

Finally, it became time to advance. Beal ordered the regiment forward. Along the way, General Hooker rode up. "You must hold those woods!" he exclaimed. Bullets went snapping and whizzing past. Mansfield wanted his men to advance in two columns, feeling it was easier to handle them that way; Beal wanted to deploy his regiment in line of battle, and as soon as Mansfield had moved out of sight he did so, the general's wishes notwithstanding. "And now came the moment of battle that tried us severely," Gould wrote, "not that there was a sign of hesitancy, or show of poor behavior, but it is terrible to march slowly into danger, and see and feel that each second your chance for death is surer than it was the second before. The desire to break loose, to run, to fire, to do something, no matter what, rather than to walk, is almost irresistible. Men who pray, pray then; men who never pray nerve themselves as best they can, but it is said that those who have been praying men and are not, suffer an agony that neither of the other class can know."[14]

They reached a rail fence and fired at the Rebels. The Rebels fired back. One of them shot Beal's horse in the head. As the colonel dismounted from the wounded animal, he was shot in the legs. His crazed mount then charged across the field and lashed out at Lt. Col. James Fillebrown, knocking him out of the battle with a fierce kick of its hind legs. Mansfield, in the confusion, became convinced that the 10th Maine was firing at Union troops. He rode over to stop them. A captain and a sergeant argued that they were shooting at the enemy. "Yes, Yes, you are right," Mansfield conceded, and then Rebel bullets struck him. Gould was standing nearby. At first he thought the bullets had hit only Mansfield's horse, but as the general dismounted, the wind blew his coat open and Gould saw blood streaming down his side. Gould and two other soldiers from the regiment helped the mortally wounded general to the rear, where he soon died.

More and more men fell. A sergeant in Company I, "a rough fearless fighter," climbed atop the fence and sat there, sword raised, to stop any Maine soldiers who might consider retreating. The bullet that smacked into him was audible the next company over. Capt. Nehemiah T. Furbish, "a wide-awake, harum-scarum fellow, full of life and joviality," had been too sick to fight at Cedar Mountain and so perhaps he felt he had to lead his color company into battle here to prove his courage. He took aim at a Rebel with his pistol, but fell dead instead. Adding to the roar of battle were the barks and growls of Major, a dog that Company H had adopted.[15]

Bull Sumner and the II Corps were right behind the XII, with Otis Howard in command of his brigade in Sedgwick's division. Around 7:20 A.M., Sumner ordered Sedgwick to move forward. Sedgwick formed his division in three lines, one for each brigade, and started them through the cornfield that Hooker's fight had left strewn with the dead and wounded. They crossed the Hagerstown Pike and then moved into the West Woods on the other side. Sumner directed the attack, Howard said later, "with an extraordinary confidence in our column of brigades and caring nothing for his flanks." He intended that as a mild rebuke of Old Bull, for commanders needed to protect their flanks, and the West Woods proved to be "a trap well set and baited." Rebels from Jackson's and Longstreet's commands lay in wait. Once Sedgwick's men marched into range, the Confederates opened a devastating fire and exploited a gap that opened between Sedgwick's division and that of William French, which had veered off to the left. The woods became a deadly hornet's nest, with shot and shell coming not only from the brigade's front, but also from its left and rear. Howard recalled sitting on his horse in the rear of his brigade, "when the round shot were crashing through the trees and shells exploding rapidly over our heads, while the hissing rifle balls, swift as the wind, cut the leaves and branches like hail, and whizzed uncomfortably near our ears." Soon enough, Sumner realized the threat to the division's flank and rode into the woods to call off his men. "Fall back," he shouted. "You are in a bad position!" The noise was so deafening that it was hard to hear anything the old general was saying, but he finally made himself understood through his violent gestures. Somehow Howard managed to extricate his brigade from the West Woods and establish a new defensive line. By that point Sedgwick had been badly wounded, and Howard received command of the division.[16]

———

Thomas Hyde was now in temporary command of the 7th Maine, with Colonel Mason and Lt. Colonel Connor both ill, "and to say I was proud and happy with my lot is far too inexpressive," he said. As part of William Franklin's corps, the regiment had been sent north from the Peninsula to support John Pope, but it did not arrive in time to provide much assistance. Hyde was not too disappointed by Pope's embarrassment. Pope had already insulted the Army of the Potomac, and had been "sized up for a braggart." But Hyde was growing disillusioned. "I am completely disgusted with the whole management of this war and so are we all," he said. "The best are losing heart."[17]

The 7th Maine had been present for the fight at Crampton's Gap, but in a support position. As the regiment marched toward the sound of fighting around Sharpsburg, it began passing streams of wounded and stragglers, a few at first, and then more, and then a flood, heading away from the fight. They passed the bloodied 10th Maine, "that splendid regiment reduced to a small squad," said Hyde. He asked about Beal and Fillebrown and learned about their wounding. Then the 7th Maine emerged from a small patch of woods, and suddenly "the whole magnificent panorama of the field of Antietam was in full view." The regiment marched past lines of dead Confederates, and Hyde saw one of his men, a Skowhegan lieutenant named Emory, leap into the air and fall to the ground. It turned out that he had been hit in the belt buckle. After driving back some Arkansas and South Carolina soldiers, the regiment dropped and hugged the ground. Some men found shelter behind the many boulders that littered the terrain. One private, a man named Knox, crept forward. On the Peninsula he had received permission to use his own gun instead of a government-issued musket, and now he operated like a sniper. He began taking down Rebels one by one until a shell fragment disabled his weapon.

It was getting late in the day, near five o'clock, and the fighting on this northern part of the battlefield had largely died down. But the Rebels had their own snipers, firing from behind haystacks at the Piper farm, just to the south. When a Maryland battery complained to brigade commander William Irwin about them, Irwin ordered Hyde to take the 7th Maine and clear the snipers out. Hyde had just seen a large body of Rebels move into that area, and informed Irwin of the fact.

"Are you afraid to go, sir!" Irwin barked. Hyde later came to believe he was drunk. ("He was a gallant man, but drank too much, of which I was unaware," Hyde wrote.) He asked Irwin to repeat his order so that the whole regiment could hear it. Irwin did. Hyde had no choice but to obey. He assembled his men and sent them into motion. They passed over a sunken road that was already piled with corpses, and down a slope toward the Piper farm. "We were moving at the double-quick down into a cup-shaped valley, fifteen skirmishers under Lieutenant Butler in front, Adjutant Haskell on Colonel Connor's big white horse on the left, and I to the right on my Virginia thoroughbred," Hyde recalled. "My feeling was first of great exhilaration, which was quickly dashed by that wretched Maryland battery, who, thinking to open over our heads, took four men out of my right company at their first shot." Hyde saw Haskell and his horse fall, then he rode out in front of the regiment just in time to see a line of the enemy rise up on the right, from behind a stone wall that ran along the Hagerstown Pike. Fortunately for the Mainers, they were moving at such a clip the Rebel volley failed to do much damage. Hyde ordered his men over to the left behind a protective rise. From there, he could see that several times their number of the enemy lay in wait. He wheeled his men past the farm buildings and into a sheltering orchard. The Rebels gave chase. Hyde's horse was hit, and the major fell to the ground. Musket balls clipped the trees and showered him with broken branches. He remounted his wounded horse as his men fired back at their pursuers. Hyde veered around to help color bearer Harry Campbell, who had been hit, and found himself surrounded by the enemy. But his men rallied to save him, and the 7th Maine fought its way out of the trap as their fellow soldiers watching from a distance waved their hats to cheer the doomed but brave charge. Of the 166 enlisted men who made the charge, Hyde reported 12 killed, 60 wounded, and 16 missing. He counted 3 of the 15 officers as killed, 7 wounded, and 2 missing. "I suppose I was fired at in that battle a thousand times, and what saved me was that Providence knew that I was an only son and my mother was a widow," he wrote home.[18]

That night, Hyde and his surviving officers wept over the regiment's losses. "We had the consolation of knowing that we had gone farther into the Rebel lines than any Union regiment that day, that we had fought three or four times our numbers, and inflicted more damage than we received, but as the French officer at Balaklava said, 'It is magnificent, but it is not war.' When we knew our efforts were resultant from no plan or design at headquarters, but were from an inspiration of John Barleycorn in our brigade commander alone, I wished I had been old enough, or distinguished enough, to have dared to disobey orders."[19]

Whether out of guilt or sincere gratitude, Irwin was more than complimentary in his official report. "No words of mine can do justice to the firmness, intelligence, and heroic courage with which this regiment performed its dangerous task," he wrote. "Their killed and wounded and their colors riddled by balls are the proud, yet melancholy, witnesses of their valor. Alone and surrounded by the enemy, they fought until nearly all their cartridges were expended. They then delivered one fierce parting volley, closed their ranks around their color, and fell slowly back to the line of battle." Irwin also singled out "the gallant soldier and gentleman, Maj. Thomas Hyde," for praise. "He led his regiment into action with spirit and courage, handled it under severe fire with judgment, and retired in compact order and with a steady front," he said. "Conduct like this requires soldierly qualities of the highest order."[20]

～～

The 7th Maine made its futile charge after the savage fighting on the northern part of the battlefield—through the cornfield and in the East and West Woods—had largely ended. There had been more terrible fighting in the center, which left a sunken farm lane that traversed the rolling countryside choked with the dead and wounded; among the dead was Israel Richardson, Otis Howard's old division commander. The main action then shifted south, where the IX Corps made attempt after attempt to cross a stone bridge that spanned the Antietam. It had approached 1:00 P.M. before the 51st New York and 51st Pennsylvania finally made a dash and forced a passage across the bridge. Now the IX Corps was in a position to move against Sharpsburg and pin Lee's army against the Potomac River. The situation was hanging in the balance for the Army of Northern Virginia. But then A. P. Hill's brigade appeared from the south, flags flying, after an epic march from Harpers Ferry. Hill arrived just in time to blunt the Union advance and end the day's fighting.

It had been a terrible and bloody day—one that remains the bloodiest single day of combat for American soldiers. Nearly 5,000 men lay dead, more than 18,000 were wounded, and some 3,000 were reported missing. When George Bicknell and the 5th Maine reached the battlefield after the fighting had ended, they found a scene straight out of hell. "Hundreds of poor fellows were lying there suffering from wounds, while the dead were scattered all over the field, lying in the same position in which they had fallen," said Bicknell. "Many bodies, even at that early season, had already commenced to mortify, and the stench was terrible. Broken gun-carriages, dead and dying horses all lay scattered around, presenting an awful spectacle. In places, the dead lay piled one upon another, some dying apparently without a struggle, while others exhibited the pain which they must have suffered by their distorted features. From some the brains were protruding, some had lost a leg or an arm, and others were literally covered with blood." The soldiers of the 5th Maine looked on the scene with horror, glad that they had been spared.[21]

John Mead Gould had been horrified by the dead Rebels he saw when the 10th Maine marched over South Mountain, but when he witnessed the fields of Antietam on the morning after the battle he realized the earlier battle "was a mere flea-bite to this field." He saw dead men everywhere. Even after the Union corpses had been removed from the field, the Confederate bodies "lay thick as grasshoppers," so many that Gould could not even estimate their numbers. "If they say 2000 on each side I shall believe it," he said. "If 4000 I shall believe it as truly. If 6000 I shall consider it correct. If 8000 I shall not dispute. If 10,000 I shall attribute it to the inability of man to grasp at the meaning of figures." Some of the bodies were swollen, the faces turned black. Other dead men appeared to be sleeping. But after he spent two hours wandering through the vast field of corpses, Gould felt a deadening of sensation. "You look at them as so much trophy, so much evidence of the days work, and of the uselessness of secession," he wrote. "It seemed as if human life was worth nothing and a man's soul a myth."[22]

Many soldiers expected the battle would resume that next day. But McClellan did not order an attack. Instead, the two battered armies remained where they were, nursing their wounds and burying their dead. Some men of the 10th Maine located the bodies of soldiers they had fought the day before, "and were not a little pleased to be able to cut buttons from the coats of men who had fallen in their attempts to kill us."[23]

Late that night, Robert E. Lee's army slipped across the Potomac River under the cover of darkness and left the field to George McClellan.

The 20th Maine came tantalizingly close to fighting at Antietam but never received the call to go into battle. Instead, it remained in the rear with the bulk of the V Corps, which McClellan held back as his reserve. The regiment received its baptism of fire two days later when McClellan ordered a cautious scouting expedition to follow the retreating Rebels. The men carefully crossed the Potomac at Shepherdstown, West Virginia, and then faced a hard climb of about 200 feet on the opposite bank. "We forded the river last Saturday afternoon about 3,000 strong," said Hezekiah Long of Company I, "and had not got our shoes on before the Rebels appeared in force on the bluffs almost over our heads and poured it into us 'right smart,' as the Western people say." Before it could do much more than return a scattered volley, the regiment received orders to fall back over the river.[24]

Harlan Bailey, an 18-year-old farm boy from Woolwich, had just crossed the river and was emptying the water from one of his boots when he received the order to fall back. As he wrote to his sister in Maine, "and away I went with one stocking on and one off." A Union battery on the other side provided covering fire that saved the 20th Maine from suffering too severely when the Rebels emerged from the woods and began shooting at the retreating soldiers from the top of the bluff. Chamberlain was sitting on his horse in the middle of the creek directing his men. "The balls whistled pretty thick around me, and splashed on all sides, but didn't touch," he wrote Fanny.[25]

Despite the regiment's steep learning curve, the 20th Maine's lieutenant colonel believed he was right where he belonged. While he missed his wife and children, he did not miss the tedium of academic life. "I feel that it is a sacrifice for me to be here in one sense of the word; but I do not wish myself back by any means," Chamberlain wrote to Fanny. "I feel that I am where duty called me. The 'glory' Prof. Smyth so honestly pictured for me I do not much dread. If I do return 'shattered' and 'good-for-nothing,' I think there are those who will hold me in some degree of favor better than that which he predicted." In the meantime, Chamberlain continued to study every military work he could find, and he asked Fanny to arrange to ship him his copy of Jomini's *Art of War*. "The Col. & I are going to read it," he said. "He is to instruct me, as he is kindly doing in every thing now."[26]

Other than his second in command, Ames had seen little encouraging about his new command, but he remained determined to whip the material he had been given into an instrument of war, whether that material liked it or not. And most of it didn't. "I swear they will shoot him the first battle we are in," Tom Chamberlain reported to his sister. "Col. A. will take the men out to drill & he will d'm them up hill and down." Chamberlain said the colonel was "about as savage a man as you ever saw."[27]

Ames must have been just as frustrated, for his men had not been raised to submit to military discipline. Just as Otis Howard had discovered on the march to First Bull Run, Ames realized that the sailors, farmers, and lumbermen from the Pine Tree State were independent-minded cusses who did not like being ordered about. "One of the most difficult things in the world for a genuine Yankee to do, was to settle down, and become accustomed to the experience of a soldier's life," remembered one of Ames's men. "He was naturally inquisitive, and wanted to know all the reasons why an order was given, before he could obey it. Accustomed to be independent, the words *go* and *come* grated harshly upon his ear. At home he had considered himself as good as any other person, and in the army he failed to understand why a couple of gilt straps upon the shoulders of one who at home was far beneath him, should there make him so much his superior."[28]

Writing to his wife on October 26, Hezekiah Long said that some of the regiment's men did not like Ames very much "as he swears at them sometimes." Long liked him well enough, though, and he thought the rest of the regiment was starting to come around.[29]

CHAPTER 7

The 19th Maine Smells Powder

Ten days ago our army lay encamped on this side of the Rappahannock—
now it is in the same place—each Regt in its old camp—but 13,000 men
have been plucked from its ranks and nothing has been gained.
—GEORGE ROLLINS, 3RD MAINE

Shortly after watching John Pope's defeated army retreat behind the Washington defenses after Second Bull Run, Abner Small and the 16th Maine received orders to break camp and join the Army of the Potomac for the pursuit of Robert E. Lee's army into Maryland. The regiment departed so hastily that it left its tents, knapsacks, and overcoats behind. None of the men realized how long it would be until they saw them again.

The 16th Maine headed north through Frederick, and then crossed South Mountain en route to the battlefield near Sharpsburg. It arrived too late to take part in the fighting, but the men did get a sobering glimpse of war's toll. Dead bodies still littered the field and the little white Dunker Church was riddled with shot and shell. "From a knoll near by I counted two hundred dirty and bloated bodies, blue and grey together. If I had looked where all the fighting had been, I should have counted twenty times as many," wrote Small.[1]

If any of these green Maine soldiers hoped to get a taste of combat, they were disappointed. Days stretched into weeks, summer slipped into fall, and, despite prodding from Lincoln, McClellan and his army remained motionless in Maryland. The 16th Maine still lacked the basic equipment—the knapsacks, tents, and overcoats—it had left behind in Washington, where it remained tangled in red tape. That had not been such a problem while the weather remained warm, but fall promised colder temperatures, increasing discomfort, and worse. Col. Asa Wildes had fallen ill (he would officially resign in January), so the task of retrieving the regiment's equipment fell to its lieutenant colonel, Charles Tilden.

Tilden was born in Castine on May 7, 1832. His father was a merchant, and it appeared his son would follow in his footsteps. But Charles was interested in military matters, perhaps because he knew he had ancestors who had served in King Philip's War and the American Revolution. In 1858 Charles joined a state militia unit called the Castine Light Infantry. After the attack on Fort Sumter, his company joined the 2nd Maine Infantry, and Tilden received an appointment as first lieutenant. He served with the regiment at First Bull Run and during the Peninsula Campaign. While still in Virginia, Tilden received word that he had been commissioned a lieutenant colonel in the newly formed 16th Maine. Clean-shaven and young looking, Tilden was "a strict disciplinarian, and a man whose sharp eye could detect instantly any appearance of cowardice, any shirking of duty, any lack of neatness, any sham of any kind," but he won the respect of his men. As his adjutant, Abner Small, wrote, Tilden was "a man who could be both brave and gentle, severe yet just."[2]

But Tilden could not manage to shake the regiment's equipment loose from the army's bureaucracy. Lacking overcoats and tents, the men looked increasingly forlorn as the weather grew colder. They shivered beneath their thin army blankets or built crude shelters from whatever materials they could scrounge, including fence rails and cornstalks. Other regiments began mocking the 16th Maine as the "blanket brigade." Disease took many of its soldiers. On October 15, out of 698 men present in the morning report, 256 men were on the sick list, 68 of them so ill they were in the regimental hospital.[3]

On October 13, Tilden entreated his brigade commander, Nelson Taylor, to provide some assistance. "I would earnestly request that the within order be forwarded with your approval, as men in my command are suffering for the want of a change of clothing, (some without shirts to their backs and many without underclothes)," he wrote. Nothing happened.[4]

In late October, Capt. John Ayer received permission to travel to Washington and retrieve the regiment's long-missing equipment. Before Ayer could return, though, McClellan finally put the army into motion. The 16th Maine received orders to strike camp and move south on a march that would have been bad enough with coats, and was made even worse by a cold, pouring rain. The men crossed the Potomac on a pontoon bridge at Berlin (present-day Brunswick), and once again trod upon the "sacred soil" of Virginia, now transformed into thick, cloying mud. The only thing that raised their spirits was a brief glimpse of McClellan as the general rode past. By the time the miserable men reached Warrenton, the rain had turned to snow. Small remembered it became so cold the canteens froze. After the regiment halted near the home of a known Rebel outside of town, some foragers discovered a stash of supplies hidden in the outbuildings. "As well try to stem the Mississippi, as that torrent of hungry men, who, regardless of discipline and rank, went through the buildings, bringing to light, not only food, but ammunition, and hogsheads of salt, stored for the rebels," Small recollected.[5]

Captain Ayer managed to wrest the regiment's belongings from the army bureaucracy in Washington and had them sent to Hagerstown, not far from Sharpsburg. But the regiment had moved on by the time the shipment arrived, and the army quartermaster in Hagerstown refused to provide transportation. Tilden sent a lieutenant to Hagerstown to see what he could do; before the quartermaster could return the regiment was on the move again.

The 16th Maine continued its physical suffering. When their division's medical director filed a report about the unit's condition on November 18, he found the men suffering from diarrhea, dysentery, bronchitis, rheumatic diseases, and fevers. He blamed the lack of sufficient clothing. "The men are without overcoats; few have more than one blanket, and their clothing unclean and almost useless," he noted. Thirty-four had no underclothes at all. "How those men suffered!" Small lamented. "Hunger, daily felt, was nothing compared with it. Men of education, of refinement, and wealth, who willingly and cheerfully gave up home, with all its love and comfort, for country, made to feel degraded for want of proper clothing!"[6]

On November 13, Tilden received permission to send Lt. Oliver H. Lowell to Hagerstown to retrieve the regiment's belongings. Thanksgiving morning arrived on November 27, and the lieutenant hadn't returned. The men of the 16th Maine had little reason to give thanks—and then Lowell arrived with the long-lost knapsacks and coats. It was as though sunlight had broken through the clouds. "Despondency gives place to a buoyancy hitherto unknown," said Small. "Shelter, food, and clothing have done their perfect work, and a feeling of satisfaction and contentment envelops the command, which does itself credit on parade, now held every night." The 16th Maine could finally shed its hated blanket brigade nickname.

The regiment had regained some self-respect, but it had yet to prove itself in battle. That opportunity would come soon enough, alongside the Rappahannock River at a place called the Slaughter Pen, where "lives went out by scores—literally were snuffed out like candles."[7]

Hiram Berry missed the fighting at Second Bull Run and Antietam. The action on the Peninsula had taken a toll on the general's health. He suffered from malaria, and his hair started falling out in clumps. He was sent behind the lines to recuperate. "I am here—that is, what is left," he wrote to his wife from Berkeley Wharf Landing on the James River. "I am not well—have been so much exposed and have worked so hard." All his former optimism about a speedy end to the war was gone, broken by the harsh realities he had witnessed on the Peninsula. "I see no end to this war at present," he wrote on July 28. He had one thing to look forward to, and that was an opportunity to take a leave of absence and see his wife and daughter.[8]

He got his wish. Berry was in New York by August 4, waiting for a steamboat that would take him home. All along the Maine coast on his way to Rockland—in Wiscasset, Damariscotta, Waldoboro, and Warren—the public greeted him with salutes and enthusiasm. A parade with a marching band and members of the local fire companies escorted him into Rockland, where the mayor made a speech. How much Berry enjoyed it is open to question. When the procession finally deposited him at his home on Middle Street, Berry appeared "much fatigued and enfeebled" and begged out of making an address because of his health.[9]

Although still weak from his illness, Berry returned to the army in September and rejoined his brigade near Alexandria. He was saddened by Kearny's death. "He was my friend and I had a great love for him, as I know he had for me," Berry wrote to his wife. David Bell Birney took command of Kearny's division. Born in Alabama to a staunchly abolitionist father, Birney had been practicing law in Philadelphia when war broke out. He became lieutenant colonel of the 23rd Pennsylvania and later its colonel, and then a brigadier general.

With McClellan in command of a reunited army, Berry felt that while the army might not win any great victories, McClellan would commit "no great blunder." It was hardly a ringing endorsement of Little Mac, but Berry slowly began regaining his optimism after the fighting at Sharpsburg, and believed that McClellan would quickly move on Richmond.[10]

His brigade underwent some reshuffling. He now commanded the 3rd and 5th Michigan, the 37th New York, which had been consolidated with the 55th New York, and a new regiment from the Pine Tree State, the 17th Maine. It was the first Maine regiment Berry had commanded since he had been promoted from the 4th. Its colonel was Thomas A. Roberts, who had served in a Portland militia company. Roberts's son Charles, a veteran of the 10th Maine, became his father's adjutant.[11]

The colonel of the 55th New York was Régis de Trobriand—or, to give his full name, Philippe de Régis Dénis de Keredern de Trobriand. He was one of the more cosmopolitan officers in the Union army. His father was a French baron who had fought under Napoleon; the baron's son became a poet, painter, and lawyer who married an American. He became a United States citizen just before he volunteered for the Union and received command of his regiment. The men seemed to like this cultured Frenchman who led them. "He seemed as one of us and had such a careless jaunty way about him which took amazingly with the men, it was so different from the stiff dignity usually assumed by our superiors after they got a star on their shoulders," said one private in the 17th Maine. De Trobriand's men, naturally enough, called him "Froggy."[12]

De Trobriand found his new brigade commander to be "a plain straightforward man, tall and broad-shouldered. His blue flannel blouse and his whole dress gave him very little of a military air. But whoever judged him from his appearance would have judged badly, for, although he had rather the appearance of an honest farmer than that of a brigadier general, he was not the less a good officer, as faithful to his duty as he was devoted to his soldiers." Berry's obvious ill health made de Trobriand wonder why "that fine race of woodsmen from State of Maine" seemed to suffer more than most from the "fatigues and privations of the war."[13]

John Haley was a private in the 17th Maine's Company I. Born in Biddeford on March 3, 1840, Haley had become bored with his job at a waterpower shop in Saco by the time the war broke out. He thought about enlisting, but didn't take the step until Lincoln issued his call for 300,000 more volunteers in July 1862. When a friend enlisted, Haley decided to take the plunge, too. He wasn't motivated by patriotism. "I lay claim to but very little of what goes by that name," he said. Nor did a hatred of slavery inspire him. He figured that by joining the army he would see some of the world and maybe witness a battle, "only I wished to be a safe distance from it—a mile at least." He also received bounties of $45 from the state, $25 and the first month's wages from the Federal government, and $55 from Biddeford.[14]

Haley's Civil War reminisces, published in 1985 as *The Rebel Yell and the Yankee Hurrah*, remain entertaining reading today. He looked upon the soldier's life with a refreshingly cynical eye, and that included his own performance. Haley rated his soldiering skills as "below criticism. Poor fighter. Achieved successful mediocrity. Present all the time."[15]

Haley's company was mostly from York and Cumberland Counties and it was fairly well educated: Haley counted 16 high school graduates, 2 college men, a pair of clergy, and 1 lawyer. The company's captain (William Hobson of Saco) was a teacher, the first lieutenant (Putnam S. Boothby of Biddeford) was a hotel clerk, and the second lieutenant (James O. Thompson of Portland) was a preacher. None had military experience.[16]

Charles Mattocks was the captain of Company A. He had been born in Danville, Vermont, but moved to Baldwin, Maine, when his widowed mother remarried a local man. At the start of the war Charles was a junior at Bowdoin College (Chamberlain was one of his professors) and he spearheaded the formation of a unit called the Bowdoin Guards. As soon as he graduated in 1862, Mattocks joined the 17th Maine as a first lieutenant. He was young, but also ambitious and intelligent, and he began earning a reputation as a diligent and disciplined soldier, although he could come across as aloof and distant to the enlisted men. John Haley, for one, didn't care for him. "I can't think of any officer I'd sooner part with, for he was very pompous and had yards and yards of superfluous red tape about him," he noted.[17]

The 17th Maine followed the trail previous Maine regiments had blazed, going to Boston, New York, and Philadelphia, and then proceeding through the secessionist hotbed of Baltimore, which still gave good Union men the willies. "As we marched through the streets many women waved handkerchiefs and flags, but my opinion is that it would be congenial to their taste to be drinking water from a cup made of a Yankee skull," Haley said. They reached Washington too late to chase Robert E. Lee into Maryland, but they could hear the cannon fire from Antietam, 63 miles away.[18]

The 17th left Washington on October 7 and learned the next day that it would form part of Berry's brigade in David Bell Birney's division. "He reminds me of a graven image and could act as a bust for his own tomb, being utterly destitute of color," said Haley of his division commander. "As for his countenance, it is as expressionless as a Dutch cheese."[19]

Joshua Lawrence Chamberlain was still enjoying himself, despite the rigors of military life. "You may imagine that I am in a suffering condition, but I am not one of that sort," he wrote Fanny on November 3. He liked sleeping on the ground with a saddle for a pillow and only a rubber blanket and shawl for warmth. He loved sitting in a tent at night and telling ghost stories with Ames, regimental adjutant John Marshall Brown, and the regiment's doctor. He even had Brown do a bit of amateur barbering and shave away Chamberlain's beard, retaining only a fierce mustache that drooped below both sides of his jaw. "You would not know me," he told his wife.

Camp life was just fine and much more interesting than academia, but Chamberlain knew very well that the real purpose of any army was to fight and he expected to see more combat before long. "We are on for Richmond once more <u>and finally</u> we shall take it this time you may be sure," he told Fanny. "But we have got to fight all our way from Fredericksburg, I suppose."[20]

Otis Howard realized he had returned to the army too soon. In October he fell ill with a serious fever and felt sick enough to request leave to go home to Maine. Even though he was feeling better by the time he reached Philadelphia, he continued north, aware of what had happened the last time he had pushed himself too quickly. He enjoyed a short reunion with his wife and children and then set out once more for the war zone. When he reached Harpers Ferry on November 6, he learned that the Army of the Potomac—quiet ever since the bloody battle of Antietam—had moved south without him. Howard borrowed a horse and an ambulance and headed off in pursuit with an aide, Capt. Eliphalet Whittlesey. Like Joshua Chamberlain, Whittlesey had been a Bowdoin professor before the war. In fact, he had taken over Chamberlain's position teaching rhetoric and oratory when Chamberlain became professor of modern languages in 1861.

Howard and Whittlesey made their way through a real Maine-style snowstorm and finally caught up to the army the next day. McClellan greeted Howard warmly, and even joked that he must have called up the blizzard, Jonah-style, so perhaps he should be sent back home.[21]

The snow turned out to be the least of McClellan's problems. Lincoln had tired of the general's apparent lethargy after Antietam and, with the midterm elections over, felt he could brave the political implications of replacing him. That evening McClellan received orders relieving him of command. Ambrose Burnside was the new leader of the Army of the Potomac.

November 8 was Howard's thirty-second birthday, but the news about McClellan dampened any inclination to celebrate. "We are frightened," he confessed to brother Charles, who was still home recovering from his wound. He called on McClellan again that day. "He appeared well, said: 'Burnside is a fine man & a man of integrity of purpose &

such a man cant go far wrong,'" Howard told Lizzie. "He also said in the course of our conversation, 'I have been long enough in command of a large army to learn the utter insignificance of any man unless he depend on a power above.'" Those were just the kind of words that Howard could appreciate. "It is not possible to be associated with Gen'l McClellan and not love him," he said.

After paying his respects to the outgoing commander, Howard visited the incumbent. Burnside told him he had been unable to sleep for the past two nights, and he looked it. He told Howard he did not consider his promotion "a fit subject for congratulation." On November 9 the army turned out to say farewell to McClellan. The outgoing commander rode along the lines of cheering soldiers with Burnside at his side.[22]

There was a great deal of sadness among the soldiers over McClellan's departure. "Evidently almost everybody was disappointed," noted George Bicknell of the 5th Maine. "Officers and men, who never blanched before a cannon's mouth, could not repress the tear when their beloved general waived them a last adieu. The excitement in camp for a few hours was intense." Even the green men of the 17th, still untested in battle, resented McClellan's removal from command of the army. "We think 'little Mac' the smartest and most ill-used person on earth and are convinced that nothing can crush the Rebellion unless he is in command," said Haley.[23]

The Thanksgiving Day that so cheered the 16th Maine was nothing special for the 17th. "[W]e munched our wormy hard tack (short rations at that), shivering over our camp-fires, and thought of the groaning boards and the good cheer we were wont to enjoy; the happy reunions and family gatherings in 'our dear old native homes,'" remembered Edwin Houghton, a sergeant in Company A. Pvt. Meshach P. Larry, a 29-year-old blacksmith from Windham, told his sister he didn't even realize what day it was until he overheard "some grumble about the poor fare for thanks giving." "I and another fellow went of[f] and got a lot of dry rails and built a big fire cooked our coffee eat our hard bread and rolled ourselves in our blankets and lay down to sleep," Private Larry said. He told his sister of another soldier who had it much worse. He had died and been buried before a package from home arrived with Thanksgiving treats, "but he was we hope marching along those streets that are paved with gold or feasting with angels."[24]

Harlan Bailey, who had joined the 20th Maine as an 18-year-old farm boy from Woolwich, didn't celebrate Thanksgiving with his regiment. Bailey had fallen ill with measles, and spent the holiday in Baltimore's Patterson Park Hospital, along with hundreds of other sick soldiers. But the situation had its compensations. Some loyal ladies from Baltimore provided a sumptuous dinner, which was "got up in the best of style," Bailey said. "The dinner consisted of mash turnip and potatoes bread and water rost pigs and turkeys cakes oysters chickens cheese jellies preserves and pies of every description. I have not told you half of what we had but have given you a faint idear of our dinner."[25]

In the camp of the 19th Maine, Thanksgiving was a "cheerless day," with the men dining on a dinner of "hard bread and salt pork." The regiment had yet to experience combat or much of anything except drilling, marching, and tedium. It had reached Washington on August 29 and remained there, drilling until it left for Harpers Ferry in early October. While encamped on Bolivar Heights above the town of Harpers Ferry, some soldiers left their fire to keep their tents from being blown away by a sudden gust of wind. While the men wrestled with the tents, the wind blew embers from their fire into a stack of artillery shells. No one was injured in the resulting explosion, but the Maine soldiers' pride suffered when the *Philadelphia Inquirer* reported that they had caused the explosion by placing the shells in their fire to support their frying pans. "Our regiment never outlived that story," said John P. Lancaster, the young Richmond farm boy. On November 21 the still-green soldiers established their camp outside Falmouth, Virginia, just across the Rappahannock from Fredericksburg, about halfway between Washington and Richmond.[26]

The 3rd and 4th Maine both belonged to the brigade of Brig. Gen. Hobart Ward, in David Birney's division. On December 3, Elijah Walker received orders from Ward's headquarters assigning his 4th Maine work that generals seemed to think best suited Maine troops—cutting down trees. Their orders were to fell enough timber to lay a 24-foot-wide corduroy road two-tenths of a mile across a swamp. Walker marched his regiment seven miles south from its campsite at Stafford Court House, between Washington and Fredericksburg, and the men set to work felling the trees and loading the timber into wagons. They started constructing the road after nightfall on December 9, working under the cover of darkness so enemy eyes would not take note of the activity. Wrestling the heavy logs into the mud on the cold dark night was a brutal, backbreaking task. Work continued the next night and into the early hours of December 11. When Walker received orders to have his regiment rejoin Ward's brigade, he knew how exhausted his men were and decided to ride off alone to report to headquarters. Once he got there he received another order demanding that the 4th Maine rejoin the brigade immediately. For the first time in his military career Walker considered disobeying an order, but he thought better of it. He managed to get his tired soldiers moving that afternoon, but the brigade had moved and they could not find it. Walker and his men ended up spending a cold night without tents or fires before they managed to catch up on December 12. By then the whole army was stirring into motion, as Ambrose Burnside had made plans to hurl his force at the town of Fredericksburg.[27]

Once he had assumed command, Burnside had moved pretty quickly to threaten the town. Unfortunately, Burnside moved faster than the sluggish army bureaucracy, which proved frustratingly inept at providing the pontoon bridges he needed to get his army across the Rappahannock River. Robert E. Lee and his army had ample time to reach Fredericksburg first and turn the hills just beyond the town into a daunting defensive position by the time the cumbersome pontoon trains arrived.

Burnside decided to have his army cross the river at two spots, one directly across from the town and the other downriver of it. He divided his force into three "Grand Divisions." The Left Grand Division was under the command of William Franklin. It consisted of two corps, the I and the VI. It would cross the Rappahannock south of town. Bull Sumner commanded the Right Grand Division, consisting of the II and IX Corps. It would make a direct assault on Fredericksburg. Joe Hooker remained in reserve with the Center Grand Division, comprising the III and V Corps. Maine troops were scattered throughout all three Grand Divisions. Otis Howard commanded a division in the II Corps, which was under Darius Couch now that Sumner had the Grand Division; one of Howard's brigades included the 19th Maine. "Gen. Howard commands our division," wrote Charles E. Nash of that regiment. "He frequently visits us, and is ever warmly welcomed. That 'empty sleeve' speaks volumes."[28]

As part of the III Corps, Hiram Berry's brigade was in Hooker's Grand Division. He had the 17th Maine in his command. The 3rd and 4th Maine were with Hobart Ward's brigade. The 2nd and 20th Maine were both in the V Corps. The 16th Maine was with Adrian Root's brigade of John Gibbon's I Corps division. There were also two Maine batteries with Gibbon, the 2nd and the 5th.

The 17th Maine got its first indications that a battle was imminent on December 11, when Union guns upstream began pounding Fredericksburg. They were trying to dislodge Confederate sharpshooters who had been killing the engineers laying the pontoon bridges. The engineers had no such trouble south of the town when they erected the two bridges for Franklin's men. On the opposite side of the river a fairly flat expanse of land stretched out toward the embankment of the Richmond, Fredericksburg & Potomac Railroad. Beyond that was the slight rise of Prospect Hill, occupied by troops under Stonewall Jackson. The land in front of it would soon earn the unfortunate but appropriate name of the Slaughter Pen.

The 16th Maine tramped across the swaying pontoon bridge on the afternoon of December 12. The sun set and the stars began to appear in the December sky as the regiment prepared to bed down for the night. "Men wrapped their blankets around them, and lay down to sleep as if unconscious of their surroundings; of the missiles of death within short range; of the fact that this is their last sleep on earth," remembered Abner Small.[29]

John Haley of the 17th Maine had listened to the pounding of the guns upstream with a sense of dread. "Instinct told us what was coming," he wrote. He went to bed on the night of December 12 with "dismal

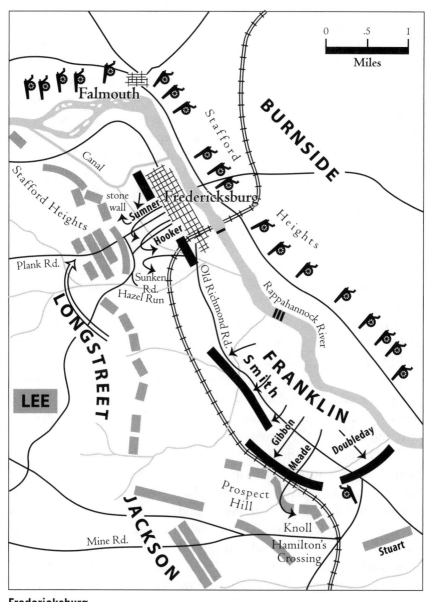

Fredericksburg

forebodings" that kept him from sleeping. He wondered what would happen to him the next day. "Possibly this might be my last night on earth," he thought. "Even worse, ere the setting of another sun I might be mangled and bleeding." Similar thoughts passed through thousands of heads that night.[30]

The morning of December 13 dawned damp and chilly, with a thick fog cloaking the landscape. When the attackers stepped off, the horses, artillery batteries, and thousands of marching men quickly turned the plowed fields into "quagmires" of ankle-deep mud. Confederate artillery began to hurl projectiles their way, and a pair of Rebel cannon to the right "made sad havoc" in the 16th Maine. Thomas S. Hopkins of Company C, a boy of only 16, dropped down by the Bowling Green Turnpike and hugged the earth as Confederate projectiles went screaming over his head. "It was a wild scene," he recalled. "The sharp rattle of musketry, the almost continuous booming of cannon, the neighing of horses, the yells of the drivers, and the sharp commands, mingling with the cries of the wounded, were enough to strike terror to the hearts of our boy soldiers."[31]

The regiment was positioned to the left and right of James Hall's 2nd Maine Battery. Small noticed how the battery's horses steamed in the cold December air, and the way its guns were splattered all over by the ubiquitous mud. Hall was mounted, and Small saw an enemy shell whizz past the captain and explode a nearby caisson. Hall, he recalled, "looked annoyed." He dismounted, carefully sighted one of his guns, ordered it fired, and then casually remounted.[32]

The 16th Maine endured the shelling for a while, and then brigade commander Adrian Root sent orders to throw down the knapsacks, fix bayonets, and advance. Almost immediately the man to Hopkins's left was hit, the ball making a "sickening thud" and knocking the soldier to the ground. "I'm shot!" he shouted. "Down to this time I had felt nervous, and my knees trembled and legs felt weak," Hopkins recalled. "I acknowledge that I was afraid, but being afraid and yielding to fear are two different things." He remembered the day when the regiment left Maine, and how his mother said she never wanted to hear that he had turned his back to the enemy. The remembrance gave Hopkins courage.

"The tears trickled down my cheeks, and I believe I could have fought a whole army."

The young soldier remembered how the air seemed to be full of shot and shell, with so many projectiles striking the ground he was constantly getting spattered with dirt. As the regiment moved toward the railroad embankment, the soldiers instinctively leaned forward and lowered their heads, as though they were pushing through a terrible storm. Suddenly, Hopkins slammed into the ground. He didn't understand what had happened, and didn't realize he had been shot. Then he felt severe pain in his groin. Fearing the worst, he would not examine the wound. He staggered to his feet and, eyes averted, used his rifle as a crutch and hobbled to the rear. Once he felt reasonably safe, Hopkins screwed up his courage to look at his injury, and was overjoyed to find it was just a bruise. A tin cup in his haversack had stopped the bullet. Later he heard stories from other men who had been saved in similar ways, one lieutenant by a tintype and another by a pocketknife.[33]

One of the first men wounded was even younger than Hopkins. Benny Worth of Company E was only 15. A shell fragment hit him in the head, but Worth stayed with the regiment despite being dazed and bloodied. "This is what I came for," he told his fellow soldiers later, showing them his wounded head.[34]

The railroad embankment in front of Prospect Hill gave the Confederates a natural defensive position. The fighting turned furious at the ditch in front of it. Sgt. George Bisbee, the former law student from Dixfield, watched two Confederates hurl their rifles, bayonets attached, at the oncoming Union soldiers, striking two of them. "These were the first and only bayonet wounds that I ever saw during my service," Bisbee said. Otis Libby of Company H was clubbed in the head with a musket and became so crazed with pain he bayoneted two Rebels who were trying to surrender. Charley Lyford was killed during the charge and his death roused brother Monroe to a killing frenzy. He stormed the embankment and stabbed one of the defenders to death with his bayonet. "Curse you, you killed my brother!" Monroe howled. Capt. Charles Hutchins of Company B, a Bowdoin graduate who had insisted on fighting even though he was so weak with fever he could barely keep up with the regiment, fell dead with bullets through his head and heart. Before the fight he had told a soldier in his company that he expected to be killed.[35]

Not everyone was so brave. When a soldier named Levi Baker fell wounded, Pvt. Oliver Creddiford of Company F saw his ticket to the rear. The powerfully built Creddiford slung Baker over his shoulder, making sure to keep the wounded man between him and the Rebel bullets, and headed for safety. The company commander confronted Creddiford and ordered him back to his position. "Captain, you must think I am a damned fool to let Baker die here on the field," said Creddiford, who kept moving.[36]

Even without Creddiford on the front lines, the Union soldiers managed to drive the Rebels from behind the embankment, and the 16th Maine sent some 50 or 60 prisoners to the rear. But during the fight, the regiments on each side retreated, leaving the Maine soldiers exposed. Tilden ordered a withdrawal. The retreat became even bloodier than the advance. The Rebel infantry followed closely and shot down the New Englanders as they moved back and out of the fight. "We almost had to charge to get out of the Confederate lines," Bisbee said. Along the way, Sgt. William Broughton of Company D—who had enlisted at the age of 16—retrieved the flag of the 94th New York and brought it to Tilden. "Men of the Sixteenth!" Tilden shouted. "I wish to take every one of you by the hand, and thank you personally for your gallant bravery."[37]

Sergeant Bisbee was hit in the arm as the 16th Maine retreated. The impact knocked him to his hands and knees but the sight of his own blood jolted him back to his feet and he made his way to the rear. A surgeon at a field hospital in a house behind the lines decided the arm needed to be amputated. Then another surgeon took a look. "Seems to me this arm ought to be saved," he murmured, almost to himself. Bisbee departed the house with both arms. Outside he noticed a pile of human limbs the doctors had tossed away—enough, it seemed, "to fill a medium sized cart." Bisbee underwent a series of operations in Washington and remained in critical condition for some time. A nurse he believed to have been Mrs. Sampson—the same Sarah Sampson who had nursed Howard in Washington and the Maine troops on the Peninsula—was especially helpful, and he felt she had saved his life.[38]

Hobart Ward took his brigade, which included the 3rd and 4th Maine, across the river in the late morning on Saturday. There they had to withstand such fierce shelling that he had most of his men move further to the rear and lie down. He then sent the 3rd Maine off to the right to support Hall and the 2nd Maine Battery. The regiment was now under the command of Moses B. Lakeman. A Boston native and the nephew of Hallowell's mayor, Lakeman joined the 3rd Maine as the captain of Company I. "Lakeman is a gallant officer, deserves such credit for his exemplary behavior, and should make an excellent Colonel, Lieut. Col. or Major," said his division commander, David Birney. "He has energy, and great decision of character." The new lieutenant colonel was Edwin Burt of Augusta, and Samuel Lee was the major. Lee, from Leeds, was Otis Howard's cousin.[39]

George Meade's Pennsylvania division had taken the lead, moving forward across the wide, muddy field. The Pennsylvanians pushed through a triangle-shaped wood that the Rebels had left undefended and broke through Stonewall Jackson's lines on Prospect Hill. There Meade waited in vain for reinforcements to arrive, until Rebel counterattacks drove his men back. When the Pennsylvanians came streaming back in disorder after their temporary success, Ward dispatched Elijah Walker and the 4th Maine forward to help two New York regiments stem the Rebel tide. "The three regiments rushed forward with great impetuosity, under a terrific fire from the enemy, who were partially hid behind a ditch," Ward reported. The Union troops forced them out and chased them back to the railroad embankment. "Here our troops received a severe check, losing over 300 out of 800 in less than five minutes," said Ward. Their momentum stalled, Ward's men retreated, taking some 200 enemy prisoners with them.[40]

The 17th Maine didn't cross the river until noon on December 13. It received orders to move at double-quick to the front, a trot of about a mile. The battle was already in progress. The 17th Maine watched Meade's men retreating toward them. Their moment of combat had arrived. Berry ordered Colonel Roberts to advance. The green, untested soldiers were still wearing their knapsacks. Roberts didn't know whether his men should throw the packs onto the muddy ground or wear them into combat, and he asked Berry what he should do. "I don't care what you do with the knapsacks, if you will only go forward." Berry replied patiently.[41]

So they did. As the Maine soldiers began their advance, Meade's retreating troops reached their lines and passed through, apparently demoralized by their repulse. Sgt. John Libby was the first of the Mainers to fall, when a shell fragment tore through his hip. The regiment kept going until it reached a slight rise, where it commenced firing. Enemy artillery shells whizzed and whirred over their heads as the Rebels sought to get their range. "This was our first experience under fire, and the sensation was not only decidedly novel, but very unpleasant," Houghton noted drily. General Berry rode up, his hat pulled down low. "Steady, 17th Maine!" he shouted. "The State of Maine is looking at you today!" Houghton remembered that Berry's words "inspired the men and gave them new courage." Haley's recollection was a little more sardonic. He said Berry's words "stirred us wonderfully, way down to the bottom of our boots, making us wish we were back home." That was probably not the effect the general desired.[42]

Ordered to lie down to escape the enemy fire, some of the men of the 17th Maine eyed their new blue uniforms, and then looked at the ground, which had been churned into thick mud, and hesitated about soiling their fine garments. The enemy fire soon "convinced them that the mud was the minor of the two evils." Around 4:00 P.M. they received orders to move ahead to support a battery and they waited for a Rebel counterattack that never came. For the rest of the day, the Maine soldiers remained where they were, lying in the mud behind the Bowling Green Road, hoping the Rebel gunners in front of them on Prospect Hill wouldn't find their range. That night the no-longer-untested regiment bedded down in the field, serenaded to sleep by cries of the wounded who lay where they fell. David Lovell wrote to his sister about the experience. "[A] battle field is a place if once seen can never be forgotten," he wrote, "the crys of the wounded and the dying is more than humanity can bare some crying for help some for water some for their friends to come and get them and not leave them there to die it is awfull."[43]

As he lay on the cold ground, listening to the sounds of agony and the occasional sound of gunfire from out of the darkness, Haley contemplated his first experience of combat. It felt like he had packed an entire lifetime into a single day. He assumed other regiments suspected the 17th Maine would falter when under fire for the first time, but the regiment had performed well. In fact, a New York regiment posted behind them to make sure they didn't break soon left the Maine boys on their own. The 17th Maine, Haley said, "behaved so well it merited the encomiums of General Berry."[44]

As for Berry, Maj. William De Lacy of the 37th New York recalled watching him at Fredericksburg, "always calm, unruffled, with a genial smile, never a harsh word, and never theatrical but he was, as he looked, always reliable, ready at all times for any emergency. All the soldiers loved him." Somehow, Berry managed to have his mail brought to him during the battle, and he sat on his horse and perused a letter from his daughter as Confederate artillery filled the sky with projectiles.[45]

Things had been bad enough for the Maine soldiers south of Fredericksburg in the Slaughter Pen. The situation was even worse to the north, around the town itself. The initial attack there was to be carried out by Sumner's Right Grand Division. The first problem Sumner faced was how to get over the river. When Union engineers attempted to span the Rappahannock with the long-delayed pontoon bridges, Confederate riflemen hidden in the buildings on the opposite shore shot them down. Even the bombardment of the city—the fire that the men of the 17th Maine heard on December 11—could not dislodge the sharpshooters from their positions. Artillery chief Henry Hunt suggested an amphibious attack, and one of Otis Howard's brigades, commanded by Norman L. Hall, volunteered to make the attempt. Following another fierce artillery barrage, members of the 7th Michigan, under the command of Lt. Col. Henry Baxter, jumped into six pontoon boats and frantically rowed and poled their way across the river. Baxter fell with a bullet through his lung, but the Union attackers reached the far bank, stormed ashore to establish a bridgehead, and drove the defenders away from the river. The

19th and 20th Massachusetts regiments followed Baxter. The engineers could now finish the bridges without molestation.

Howard's division of Couch's corps was the first to cross over into the town, which the men found wrecked and smoldering from the artillery barrage. On the north side of the river, the band of the 127th Pennsylvania decided to boost morale by striking up a tune, "but just as the instruments were put to their mouths a shot struck right among them and they fell on their faces, then scattered, so our only music was cannon and musketry fire," Howard wrote his wife. It was beginning to get dark, but Howard pushed his regiments forward against an increasingly deadly fire. The men reached Princess Anne Street, the third street up from the river, when Howard halted and sent out pickets. Union soldiers soon began looting abandoned homes. "Our men were in the houses & pillaging & destroying went on to some extent," Howard admitted to Lizzie. "A few men got into wine cellars & got pretty drunk."[46]

The pillaging was pretty widespread. "Few men recrossed the river at the close of the battle without bringing back some trophy by which to remember the city," remembered a soldier from the 19th Maine. "Some of the boys slept on feather beds spread in the streets. There were no very stringent orders—certainly none that were obeyed— against going into the residences and helping oneself." It was not the Army of the Potomac's finest hour, but no doubt many soldiers felt the support Fredericksburg's citizens gave to the Rebels justified the destruction.[47]

The divisions of William French and Winfield Scott Hancock followed Howard over the bridges the next day, in preparation for an attack planned for December 13. It promised to be costly. Lee had a strongly fortified position on a ridge behind town called Marye's Heights, and his artillery had been carefully positioned to turn the plain below into a killing field for any Union attackers. At the base of the hill, James Longstreet's infantry took up a natural defensive position behind a stone wall, where it could add its rifle musketry to Alexander's hail of metal. The Union soldiers didn't stand a chance.

That night Howard sat on the floor in the shattered house he was using for headquarters and wrote a letter home, with a young black child named Tom holding up the portfolio he was using as a writing desk.

Charles Howard, who had just rejoined his brother after recovering sufficiently from his Peninsula wound, was sleeping nearby. At some point, Howard made a late-night circuit of his division. Samuel Smith of the 10th Maine recalled hearing a stir in the darkness as an officer came walking along the lines. The men lifted their heads to see who it was. "General Howard, boys, General Howard," he told them. Smith said that "the sound of his voice and the knowledge that he was there seemed to give the men some assurance." In the morning, an old woman from town served him and his staff breakfast and Howard had a short reading of scripture before embarking on the very unchristian behavior of war.[48]

French's division was the first to try storming the Confederate defenses. His men were slaughtered. Then it was Hancock's turn. His men fared no better. Howard climbed up with Darius Couch into a church steeple that offered a bird's-eye view of the fighting. It was a terrible sight. "Oh, great god!" Couch cried in agony, "see how our men, our poor fellows, are falling!" He wrote later, "I had never before seen fighting like that, nothing approaching it in terrible uproar and destruction." No Union soldiers even reached the stone wall at the base of Marye's Heights, and the dead and wounded quickly littered the open ground leading up to it.[49]

After the soldiers of French and Hancock made their fruitless attempts to reach the wall, it was Howard's turn to sacrifice his soldiers. Col. Joshua Owen's Philadelphia brigade went first, followed by that of Norman Hall. Col. Alfred Sully's brigade—which included the 19th Maine—remained behind as a reserve, but Howard was soon compelled to start sending Sully's regiments forward to support his other brigades. "My regiments began to fire when each in its turn reached the general line of battle, so that the rattle of musketry for hours was unceasing," Howard wrote.[50]

In his report, Sully made special mention of the Maine soldiers, "who for the first time smelt gunpowder, and apparently did not dislike the smell of it." The 19th Maine smelled powder, but it did not receive the opportunity to burn any. Commanded by Col. Frederick Sewall, one of Howard's former aides (and the same Bath lawyer who had sworn in Thomas Hyde and his friends), the green regiment formed with its brigade in front of Marye's Heights and prepared to add its own names to the growing number of the dead and dying. But the attack was called off and the 19th Maine's baptism of fire was delayed for another time. The experience was still nerve-racking. John P. Lancaster of Company A was pleased to find he was not afraid, at least not this time. "I do not think I dodged a single shell or musket ball there, for I was a soldier and I thought it would be cowardly to dodge," he said. "But for all that I could not help thinking of home, and wishing that I was there, and wondering how people of the intelligence and humanity of the American people could consent to submit a dispute to the arbitrament of war."[51]

Howard's division lost 64 officers and 813 men by the time it was relieved by some of Hooker's men around 2:00 A.M. The attacks, Howard said, had been a "hopeless sacrifice." The next day he returned to the church steeple with Crouch and surveyed the battleground. They had a clear view to the sunken road behind the stone wall, "and saw the ground literally strewn with the blue uniforms of our dead."[52]

⁓

While Sumner's Grand Division was being slaughtered in futile attacks against the stone wall, the 20th Maine waited on the opposite shore of the Rappahannock, held in reserve as part of Hooker's force. Chamberlain received permission to ride to the big brick Lacy house that stood on a bluff across the river from Fredericksburg, and he watched with fascination a scene that "was grand beyond anything I ever witnessed or expected to witness" as the Union cannon pounded the town and the engineers struggled to build their bridges. "Antietam was not anywhere equal to it, because more spread; this is all gathered into one focus," he told Fanny. On December 13, from their position on the bluff, the men of the 20th watched the Union attacks break and fall apart as they crossed the killing field. "There we stood for an hour, witnessing five immortal charges," Chamberlain remembered years later. "Tears ran down the cheeks of stern men, waiting, almost wishing, to be summoned to the same futile, glorious work."[53]

Those stern men soon got their wish, and they began marching across a swaying pontoon bridge and into town. Once across, the men threw down their knapsacks and prepared to move into the battle. "God help us now," Ames said. "Colonel, take care of the right wing! Forward the Twentieth!" The 20th Maine advanced. "The dead and wounded lay thick even here, and fragments of limbs were trampled underfoot," Chamberlain said. It was near sunset. "On we charged over fences and through hedges—over bodies of dead men and living ones—passed four lines that were lying on the ground to get out of fire—on, to that deadly edge where we had seen such desperate valor mown down in heaps."[54]

"The air was filled with iron hail," said Theodore Gerrish. "It was the first baptism of fire that our regiment ever received, but with the inspiration derived from such a man as Colonel Ames, it was a very easy thing to face danger and death." The Mainers fired a volley in the direction of the Confederates, and then took shelter behind a slight ridge that provided minimal protection. "Above us and almost within speaking distance was line after line of earthworks filled with rebels, while above them was the artillery vomiting fire and death incessantly," Gerrish wrote. "The utter impossibility of taking the rebel position was manifest to every man in the regiment, but we blazed away at the enemy, and they at us." Night fell and with it the temperatures. Chamberlain and Adjutant Brown fruitlessly searched for blankets or overcoats they could take from men who had fallen. Later that night a soldier on a similar errand yanked Chamberlain's cape from over his face, thinking he was a corpse, but he must have been startled to find living eyes staring back at him. Above the soldiers on this miserable and cold December night, the northern lights swirled and danced across the sky.[55]

The men remained in their position through the whole next day, sheltered behind the low ridge on the battlefield, unable to raise even a head above the crest lest they fall victim to Rebel sharpshooters. "No man could stand, without being shot down—troops ordered to our relief could not come up without being annihilated—the aides that sought to bring us orders riding at full speed had their horses shot from under them the instant they reached the crest behind us," Chamberlain said.[56]

The regiment was finally relieved on the second night and allowed to move back under the cover of darkness into the shattered town. Its experience at Fredericksburg had not been as bloody as the charges in front of the wall, but the 20th Maine had done some nerve-racking work. "Never did officers or men perform such perilous duty as mine had done for the past thirty-six hours," reported brigade commander Stockton. "The din of battle, the charge, and contest try most men's nerves, but that is nothing to what it is to be compelled to lie all day, scarcely sheltered at all, exposed to the shells and musketry of an ever-watchful enemy."[57]

The 20th Maine made one more visit to the front lines at Fredericksburg, when it received orders to move up on the night of December 15 and remain in place while the rest of the army moved silently back over the Rappahannock on the pontoon bridges, which were covered with dirt and brush to muffle the sounds of retreat. In a *Cosmopolitan* article about his Fredericksburg experiences published in 1912, Chamberlain recounted some stories that might owe more to drama than truth. He said he encountered a soldier digging quietly in the darkness, and started to rebuke him for being on the wrong side of the trenches—until he realized the man was a Confederate. "Dig away then, but keep a sharp lookout!" Chamberlain bluffed, and then he quietly slipped back to his own lines. In another incident, he said, a staff officer arrived and loudly told the Union soldiers to get out, that the rest of army was already across the river. Thinking quickly and hoping to lull any suspicions by eavesdropping Rebels, Chamberlain loudly rebuked the messenger for being a Confederate trying to sow panic in the Union ranks. The ruse, if it really happened, must have worked, for all remained silent on the Yankee front until the 20th Maine and the other regiments of the rear guard quietly disengaged from their perilous spot and slipped away to join the rest of the Army of the Potomac on the opposite bank.[58]

<hr />

South of town on Sunday, December 14, the two sides gathered as many of their wounded as they could under a flag of truce. That night there was some excitement when the pickets reported an enemy advance, but all was soon quiet again. The next morning at four o'clock the soldiers were awakened and given rations: hardtack, pork, coffee, sugar, and some whiskey. The rest of Monday remained reasonably uneventful, with another flag of truce allowing the recovery of more wounded. Confederate general D. H. Hill sent a note through the lines complimenting Berry on the way he had handled his men. There was even time for mail call. The Union soldiers prepared to spend another night bedded down on the cold battlefield, but sometime around 10:00 P.M. they received orders to move silently to the rear. Anything that could clank—cups, canteens, knives, and forks—was carefully packed away, and under the cover of darkness the 17th Maine and the rest of Franklin's men slipped away, stole across the pontoon bridges, and returned to the northern bank of the Rappahannock. Capt. William Hobson of Company I recalled seeing Berry on his horse, watching his men cross over to safety. "Ah, boys, I've got you out of a bad scrape," the general told them.[59]

The 17th Maine set up in Camp Pitcher, named after Maj. William L. Pitcher of the 4th Maine, who had been killed in the battle. Having his name attached to the camp was a dubious honor at best. "This officer was held in high esteem in his regiment but he derives no honor from having his name associated with a hole like this," said Haley. The men there suffered from bad water, poor rations, and overall unhealthy conditions. Disease began to take its inevitable toll.

General Birney admitted the regiment into the Order of the Red Patch, named after an insignia Kearny had created to identify his men. "Kearney [sic] was a wild Irishman from New Jersey, and a goodly portion of the division are the same," said Haley. "Then there are three Maine regiments, the 3rd and 4th, and now the 17th. Our troops from Maine prove themselves as good as the best, and that is the record they have received from all who have commanded them."[60]

On December 20, George Rollins, the young Vassalboro student in the 3rd Maine, wrote to his sister to describe his experiences in the fighting. "I suppose you have read the particulars of the battle of Fredericksburg and know something of the awful slaughter of Saturday last," Rollins said. "The account is enough to make one shudder by perusal and it seems terrible to make such havoc among men for nothing. Ten days ago our army lay encamped on this side of the Rappahannock—now it is in the same place—each Regt in its old camp—but 13,000 men have been plucked from its ranks and nothing has been gained."

Rollins told his sister how he had crossed the Rappahannock on a pontoon bridge, and went immediately into the fight. "Dead and wounded men & horses lay in every direction," he said. "The shells were flying right busily—dropping a man here and there but we cold not mind that for our business was with the enemy." His regiment was sent plodding through the mud over to their right to support the fellow Mainers of James Hall's battery. Artillery fire went whistling over their heads. Sometime around 3:00 P.M. Rollins watched Union infantry in a desperate fight with advancing enemy troops. More and more bullets filled the air and splattered into the mud around the 3rd Maine. "Our men began to get hit," said Rollins. "At last it became too hot for the battery and it commenced leaving." The 3rd Maine retreated with the artillery, and then faced around once more to check the advancing enemy. "I had just got turned about ready to give Mr. Rebel a shot when thump went a bullet into my elbow," Rollins reported. "The arm dropped to my side useless so I started for the rear."

Rollins told his sister he planned to stay with the regiment until he got paid, then find his way to a hospital in Washington—the city whose sights had so thrilled the excited young soldier the year before. Three days later Rollins was admitted to Lincoln General Hospital. He died there on January 4. The "thump" of the bullet slamming into his elbow had been his death knell.[61]

The 16th Maine, like other regiments in the Army of the Potomac, began settling in for another winter encampment. Its soldiers constructed winter huts, made furniture from whatever boxes and barrels they could find, constructed rude chimneys, made beds with pine bough mattresses, and prepared to wait until spring for further campaigning. Then, on January 14, orders came to destroy everything that couldn't be transported and prepare to march. One member of the 16th Maine's Company C took his carefully crafted furnishings and buried them in a grave. He held a funeral ceremony, with appropriate readings, and marked the site with a headstone.[62]

"I dread the scenes of another bloody field," Holman Melcher of the 20th Maine wrote to his brother on January 17 as the army stirred into activity. "I dread the carnage that must be the result of the meeting of these two great armies, armed as they now are. I shrink from the ghastly wounds that will meet our vision as we rush over the noble fallen." But Melcher reassured his brother that he was not losing his courage or becoming fainthearted. He intended to do his duty and if he had to die, he would be at his post and with his face to the enemy.[63]

The activity marked the launch of what became known as the "Mud March," Burnside's attempt to move up the Rappahannock and surprise Lee with a flank attack. Instead, it was Burnside who was surprised—by a fierce, unrelenting deluge of rain. The torrential downpour turned the roads to bottomless mud pits, sinking cannon and wagons to their axles and, according to stories, mules to their ears. The impassable roads thwarted all attempts to move the army. Burnside had to call the whole thing off. The wet, weary, and mud-splattered army returned to its previous encampments. The soldier from Company C dug up his belongings and went back to the business of surviving the winter. There would be plenty of opportunities for fighting in the spring.

CHAPTER 8

Hooker Takes Command

There is a growing desire for peace expressed by all the soldiers they feel that this toil and suffering is not for the Union, but for the advancement of political schemers, and army contractors who for gain, would <u>steal the coppers from</u> a dead soldier's eyes after cheating him out of his daily bread while living.
—FRELAND N. HOLMAN, 1ST MAINE CAVALRY

So far, defeat and humiliation had dogged the Army of the Potomac. Over two years of war, it had seen the tenures of three different generals-in-chief—Scott, McClellan, and now Halleck—while the army itself had already gone through two commanders, not to mention the efforts of Irwin McDowell and John Pope. The fate of its third commander appeared to hang in the balance. Fredericksburg had certainly been a defeat and the Mud March a humiliation. Morale in the army plummeted. Two of Burnside's officers, William Franklin and Baldy Smith, took it upon themselves to write directly to the president to explain their differences with Burnside. Two other officers from the VI Corps, brigadier generals John Newton and John Cochrane, traveled to Washington and met personally with the president so they could warn against another offensive under the army's current commander.

Bad morale wasn't restricted to officers, either. By January 15, a 41-year-old farmer from Saco named Orsamus Symonds had seen enough, and he decided to write to Abner Coburn, the newly elected

Maine governor, about the state of affairs in the army. "I have been on the field in battle in the hottest of the fight," wrote Symonds, who was with the 17th Maine. "The horrors of that was awful but it was not half the misery of this war the deaths in camp and hospital is enormous." The newspapers, Symonds wrote, may say that the men were ready for another fight, but he insisted that was not true. "I will sacrifice my life on this statement there is not one in each 100 000 that would ever lift the gun again if they could get rid of it in any way they are all most insane to get this thing closed up somehow. . . . all our battles in this state have been a wholesale slaughter of men." Symonds told Coburn that there was "an awful neglect somewhere on the part of some department." Unless something was done, Symonds said, "we all die in this miserable condition."

Apparently convinced that nothing could or would be done. Symonds deserted six days later. He was one of thousands of Union soldiers who fled the army on "French leave."[1]

Some of the soldiers in the 19th Maine wanted out so badly they began "accidentally" wounding themselves—shooting themselves in the hand, or chopping off a finger or toe—just to get sick leave. The situation became so dire Col. Frederick Sewall felt compelled to issue an order forbidding any more accidents in the regiment.[2]

Freland N. Holman, a private in Company L of the 1st Maine Cavalry, was thoroughly disgusted with everything. "There is a growing desire for peace expressed by all the soldiers," he wrote home at the end of December. "They feel that this toil and suffering is not for the Union, but for the advancement of political schemers, and army contractors who for gain, would steal the coppers from a dead soldier's eyes after cheating him out of his daily bread while living.

"This state of things cannot endure forever, this army of corruption will one day be shown up to the American people in its true character."[3]

It was time for change. Ambrose Burnside had been given his chance, and he blew it. Now, despite severe misgivings, President Lincoln picked Joseph Hooker to take his place. Hooker was a fighter, but he also had a reputation for undermining his superiors while inflating his own reputation, and for possessing a somewhat lax morality. Charles Francis Adams, a cavalryman who also happened to be the son and grandson of presidents, described Hooker's headquarters as "a combination of barroom and brothel." This was not the kind of person of whom General Howard— the "Christian General"—or his equally pious brother Charles could approve. Charles wrote to his mother and said he felt "sad" about the new commander. "He is intemperate and profane. I know not what will become of us." Writing to Lizzie about Hooker's promotion and Lincoln's removal of Generals Sumner and Franklin, Otis Howard said, "Hooker is not believed to be as good man morally as either of the others, but if God is proposing to use him as his fit instrument we will work on & wish for His will."[4]

Hooker defied such low expectations by quickly whipping the army into shape. "Whatever may have been Hooker's shortcomings, he was an excellent organizer," noted John Day Smith of the 19th Maine. "The men's rations were improved, new clothing was issued and regular battallion and brigade drills were instituted. New life was instilled into all departments of the army. The cavalry was for the first time brought forward and used as an important arm of the service, desertions practically ceased and a new spirit was infused into the body of the soldiery." Hooker issued distinctive badges to identify each of his corps, similar to what Phil Kearny had done for his division. Hooker also started a policy of allowing soldiers to go on furlough, another boost for morale.[5]

There was a story in the 5th Maine about an occasion shortly after Hooker took command when two officers rode into camp and took seats by a fire. The Mainers suspected they were cavalrymen. "Well, boys, how do you fare nowadays," one of them asked a soldier.

"Hard," the soldier replied, and showed the stranger the moldy, tough bread the men were forced to eat.

"Little rough," the stranger replied, and then the two horsemen saddled up and rode off. The next day the regiment received a supply of soft, fresh bread. The inquisitive stranger had been none other than Fighting Joe Hooker, inspecting his new command.[6]

John Lenfest, a private in the 20th Maine's Company E, was a farmer from Union who had enlisted at the relatively advanced age of 40. On March 10, 1863, he wrote to his wife and told her he had never weighed more in his life. "We live better since old Joe Hooker has comand of the

Army of the Potomac," he said. "We git potatoes twise a weake fresh beaf and beans and flower."[7]

Even Charles Howard began to gain a grudging respect for the intemperate and profane man who now held the reins of command. "Our army constantly feels the presence of Hooker as an energetic and stirring General," he wrote to his mother on February 19. "He will yet, I confidently believe, strike a hard blow at the Rebellion."[8]

For George P. Wood, a soldier in Company H of the 4th Maine, the jury was still out. "I like Hooker better than I did at first," he wrote to his family on March 30. "Still I cant have the confidence in him that I did in McClellan. One thing if he goes into a fight he will not budg a hair as long as he has a Regt left." On the other hand, John Mead Gould of the 10th Maine was impressed by Hooker the first time he saw him in person. "He is unmistakably a great man," Gould noted on March 19. "The way he sits in his saddle and every motion he makes shows it. I am content to be under such a general."[9]

In the 20th Maine, Adelbert Ames continued meting out strict discipline. He even punished men who didn't adequately wash their hands and faces by putting them on guard duty, where they had to pace back and forth with a rail over their shoulders. "Some of them complain bitterly because they have to 'lug poles' all day," Holman Melcher observed. "But make up their minds, that it is better to wash their face in [the] future." Melcher, who received a promotion to lieutenant in April, noted a marked improvement in the regiment's appearance and morale, and he gave credit to Ames—"a very strict, stern man, but a noble officer, brave and decided."[10]

Lt. Col. Selden Connor was in temporary command of a much reduced 7th Maine, which was now in the VI Corps division of another Mainer, Maj. Gen. Albion Howe. A somewhat cantankerous man who would be sidelined later in the war following his criticism of Generals Sedgwick and Meade, Howe hailed from the town of Standish, north of Portland. He had graduated eighth in the West Point class of 1841. He later fought in Mexico and against Native Americans in the West, and was one of the soldiers that Robert E. Lee brought with him to Harpers Ferry to quell John Brown's raid in 1859. After commanding artillery on the Peninsula, Howe received a brigade during the Seven Days' Battles and the Maryland Campaign. He was advanced to division command before Fredericksburg, but did not see any action there. Howe had short hair and a mustache and radiated an air of bulldog obstinacy. He was not popular in the army. One of his officers noted Howe's "unsocial disposition" and said he "was not a commander under whom one would desire very ardently to serve."[11]

His division commander's sour disposition notwithstanding, Connor felt cautious optimism. "The army never was in better shape than now; I think it lacks the enthusiasm that pervaded it when we commenced the Peninsular Campaign but it has a cool, dogged determination which perhaps is better," he wrote to his father on March 25. "Gen. Hooker is gaining strength and popularity every day with the army, and we hope and expect that he will not be found wanting when the day of trial comes."[12]

Turmoil was not restricted to general officers. The 19th Maine went through a period of intrigue under Col. Frederick Sewall, who did not appear to be popular with his men. "Our old Col. cares no more for his men than you would for a good dog in Maine," Wilbur M. Clifford complained in an October letter home. Increasingly, Sewall raised the ire of Henry W. Cunningham, the regiment's major. Cunningham hailed from Belfast, and he believed the colonel favored men from around Sewall's home in Bath. Cunningham also desired to see his son, Edward, a second lieutenant in Company D, receive a promotion. It's possible that Cunningham also knew that Sewall had expressed reservations about him because he used "spirituous liquor." Sewall had served under Howard, after all. (But even the most virtuous man can stumble. In November Clifford noted that Colonel Sewall had gotten drunk in Warrenton, and the next day ordered the regiment assembled so he could ask for its forgiveness.)[13]

Whatever the motivations, Cunningham had been keeping Adjutant General Hodsdon and Governor Washburn informed of the regiment's doings with chatty letters that paid special attention to the deeds of the Cunninghams and the shortcomings of Colonel Sewall. Whenever possible, he pushed for the promotion of Company D's captain, William Folger—not necessarily because he liked Folger, but because his promotion would open the captaincy for Edward Cunningham.

The situation reached a slow boil in the winter of 1863, when it became apparent that Sewall's health would force him to resign. Two factions emerged within the regiment. Sewall wanted Lt. Col. Francis Heath to replace him as colonel, with Cunningham moving up to lieutenant colonel and Capt. James W. Welch to major. Cunningham wanted the colonelcy for himself, with Heath remaining as lieutenant colonel, and Folger becoming major. Captain Welch complained that Cunningham was pulling strings back in Maine, writing letters "to all of his friends in the Legislature" and arranging for a furlough so he could apply pressure in person. In any event, Cunningham's machinations fell short, for when Sewall resigned in February, Heath became the new colonel.[14]

Promotions weren't the only reason for discontent. President Lincoln's Emancipation Proclamation, issued on January 1 and freeing all slaves within rebellious territory, created consternation among some Maine soldiers who had enlisted to restore the Union, not end slavery. Joseph Nichols, lieutenant in the 19th Maine's Company C, tendered his resignation because of it. Nichols was a Democrat from Phippsburg and he apparently believed his resignation would not be accepted and made the gesture to curry favor with fellow Democrats back home. His resignation was rejected, but then Nichols was court-martialed and cashiered from the army.[15]

On the other hand, Granville M. Baker, a soldier from Standish in the 20th Maine's Company D, heartily approved of the plans for African American soldiers. Writing to Governor Coburn on February 20, 1863, Baker averred that he was "firm in his patriotism and love of country, and deems the plan of arming the negro and bringing him into the field as an auxiliary force on the speedy suppression of the rebellion a first and wise measure." In fact, Barker wanted to be considered for a captaincy in a colored regiment.[16]

General Howard had also been thinking about the status of the slave. In a letter he wrote on New Year's Day he informed Lizzie that he had sent a "hasty article" to the *New York Times* outlining his reasons why he thought slavery needed to die. "At times I have been able to apologize for Slavery, but have always felt that it was a blot upon us," Howard told the *Times* readers. Now, he said, "we have no alternative; we must destroy

Slavery root and branch; we must do it in order to '*subjugate*' the persistent enemy of Republican government." It's possible a little self-interest was involved in the letter, too—Howard's biographer, John A. Carpenter, speculated that the general may have been publicly aligning himself with the administration's policies now that his promotion to major general of volunteers was awaiting approval. Whatever his motivations for the letter, it appears Howard sincerely wanted to see the institution come to an end. "Slavery dies hard and costs us a bitter sacrifice, but I hope and trust we haven't invested our blood and treasure for naught," the future head of the Freedmen's Bureau wrote his wife on January 4.[17]

Later, Howard wrote home with a sad story about a young "contraband," one of the slaves who had escaped to freedom within the Union lines and who worked around the camp. The young man, whose name was Andrew, had been returning to camp on horseback with a load of laundry when a soldier from the Irish Brigade stopped him and demanded the animal for himself. Andrew refused, explaining that he was on an errand for General Howard. The soldier cursed, raised his musket, and shot him. Andrew managed to ride back to camp, but doctors had to amputate his arm at the shoulder the next day. He died shortly afterwards. "He was a good boy, kind and thoughtful at all times & I believe a follower of Christ," Howard told Lizzie. The killer was not identified. "In the Irish brigade, they are so clannish that they will secure each other from all deserved punishment," the general complained.[18]

Charles Howard had something else on his mind—he was "smitten." In February the general's youngest brother and trusted aide visited West Point, where he reconnected with Jeannie H. Grey, a young woman who had known Otis and Lizzie there. Back in December 1861 Grey had written to Otis requesting his help in getting a commission for a friend. In her letter she also detailed her financial woes, and explained that she was trying to borrow enough money to build her own house. This alone was fairly progressive for a woman in the nineteenth century, but even more surprising was the way she ended up raising the money. In 1863 Jeannie published a romance novel under the pseudonym Hearton Drille and titled *Tactics; Or, Cupid in Shoulder Straps. A West Point Romance*. None of this appeared to please the straitlaced Howard family. Rowland,

Otis, Lizzie, and the Howards' mother all disapproved of any match with the free-spirited, independent, and outspoken Miss Grey. Lizzie must have been especially critical in her correspondence with her husband, for Otis had to stop letting Charles read her letters. Otis, in fact, was the sole voice of reason, counseling his family that too much resistance might only drive Charles to propose. "Now darling the prospect is Jeannie may become a sister," Otis wrote Lizzie on March 18. "My heart rebelled a little at first, but Charles has good taste & good sense and may like things different from you & me and he will say 'no interference.'" The universally negative reactions did put the brakes on any romance, and by the end of March Charles told Otis he would probably stop writing to Miss Grey.[19]

Hiram Berry had inspired his men on the battlefield, but off it he was still in bad shape. He lost so much hair he had his head shaved. When John Haley of the 17th Maine spied the newly shorn general, he found his appearance "startling." The fighting at Fredericksburg had taken a toll on Berry mentally, too. The 4th Maine's Elijah Walker recalled how Berry had approached him the morning after the battle, put his head on Walker's shoulder, and wept so bitterly he could not speak. Two staff officers gently ushered the general away. "One hour later he was in his saddle, directing his brigade, as cool and calm as though nothing had happened," Walker said. After the Mud March debacle, Berry admitted that he was "well-nigh used up."[20]

Despite the death and heartbreak, Berry still showed glimmers of what his biographer called his "inordinate love of fun." One practical joke that amused the general was to ride up behind some unsuspecting staff officer, reach down, and sweep the kicking and squirming man up onto his saddle and carry him into camp. The stunt didn't work out so well when Berry tried a variation on the wife of the assistant adjutant general, who was visiting her husband. She had been out riding when she heard horsemen approach. Fearing they were Rebel cavalry, she desperately tried to escape. One rider rode up from behind, snatched her from the saddle, and shouted, "Surrender!" The poor woman struck at her captor with her riding whip before bursting into tears of fright. The horseman, of course, was Berry. He immediately released his poor victim and stood before her "in abject remorse, overwhelming her with apologies."[21]

Berry did receive some good news during the winter. Gen. Charles Hamlin, the vice president's son, had been lobbying to get him a promotion. He had gained glowing notices from Joseph Hooker ("He is practical, intelligent, enterprising, intrepid and devoted," Hooker wrote), and Samuel Heintzelman ("He has always performed his duties with energy and good judgement"). On January 22, 1863, Vice President Hamlin wrote to inform Berry of his promotion to major general. He received command of Joe Hooker's old division, which was now part of the III Corps.[22]

The III Corps' previous commander, George Stoneman, had taken command of the new cavalry corps and was replaced by Maj. Gen. Daniel Sickles. Like Berry, Sickles was a Democrat, a product of New York's Tammany political machine. He was a rake and a rogue, a man to whom the tag "notorious" seemed to fit naturally. While serving as an aide to James Buchanan when the future president was envoy to Great Britain, Sickles had allegedly brought his mistress, a prostitute, to England with him. There was nothing alleged about what he had done on February 27, 1859, when he was serving in Congress. In Lafayette Square, just across from the White House, he had shot his wife's lover to death. The lover was Barton Key, U.S. attorney general and the son of Francis Scott Key of "Star Spangled Banner" fame. Acquitted thanks to the first successful use of the temporary insanity defense, Sickles had further shocked society by taking his wife back, only to neglect her once again.

When war broke out, Sickles had raised a unit of New York soldiers he called the Excelsior Brigade and offered his services to the nation. It did not matter that he had no military experience. The Lincoln administration needed as much support from Democrats as it could muster, and Sickles received a commission as a brigadier general. He may have lacked military training, but Sickles proved to be an aggressive fighter, and his notoriety meshed well with the attitudes at Hooker's headquarters. Hooker had a reputation for liking the ladies and the bottle; his chief of staff, Daniel Butterfield, was shadowed by allegations that he had burned down buildings in his native upstate New York; and now Dan Sickles had been added to the Army of the Potomac's inner circle. Charles Francis Adams called it "the drunk-murdering-arson dynasty."[23]

Not everyone shared Adams's opinion of Sickles. John Haley of the 17th Maine liked him just fine and said the rest of the corps did, too. "He is every inch a soldier and looks like a game cock," Haley noted. "No one questions his bravery or patriotism. Before the war he killed a man who had seduced his wife. A person who has the nerve to do that might be expected to show good qualities as a general where daredeveiltry is a factor."[24]

Berry got a division, but Otis Howard received a corps. He first took over the II Corps when Darius Couch moved up to take command of the Grand Division following Sumner's removal. When Hooker abolished the Grand Divisions, both generals returned to their original positions, Couch to the II Corps and Howard back to his division. Otis was fine with that, vacillating as he often did between ambition and insecurity. "I do feel almost startled at my own littleness, but I hope for the sake of my own command I am held in higher esteem by others than I hold myself," he admitted to his wife. But ambition won out when Sickles— whom Howard outranked—received the III Corps. Howard complained to Hooker and received a promotion to head of the XI Corps. Brother Charles was promoted to major and given permanent placement as Otis's aide-de-camp.[25]

Howard's corps was a new addition to the Army of the Potomac. It had originated as the I Corps under John Frémont and then became part of John Pope's Army of Virginia. It did not join the Army of the Potomac until after Fredericksburg. The corps had a large proportion of Germans and soldiers of German descent, who took pride in being commanded by Franz Sigel, Frémont's successor, who had fled his native Germany during the political turmoil of 1848. Insulted by the fact that his corps was the smallest in the army, Sigel opted to resign after Hooker took command.

Howard and the XI Corps was not a match made in heaven. The German soldiers in the corps had taken pride in fighting beneath one of their own but they did not appear to look too favorably on their young, Bible-thumping commander. As one writer put it, "Howard was a West Point–trained, evangelizing New Englander who spoke no German, knew little about the cultural values of his German troops, and cared more about their souls' salvation than their morale." None of this endeared him to his men.[26]

One German who had reason to look askance at Howard's promotion was Carl Schurz, who had commanded a division under Sigel and hoped to replace him at the head of the corps. Like Sigel, Schurz had fled Germany in 1848 when the revolutionary forces opposing the Prussians had been defeated. In the United States he became known as a skilled orator and a vocal opponent of slavery. President Lincoln appointed him the U.S. minister to Spain but Schurz did not stay there long. He returned to the United States early in 1862 and received a commission as a brigadier general. He fought in the Shenandoah Valley under Frémont and at Second Bull Run under Pope. A bespectacled man with thick hair and beard, Schurz may have looked more like a European revolutionary than an American general, but he had fought well enough at Second Manassas.

In his memoirs, Schurz professed to have been unimpressed by his new corps commander, whom he described as "a slender, dark-bearded young man of rather prepossessing appearance and manners." Schurz conceded that Howard was brave—his empty sleeve testified to that—but doubted his intellect. "A certain looseness of mental operations, a marked uncertainty in forming definite conclusions became evident in his conversation," Schurz said. "I thought, however, that he might appear better in action than in talk." Schurz said he came to like Howard, but the men in the corps did not. "They looked at him with dubious curiosity; not a cheer could be started when he rode along the front," Schurz wrote. "And I do not know whether he liked the men he commanded better than they liked him."[27]

Schurz was just one of the officers who added a distinctly cosmopolitan flavor to the XI Corps. Adolph Von Steinwehr commanded the Second Division, and the corps' brigade commanders included Col. Leopold von Gilsa, Col. Adolphus Buschbeck, and Brig. Gen. Alexander Schimmelfennig. Howard was aware of the distance between him and his men, knew "there was much complaint in the German language at the removal of Sigel," and that he "was not getting the earnest and loyal support of the entire command. But for me there was no turning back."[28]

In the 17th Maine, an ambitious private from Company A named Charles O. Blackstone was growing tired of his lowly place in the regiment. On January 7 he wrote his father a letter. "I entered the army as I would any other school, and that with similar motives," Blackstone said. "I have gone through with the preliminaries, and have become dissatisfied with my present position on account of my acquaintance with men and things with whom I have been brought in contact. It is my intention now, to rise a little, and I shall require some of your assistance." He had heard that the 18th Maine was going to be transformed from infantry to heavy artillery and wanted his father to use his connections at home to get Charles a commission in the regiment. Blackstone's father must have done his son's bidding, for letters soon began arriving in Augusta recommending his son. Young Charles was also doing his part, for Charles Mattocks, the captain of his company, wrote Governor Coburn to recommend Blackstone, and soldiers in the regiment circulated a petition for him. All seemed on track to satisfy the young private's ambition.[29]

The 7th Maine had been so decimated at Antietam, following Irwin's alcohol-inspired orders, that McClellan personally ordered it back to Maine to refit and recruit new soldiers. Hyde returned to the field in February. After his taste of regimental command, he began chafing under the control of Col. Edwin C. Mason, the no-nonsense old soldier who had returned to lead the regiment. The feeling was probably mutual. In fact, after Antietam the colonel placed Hyde under arrest, ostensibly because the young major had not kept him sufficiently informed about the battle. (Hyde believed he angered Mason by recommending several of the regiment's sergeants for promotion without consulting him.) In any event, Hyde avoided further conflict when he received a promotion to the staff of VI Corps commander Baldy Smith. Once Smith was sent packing following his machinations against Burnside, Hyde was appointed to the staff of Smith's successor, John Sedgwick.

Sedgwick's soldiers called him "Uncle John." He had been born in Connecticut in 1813 and graduated from West Point in 1837. He had battled the Seminoles, fought under Zachary Taylor and Winfield Scott in Mexico, and served in the 1st Cavalry when it had been commanded by Robert E. Lee. Once war broke out, Sedgwick gained the rank of brigadier general, was promoted to major general, and was wounded both on the Peninsula and at Antietam. He was considered to be capable and dependable, but cautious. The members of his staff looked upon him as a father figure. "A lion in battle, but with the harness off, gentle as a woman, unselfish as a saint," was how Thomas Hyde described him. "Surely those of us who made his military family then can look back upon no greater privilege, no more lasting recollection, than being permitted to enjoy his confidence and appreciate his simple greatness."[30]

As April 1863 neared its close, it became increasingly apparent to the Army of the Potomac's soldiers that a movement was imminent. It became equally clear that the 20th Maine was going to miss the excitement. Smallpox had broken out in the regiment. The disease was dangerously contagious, especially in an army with so many men who had never ventured far from home and had never been exposed to various illnesses. Instead of preparing for battle, the regiment went into quarantine. Signs were posted around the 20th Maine's camp, and the word was that the regiment would remain isolated for at least two weeks. Many soldiers would have been perfectly happy with a legitimate excuse to miss combat, but it frustrated Joshua Chamberlain. "If in the meantime there is a battle, & I am left here in a pesthouse, I shall be desperate with mortification," he wrote to his wife on April 24. He sought to get placed on the staff of some general—any general—so he could play a role in the upcoming fight.[31]

Ames also itched to see combat. He had been angling for promotion and had already received a ringing endorsement from Joe Hooker. "I know of no officer of more promise, and should he be promoted I feel no doubt but that he will reflect great credit upon himself and his State," Hooker wrote to Hannibal Hamlin in November. Hiram Berry had echoed that praise in his own letter to Hamlin. "Colonel Ames is a soldier and a good one," he wrote. "He has already won a name by his bravery and skill on the battle field, that any man may well be proud of." Berry also mentioned that Ames was "an excellent disciplinarian."[32]

Ames agreed. "Up to the battle of Fredericksburgh I have been somewhat disliked by my men and officers, but at that battle the feelings in the Regt. changed completely," he wrote to his parents. "I was the only Colonel in the brigade who when in front of his Regt. and *led* his men into the fight. All of my men who were killed and wounded (thirty-six) were in rear of me when struck. My men now have confidence in me; and the battle taught them the necessity of discipline."[33]

However, word was spreading back in Maine that Ames was *too* strict. To counter this, in February the regiment's officers felt compelled to draft a letter addressed "To Whom It May Concern" and sent it to John Hodsdon. "It has been unjustly represented that the Regiment has been subjected to hard and unnecessarily severe discipline, & that the health of the men has been broken down through the fault of the commanding officer," the letter read. The real problem, the officers explained, was that the regiment was ordered into the field before it was ready. If the men suffered as a result, it was not Ames's fault. "To us he has been universally kind & courteous. He has spared no exertions in the instruction of officers & men. It is due to him that the Regiment is so well drilled & effective—that it has been able to face the fire of the enemy with maneuvering lines, & fully to sustain the proud reputation of the state of Maine." The real charge against Ames, these officers said, is "the exact & faithful performance of his duties."[34]

There was also the danger that an unscrupulous soldier could interpret Ames's strictness differently, and use it as an excuse for his own cruelty. This might have been the case with quartermaster Alden Litchfield. In February 26, 1863, Isabella Fogg—a resident of Calais who had joined the Maine Camp Relief Association to aid the soldiers—wrote to the authorities in Falmouth to register a complaint about Litchfield. She said "a more wicked, profane, cruel, unprincipled man, I think could not be found in the State of Maine." Fogg complained that the quartermaster forced sick men who could barely walk to leave their tents and stand guard in the pouring rain over the horse of the regimental surgeon—"as if the loss of a horse, was to be compared with the life of one of the brave sons of Maine." Fogg also said Litchfield ordered some soldiers to bury the body of one of their comrades, telling them that if they were not quick enough about it "he would cause a hole to be dug in which to inter them." Even worse, he claimed he was simply carrying out Ames's orders, which Fogg said she knew to be a lie.[35]

In his history of the 20th Maine, Theodore Gerrish tells another story about the quartermaster, whom he described as "a large, rough, overbearing man, one who disgraced his uniform every day by his brutal treatment of the men." Gerrish detailed how Litchfield ordered Sgt. George H. Buck to chop some firewood for him. Buck, who was sick and exempt from such work, refused. Litchfield knocked him to the ground, kicked him, and reported him for refusing orders. Buck was summarily reduced to private. It would take a new commanding officer to offer him some form of redemption.[36]

In the meantime, Ames, like Chamberlain, sought a way to participate in the coming battle. He had better luck than Chamberlain and managed to get himself appointed to the staff of V Corps commander George G. Meade.

⌁

The president of the United States visited in April. Lincoln, his wife, his son Tad, and other members of a small entourage traveled down the Potomac on a steamer and then boarded a train for the final leg of the journey to the Army of the Potomac's headquarters. There Lincoln consulted with Hooker and reviewed portions of his command. Many of the soldiers were somewhat amused to see the president's lanky form mounted on a horse that seemed too small for him. "There was a fearful disproportion between the length of his legs and the height of the horse," noted John Haley. "It seemed as if nothing short of tying a knot in them would prevent them from dragging on the ground." John Mead Gould was similarly unimpressed by the commander in chief. In his diary he wrote, "The President wore an immense stove-pipe hat and cut a comical figure enough, or as some of the boys said, 'There's a deserter from a comic almanac' and it did look as if the President was a man got up in imitation of his picture rather than the pictures being likenesses of him." For his part, Lincoln departed Hooker's camp with a sense of foreboding. He felt that maybe Joe Hooker was feeling a bit overconfident.[37]

Pvt. Henry H. Hunt of the 5th Maine Battery (not related to the Henry Hunt who served as the army's artillery chief) took advantage of the cavalry review to ride over and get a look at the president. He pushed his way through the crowd until he was close enough to observe Lincoln, whom he thought was "very pale and haggard—looked weighed down by care." Hunt then amused himself by studying the officers around him. "Such a collection I never saw before: some mere boys with Colonel's straps and some officers so drunk that they could hardly sit in their saddle, others passing their flasks around among their friends." Hunt found it all laughable, "though it is shameful that whiskey should be so much a thing among the officers of the army."

"I supposed that after this review we may expect something will be done," Hunt wrote home to his mother in Gorham. "I have seen Gen. Hooker several times lately. I like his appearance very much—he looks like a man of great firmness & decision. I hope he will be more fortunate than Burnside in the handling of this army—and he already has one advantage over him, that of the confidence of the soldiers."[38]

CHAPTER 9

Howard Gets Flanked

*It was a terrible gale! the rush, the rattle, the quick lightning from a
hundred points at once; the roar, redoubled by echoes through the forest;
the panic, the dead and dying in sight and the wounded straggling along;
the frantic efforts of the brave and patriotic to stay the angry storm!*
—MAJ. GEN. OLIVER OTIS HOWARD

The battle of Chancellorsville was the low point of Oliver O. Howard's
military career. More than any other Union officer—except for Joseph
Hooker—Howard must shoulder the blame for the Army of the Potomac's debacle in the tangled Wilderness in May 1863. Yet Howard somehow survived the disaster, while the German troops under his command
became the scapegoats. As one historian noted, Howard's career "must
constitute one of the great paradoxes of American military history: no
officer entrusted with field direction of troops has ever equaled Howard's
record for surviving so many tactical errors of judgment and disregard of
orders, emerging later not only with increased rank, but on one occasion
with the thanks of Congress."[1]

Perhaps he had God on his side.

Torrential rains postponed Hooker's plans to take the offensive, but
the army finally began moving on April 27. The army commander hoped
to accomplish what Burnside had tried and failed to do with his Mud
March—move the bulk of his force north up the Rappahannock, cross
the river, and outflank Lee's forces in Fredericksburg. Hooker sent the

V, XI, and XII Corps off on the flanking maneuver. The I, III, and VI Corps moved south of Fredericksburg, to the area where Franklin had crossed back in December, to focus Lee's attention there. Hooker also wanted his new cavalry corps, under the command of George Stoneman, to make a raid in the rear of Lee's army and disrupt his communications. John Gibbons's division of the II Corps remained at Falmouth, directly opposite Fredericksburg.

Howard's XI Corps took the lead on the march north. Starting around 5:30 A.M. on April 27, the corps quietly left its winter camps, without any pomp and circumstance that could potentially alert the Rebels that the Army of the Potomac was finally stirring. The men carried rations for eight days and had been ordered to leave behind anything they didn't need. Before long, following a tradition established early in the war, soldiers began tossing away items they no longer considered essential. Coats, blankets, cookware, and other such things began accumulating along the sides of the road.

During the march, Hooker rode by and expressed irritation that Howard's corps was not traveling lightly enough. He had expressly ordered that supply trains were to be kept to a minimum, and Howard's were slowing the rest of the army. Howard blamed subordinates who had snuck in some extra wagons with additional supplies. This was his "first mortification" of the campaign.[2]

In the I Corps, the 16th Maine left its camp on April 28 and moved south. During the march, rumors passed from soldier to soldier that a distinguished visitor was going to review them. The regiment halted in a field, and the distinguished visitor approached, holding on for dear life atop a bucking, uncontrollable horse. It was Abner Coburn, Israel Washburn's successor as governor of Maine.

Born in what is now Skowhegan in 1803, the second of what would be 14 children, Coburn had started life in humble circumstances. He learned the value of hard work at an early age and never forgot it. As a young man he served as an assistant to his surveyor father and started his own business at the age of 22. Father and son branched out from surveying by purchasing land along the Kennebec River to harvest timber and became hugely successful in the lumber business. Abner later expanded into railroads and became president of the Portland and Kennebec line. He served in the Maine legislature as a Whig and later helped found the Republican Party in the state. Washburn was preparing to complete his second one-year term in 1862 when Coburn won election to the governorship and took office in January.[3]

No matter his accomplishments back in Maine, the governor did not make a good impression in Virginia. The soldiers couldn't tell whether to cheer or laugh at his undignified arrival. Colonel Tilden had to help Coburn dismount from his overexcited mount. The governor gathered himself and then walked up and down the ranks, shaking hands with the men and asking them what they ate. Addressing Tilden, the governor asked, "Colonel, you keep a rooster, don't you? I keep a private rooster myself, and I want all my colonels to keep one." Then Coburn climbed back on his horse and departed, leaving the men somewhat baffled.[4]

John Haley was similarly unimpressed when Coburn stopped by the 17th Maine. "Governor Coburn is, without exception, the most wretched speechmaker that ever burnished the cushion of the governor's chair," he decided. "He acted more like a great, blubbering school boy than like the Governor of Maine."[5]

❦

Howard's corps crossed the Rappahannock on a pontoon bridge at Kelly's Ford in the late afternoon of April 28, and was splashing across the Rapidan at Germanna Ford late the next night. On Wednesday, April 30, Howard rode ahead of his corps to a crossroads in the area of tangled forests, boggy runs, and tiny clearings called the Wilderness. The intersection was called Chancellorsville, but it was a poor excuse for a "ville." There was no town or even hamlet. There was only the home of the Chancellor family, a fine brick building that stood at a crossroads. Two roads, the Orange Turnpike and the Orange Plank Road, converged just to the west of the Chancellor house near a place called the Wilderness Tavern. From there they continued as a single route eastward until the Plank Road veered off to the south just beyond Chancellorsville. The two roads rejoined farther east, then continued on past Salem Church and into Fredericksburg.

Howard found that George Meade and the V Corps were already at the crossroads, and he reported to Henry Slocum, commander of the XII Corps. Slocum told Howard to position his command on the right of the gathering army along the Orange Turnpike. Slocum would post his corps to Howard's left, continuing the line to Chancellorsville. The bulk of Couch's II Corps soon arrived, and Sickles and the III Corps, which had withdrawn from its position with the force south of town, were on their way north.

Hooker's army had stolen a march on Robert E. Lee and was now in the enviable position of threatening the Rebel army's flank. So far, his plan had been a near-complete success. Hooker reached Chancellorsville on the evening of April 30. The progress his army had made pleased him so much he was moved to issue General Orders No. 47. The enemy, he said, "must either ingloriously fly or come out from behind his entrenchments and give us battle on our own ground, where certain destruction awaits him." The only flaw was a dearth of results from the cavalry arm, Stoneman's raid having been delayed by the rains and high rivers.

By the next day, though, Hooker's confidence seemed to be wavering. The V, II, and XII Corps had begun moving down separate roads in the direction of Fredericksburg, only to receive orders from Hooker to reverse course and entrench around Chancellorsville. The generals complied, but not without some grumbling.

On May 2 Meade and V Corps held the army's left. The II Corps came next, forming at almost a right angle on Meade's right. Slocum's XII Corps connected with Couch's right at another right angle, forming a salient around the Chancellor house. Howard's XI was on the far right, forming an almost straight line along the Orange Turnpike and facing south. Sickles and his III Corps, which included Hiram Berry's division, had reached Chancellorsville late on May 1. Some of his corps filled a gap between the XI and II Corps, with the rest waiting behind the Chancellor house as a reserve.

Howard's corps had three divisions. Charles Devens Jr. commanded the First Division; the Second was under Adolph von Steinwehr, and Schurz had the Third. Devens's division held the right of the line—the right of the entire army, in fact. Devens had been a Massachusetts lawyer when war broke out, and he used his militia experience to get a major's commission in a 90-day regiment. As the colonel of the 15th Massachusetts, he had experienced a brush with death when one of his uniform buttons deflected a Rebel bullet at the battle of Ball's Bluff. He was also wounded at Fredericksburg, where he commanded a brigade in the VI Corps. According to Schurz, the cold and austere Devens was not well liked by his division, in part because he had replaced the popular Nathaniel McLean, a thickly bearded Ohioan who had been bumped down to brigade command.

Devens had two brigades, under Leopold von Gilsa and Nathaniel McLean. Von Gilsa's brigade was on the far right of the division, and hence held the entire army's right flank. Von Gilsa was another German refugee; at one point he had been forced to make a living playing piano in New York music halls. He also displayed a mastery of swearing in German. Howard apparently did not think much of him, at least in retrospect. In his autobiography, the best that Howard could say about von Gilsa was that "he made a fine soldierly appearance" for drills and reviews. At Chancellorsville, von Gilsa's right was "in the air," with nothing anchoring it but the woods and thickets of the Wilderness. Most of the brigade was facing south along the turnpike, with two regiments at the end of the line bent at a 90-degree angle from the rest of the line and facing west.[6]

McLean's brigade was next in line, also looking south over the turnpike. Schurz's division was next, and then Steinwehr's. Francis Barlow's brigade of Steinwehr's division served as a reserve. Howard made his headquarters in a building known as Dowdall's Tavern, the home of another member of the Chancellor family. He must have felt secure about his position, for when Brig. Gen. Charles Graham, who commanded a brigade in the III Corps, arrived at Howard's headquarters on May 1 with orders to post his men as pickets, Howard replied that he "needed no assistance." Graham took his men and returned to the Chancellor house. Howard's confidence might have been justified had the Rebels attacked from the south—but, unfortunately for the XI Corps, they did not.[7]

Hooker was correct about one thing—his movements did draw Lee out from behind his entrenchments, but not in a manner that anyone in the Union army expected. Lee had seen through the Union feint south of town, and realized that the real threat lay around Chancellorsville. Early

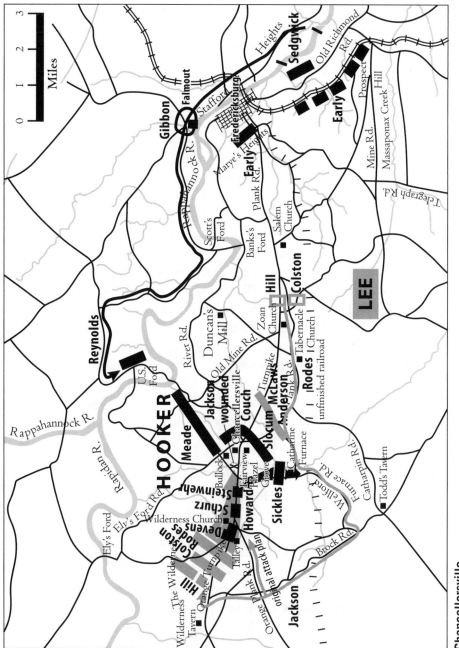

Chancellorsville

on May 1, Stonewall Jackson began moving his men out from behind Fredericksburg to meet this new threat. One of Jackson's divisions, under the command of Jubal Early, remained behind. That night, Lee and Jackson made plans for Jackson to take his corps on a wide-ranging march around the Union army and fall on its unsuspecting right flank—the position held by Oliver O. Howard's XI Corps.

Hiram Berry, whose division initially went south of Fredericksburg with the rest of the III Corps, felt a sense of foreboding about the campaign. He told quartermaster James F. Rusling he did not think he would come out of it alive, and he gave him some of his papers and asked him to make sure his body was recovered and sent back to Maine. On the night before the III Corps moved north from Franklin's old crossing spot to join the flanking force, another member of Berry's staff thought the general seemed "greatly depressed." Berry mentioned that he was anxious to receive mail and get word about his wife and daughter. The officer volunteered to make the 18-mile round-trip to the rail station at Stoneman's Switch and fetch any letters waiting there. When the aide returned around 2:00 A.M. he found Berry still waiting anxiously. The general took his letters and sat down on a log before a fire to read them. He showed Rusling a photograph he had received of his daughter. "Now I will try to get some sleep," Berry said, "as I look for warm work in the morning.[8]

As the sun rose on May 2, Joe Hooker arrived along the XI Corps line to take a look at its defenses. He appeared impressed. "How strong! How strong," he said. Yet he must have developed some reservations, for later in the day he had an order sent to Howard, warning him that his preparations had been made with the idea that the enemy would make a frontal attack. "If he should throw himself upon your flank," said Hooker's message, the commanding general "wished you to examine the ground and determine upon the position you will take in that event, in order that you may be prepared for him in whatever direction he advances." Hooker advised Howard to keep "heavy reserves well in hand to meet this contingency. We have good reason to suppose that the enemy is moving to our right. Please advance your pickets as far as may be safe, in order to obtain timely information of their approach." Hooker then sent a second, similar message to both Howard and Henry Slocum, whose corps was next in the Union line. "The right of your line does not appear to be strong enough," Hooker warned. "No artificial defenses worth naming have been thrown up, and there appears to be a scarcity of troops at that point, and not, in the general's opinion, as favorably posted as might be."[9]

Sometime around noon, Howard complained of fatigue and said he wanted to catch some sleep. He instructed Schurz to wake him if any urgent dispatches arrived. When Hooker's directive to watch the flank arrived, Schurz said, he immediately took the message to Howard. The second warning arrived shortly afterwards. Howard said he did not recall seeing any such messages. In any event, he claimed, he had gone ahead on his own initiative and done what the message had instructed to protect his flank.

That would have surprised Schurz, who said he pointed out to Howard the weakness of his right. "Do you not think it certain that the enemy, attacking from the west, will crush Gilsa's two regiments, which are to protect our right and rear, at the first onset?" he asked. "Is there the slightest possibility for him to resist?"

As Schurz remembered it, all Howard had to say was, "Well, he will have to fight."[10]

The Federals had received their first hint that something was up around eight o'clock, when a long column of Confederates became visible to the south through a gap in the trees near a place called Catherine Furnace. The reports reached David Birney, who commanded a division in the III Corps, and he sent word to Dan Sickles, his corps commander. Sickles ordered his artillery to shell the enemy soldiers.

Eager for a fight, Sickles had Berry send out two of his regiments to see what the enemy was up to, and he asked Hooker for permission to do more. With Hooker's blessing, Sickles advanced Birney's and Amiel Whipple's divisions, with Hiram Berdan's sharpshooters as skirmishers. By the time Sickles reached Catherine Furnace, almost all the Confederate column had marched off into the woods, leaving only the 23rd

Georgia behind to be captured. It was possible that Jackson was marching to attack the army's right; it was also possible that Lee was retreating.
Hooker apparently believed the second interpretation, and when Howard
returned to his headquarters later in the day, he did, too.

Carl Schurz did not share that optimistic interpretation. He rode
over to Dowdall's Tavern to tell Howard he thought Jackson was preparing to attack their right—he even stopped along the way to tell Capt.
Hubert Dilger to find some good westward-facing positions for his artillery battery. Howard would have none of it. Lee was retreating, he said.
"I was amazed at this belief," recalled Schurz. "Was it at all reasonable to
think that Lee, if he really intended to retreat, would march his column
along our front instead of *away* from it, which he might have done with
far less danger of being disturbed?" Howard remained unconvinced.[11]

Increasingly desperate, Schurz moved three of his regiments so they
would be better positioned to resist an attack from the west. Howard,
he said, did not object. Other than that, along with the digging of some
shallow entrenchments and a movement of the artillery reserve, nothing
else was done to improve what Schurz called the XI Corps' "absurdly
indefensible position." It was made even more difficult to defend when
Hooker asked Howard to send Barlow's brigade forward to support Sickles. Howard, who had intended to keep Barlow as his reserve, "deemed
it of sufficient importance" to accompany the brigade on Sickles's expedition personally.[12]

<hr/>

The blow fell sometime after 5:00 P.M. Jackson's men had indeed headed
south at Catherine Furnace, but only until they reached a road that ran
north toward the Orange Turnpike to the west of the XI Corps' position.
Jackson placed his men—the divisions of Robert Rodes, Raleigh Colston,
and A. P. Hill—in long lines of battle that extended north and south of
the turnpike and easily overlapped the unsuspecting XI Corps off to the
east. Then Jackson ordered his men forward. The Rebels pushed their
way through the woods and thickets that separated them from Howard's
mostly unsuspecting men. Animals fled the lines of humans forcing their
way through the tangled growth and burst out of the woods to scamper

through the camps of Howard's men, many of whom had stacked their arms and were playing cards or cooking food. There was the sound of gunfire, the warning shots of the pickets, and then Jackson's soldiers burst out of the woods like a whirlwind. The surprise was so complete, said one soldier from the 153rd Pennsylvania, in von Gilsa's brigade, "some of our men were shot in the back while sitting on their knapsacks."[13]

Von Gilsa's brigade didn't stand a chance against the onslaught; division commander Devens—drunk, according to some accounts—received a serious wound in the foot and was eventually forced to relinquish command. Like dominoes, his brigades fell back and sowed more chaos and confusion in the divisions of Schurz and Steinwehr. Many of the men broke and ran from the onslaught. "Down the road towards Chancellorsville, through the woods, up every side road and forest path, pours a stream of fugitives," wrote Lt. Theodore Dodge, the adjutant of the 119th Pennsylvania, a largely German regiment in Schurz's division. "Ambulances and oxen, pack-mules and ammunition-wagons, officers' spare horses mounted by runaway negro servants, every species of the *impedimenta* of camp-life, commissary sergeants on all-too-slow mules, teamsters on still-harnessed team-horses, quartermasters whose duties are not at the front, riderless steeds, clerks with armfuls of official papers, non-combatants of all kinds, mixed with frighted soldiers whom no sense of honor can arrest, strive to find shelter from the murderous fire."[14]

Howard had just returned to his headquarters from his expedition with Barlow when he heard "the ceaseless roar of the terrible storm" from the right. He sent messengers to find out what was happening and rode out to find a central position behind Schurz's lines. It wasn't long before men came rushing past him in a panic. Howard compared it to "all the fury of the wildest hailstorm." "It was a terrible gale!" he recalled, "the rush, the rattle, the quick lightning from a hundred points at once; the roar, redoubled by echoes through the forest; the panic, the dead and dying in sight and the wounded straggling along; the frantic efforts of the brave and patriotic to stay the angry storm!" Howard made some frantic attempts to reform his line to face this new threat, but it was no use. It didn't help that the general's horse, caught up in the panic, threw its rider to the ground. One of his aides, Capt. Frederick Dessaur, was shot and killed. Howard dashed about the battlefield, trying to stem the flood, to little effect. "Such a mass of fugitives I haven't seen since the prior battle of Bull Run," Howard told Lizzie. Years later he told a reporter that he "wanted to die. It was the only time I ever weakened that way in my life, before or since; but that night I did all in my power to remedy the mistake, and I sought death everywhere I could find an excuse to go on the field."[15]

While many of the surprised soldiers did break and run, many others did what they could to stem an overwhelming tide. The battery under Dilger—"one of those handsome, hearty, active young men that everybody liked to have near," in Howard's estimation—fought bravely and well, as did the men of Col. Adolphus Buschbeck's brigade of Steinwehr's division, who managed to temporarily check the Rebel advance for a half hour or so. Anything that delayed the Rebels was a great help, for time was of the essence. Jackson had unleashed his attack late in the afternoon and his daylight hours were limited. Stonewall continued to order his men forward even as the sun set and night fell. A bright moon provided some light, but night fighting always brought the potential for confusion once it became difficult to separate friend from foe. Jackson learned that lesson all too well when he rode in front of his lines to personally reconnoiter the terrain to his front, and was mortally wounded by his own troops as he rode back.[16]

Years later, in his memoirs, Howard said he had done everything possible with the XI Corps at Chancellorsville. "I may leave the whole matter to the considerate judgment of my companions in arms, simply asserting that on the terrible day of May 2, 1863, I did all which could have been done by a corps commander in the presence of that panic of men largely caused by the overwhelming attack of Jackson's 26,000 men against my isolated corps of 8,000 without its reserve thus outnumbering me 3 to 1."[17]

Howard did have a point. Jackson's men greatly outnumbered the XI Corps. In addition, Howard's reserve—Barlow's brigade—had been taken from him, and much of the III Corps, which would have been in position to act as support, had gone south in its futile pursuit of Lee's "retreating" army. Hooker did warn Howard about a flank attack in the morning, but his fears on that score had subsided by afternoon when he had Howard send his reserve force in pursuit of Lee's "retreating" army. Howard and the XI Corps should not bear the full blame for the events of May 2. Yet it's also true that Howard had not done enough to protect his flank from an attack from the west. He displayed little initiative. His soldiers paid the price.

—◆—

Fortunately for Hooker's army, Hiram Berry's III Corps division had not gone with Dan Sickles on the pursuit of the "retreating" Rebels. On the evening of May 2, it was still waiting in reserve behind the Chancellor house when Berry detected the growing sounds of pandemonium from the army's right. "The firing became hard and harder and the enemy seemed to approach," wrote Col. Robert McAllister of the 11th New Jersey from Berry's division. "In a moment we were to arms and moved rapidly forward to the Plank road, past General Hooker's headquarters. As I looked up the road I beheld the 11th Army Corps coming down it, wagons, ambulances, horses, soldiers armed and unarmed, pell-mell, real Bull Run style. We now had to throw ourselves into the breach or all was lost."[18]

As the shattered remnants of Howard's corps fled down the Plank Road and past the Chancellor mansion in disorganized panic, Hooker rode up to Berry and told him to throw his men into the breach. Howard also arrived, looking "despondent and downcast," and spoke with Berry. The two generals decided they would position their men astride the Plank Road, with Berry responsible to the north and Howard to the south.[19]

Berry quickly began to push his troops forward and form them into a line perpendicular to the Plank Road. The brigade of Brig. Gen. Joseph Revere—Paul Revere's grandson—formed the first line, along with some of Joseph Carr's brigade. The rest of Carr's brigade formed a second line. Ahead, not 200 yards away, were Confederate soldiers under A. P. Hill, and Berry's pickets captured some of them. Working with his chief of artillery, Thomas Osborn, Berry placed two batteries behind his lines in a position to fire over the heads of his troops, and moved two cannons right up to the front line. Berry rode up to Colonel McAllister as he positioned his men. "Now, Colonel, you do your very best," the general said.

"Yes, General, I shall," McAllister replied. "That noble and brave man rode along the lines of battle that night wherever there were points of danger, and words of comfort and encouragement fell from his lips," he recalled. The bright moonlight streamed from the heavens, and between the blasts of artillery, the Union soldiers could hear sounds of the enemy emerging from the shadows. It was a tense and watchful time. McAllister remembered the beauty of the spring night, the brightness of the moon and the sharp contrast of the shadows. But the quiet never lasted long. "All would be still and calm one moment, then crack! would go a gun, followed by many others, telling us we were again attacked and our pickets engaged, soon followed by a tremendous roar of musketry. The enemy marched in front of us and were determined to break our lines." A. P. Hill's division renewed the offensive around 10:30 P.M., but Berry's artillery was able to wreak havoc in the enemy ranks, and the Rebels fell back.[20]

John Haley of the 17th Maine also recalled the beauty of the spring night. He and the other soldiers of Birney's III Corps division had moved south during the day to pursue the Rebels seen at Catherine Furnace. Late in the day they had heard the sudden tumult that marked Jackson's attack on Howard's flank. Now Sickles found himself in an exposed position, with Jackson's men moving in his rear. He needed to move back to rejoin the rest of the Union army, and chose to make a night march.

Birney's division set off down a narrow road that ran through the woods. "As we moved out into the road, our bayonets glistened in the moonlight like the rising and falling of waves," Haley recalled. "It was a magnificent sight, not soon to be forgotten." The men marched on through the bright, moonlit night. Suddenly the silence was shattered by crash of gunfire, "terrible volleys of musketry on both sides of the road," said Capt. Charles Mattocks. "Such a whistling of balls one seldom hears." The firing was too high to draw any blood, but it created panic and confusion. Men scurried for the rear; Haley claimed that brigade commander Hobart Ward rode over two of his own soldiers as he sought safety. The initial fire had come from Rebels, but as the confusion and panic spread, it became impossible to separate friend from foe. Union soldiers fired in the direction of what they felt was the enemy, killing and wounding men from their own side. Finally the gunfire trickled to an end and silence reigned once more. Rather than risk another confusing nighttime encounter, Sickles's men halted for the night and waited for dawn.[21]

When the sun rose on Sunday, May 3, it found the Army of the Potomac pummeled and embarrassed, but not yet defeated. The Rebels' flank attack had wreaked havoc in the XI Corps, but the rest of the army remained in reasonable shape. Jackson's wounding had taken the wind out of the Confederate attack, and Berry's timely support had allowed the Federals to stabilize their lines and save the army from collapse. In fact, Hooker's position was not so bad at all. Lee's army was dangerously divided, with the Union forces standing between Jackson's wing and the rest of the Confederates. The field was not yet lost.

That morning Captain Rusling found Berry sitting on a stump by the side of the road. He made a joke about the general's earlier presentiment of death. "Rusling, the battle is not over yet," Berry replied.[22]

The Confederates proved Berry right. Despite the loss of Jackson—cavalryman Jeb Stuart now commanded Stonewall's corps—the Rebels renewed the fighting at daybreak, and pressed Berry's line along the Plank Road just west of the Chancellor house. The 3rd Maryland, a regiment from the XII Corps, fell back on Berry's left, exposing Revere's brigade to a flank attack. The Rebels stubbornly forced Revere back as well.

It was sometime around seven when Berry rode across the Plank Road to talk to Gershom Mott, who commanded one of his brigades. The generals conversed for a time and Berry was crossing back over the road when a Rebel sharpshooter hidden in a tree got him in his sights. The bullet found its target. It hit Berry in his arm, passed through his body, and stopped near his hip. It was a mortal wound. His staff picked up the dying man and started to take him off the battlefield. "My wife and child!" he whispered. His aide L. G. Benedict said Berry's last words were, "Take me from the field, Benedict." And then Hiram Berry died. He was 38 years old.

Hooker rode up minutes later. "My God, Berry, why was this to happen?" he cried. "Why was the man on whom I relied so much to be taken away in this manner?" He had the body sent to the rear. Members of the 4th Maine, Berry's old regiment, were marching by as the general's corpse was being taken away. They insisted that the stretcher bearers stop and place their burden on the ground. Then each man filed by and "kissed the cold brow of the man they had loved and had first followed into battle, and then silently and tearfully took their places in the ranks." Quartermaster Rusling ordered the construction of a coffin and had it draped with Berry's headquarters flag.[23]

In the confusion following Berry's death, Revere believed he was in command of the division, and decided, on his own initiative, to retreat, an action for which he was later court-martialed. Adding to the Union army's woes, Hooker himself was nearly killed shortly afterwards. Earlier, he had ordered Sickles to withdraw from an exposed position called Hazel Grove, and the Confederates had quickly moved in and set up artillery there. A shot fired from a Rebel cannon at Hazel Grove struck a pillar of the Chancellor house while Hooker was leaning against it. The force of the blow knocked the general unconscious. Hooker suffered from the effects of the concussion for hours afterward and the Army of the Potomac drifted rudderless as the fighting around Chancellorsville reached a bitter intensity. The Confederates of Jackson's corps slowly forced the Union defenders from their lines into a new defensive position behind the Chancellor house, which was now in flames. "Worst of all was the shelling," said Charles Mattocks of the 17th Maine. "One shell burst in my Co. as we lay on our faces, and made fearful havoc in the ranks." It almost tore the thighs off two corporals, wounded two others, and nearly tore off the heel of a third. "I was lying behind them, and so bad a set of wounds I have not seen together."[24]

Charles O. Blackstone, the ambitious private who had been seeking a promotion in the heavy artillery, was one of the wounded corporals. He had moved one rung up the ladder of promotion when he was promoted to corporal on April 1, but that was as far as he would rise, for he would not survive his terrible wound.[25]

One Union battery making a doomed resistance against the Rebel tide was George Leppien's 5th Maine Light Artillery. On the morning of May 3, Leppien's men unlimbered near the Chancellor house, and immediately became a prime target for Confederate artillery posted at a clearing called Fairview—even closer to Hooker's headquarters than Hazel Grove was. A storm of shell began sweeping the area. Limbs and branches from the sheltering trees, severed by the artillery fire, rained down on the soldiers. Enemy shells ricocheted across the hard ground, killing and mangling men and horses. "Even before we could get into position our horses and men went down like grass before the scythe," recalled Pvt. John Chase, a "rugged farm boy" who had been working as a soap boiler in the Augusta area before enlisting in the battery. One limber exploded. A shell hit Leppien, still mounted, and nearly tore off his foot, a wound that would kill him. General Couch saw the battery's situation and ordered Lt. Edmund Kirby of the 1st U.S. Artillery to take Leppien's place. Kirby had just ridden up to assume command when a Confederate cannonball ripped off his horse's leg and threw him to the ground. Kirby asked for a pistol and shot his horse; moments later another ball crushed his thigh and left him dying. When soldiers tried to move him to the rear, Kirby told them, "No! Take off that gun first." Only a single cannon remained in action, with only two men—Private Chase and Cpl. James Lebroke—able to keep it in operation. Chase frantically sponged out the barrel and then rammed home the charge while Lebroke fired the gun.[26]

General Hancock decided enough was enough and ordered infantry to help remove what remained of the battery. Col. St. Clair Mulholland of the Irish Brigade's 116th Pennsylvania moved forward to assist. "Up to that time I had no use for an Irishman," Chase recounted later, but when he saw the regiment coming to his assistance, "I can assure you, my friends, that I loved an Irishman then." With the help of the Pennsylvanians, Chase and Lebroke rolled their cannon back to safety. Chase later received the Medal of Honor for his actions at Chancellorsville; he would go through an even worse ordeal with the battery at Gettysburg.[27]

In the meantime, John Sedgwick's VI Corps had remained south of Fredericksburg, hopefully presenting enough of a threat to keep Lee worried about that part of the battlefield. One of Sedgwick's regiments was the 5th Maine, which formed part of Joseph Bartlett's 2nd Brigade of William T. H. "Bully" Brooks's division. The regiment had stirred from its camps on April 28, and at daybreak the next morning was part of the force that crossed the Rappahannock in pontoon boats. "It was a bold undertaking; not a man flinched but gallantly came to the work," reported Col. Clark S. Edwards. "In an incredible short time, Brook's Division was all over, and deployed in lines of battle." Once the enemy pickets had been driven back, engineers began constructing the bridges and had completed the spans by noon.[28]

After the I and III Corps had moved off to Chancellorsville, Sedgwick and his 24,000 men remained on the south side of the Rappahannock below Fredericksburg. If it weren't for the threat of imminent death hanging over their heads, the soldiers could have basked in the lovely spring weather on Saturday, May 2. From somewhere behind the enemy lines, they could hear a Southern band playing "Dixie," over and over again. When it stopped, a Union band answered with "The Star-Spangled Banner." The impromptu musical competition ended when the opposing pickets opened fire and the Federals began advancing across the fields toward the daunting presence of Prospect Hill. This was part of the "demonstration" that Hooker wanted Sedgwick to make. Later that day, as Jackson's men were preparing to pounce on the XI Corps, Sedgwick received orders to turn his demonstration into an actual attack, capture Fredericksburg, and then move up the Plank Road to link up with Hooker at Chancellorsville.[29]

The 5th Maine was roused in the predawn hours on Sunday. It was a beautiful spring morning—"almost too lovely in which to engage in blood and carnage," remembered George Bicknell. Firing erupted from upriver. As the sun began to rise, the 5th Maine moved into the shelter of a ravine and waited there for a couple of hours. As soon as they moved out, the opposing forces engaged in a terrific artillery duel, with the Rebels getting the worst of it.

"Now commenced hot work," wrote Bicknell. Bartlett and his brigade were going to advance on Fredericksburg from the left. The brigade moved forward and passed through another ravine. This turned into a death trap, with Confederate artillery finding it an ideal target. "Never did mortal witness a more fearful fire or more severe destruction in some a brief space," Bicknell recalled. Brigade commander Bartlett remained on horseback throughout the barrage. "Noble men, noble men," he exclaimed as he watched his soldiers. One Rebel shell grazed a Maine soldier who was lying prone. The shell tore off the man's haversack, sending the contents flying through the air and the soldier tumbling across the ground. Amazingly he was unhurt. "Golly boys," he said, eying the scattered contents of his pack, "five days' rations gone to thunder." Those around him, temporarily forgetting their danger, roared with laughter. They finally found shelter in a streambed, but not before Bicknell suffered a head wound that would keep him away from the regiment for several months.[30]

Selden Connor and the 7th Maine, part of Thomas Neill's brigade of Albion Howe's division, also approached the hills behind Fredericksburg from the left, but closer to town. It was around noon when General Neill approached Connor and told him to have his men throw down their knapsacks and prepare for combat. Before they could get ready, firing erupted to the right, and Connor realized the Union attack had already started there. He ordered his men to move at double-quick. They charged down a steep slope and across the boggy morass of Hazel Run. "I rode my horse throughout," said Connor. "I went down a hill as steep as a roof and through a swamp up to my horse's belly." The Confederate guns found their range and men began to fall. Those who made it through the fire reached the heights after a run of about a mile, panting and exhausted, only to find Union troops already there. Firing to the left told Connor that the 33rd New York of his brigade was in trouble, and despite the pleas of his officers to give the regiment 15 minutes to catch its breath, Connor prodded his men to their feet and sent them to aid the New Yorkers. They advanced with a yell "and rattled away at the rebs who shortly turned tail." Said Connor, "It was one of the most brilliant things of the war."[31]

The firing Connor had heard to his right was the start of the Union assault on the stone wall that had proved such a fatal obstacle back in December. Behind it was Jubal Early's division and men from William Barksdale's Mississippi regiment. "It was once felt that a desperate encounter was to follow, and the recollections of the previous disaster were by no means inspiriting," wrote one Union officer. On the right, under the command of George Spear, the 61st Pennsylvania took the lead in the front of the 43rd and 67th New York and the 82nd Pennsylvania. The 7th Massachusetts and 36th New York formed the center column. And on the left was Hiram Burnham, formerly the commander of the 6th Maine and now at the head of the "light division" of the VI Corps.[32]

As his forces prepared to make the attack on the heights, General Sedgwick turned to his aides. "Now, young gentlemen, here is a chance for you to distinguish yourselves by leading the storming columns," the general said, joking. Henry Farrar, a young man from Bangor, took Sedgwick seriously, and spurred his horse ahead to take the lead. Hyde galloped after him to explain that the general had been kidding. Farrar always told people afterwards that Hyde saved his life at Fredericksburg.[33]

Hyde trotted off to accompany George Spear in the attack on the right. It soon turned into a repeat of the disaster of 1862 as the Confederates focused a storm of shot and shell on the approaching Federals. "Colonel Spear was killed," Hyde reported, "and the loss was so heavy and sudden that the column was checked and thrown into confusion in the narrow road, down which grapeshot seemed to be searching for everybody." The scattered force was attempting to regroup for another try when Hyde turned to look at Marye's Heights and saw something that filled his heart with joy—the flag of the 6th Maine flying at the summit.[34]

Back in 1839, when the conflict over Maine's border with British Canada had threatened to flare into war, Hiram Burnham of Cherryfield in Washington County had commanded a militia company known for its discipline and precision at drill. Burnham had not seen any fighting then, and he had to wait for more than two decades before he finally did. By then he had become a lumberman and an active member of his community, serving as coroner and a county commissioner. "His leadership among the logging fraternity was unquestioned and his men looked up to him as both a father figure and the leader of the pack," wrote James H. Mundy in his history of the 6th Maine. "Even at fifty he was a stocky and robust figure and his men lovingly referred to him as the 'Grizzly.'"[35]

When the war started, Burnham raised a company for the 6th Maine and became its colonel after its original commander, Bangor lawyer Abner Knowles, had proven his ineptness and resigned in December 1861. A few days before Chancellorsville, Burnham was elevated to command of the "light division." In reality, it was more the size of a brigade and consisted of the 5th Wisconsin, 31st and 43rd New York, 61st Pennsylvania, Burnham's own 6th Maine, and the 3rd New York Independent light battery.[36]

When Burnham received his orders to storm Marye's Heights, he rode back to his troops. "Boys, I have a government contract," he shouted.

"What is it?" they shouted back.

"One thousand rebels, potted and salted, and got to have 'em in less than five minutes," Burnham replied. He ordered his men forward. He had the 5th Wisconsin act as skirmishers, with the 6th Maine behind them and to the right, and the 31st New York to the left. The 23rd Pennsylvania followed in support.[37]

With Burnham moved up to command the light division, Lt. Col. Benjamin Harris, a lumberman from Machias, led the 6th Maine. His orders were for his men to advance at double-quick with weapons uncapped, not stopping to fire until they reached the stone wall. Charles Amory Clark, the former Foxcroft Academy student who was now the adjutant for the 6th Maine, jumped to his feet and shook hands with Maj. Joel Haycock. "God bless you," they said to each other, and then turned toward the Confederate lines and charged the works. "Artillery and musketry poured a fire upon us which seemed to make the whole atmosphere hot and lurid," Clark recalled.

"It was a race with death, but with all this terrible tension we were under we kept our formation, the lines closing up as they were thinned by the firing," said Lt. Wainwright Cushing. "How anyone should escape being struck in this hail of lead seemed to me a wonder." Cushing did not escape, and he fell to the ground with a shot to the thigh. Haycock was shot and killed. Sewall Gray of Company A, the student with whom Clark had vied to be the first man from Piscataquis County to enlist, died in front of the wall. Those who survived the charge stormed over the barricade and fought savagely with the Confederate defenders. George Brown, a private in Company K, bayoneted two Rebels and then clubbed a third with his musket. The enemy fled from the onslaught, and the Union soldiers pursued them up the heights. Clark didn't recall a single shot being fired during the charge. "Our success was glorious, but we had paid for it dearly," he said. Out of the 400 men in the 6th Maine, 128 were killed or wounded. Thomas Hyde noted the costs when he saw the green hill of Marye's Heights "dotted all over with still forms in blue."[38]

Capturing Marye's Heights had been a triumph, but Sedgwick still had to push west down the Orange Plank Road and attempt to link up with Hooker at Chancellorsville, some 11 miles away. He found his route blocked by Rebels at Salem Church, around the halfway point. Lee had sent the division of Lafayette McLaws and William Mahone's brigade scurrying east, and a brigade under Cadmus Wilcox had hurried over from nearby Banks Ford to meet this new threat. Fighting erupted later in the afternoon and continued until dusk. Sedgwick was unnerved by the greater-than-expected resistance and concerned by the lack of any support from Hooker. Making matters worse for the Federals, Early took advantage of the vacuum left by Sedgwick's departure from Fredericksburg and rushed his men back to reoccupy Marye's Heights. Sedgwick was now between two forces of Rebels.

John B. Gordon's brigade of Early's division moved up the road in pursuit of Sedgwick. Virginians under William "Extra Billy" Smith followed. Some of them, the 58th Virginia, clashed with the 7th Maine. Connor reported that his men captured 80 prisoners and the Virginians' flag, "routing them completely." The men of the VI Corps might have gained a little confidence from the encounter, but it appeared the Rebels were feeling equally confident. The prisoners told Connor the Federals would "have to skedaddle out of that before night or Lee would drive us into the river." Feeling squeezed on two sides, on the morning of May 4

Sedgwick decided to pull his men back into a horseshoe-shaped defensive line that shielded Banks Ford on the Rappahannock. He would wait there until he received some support from Hooker.[39]

Thomas Hyde remembered dropping by his old regiment later that day and chatting with Connor and Capt. John Channing. Connor turned to him and said, "Its five o'clock now, Major: if the rebs want anything to-night it's time for them to commence." The words were hardly out of his mouth before the sound of the Rebel yell shattered the late-afternoon stillness, and 11,000 Confederates, arrayed in neat lines of battle, flags flying, emerged from nearby woods and attacked the Union line "in overwhelming force." Hyde watched as brigade commander Thomas Neill ordered a charge—mistakenly, Hyde thought—down a hillside and across terrain broken by ravines that ensured the Union soldiers could not maintain their lines. "I took the right of the regiment, and it was soon cut in two, we going down one ravine and Colonel Connor down the other," Hyde wrote. "General Neill and staff were all *hors de combat* and Colonel Connor wounded in less time than it takes to tell it, and the little brigade had smashed itself to pieces against ten times its numbers." Connor's wound was minor—a bullet had passed through his coat and pants, creased his thigh, and became embedded in his saddle. "That is what I call a 'close shave,'" Connor told his father. Hyde rode off to find Sedgwick, who ordered him to bring up reinforcements. By the time he had done so, stiffening Union resistance and growing Rebel confusion had halted the enemy advance.[40]

With no aid coming from Hooker at Chancellorsville, Sedgwick decided to take his corps across Banks Ford on pontoon bridges that had been erected there. As the corps started the long, tedious process of crossing, the 6th Maine took part in a rearguard action to prevent the Rebels from capturing a steep bluff that overlooked the bridges. That night Charles Clark embarked on a scouting expedition, approaching so close to a Rebel camp he could see the enemy soldiers, illuminated by the bright moonlight, preparing for an attack. He returned to his regiment and repositioned his men to meet it. "There was a sharp fight of ten or fifteen minutes, and the night was filled with wild outcries and uproar," he recalled. The 6th Maine managed to hold off the enemy this time, but the outcome of a second attack appeared doubtful. With Lieutenant Colonel Harris cut off from the regiment by the enemy, Clark took matters into his own hands and issued orders to prepare for a silent withdrawal down the formidable bluff. Clark tried to make the descent on horseback and quickly regretted the decision. His mount began sliding and tumbling down the incline and then falling through the air. Clark grabbed desperately at some branches, and managed to scramble into a tree. He slid down the trunk to the base of the bluff. He expected to find his horse at the bottom with a broken neck, but the steed was waiting for him, a little bruised and sore, but intact. Up above them, the Confederates pushed forward, only to find their quarry had slipped away. Clark and the rest of the regiment made their way to the river and passed over the pontoon bridges to safety; Burnham, Clark said, cried with relief when he heard his old regiment had escaped. Clark later received the Medal of Honor for his actions.[41]

Joe Hooker was done fighting. Late on the night of May 4 he called his corps commanders together for a meeting. Hooker had already decided he wanted to take his army back across the Rappahannock, but he wanted to gauge their opinions. Perhaps he hoped they all shared his desire to break off from the fight. After outlining the situation, Hooker left the tent so his generals could talk among themselves. Meade was for continuing the fight (but only, Hooker claimed, because he felt the army would not be able to recross the river without a battle). Reynolds, whose I Corps had arrived too late to take much of a part in the battle, fell asleep after saying he'd follow whatever Meade advocated. Sickles advised crossing. Couch was somewhat ambivalent, due to his doubts about Hooker's abilities. Howard was adamant that the army should stay and fight. He said his corps was largely responsible for the situation in which the army found itself, and he was for an advance. "His opinion was received for what it was worth," Hooker said later. When Hooker returned to the tent, he announced that the army would recross the river. His campaign was over.[42]

By the time the men began trooping across the pontoon bridges late on May 5, the bucolic spring weather had given way to torrential rainstorms. The rising water threatened to sweep away the bridges, giving hope to Couch and Meade that they might be forced to fight a battle after all, Hooker's orders notwithstanding. But Fighting Joe, already back on the north side, sent a messenger repeating his demand that the army cross the river.

The 17th Maine was just one of the regiments who stood in the mud and the pouring rain, waiting for their turn to cross over the increasingly precarious pontoon bridges. John Haley remembered how the soldiers would shuffle forward, and then "stand still and shiver." In his history of the regiment, Edwin Houghton remembered "sitting in a pelting rain, by a poor fire, in a chilly night darker than Egyptian darkness, trying to kill time by relating incidents pertaining to our civil life." As May 6 dawned, the regiment was still on the river's south side. By eight o'clock the regiment had finally crossed, "thankful to have escaped from another disastrous attempt to go to Richmond via Fredericksburg." The men of the III Corps were slogging their way back toward their old camps when they passed men from the XI Corps and "exchanged greetings of a highly uncomplimentary nature." Unlike many, Haley did not blame the ordinary soldiers of the XI Corps, but he did hold their commander accountable. "General Howard should have been prepared, but he wasn't; hence these jeers."[43]

George Bisbee, the sergeant from the 16th Maine who had nearly lost his arm at Fredericksburg, had gone to extraordinary lengths to return to his regiment before Chancellorsville. After a 30-day furlough in Maine, Bisbee learned that he had received a commission as second lieutenant. He traveled back to Washington, but the doctors there refused his requests for a pass to the front. Bisbee then accepted a discharge, pocketed his back pay, and decided to set out for Virginia and find the 16th Maine on his own. He went to the U.S. Capitol, tracked down Vice President Hamlin—who was a friend of his father's—and got a pass from him. Then Bisbee boarded a train to Virginia, found his regiment, sought out the mustering officer, reenlisted, and accepted his commission.[44]

The 16th Maine had a relatively quiet Chancellorsville. As part of John Reynolds's I Corps, it had moved south below Fredericksburg before receiving orders to join the main part of Hooker's army to the north. The regiment reached the field after Jackson had routed the XI Corps, and its soldiers encountered many stragglers from Howard's demoralized command as they took up a position to the Union army's right. They listened to the roar of battle on other parts of the line as they waited for their turn to fight. It never came.

Abner Small, the regiment's adjutant, did experience some excitement at Chancellorsville when he had volunteered to ride out and examine the situation along the Rapidan River. Small and an orderly rode past the pickets and beyond the cavalry vedettes without incident and continued on through quiet countryside until they reached the river. On the way back, though, the two men nearly rode into a line of Rebel soldiers that had formed across the road they were taking. "There was but one alternative; it was either prison or the Union lines," Small recalled. The Mainers spurred their horses and went galloping past the startled Rebels. "Halt, you damned Yanks!" one of them yelled, and gunfire split the air. Fortunately for the damned Yankees, the Confederates missed their targets, and the two Union soldiers made it back to their lines to report.[45]

In the dark and rain of the predawn hours of May 6, the 16th Maine crossed over the Rappahannock at United States Ford and marched back to Falmouth, where the soldiers collapsed in the mud. Cold, wet, and exhausted, Bisbee accepted his first and last drink of commissary whiskey. He had never tasted kerosene before, he said, but he figured the burning sensation from the whiskey must have been similar.[46]

—•—

On May 8, Capt. Charles Mattocks went to the hospital to visit the wounded men from his company. "I find that Corporal Blackstone cannot live," he wrote in his journal. "He has a terrible wound in the thigh, it being carried away bone and all, by that murderous shell. I very much doubt if he lives forty-eight hours. He bears up under his sufferings like a hero, and seems willing to die. He thinks he has fallen in a good cause, and so he has, but still it seems sad to see so young and ambitious a fellow die here away from friends and home." Blackstone died the next day. His campaign to get a commission in the heavy artillery died with him.[47]

⌁

Hiram Berry's body was taken to Washington for embalming, and then by steamer to Portland, where it lay in state at city hall. From Portland, the steamer *Harvest Moon* took the coffin to Rockland. Berry returned home on a lovely spring day. Once the steamer came into view at the mouth of the harbor, a cannon fired from the city, and followed up with a shot each minute. Stores and businesses closed, and the citizens of Rockland flocked to the waterfront to await the *Harvest Moon*. An honor guard from the 7th Maine accompanied the hearse through the crowded but silent streets to the general's home, where the body was placed in the parlor. His battle sword and the sword the 4th Maine had presented to him lay on a table next to the coffin. He was buried in Achorn Cemetery the next day. The bright spring weather had turned gloomy, "as through sympathizing with the mournful scene beneath." Among the mourners was Vice President Hamlin, who was serving as a private citizen in the Bangor Fusiliers.[48]

Before Berry's death, there had been rumors that Hooker intended him for a corps command. Supposedly his name had come up as a possible future commander of the Army of the Potomac. Instead, the former lumberman, businessman, and mayor had become just one more of the hundreds of thousands of Americans who gave up their lives in the American Civil War.

But even among all the death and suffering, there was new life and joy. Otis Howard received some good news when he learned that Lizzie had given birth to a boy, their fourth child. The baby was conceived shortly before the wounded Howard left Maine to resume his life as a warrior. "God is indeed good to us, my precious wife," Howard wrote on May 9. The baby had arrived on May 3, which Howard called "the day of the most terrific battle I ever witnessed." To Howard, that timing suggested the perfect name. "The battle was Chancellorsville," he told Lizzie, so he suggested they name the baby Chancellor, and call him Chancey. And, strangely enough, that's what they did.[49]

CHAPTER 10

The Army Moves North

Oh, it was grand! and many a man who was in that charge has at times fancied that if he were allowed to choose, he would say, "Let me bid this world good-by amid the supreme excitement of a grand, exultant, successful cavalry charge like this!"
—EDWARD TOBIE, 1ST MAINE CAVALRY

Less than two weeks after they had marched out with such optimism, the men of the Army of the Potomac were back in their old camps, feeling the sting of yet another humiliating defeat. Their commander tried to put the best face on things by issuing General Orders No. 49. "We have added new laurels to our former renown," Hooker claimed. "We have made long marches, crossed rivers, surprised the enemy in his intrenchments; and whenever we have fought, we have inflicted heavier blows than those we have received."[1]

If he appeared sanguine on the surface, inwardly Hooker must have been seething. The XI Corps offered an obvious scapegoat. Years later Hooker erupted when he talked to a reporter in San Francisco about Otis Howard. "He's a very bad man, but he's a pious character," said Hooker. "He was always a woman among troops. If he was not born in petticoats, he ought to have been, and ought to wear them. He was always taken up with Sunday Schools and the temperance cause. These things are all very good, you know, but have very little to do with commanding army corps.

He would command a prayer meeting with a good deal more ability than he would an army."[2]

Howard knew he and his corps had failed, and he understood that the rest of the army believed it, too. On May 10 he felt compelled to issue a general order acknowledging "a feeling of depression" in the corps. "Some obloquy has been cast upon us on account of the affair of Saturday, May 2," he said. "I believe that such a disaster might have happened to any other corps of this arm, and do not distrust my command." He said the events of May 2 would be a learning experience, and felt that his officers and men were eager for another chance to prove their worth.[3]

Despite the bad feelings, Howard received no official blame for the Chancellorsville debacle, and he retained his command. "I must expect a few hits as my corps did not do well," he admitted to Lizzie, but he was not so willing to shoulder much personal blame. "I am conscious of having neglected no precaution and yet our right was turned in the thick woods and an overwhelming force hurled upon the flank & rear." He suspected that politics might play a role in the criticism sent his way. Back in April he had been approached with the suggestion that he run for governor of Maine as a Republican. Howard had rebuffed the proposal, but suspected that if word leaked out and political foes wanted to damage his reputation, Chancellorsville provided a perfect cudgel.[4]

When brother Rowland wrote and asked if his spirits were flagging, Otis responded with an emphatic "<u>No.</u>" He still believed that the war and all its reverses were part of God's plan, and that Stonewall Jackson—despite his success against Howard—had been fighting for the wrong side. Still, he nursed doubts about the moral fitness of the Union's generals. "Would that you would plead with our Father to correct the soul of Gen Hooker," he wrote to his minister brother. "It is just what we need." Even more discouraging were the rumors that Dan Sickles might be elevated to army command. "If God gives us Sickles to lead us I should cry with vexation & sorrow and plead to be delivered," Howard told Rowland. He even contemplated resigning, but felt he couldn't leave before the work was done. Nor did he want to disappoint the many devout Christians who looked to him as their representative in the army.[5]

Howard was aware that many people laid the blame for Chancellorsville on him and the XI Corps, and he let Hooker know that he would understand if he wanted to replace him. Realizing that the army's commander was a very "politic man," Howard knew perfectly well that Hooker would sacrifice him "the moment he deems it necessary." Until that happened, Howard would make sure his men were drilled, trained, and prepared so that a debacle like Chancellorsville never happened again.[6]

Hooker was also disgusted by the performance of his cavalry under George Stoneman. Sent to cut off Lee's communications and harass his supply lines, Stoneman's cavalry had accomplished little of lasting effect. In Hooker's estimation, "no officer ever made a greater mistake in construing his orders, and no one ever accomplished less in so doing." The cavalry, he said, "seriously embarrassed me in my subsequent operations." When Stoneman requested sick leave, Hooker was more than happy to grant it—and then he extended it indefinitely.[7]

The Union cavalry had endured a somewhat bumpy ride to this point in the war. At the start of the conflict, government authorities doubted there was any need for new cavalry, believing that the war was certain to be over before there was time to raise and train expensive cavalry regiments. Once Bull Run shattered those optimistic expectations, a call went out from Washington for Maine to raise more regiments beyond its initial ten. Among them was to be a regiment of cavalry. In October 1861, Adjutant General Hodsdon placed advertisements in the state's newspapers calling for horses. "The horses must be sound in all particulars, from 15 to 16 hands high, not less than five nor more than nine years old, color to be Bay, Brown, Black, and Sorrel, good square trotters, bridle-wise, and of size sufficient for the purpose above named," read Hodsdon's ad. "A small proportion of grey Geldings and dark Mares will be purchased. The Horses must be well shod."[8]

The first soldier to sign up for the new cavalry regiment was a young man from Thomaston named Jonathan Cilley. He was a Bowdoin graduate and the son of a Maine congressman killed in a duel by Kentucky congressman William Graves in 1838. Young Cilley was three years old at the time of his father's death, and it seems he grew to blame the entire South for his misfortune. The "same powers" that killed his father were now seeking to destroy his country. When war broke out, Cilley tried raising a battery, but Washington said it had enough artillery. Cilley became the first man to enlist in the 1st Maine Cavalry instead, and took command of Company B.[9]

Calvin Douty of Dover was not in such a hurry to sign up. At the age of 48 he was much older than the typical volunteer. He had already served three terms as the sheriff of Piscataquis County and was the father of three surviving children. His wife did not want him to join the army, but after Bull Run Douty decided the needs of his country outweighed his personal concerns, he joined the 1st Maine Cavalry as a major.[10]

Other soldiers signed up from all over the state, until the regiment's 12 companies had representatives from all 16 counties. Somewhat ironically for budding cavalrymen, when they reached Augusta they first had to bed down in the horse stalls at the agricultural fairgrounds. They endured winter in Augusta with temperatures plummeting to 20 below zero and snow drifting six feet high. More than 200 men either died or had to leave the regiment because of illness.

Douty suffered a different kind of loss during that miserable winter. His youngest child, a 15-month-old son, died of diphtheria in December; a nine-year-old son followed him to the grave eight days afterwards. Of his six children, five had died.[11]

The first time the raw cavalrymen drilled on horseback was amusing only in retrospect. Men and horses were both inexperienced, and it showed. "There was kicking and rearing, and running and jumping, and lying down and falling down, on the part of the horses, and swearing and yelling, and getting thrown and being kicked, and getting hurt and sore in various ways, by the men," wrote regimental historian Edward Tobie. Charles E. Gardiner, a 20-year-old from Palermo, received a particularly testy mount. Gardiner fumed when the other men in his company made fun of his inability to control his horse, but he got the last laugh. After the men were dismissed, he rode his horse up and down the track at the fairgrounds until the animal finally submitted to his will.

Like his horse—and many other soldiers—Gardiner had his own difficulties with authority figures. "The first and hardest thing for me to learn was to submit to orders and whim of the non-commissioned officers," he wrote. "What used to make me angry was that I was not allowed to give them any back talk, but must obey all orders however rediculous [*sic*] they might seem to be."[12]

The regiment's first colonel was John Goddard of Cape Elizabeth. A stern-looking man with a moustache, thick sideburns, and pouchy eyes, he was a strict disciplinarian and a rigid moralist. He forbade swearing in the regiment, forcing the soldiers to find acceptable substitutes. "General Jackson!" became a favorite malediction. Goddard also decreed that any soldier who did not sign a temperance pledge would not be promoted. "It has been said that the regiment would not have won the proud position which it did, but for the severity of the discipline of the five months in Augusta," wrote Edward Tobie. But in the eyes of his soldiers Goddard proved to be "an arbitrary, haughty man" who treated the men "as he had been accustomed to rule his back-woodsmen and river drivers." Charles Gardiner thought he was little more than "a pompous old lumberman." Some of his officers went to the governor and complained about the colonel, saying they would resign rather than serve under him. Washburn dealt with the crisis by asking Goddard to resign instead. Goddard, preferring to tend to his business interests back home, complied. Samuel H. Allen of Thomaston replaced him.[13]

The regiment finally left Augusta on Friday, March 14, 1862. The train had hardly gone a dozen miles before a car jumped the track and tipped over, but fortunately no one was injured. The rest of the journey to Washington passed without incident. There, the regiment was split up, with Douty taking five companies to Harpers Ferry to serve under Nathaniel Banks and the rest remaining in Washington.

Douty's portion of the regiment saw its first action in the Shenandoah Valley while fighting in Banks's ill-fated campaign against Stonewall Jackson. On May 24 Jonathan Cilley, the first man to sign the rolls, also became the regiment's first battle casualty. Cilley was leading his men outside the town of Middletown when Rebel shells began crashing through the trees above them. He had just assured his troopers they had nothing to worry about when Cilley was struck, "falling from his horse in much the same deliberate manner in which a squirrel falls to the ground when shot." Although Cilley survived, his wounding sent a temporary panic through his men. One sergeant rode off and took shelter behind a nearby church; asked why, he said "he didn't know what else to do."[14]

Charles Gardiner saw his first fighting that day as well. 'I wont say I was not scared, for I was; and I contend that no man, unless he is a fool can withstand shells shrieking and bursting around him without feeling some scared and for a moment wishing he were at home," he said. "However I made up my mind that I would face the music and at the first chance give the enemy the same medicine they were giving us." Gardiner was one of the men in a battalion of five companies who got hemmed in on a road lined by stone walls and choked by Union wagons and other cavalry. The dust was so thick that Gardiner could not see beyond his own horse, one reason why the Union cavalrymen did not realize they were riding straight into the mouths of Confederate cannons. They made a perfect target, and the carnage was terrible. Gardiner's horse stumbled and Gardiner went flying over its head. His horse fell on top of him. Men were groaning and swearing all around him in the dust and confusion. After Gardiner managed to squirm out from under his horse he felt as though his back was broken, but he was able to crawl through a gap in the stone wall alongside the road and hide in the grain field on the other side. He avoided capture for three days before a squad of Confederate cavalry scooped him up. He received a parole after a spell on Richmond's Belle Isle.[15]

The 1st Maine Cavalry had seen some action, but the regiment had not made much of an impact. At Cedar Mountain it did little but endure Rebel shelling. Other than trying to stop the growing number of stragglers, it was not actively engaged at Second Bull Run. During the pursuit of Lee into Maryland, the Maine cavalry got no further than Frederick, where it fought a small skirmish with cavalry under Fitzhugh Lee. Company G was assigned as guard to Maj. Gen. Jesse Reno of the IX Corps, but it could not prevent him from receiving a mortal wound during the fighting on South Mountain.

By November 11, the regiment had returned to the "sacred soil" of Virginia, Burnside had replaced McClellan at the head of the army, and

Calvin Douty had grown tired of the way his regiment was being used. Writing to Governor Washburn, he complained that "we are not rendering any marked service but are broken up into squads of from four to twelve men each and scattered throughout our Army of the Potomac as 'orderlies' and cattle drivers, and our companies are by these details reduced to about twenty men each for duty." He compared the regiment's duties to that of an "errand boy." He wanted to go out west with General Nathaniel Banks so his men would get a chance to fight.[16]

Douty's request was not granted. At the battle of Fredericksburg, the cavalry once again had little to do but display its courage while standing under fire. Its brigade commander, Brig. Gen. George Bayard, was mortally wounded during the fighting, but his death was somehow symbolic of the way his cavalry was employed—Bayard was struck while reclining against a tree at Maj. Gen. William Franklin's headquarters.

The 1st Maine's role was typical of the way the Army of the Potomac used its cavalry in general. The Rebel cavalry aggressively scouted and screened, none more aggressively or with better results than the troopers under Maj. Gen. J. E. B. "Jeb" Stuart. Union army commanders, by comparison, had failed to match the Confederates' employment of their mounted troops. "Who ever saw a dead cavalryman?" was a derisive question bandied about among Union soldiers.

All that began to change once Hooker took command of the Army of the Potomac and placed his newly formed cavalry corps under Stoneman. The 1st Maine Cavalry became part of the new corps' 3rd Division under Pennsylvanian David McMurtrie Gregg, in the brigade commanded by Col. Judson Kilpatrick.

Thanks to its reputation for temperance, the 1st Maine Cavalry had become known as the "Puritans." It is highly unlikely that the word was ever used in connection with its brigade commander. Judson Kilpatrick, who gained the nickname "Kill-Cavalry" for his profligate use of his men and horses, was known as a notorious rake and rogue with a burning ambition to gain a general's star. Historian Edwin B. Coddington acknowledged that Kilpatrick "was known more for his reckless bravery than his brains," and some felt that he was braver with others' lives than his own. Biographer Samuel J. Martin noted that Kilpatrick's enemies perceived him to be "a coward—an egotistical, lying, sadistic, philander-ing, thieving miscreant whose lofty reputation had been gained by words, not deeds."[17]

The division commander was less colorful, but steadier. Gregg was a sad-eyed Pennsylvanian with a big, spade-shaped beard. His first cousin was the state's governor, Andrew Gregg Curtin, but the general owed his position to ability, not family connections.

There were changes within the regiment, too. Douty officially became the commanding officer after Colonel Allen resigned. Capt. Charles H. Smith advanced to lieutenant colonel, and Capt. Stephen Boothby became major. And thus organized, the 1st Maine Cavalry set out to help Stoneman wreak havoc during Hooker's Chancellorsville campaign. "On this expedition there was some fighting, plenty of hard marching, a loss of sleep, and a want of rations which tested the physical endurance of the men more severely, perhaps, than any other service during the whole four years of the regiment's history," said Tobie. And while Stoneman's efforts failed to impress Hooker, the men of the 1st Maine Cavalry remained proud of what they had done. In his history of the regiment, Tobie said "it was ever after a matter of pride with the boys that they were on 'Stoneman's Raid.'" Another history of the regiment went so far as to say that the raid was "one of the most remarkable achievements in the history of modern warfare."[18]

After Hooker sent Stoneman away on his indefinite leave, he replaced him with Maj. Gen. Alfred Pleasonton. The new cavalry head was a bit of a dandy, with a carefully groomed mustache and a taste for straw hats. Pleasonton also gained a reputation as a relentless self-promoter who didn't hesitate to exaggerate his own deeds. But he didn't take long to demonstrate that the Union cavalry was coming into its own.

In June, when intelligence indicated that the Confederates had assembled a large force of cavalry in the vicinity of Culpeper, apparently planning for a raid, Hooker ordered Pleasonton to do something about it. Hooker was not aware that the Confederate activity meant Lee was preparing for another push north. Nor did he know that Jeb Stuart, a man who loved pomp and circumstance, had just conducted a grand review of his command near Brandy Station, a depot on the Orange &

Alexandria Railroad about six miles from Culpeper and not far from the Rappahannock River. Pleasonton didn't know it, but his move came at the perfect time to give Stuart a rude surprise.

The 1st Maine received orders to move out on June 8. Dust clouds visible in the distance showed that the Rebels were moving, too. The Maine horsemen bivouacked in the vicinity of Kelly's Ford on the Rappahannock. That evening, the officers received an invitation to Kilpatrick's headquarters. "General Kilpatrick loved a good, social time almost as well as a fight," recalled Capt. Charles Ford of Company K. When the Maine officers arrived, they saw a mysterious object covered by a poncho near Kilpatrick's tent. An aide whipped the poncho aside to reveal a vessel filled with whiskey punch. Realizing there were always "honorable exceptions" to their pledges of temperance, the Maine Puritans unbent enough to pass an hour of toasts, songs, and speeches. When it came time for the 1st Maine to offer a toast, an officer raised his glass and said, "Here's hoping we will do as well at Brandy Station to-morrow as we are doing at the whisky station to-night." Kilpatrick proclaimed it the best toast he had heard all evening.[19]

The festivities concluded, the officers and the men bedded down, their horses' bridles wrapped around their wrists. They were roused around midnight and told to be ready to move at three o'clock. The hour came, and passed, and the regiment still waited. The soldiers grumbled. They had been told not to light fires to make coffee because the smoke would give away their presence.

Dawn had broken by the time the Maine cavalry finally saddled up and moved out on June 9. As they waited for their turn to cross the Rappahannock, they could hear artillery from somewhere upriver. Once across, they broke into a gallop down forest trails, the thudding hooves sending up clouds of dust that coated the whole command. Suddenly the horses emerged from the woods into a large field. In front of them was "a grand, moving panorama of war," a chaotic confusion of charging horsemen and flashing sabers. "It was a scene to be witnessed but once in a lifetime, and one well worth the risks of battle to witness," said Tobie. It was, in fact, the largest cavalry action to take place in North America.[20]

The battle of Brandy Station had opened to the north—the sounds of firing earlier that morning had come from the area around Beverly Ford, where Brig. Gen. John Buford's Federal cavalry division had surprised the Confederates in the predawn hours. They sent the Rebel cavalrymen dashing back in the direction of Fleetwood Hill, the eminence above Brandy Station where Jeb Stuart had his headquarters. The battle continued through the morning. Stuart managed to recover and rally, only to be surprised again by the sounds of battle to his south: Gregg's division, including Kilpatrick's brigade, had finally entered the fight.

Kilpatrick sent his first two regiments, the 2nd and 10th New York, charging forward toward the tracks of the Orange & Alexandria Railroad and Fleetwood Hill beyond. They collided with Rebel cavalry under Brig. Gen. Wade Hampton, and came reeling back. If Kilpatrick had been nourishing dreams of winning glory and promotion on this field, they were rapidly fading. He displayed considerable agitation when he rode up to the 1st Maine. "Colonel Douty, what can you do with your regiment?" he demanded.

"I can drive the rebels to hell," Douty replied. He ordered his men forward.[21]

"Oh, it was grand!" wrote Tobie, "and many a man who was in that charge has at times fancied that if he were allowed to choose, he would say, 'Let me bid this world good-by amid the supreme excitement of a grand, exultant, successful cavalry charge like this!'" As they galloped across the field, the Maine cavalrymen could see a little house on the hill, with an artillery battery in front of it. They headed in that direction, driving the enemy before them. The Rebels, Kilpatrick reported, "could not withstand the heavy saber blows of the sturdy men of Maine."[22]

"Increasing their speed the regiment thundered on, the faces of the men gleaming with fierce excitement, and as they advanced every nerve strung to its utmost tension, heedless of the battle now raging all around them, equally heedless of those rapidly worked guns on the hills beyond, whose screaming shells were bursting all about them with fearful explosions, sending masses of fragments hurtling through the air in every direction," Charles Ford recalled. "Neither the shouting of orders nor the crack of small arms could scarcely be heard for the terrible din." As the men and their horses thundered up and over the raised bed of the Orange & Alexandria Railroad, one soldier and his mount went somersaulting down the other side, the man delivering a volley of oaths—perhaps shouts of "General Jackson!"—all the way down.[23]

On the other side of the railroad, the Maine men smashed into the 4th Virginia. Amid the dust clouds, sabers slashed, small arms cracked, horses whinnied, and men cursed. The Rebels broke and fell back. The 1st Maine regrouped and renewed its charge, energized by the frenzy of battle. The riders reached the top of the hill, charged past the battery there, and galloped so far that Rebel forces began to regroup in their rear. Douty had become separated from his men in the fight with the 4th Virginia, so Smith took charge of reforming the regiment and readying it for a dash back to safety. The Northerners wheeled their horses and fought their way through the reformed enemy lines. At one point Smith was leading his men directly toward the battery they had charged beyond, and he could see the enemy gunners frantically reloading. At the last minute, Smith and his men veered sharply to their right, and the battery's fire tore through empty air. The regiment made its way back to its own lines, but with a loss of some 46 killed, wounded, and missing.[24]

After a long day of combat, Pleasonton was satisfied with what he had accomplished, and he sent orders for his forces to withdraw around five o'clock. He had not defeated the Rebel cavalry, which had fought tenaciously after its unpleasant surprise, but he had demonstrated that the Union cavalry was now a force to be reckoned with. Lt. Colonel Smith believed the battle marked the 1st Maine Cavalry's "christening" because it marked "the first time it was ever solidly engaged, and the first time it had ever tasted, in any satisfactory manner, the fruit of victory."[25]

Brandy Station wasn't solely a cavalry battle. Pleasonton also had two brigades of infantry to support his horsemen. One of them was a brigade under newly promoted brigadier general Adelbert Ames. His lobbying for promotion had paid off, and following the Chancellorsville disaster Howard had requested that Ames take a brigade in the XI Corps, feeling his men could use a taste of his fellow Mainer's discipline. For the movement against Brandy Station, though, Ames was given five hand-picked regiments—the 86th and 124th New York, 33rd and 2nd Massachusetts, and the 3rd Wisconsin—taken from different corps for this special assignment. The brigade crossed the river in support of Buford at Beverly Ford, where they beat back an attack by Confederate cavalry. Ames's men then moved forward and encountered an even larger concentration of the enemy. They held their own until receiving orders to withdraw. "The entire command was engaged more or less the entire day, and always with success," Ames reported. "The conduct of all was admirable."[26]

It had been a gratifying debut for the new brigade commander. Pleasonton reported, "The marked manner in which General Ames held and managed his troops under a galling fire of the enemy for several hours, is entitled to higher commendation than I can bestow."[27]

Ames then returned to his own brigade, composed of three Ohio regiments—the 25th, 75th, and 107th—and the 17th Connecticut. Brig. Gen. Francis C. Barlow was his division commander. Barlow had yet to turn 29, but he looked even younger. Clean-shaven and with a defiant tilt to his chin, he seemed more like a petulant student than a brigadier general. "His men at first gazed at him wondering how such a boy could be put at the head of regiments of men," remembered Carl Schurz. "But they soon discovered him to be a strict disciplinarian, and one of the coolest and bravest in action. In both respects he was inclined to carry his virtues to excess."[28]

Barlow had experienced a somewhat eccentric upbringing. His father abandoned the family when Francis was a boy, and Barlow's mother, Almira, took her three sons to live with her on the utopian Brook Farm in West Roxbury, Massachusetts, where they came to know luminaries such as Ralph Waldo Emerson and Henry David Thoreau. But Almira's free-living ways proved too much even for utopians, and she was asked to leave the farm. Francis went on to attend Harvard, where a schoolmate recalled, "He then, and ever afterwards, spoke his thoughts without restraint, and with a singular and almost contemptuous disregard of consequence." Barlow was practicing law in New York when the war began. He married Arabella Wharton Griffith—she was 10 years his senior, which led to some comment—on April 20, and left for war the next day as a captain in the 12th New York State Militia Regiment. By the time of the Peninsula Campaign Barlow was colonel of the 61st New York, where he earned the appreciation of brigade commander Howard. Barlow himself was badly wounded fighting at the Sunken Road at Antietam.

Barlow had already earned a reputation as a strict disciplinarian by the time he gained division command after Chancellorsville. "As a task-master he had no equal," remembered one of his soldiers. "The prospect of a speedy deliverance from the odious yoke of Billy Barlow filled every heart with joy." Barlow wore a larger-than-usual sword, he said, because when he hit stragglers he wanted it to hurt. He did not like stragglers. Nor did he much care for Germans. "You know how I have always been down on the 'Dutch' + I do not abate my contempt now," he wrote to his mother after Chancellorsville, although he admitted some "Yankee" regiments had performed just as poorly as the Germans. One thing he did like was fellow disciplinarian Adelbert Ames, whom he considered "a most admirable officer." It appears that Ames shared Barlow's disdain for Germans; General Howard would later note that he was "almost uncivil to them."[29]

—◦—

Ames's promotion left Joshua Lawrence Chamberlain in command of the 20th Maine. As with the 19th Maine, the change of command didn't happen without some friction, thanks to the regiment's major, Charles D. Gilmore. A Bangor native and former sheriff of Penobscot County, Gilmore had enlisted as a captain in the 7th Maine and had been wounded on the Peninsula when a shell crashed into the fence he was sitting on, throwing him to the ground. Perhaps this experience rattled Gilmore's nerves, for after he became the 20th Maine's major in August 1862, he displayed a talent for falling ill whenever combat loomed. Ellis Spear reported with disgust that "Gilmore had skulked in every action in which we had been engaged, & had taken no part. But he was, (as we did not so well know then) a schemer, and with some political influence."[30]

When Ames received word of his promotion, he summoned Captains Spear and Samuel Keene to his tent. He told them that Chamberlain would be promoted to colonel. Major Gilmore, Ames said, "was not fit for the service." To spare Gilmore from humiliation, Ames planned to promote him to lieutenant colonel and then have him resign. Spear would then become the regiment's lieutenant colonel and Keene its major.

As the two captains left Ames, Tom Chamberlain approached them and said he had seen Gilmore eavesdropping outside the tent. "I wonder now how we could have been so stupid as not to see that he could not be trusted & why we did not at once proceed against him, or at least inform Ames of the sneaking act," Spear said later. For Gilmore did not resign and remained as the 20th Maine's lieutenant colonel. But even as second in command, he managed to become sick whenever battle threatened.[31]

Almost immediately, the 20th Maine's new colonel had to deal with a crisis. It stemmed from the confusion about enlistments that had long plagued the Union armies. This time it involved the 2nd Maine. Most of its men had signed up for two years of service, and when that term ended in May 1863 they headed back home. A minority, whether they knew it or not, had signed papers requiring them to serve a full three years. They believed they should be allowed to return to Maine with their comrades. The army believed otherwise. The disgruntled men refused to bear arms, so division leader James Barnes sent them to the 20th Maine as prisoners with orders to Chamberlain to deal with them harshly.

If Ames had still been in command, there's little doubt he would have tried to break the recalcitrant men to his will. Chamberlain, however, was made of different stuff. For one thing, he sympathized with the prisoners and believed they had been willfully misled by their recruiters. On May 25 he wrote to Governor Coburn, who had returned to Maine following the visit that had brought him such derision. Chamberlain told the governor that the transfer had been so badly handled it had provoked the soldiers to a rebellious state. "They need to be managed with great care & skill; but I fear that some of them will get into trouble for disobedience of orders or mutiny," he told the governor. He said he would obey his orders, "but I sincerely wish these men were fairly dealt with by those who made them their promises."[32]

The new colonel did manage the men of the 2nd Maine with great care and skill. He called them together and said he would treat them "as soldiers should be treated." He said he could look into their cases and "that they should lose no rights by obeying orders." Looking back on the incident years later, Chamberlain was pleased to report that all but a handful returned to duty, and that some of them more than proved their worth with the 20th Maine.[33]

———

Following the fight at Brandy Station, Pleasonton decided to reorganize his cavalry corps. The 1st Maine left Kilpatrick's command to become part of the third brigade under Col. J. Irwin Gregg, a cousin to division commander David Gregg. The brigade's other regiments were the 10th New York and 4th and 16th Pennsylvania.

Stuart's surprise at Brandy Station had been an embarrassment to the Rebel cavalry commander, but it had not caused any significant changes to Lee's plans. His army began its move north, although Joe Hooker remained mystified as to exactly where it was going. Was Lee making another foray into Maryland? Into Pennsylvania? Did he plan to threaten Washington? It was now Pleasonton's responsibility to function as the army's eyes and ears and report on the enemy's movements.

Following a hard, hot 20-mile ride from Manassas Junction, the 1st Maine Cavalry reached the hamlet of Aldie on the afternoon of June 17. Aldie was in Loudon County, Virginia, on the eastern side of the Bull Run Mountains. On the western side lay the Blue Ridge, and beyond that was the Shenandoah Valley. Roads passing west through Aldie crossed over the mountains via Ashby's and Snicker's Gaps. If the Union cavalry-men could make their way west, through the towns of Aldie, Middleburg, and Upperville, and then through the gaps over the Blue Ridge, they could look into the valley and see what the Army of Northern Virginia was up to. Jeb Stuart and his cavalry, presumably still smarting from the surprise and near-defeat at Brandy Station, were determined to keep the Federals from prying.

Fighting was already raging outside Aldie when the Maine cavalry reached town. Their former brigade commander, Kilpatrick, had begun the battle earlier that afternoon by throwing his men piecemeal against Rebel cavalry under Col. Thomas Munford. Kilpatrick's men had gotten the worse of the encounter, especially the 1st Massachusetts, which suf-

fered 77 casualties when it charged headlong against dismounted Rebel
cavalrymen behind a stone wall. Once again, things were looking bad for
Kilpatrick, and once again he turned to the 1st Maine, even though it
now belonged to Gregg's brigade.

Henry C. Hall, then a lieutenant in Company H, recalled how Kilpatrick, covered with dust and sweat, looked like "a ruined man" as he
rode back with his routed cavalry. Darkness was falling, and it appeared
the Confederates would win the day. "What regiment is this?" Kilpatrick
demanded as he reined up by Companies D and H, under the command
of Capt. Andrew Spurling. When the men shouted they were from the
1st Maine, Hall said the effect on Kilpatrick was "electric." "Forward,
First Maine!" he shouted. "You saved the field at Brandy Station, and
you can do it here!" With a shout, the Mainers charged forward into the
night and toward the Rebel cavalry. The two forces crashed together, and
after a flurry of shots and sabre slashes, the Rebels retreated. The Union
horsemen followed. It was now so dark that Hall almost slashed a private
from his own company before he realized who he was. The private had
been shot in the arm, and Hall used his saber to knock the pistol from
the hand of the Rebel who had shot him, then slashed the enemy horsemen over the head. Another Rebel charged over and raised his saber for
a blow, but Hall yanked his horse to the side and dodged it. He resumed
his pursuit of the fleeing enemy, but then his horse stumbled and fell,
sending Hall tumbling into a ditch. His horse galloped riderless into the
night; Hall took a new mount from a captured Rebel.

The battle ebbed and flowed, but reinforcements from the 4th New
York and additional companies of the 1st Maine under Captain Boothby
shifted the tide in the Union's favor. Boothby, who had long, blond
hair and gold-rimmed glasses, was "rather a small man physically, but
weighed a ton in a fight," recalled a comrade. When in battle he shed
his natural reserve and his language became "exceedingly forceful." "God
bless you, Boothby! Hold them! Hold them!" cried Kilpatrick. Hall
recalled that "the very air was blue with flashing words that fell from
fearless Boothby's lips."[34]

Colonel Douty entered the fight a bit later, and went charging after
the retreating enemy alongside his men. Pvt. William S. Howe, a Baptist

minister before the war, recalled looking off to his side into an open field. Through the clouds of dust thrown into the air by the pounding hooves, he saw a lone horseman "charging up the line leaping fences and every obstacle that lay in his path." It was Douty. Stretched across the top of a hill was a stone wall that bent at a right angle. Hall saw Douty ride toward the wall, sword raised. Then enemy soldiers rose up from behind the wall and unleashed a volley. Douty fell dead. Bullets also hit Howe and his horse, but the private was able to rein around the fallen colonel and gallop back to Boothby. He told him he thought the colonel was dead. Boothby urged the regiment forward again. "Inside of two minutes the life of this indomitable hero was avenged, the heights captured, and Colonel Doughty's body recovered from that point where I last saw him in life," said Howe. Douty had been shot twice, and either wound would have killed him.[35]

The Rebels fell back, so the Federals returned to Aldie for the night. Smith took over the regiment, with Boothby second in command.

The Maine cavalry clashed with the Rebels again at the little town of Middleburg, on the other side of the Bull Run Mountains and farther west along the road to Ashby's Gap. Pleasonton still wanted to push over the Blue Ridge and observe Lee's movements, and Stuart remained equally determined to stop him. On June 18 the Rebels routed the 1st Rhode Island Cavalry under Col. Alfred Duffié and took a defensive position outside Middleburg on a height now called Mount Defiance. The 1st Maine Cavalry arrived the next day and attacked up the Ashby Gap Turnpike. Two companies under Boothby, C and G, charged down the road, and up the slope. A countercharge by the 9th Virginia hit their flank and drove them back down the hill.

Union reinforcements arrived, and another charge pushed the enemy off the heights. Two Maine companies stayed to the left of the road and moved into some woods held by Beverly Robertson's dismounted Rebel cavalry. They pushed the Rebels from the woods and dislodged more positioned behind a stone wall, capturing 25 of them. Colonel Smith called it "a daring feat, but gallantly performed." The Rebels fell back stubbornly, and the Federals followed until darkness fell. Once the fighting ended for the night, Sgt. Alexander McDougall of Company K, a farmer from Fort Fairfield, was amazed to find his clothing had been pierced by 17 bullets, none of which had touched him.[36]

Stuart's forces had been pushed back once more, but the Rebels still prevented Pleasonton's cavalry from observing what Lee was doing in the valley beyond. Pleasonton, frustrated by the enemy intransigence, requested the loan of some infantry, and Hooker gave him a division of the V Corps. One of its brigades was commanded by Col. Strong Vincent.

Born in Waterford, Pennsylvania, Vincent was a lawyer who had just turned 26. A Harvard man, he had been practicing law in Erie when war broke out. He had a patrician air about him, with a serious face, curly, upswept hair, and luxurious sideburns. He had commanded the 83rd Pennsylvania at Chancellorsville and was new to brigade command. Outside Middleburg he received orders to use his four regiments—his old 83rd Pennsylvania, the 16th Michigan, the 44th New York, and the 20th Maine—to push the Rebel cavalry out of their positions in the fields west of the town. The 20th Maine, however, would have to go into the fight without its newly minted colonel. Chamberlain had become a casualty of the hard marches and brutal heat and had fallen to sunstroke. Lieutenant Colonel Gilmore, much to Spear's disgust, followed his usual pattern and reported himself ill. Vincent gave command of the regiment to the 44th New York's Col. Freeman Connor.[37]

On June 21 the regiment broke camp bright and early and began a relatively easy march of seven miles from Aldie. Past Middleburg they found Stuart's cavalry waiting for them behind a small waterway called Goose Creek. Vincent arranged his regiments in line of battle and ordered them forward. Enemy artillery began lobbing shells their way, firing too high at first but gradually finding the range. One shell exploded over Holman Melcher's company, wounding several men. A shell fragment struck Melcher in the knee. It did not draw blood, but hit with such force that Melcher feared his leg was broken. Another soldier was less fortunate; Ellis Spear watched a shell strike the soldier and nearly tear off his leg, the limb remaining attached by what appeared to be a single tendon.[38]

Vincent began his attack by advancing the 16th Michigan against dismounted cavalrymen sheltered behind stone walls. Pleasonton told him to send more soldiers, and Vincent complied by ordering the 44th New York and the 20th Maine forward, and having the 83rd Pennsylvania take a concealed route through some woods to the left. "The movement was entirely successful," Vincent reported, and the enemy fell back from their stone walls. "Our brigade advanced with such coolness and rapidity that it frightened the enemy and away they went before our lines got within rifle range," Melcher reported. "They made several stands but would not remain long enough to allow us to get near enough to open upon them with rifles." Walter Morrill of the regiment's Company B was surprised when he spotted a man he knew among the Rebel prisoners. He had worked with him on the Penobscot River back in Maine.[39]

Once Vincent's brigade dislodged Stuart from his position west of Middleburg, the Rebel cavalry fell back to the town of Upperville and resumed its stubborn blocking action. Once again, Judson Kilpatrick lived up to his nickname by sending repeated attacks against the enemy in fighting that raged through the streets. Kilpatrick, his brigade badly cut up, told Pleasonton, "If I had the 1st Maine, they would go through." Pleasonton gave him what he wanted.

Capt. George M. Brown received orders to report with Companies E and M to Kilpatrick. He found him just outside of town. "Captain, I want you to go through this town and drive those fellows out," Kilpatrick said. The trot through Upperville turned into a charge when an enemy howitzer came into view and fired canister at close range. "I must admit that when the order to charge was given and the grape-shot went howling over our heads, I shut my eyes, as I did not wish to see who went down," recalled a soldier from Company M, "but it was only for an instant, and then it seemed that I heard but the gallop of one mighty horse, as we thundered down the streets of that quiet town." The enemy artillerymen abandoned their gun and ran. The Maine cavalrymen went flying past the howitzer in pursuit. On they went, the Union horsemen pushing the Rebels, the Rebel cavalry rallying and pushing back, until finally the Confederates broke off the fight and moved away. "Those Maine men would charge straight into hell if ordered to," said Kilpatrick.[40]

Still, the fight had been at best a qualified success. Despite the Union cavalry's efforts, Stuart's forces had kept Lee's army safe from observation. On July 25, their job of screening Lee's infantry completed, Stuart and his horsemen set off on a still-controversial ride around the Union army. Late on June 27, the 1st Maine Cavalry left Virginia behind, too. "Crossing the Potomac at Edward's Ferry, we were in God's land once more," said Charles Gardiner. "Getting out of old Virginia was like getting out of a graveyard into Paradise. We were welcomed all the way, the citizens met us with bread, milk, butter, and all kinds of fruit, and bade us Godspeed on our way."[41]

＊＊＊

While Joshua and Thomas Chamberlain were fighting with the Army of the Potomac, their brother John remained behind in Bangor. He was 10 years younger than Joshua—whom he still called Lawrence—and three years older than Tom. (Another brother, Horace, had died in 1861 of tuberculosis. Sister Sarah had been born between John and Horace.) Like Joshua, John had graduated from Bowdoin, but he had gone on to study at the Bangor Theological Seminary. He was still there when his brothers began writing and asking him to visit them in Virginia. They promised to have a horse waiting, saddled up and ready to take him to camp, once he reached the railroad station at Stoneman's Switch, near Falmouth. So, on June 1, 1863, John set out from Bangor on a journey south.

In Boston he stopped at the office of the Christian Committee, an organization formed in 1861 by leaders of the YMCA to supply the religious needs of Union soldiers. The commission's volunteers distributed religious literature to the armies, provided food and (nonalcoholic) drink, and cared for the wounded. John volunteered his services as a Christian Commission delegate. He said he felt it was his duty to do so. He also knew that commission delegates received railroad passes to reach the armies in the field, which must have provided some additional motivation.

John Chamberlain's reunion with his brothers, though, was some time coming. There was no horse waiting for him at Stoneman's Switch—the V Corps, and with it the 20th Maine, had already moved up the Rappahannock away from Falmouth. John dutifully did his work for the commission at various camps in Virginia, where he ran into several acquaintances from Maine, including "Tommy" Hyde and the

Howards. (John Chamberlain and Charles Howard had been classmates at Bowdoin.) He also began learning firsthand about the "unspeakable suffering of war." One "hard case" he ministered to was Dexter Boydon, a Vermont soldier who had nearly died of typhoid fever early in the war, recovered in time to be wounded and left for dead on the Peninsula, was badly wounded again at Antietam, and was shot through the body at Fredericksburg and left on the battlefield for four days. "He had read his own obituary and this I call a hard case," Chamberlain noted.[42]

In a V Corps hospital Chamberlain found several men from the 20th Maine. They complained about how Ames had treated them like dogs, but had only praise for John's brother, the new colonel. They marveled at the way he willingly threw off his coat and helped build breastworks alongside the men. But John couldn't catch up to his soldier brothers before the Army of the Potomac headed off in pursuit of Lee. Instead, John helped pack up supplies at Aquia Landing on the Potomac and then caught a boat back to Washington. There he ran into Rowland Howard, who was also doing volunteer work for the Christian Commission. The two Mainers (and fellow Bowdoin and Bangor Theological Seminary students) struck out together in a mail wagon for Otis Howard's head-quarters, somewhere near Leesburg. It was an anxious trip, for both men had been warned that Confederate guerillas infested the region. It seemed their worst fears were going to be realized when a company of horsemen stopped the wagon in a desolate part of Virginia, but much to Chamberlain and Howard's relief, they turned out to be Union cav-alry and provided an escort. When Chamberlain reached the XI Corps, he ran into Ames, who gave him a gift to bring to his brother. Charles Howard arranged transportation to the V Corps.

John Chamberlain finally caught up with the 20th Maine at Aldie. His arrival in camp was such a surprise that Ellis Spear could only stare at him "in mute astonishment" before recovering himself and telling John his brother the colonel was sick with sunstroke. John sought out Law-rence and found him "looking poorly." His brother Tom then took him on a tour of the Aldie battlefield and pointed out the spot where Calvin Douty had fallen. When the regiment resumed its march the next day, John tried to persuade Lawrence to keep out of the rain by riding in an ambulance, but the colonel refused. He said he wanted to ride like a man. And so it was that three Chamberlain brothers headed north together in pursuit of Robert E. Lee and the Army of Northern Virginia.[43]

———◆———

On June 3, the 17th Maine received a new brigade commander. He was Régis de Trobriand, the French aristocrat who had commanded the 55th New York under Hiram Berry. David Bell Birney still commanded the division and Dan Sickles remained in command of the III Corps.

There was some turmoil swirling in the regiment's upper levels. Its original colonel, Thomas Roberts, suffered from ill health and had not been present for duty at Chancellorsville until the fighting was over. He finally resigned in June, leaving Lt. Col. Charles Merrill in temporary command. Merrill, a Bowdoin graduate and Portland lawyer before the war, had served with Roberts in a militia unit back home, and it seems there was bad blood between them. Perhaps the ill will trickled down through the regiment, or maybe its soldiers knew that Merrill had a brother who was fighting for the Confederacy, because a movement began to secure the colonelcy for Maj. George West—a move that was doubtlessly spearheaded by George West. He had been born in Massachusetts and gained military experience with militia there, but West later moved to Maine's Aroostook County to take up work as a lumberman. He had begun the war as a captain with the 10th Maine. He had since advanced to major in the 17th, but he had his sights set on higher rank.[44]

As has had happened with the 19th Maine, letters and petitions began traveling from the army to the governor, recommending West and tearing down Merrill. A petition drawn up on May 23 and signed by 21 officers claimed that Merrill had taken the colors and gone to the rear during the fighting at Chancellorsville on May 3, and he had returned to the regiment only after his brigade commander ordered him to. That behavior, the petition said, "was such as to destroy all our confidence in his bravery." On the other hand, Generals David Birney and Hobart Ward both wrote to Coburn to recommend Merrill, and other soldiers testified to his bravery at Chancellorsville as well.[45]

"Col. Merrill was a kind, fatherly man, abounding in good qualities and he didn't fancy the domineering and reckless ways of West," noted John Haley, who appreciated West's military skills, but thought he was cold and ambitious. "We admired his smartness and military genius, but as a man, we despised him as thoroughly he did us." For the time being, Merrill remained in charge, even though his courage on the battlefield had been questioned.[46]

Rumors soon began passing through the ranks that Lee's army was on the move, and the Army of the Potomac would soon follow. The 17th Maine received its orders on June 11, and bugles announced that the time had come to break camp. The regiment was on the road by 4:00 A.M. The heat was "fearful," remembered Haley; in true army fashion, stragglers began falling out on the side of the road. The long marches in the sweltering heat and clouds of dust became so tortuous that men began spreading a rumor that they were being driven so hard because two generals had placed a bet on whose division could cover the most distance.[47]

June 15 was "a most horrible march," said Charles Mattocks. For Haley, it felt like marching in an oven, with the heat so bad "we soon felt as if we could boil or bake eggs in our caps." Men began to fall out of the ranks, their tongues swollen and their eyes rolling back in their heads. Mattocks had only seven men left in his company when they finally stacked arms at the end of the march. Along the way his brigade had nearly exchanged friendly fire with pickets from regiments that had come out from Washington. The encounter became a reunion of sorts, as the soldiers of the 17th Maine found old friends within the 25th and 27th Maine regiments, camped nearby. These were nine-month regiments, assigned to the defenses of Washington, now under Heintzelman's command. "They seem to think us heroes, and we make no serious objections," said Mattocks.[48]

Onward they toiled. On June 17, the regiment camped near Centreville and the men could hear the distant firing from the cavalry battle at Aldie. On June 19, they advanced to the tumbledown hamlet of Gum Springs, arriving at midnight as the heavens opened in a downpour that turned the roads to mud. In the rain and the darkness the soldiers could barely see the men standing next to them, and they tripped over every hole and obstacle. The brigade stayed put at Gum Springs for several days, so some soldiers used the time to boil their clothes and kill the lice that infested them. The only excitement occurred when someone stole a nice ham from the tent of Capt. William Hobson of Company I. Hobson threatened dire retribution upon whoever was responsible. The culprit, however, remained at large.[49]

June 25 was another rainy day, and the regiment pulled up stakes once more and continued north. Around 3:00 P.M. it reached the Potomac River at Edwards Ferry and began crossing the pontoon bridge to Maryland.

But the day's marching was not over. The brigade kept going, and going. Periodically, staff officers would ride up and tell the footsore soldiers there were only 2 more miles to go—a claim they repeated over the course of another 15 miles. It started to rain again. Marching through the drizzle, the men reached a viaduct over the Monocacy River. When a mule halted and stubbornly blocked passage of the narrow span, soldiers had no compunction about heaving the still-loaded animal over the side to drown. The 17th Maine finally stumbled into its camp late that night, with most of the men too tired to pitch tents despite the downpour. They had traveled around 30 miles.[50]

On the positive side, the Union men found the attitude of the local inhabitants to be a marked improvement over the scowling hostility they had faced in Virginia. Now, instead of offering sneers and insults, the locals greeted the Union soldiers with cheers and patriotic songs. "There is not that sourness in the countenance of every passer-by which greeted us in our wanderings over the 'sacred soil' of the 'Old Dominion,'" noted Mattocks. When the Union soldiers marched through Frederick, residents displayed flags and bunting from their homes and came out to give officers flowers and wreaths.[51]

That night the 17th Maine stopped about seven miles beyond Frederick. Word began circulating that Joe Hooker was no longer in command. He had been replaced by George Gordon Meade, the commander of the V Corps.[52]

Otis Howard went to visit the new army commander after the XI Corps reached Frederick late on June 28. When he entered the general's tent Howard found Meade with his coat off—the stifling heat trumped army formality. Howard extended his hand. "How are you, Howard?" Meade asked. Howard thought Meade seemed more excitable than usual. Howard was aware of how young he must have seemed to the commander, for Meade had graduated from West Point in 1835, when Howard was four years old. "To me, of course, he stood in the light of an esteemed, experienced regular officer, old enough to be my father, but like a father that one can trust without his showing him any special regard," Howard said. "So we respected and trusted Meade from the beginning."[53]

One of the generals Meade trusted was John Fulton Reynolds, the man who, back in April 1861, had advised Howard to accept the colonelcy of the 3rd Maine. Since then Reynolds had become one of the Army of the Potomac's most respected officers and the commander of the I Corps. "Brave, kind-hearted, modest, somewhat rough and wanting polish, he was a type of the true soldier," said one of his aides. He was tall, with dark hair, beard, and eyes, and flashing white teeth, high cheekbones, and a temperament that could be described as "taciturn." Reynolds had reportedly turned down an offer to replace Hooker at the head of the army. Meade, who had served under Reynolds earlier in the war, liked and trusted his fellow Pennsylvanian. So had Hooker, who had entrusted Reynolds with an entire wing of the army, consisting of his own I Corps, plus those of Sickles and Howard. Meade kept Reynolds in that role and sent him and the I Corps north into Pennsylvania, toward the town of Gettysburg. Howard followed with his XI Corps. On June 29, he reached the Maryland town of Emmitsburg, just south of the Pennsylvania border, after a "wearisome" march of some 20 miles on a rainy day over muddy roads.[54]

That same day, the 17th Maine established its camp outside the Maryland village of Taneytown, where the locals treated the soldiers like a combination of conquering heroes and sideshow attractions. "Ladies and young girls distributed beautiful bouquets of flowers to the officers and soldiers; groups of fair damsels, bewitchingly posted in conspicuous places, sang patriotic airs, as the 'boys in blue' marched by, and the passage of troops being a novelty, the citizens turned out *en masse*," recalled Edwin Houghton. "Long after tattoo, groups of ladies and gentlemen were promenading through our camps, actuated by a curiosity to see how soldiers really lived in the 'tented field.'"[55]

They passed June 30 in Taneytown, and were even mustered in to receive their pay. That afternoon they marched to Emmitsburg, a town that apparently did not share the pro-Union sympathies that men had experienced earlier. "It has never fallen to my lot to see such a malignant set of countenances," said Haley.[56]

"I should not be surprised if we begin the month of July with a fight," Charles Mattocks wrote in his journal. "We are now close upon the enemy, and I somewhat think there will be a few guns fired July 1st."[57]

On the night of June 30, Howard was about to go to bed at his headquarters at a Jesuit college in Emmitsburg when he received a summons from Reynolds. He wanted Howard to meet him at Moritz Tavern, where Reynolds had stopped for the night. It was about six miles away, near Marsh Creek. Howard and his brother Charles found Reynolds in a small farmhouse that was nearly empty of furniture. "General Reynolds was a tall, vigorous man of quick motion and nervous temperament," Charles Howard recalled. "That night he was somewhat paler than usual and seemed to feel anxious or at least to keenly alive to the responsibility resting upon him."[58]

There was one table in the room where they talked, and it was piled with maps and messages. The two generals went through the dispatches from headquarters and discussed the possibilities of battle. Howard left around eleven. He recalled thinking that Reynolds seemed depressed, almost as though he had received a foreshadowing of what was going to happen the next day. Back at his headquarters, Howard got only about an hour's sleep before an orderly woke him with orders, directed to Reynolds, about the army's movements. The I and XI Corps were told to move north to Gettysburg.[59]

CHAPTER 11

The 16th Maine Gets Sacrificed

*The boys fought like the d_____ never better. You may judge when I tell
you that many of our horses were not shot but bayoneted that it was
a close and desperate struggle for our guns two of which they actually
had hold of at one time. I have seen hard fighting before and been badly
smashed up, but I never saw a battery taken from the field and its guns
saved in so bad a state as the Old Second came off that day.*
            —JAMES A. HALL, 2ND MAINE BATTERY

Capt. James Hall and the 2nd Maine Battery had no idea what the day
had in store for them when they left Marsh Creek with the rest of the
I Corps early on the morning of July 1. Hall, a stolid-looking 27-year-
old redhead with a bushy walrus mustache and hazel eyes, had entered
service with the battery as a lieutenant back in November 1861. He
advanced to command when the unit's original captain, former Maine
adjutant general Davis Tillson, was promoted. On July 1 Hall had six
three-inch ordnance rifles in his battery, with 127 men and officers
reporting for duty.[1]

The battery followed Lysander Cutler's brigade north on the four-
mile march to Gettysburg. Cutler was from Massachusetts, but as a
young man he had been a schoolteacher in the Penobscot County town
of Dexter, and he had established his authority on the first day with "a
thorough flogging of every bully in the school." He later served as a militiaman and in the Maine senate. After losing everything in the financial

panic of 1856, Cutler pulled up stakes and relocated to Wisconsin, and he entered the war as the colonel of a regiment from that state. A newspaper reporter described the 56-year-old Cutler as "an elderly gentleman, spare of frame, with silvery hair, a beard nearly white, and beneath heavy eyebrows of an iron-gray color, are keen, penetrating dark eyes." He was a strict disciplinarian "and stern and unflinching in exacting the performance of all duties," as one of his men recalled. One of his first moves as colonel of the 6th Wisconsin was to weed out any officers he felt weren't competent by having them take an examination and removing any who did not pass. This aroused "much bitter feeling in the regiment," but also increased its efficiency. Cutler was wounded in the thigh at Second Bull Run and later promoted to brigade command.[2]

As Hall's battery—his six guns and all its personnel, horses, caissons, and limbers—went clattering by the Lutheran Seminary on a ridge just west of town, James M. Sanderson of John Reynolds's staff came galloping up. Reynolds wanted to see Hall immediately. Hall found the general near a barn alongside the Chambersburg Pike. Hall thought Reynolds seemed "extremely anxious."

The fighting had already started. Sometime around 7:30 A.M., cavalry under Maj. Gen. John Buford fired the first shots in what became a delaying action against advancing Rebels of Harry Heth's division, who were marching east on the Chambersburg Pike toward Gettysburg. Buford's men put up a stubborn defense and managed to delay the Confederates until the first elements of the I Corps began to arrive. Reynolds was with them. He had been pushing the I Corps, under the command of Maj. Gen. Abner Doubleday while Reynolds commanded the army's left wing, to support Buford's beleaguered cavalry. Rebel artillery down the pike started shelling his men, and Reynolds wanted Hall to do something about it.

James Wadsworth, the wealthy New Yorker who commanded the corps' First Division, was with Reynolds. Wadsworth, who had been defeated in the New York gubernatorial campaign the previous fall, was 56 years old, with thinning white hair and sideburns that framed a solemn, patrician face. Reynolds told him to bring up some infantry support to protect Hall's right. He next turned to Hall. "I desire you to damage the Artillery to the greatest possible extent, and keep their fire from our infantry until they are deployed," he said. He promised to pull Hall back from his position, which was too advanced for artillery. Reynolds then rode off to the left, where the Iron Brigade was coming up. Within minutes he was dead, shot from his horse as he was ordering the brigade forward into Herbst's Woods.

Hall turned and joined his battery, which had come rumbling up. His men rapidly unlimbered the guns and began engaging the enemy artillery farther down the pike. Reynolds had been right—the battery was in a very advanced position and it made Hall nervous, even with two regiments of Cutler's brigade that Wadsworth had assigned providing support. The time was around 10:45 A.M.[3]

General Howard was up before dawn on July 1 to begin preparations to send his three divisions—under Francis Barlow, Adolph von Steinwehr, and Carl Schurz—forward toward Gettysburg. The long columns of men finally set out around 8:30 A.M. for the 11-mile march. After some morning showers, the day was promising to be hot and dusty. Howard rode along the Emmitsburg Road ahead of his corps, and he often had to detour through woods and fields to avoid the wagons and men of the I Corps. He had two Howard brothers with him on the march—his brother the major, and his minister brother Rowland, who had reached the XI Corps on June 24 with John Chamberlain as a member of the United States Christian Commission. Rowland had never experienced combat. He was excited by the "pomp and circumstance" of an army on the march, and the way the men waved their banners as they approached the Pennsylvania border.

The general remembered coming within sight of Gettysburg with his entourage at around 10:30 that morning. He could hear the roar of artillery and the ripping sheets of musketry ahead. For Rowland, the sound of the guns "excited a thrill of patriotic emotion."[4]

The rest of his corps was still coming up, so Howard spent some time examining the terrain. He rode through a peach orchard to the right of the Emmitsburg Road, and then along a ridge that ended on a hill south of town that was crowned by Evergreen Cemetery. He was there when a messenger arrived from Reynolds with confirmation that the battle had started.

Howard wanted to find a good spot to place his men. He thought the hill with the cemetery would suit his purposes. The rise sloped down to the southern fringe of Gettysburg, a town of about 2,400 people and home to Pennsylvania College. It was the seat of Adams County and provided a central hub for a road network that radiated in all directions. Two of the spokes, the Baltimore Pike and the Taneytown Road, came up from the southeast and south and passed by Cemetery Hill. The Emmitsburg Road reached Gettysburg from the southwest, while the York Pike entered town from the northeast and became the northwesterly-running Chambersburg Pike on the other side of town. The Hagerstown (Fairfield) Road headed west; the Hanover Road east. All these roads could serve as vital lifelines for armies that needed to move men, equipment, and supplies to and from a battle. North of the town were broad fields that stretched out to a prominent rise called Oak Hill. A series of low, parallel ridges ran north to south, like waves. Howard was on Cemetery Ridge. To the west he could see Seminary Ridge, named after the Lutheran Seminary that sat astride it on the town's western outskirts. Beyond that was McPherson Ridge. As Howard faced the town, he could see another high point off to his right called Culp's Hill. Behind him, to the south, Cemetery Ridge descended to a low, swampy area before rising again to end at a pair of hills called by various names but known to history as the Round Tops. "Here was a broad view which embraced the town, the seminary, the college, and all the undulating valley of open country spread out between the ridges," Howard said. "There was a beautiful break in the ridge to the north of me, where Culp's Hill abuts against the cemetery, and touches the creek below. It struck me that here one could make a strong right flank." He turned to Theodore Meysenberg, his adjutant. "This seems to be a good position, Colonel," he said.

"It is the only position, general," Meysenberg replied.[5]

The pious, one-armed general from Maine had made a decision that would have enormous ramifications for the Union army at Gettysburg.

For the rest of his life, Howard believed that his decision to post his men on Cemetery Hill was the key to the Union victory at Gettysburg. It was his redemption for the disaster at Chancellorsville. He objected when one of Reynolds's aides, Joseph George Rosengarten, claimed that Reynolds had made the decision and told one of Howard's aides to have the general occupy Cemetery Hill. Howard refuted that account. The only aide of Howard's who had spoken with Reynolds that morning was Capt. Daniel Hall, and Hall, he said, had received no such instructions. "General Reynolds gave no order whatever in regard to occupying Cemetery Hill, nor did he make any allusion to it," Hall affirmed.[6]

The weight of evidence tilts in Howard's favor, although not everyone was convinced. Abner Small, who developed a poor opinion of Howard's generalship, believed that Reynolds should receive the credit. "General Howard's memory is conveniently defective," Small averred, "as it would otherwise conflict with his claim to the championship of Gettysburgh."[7]

After looking over the cemetery ground, Howard rode into town to find a better vantage point. The belfry at the courthouse on Baltimore Street looked promising, but he couldn't find a ladder to climb up. Just across the street, on the corner of Baltimore and West Middle Streets, the Fahnestock Brothers dry goods store occupied a three-story building with a balcony accessible via a trap door. Young Daniel Skelly was on the platform with several other people when he looked down and spotted the general and his staff trotting north down Baltimore Street. He went down to offer the use of the Fahnestock "observatory." Howard passed through the store, climbed a stairway, hurried through a lumber room, climbed another stairway, and emerged on a balcony that provided a sweeping view of Gettysburg and its environs. He could see Buford's cavalry to the northwest, Wadsworth's men fighting around an unfinished railroad cut near the Chambersburg Pike, and Doubleday's division moving out in the direction of Oak Ridge to the north. As he and his staff compared what they saw with their maps, a cavalryman reined up in front of the store. Skelly recognized him as George Guinn of Cole's Maryland Cavalry, who lived not far from Gettysburg. "General Reynolds is wounded, sir," the horseman shouted to Howard.[8]

A few minutes later another rider arrived with even worse news. Reynolds was dead. Howard was now the senior officer on the field. "My heart was heavy and the situation was grave indeed!" he recalled. He began sending orders about the placement of the available troops, dispatched messages to various officers to bring their men up, and informed General Meade—still back in Taneytown—about the developing circumstances. He sent a message to General Schurz telling him he now had command of the XI Corps and that Alexander Schimmelfennig should take over Schurz's division. Young Skelly remembered that the general appeared "perfectly calm and self-possessed." After descending from the balcony, Howard even found time to offer a few reassuring words to elderly Mrs. Samuel Fahnestock. Then he rode back to the headquarters he had established on Cemetery Hill, where he found Schurz waiting for him by the arched brick gatehouse. Howard told him to take his men forward to the fields north of town.[9]

Barlow's division had taken the shortest route from Emmitsburg, but the Third Division, now under Schimmelfennig, had moved faster and arrived first. Corps commander Schurz had Schimmelfennig's men march through town to the fields beyond, where they could form on the right of the I Corps and perhaps establish a position on Oak Hill. When Barlow arrived with his men, including Adelbert Ames's brigade, Howard rode with them through town while the batteries of Hubert Dilger and William Wheeler went clattering through the streets behind. Howard saw that most of the residents had taken shelter from the impending storm of battle. One exception was a young woman who stood outside her house and waved a handkerchief at the Union troops, eliciting cheers from the soldiers as they passed.[10]

On the Chambersburg Pike, James Hall's situation was growing increasingly dangerous. His guns were dueling with the enemy artillery on his front when, to Hall's shock and surprise, Rebel infantry appeared as if out of nowhere on his right, only about 50 yards away. They had emerged from the unfinished railroad cut that sliced through the landscape, a deep gash that provided the enemy soldiers with cover as they approached. Hall ordered his guns to pivot to the right and they opened on the Confederates—Mississippians of Joseph Davis's brigade—with double canister.

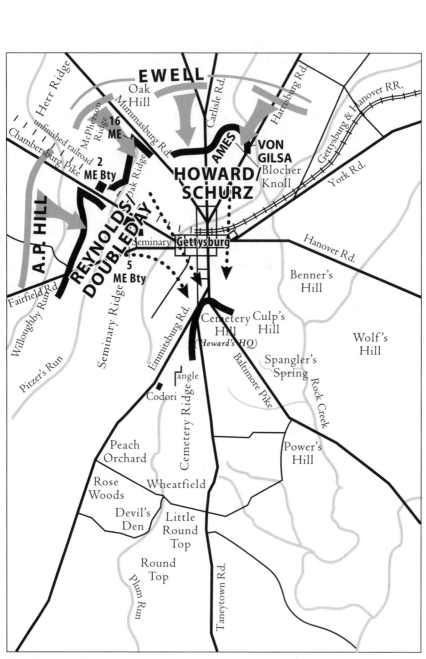

Gettysburg, July 1

Even as the battery fired at the advancing enemy, Hall was enraged to see his infantry support fall back. Enemy skirmishers soon had his range, and his men and horses began to fall. The enemy fire became so intense that for years afterwards Sgt. Charles E. Stubbs remained convinced that the Rebels were using some kind of "explosive bullets." Hall decided his men had taken enough punishment. "Feeling that if the position was too advanced for infantry it was equally so for artillery," Hall reported later with some asperity, he decided to withdraw. He ordered Lt. William Ulmer to move his two guns back to the next crest, where he could fire at the men in the railroad cut. By the time Ulmer had relocated, enemy fire was taking a heavy toll and the artillerymen had had to roll one of the cannons off by hand. Hall ordered his four other guns to the rear. The crews pushed the cannons down the slope and attached them to their limbers. "From where we limbered up to the point of going into Cashtown [Chambersburg] road, it was <u>hellish</u>," Hall recalled. "The scattering rebels along the R.R. Cut that had had been firing upon me, the moment they saw we were getting away, rushed forward and fired as rapidly as they could." The retreating artillery reached a sturdy fence with only a single narrow passage through, so the guns had to file through one at a time. Hall's horse was shot in the rump at the barrier as the beleaguered gunners struggled to save their cannons. Enemy soldiers swarmed up and bayoneted the horses of the last gun. Hall realized he would have to leave it behind.[11]

The rest of the battery moved back toward the relative safety of Seminary Ridge. Along the way Hall encountered Wadsworth and the two men had an "animated" discussion. Hall told the general he thought it was cowardly to remove the troops from his right. Wadsworth told him to move back. Hall said he wanted to save his stranded gun. The general replied, "snappishly," Hall thought, to lose no time in preparing to cover the army's retreat. Hall did send five of his men to retrieve his gun, but they never returned.

All was confusion. Hall was moving his battery back to Cemetery Hill when a messenger arrived from Wadsworth and told him to return to a position on Seminary Ridge. Hall dutifully reversed course, but as soon as he reached the indicated spot, he could see it was about to be overrun. He reversed course again. Then he ran into Col. Charles Wainwright, head of the I Corps artillery. Wainwright mentioned that Hall's abandoned gun was still on the field. This must have stung Hall's pride—losing a gun was shameful—because the captain rounded up two men and some horses and went back to retrieve it. The rescue party found the cannon between the lines and exposed to fire from both sides. Hall and his men had to scurry back behind a sheltering bank several times before they could manage to cut the gun loose from its dead horses and push it out of danger. Mission accomplished, Hall moved his battery back through town and to Cemetery Hill. He may not have been pleased with the final results, but he was proud of the way his men had behaved. "The boys fought like the d____ never better," he told John Hodsdon, "You may judge when I tell you that many of our horses were not shot but bayoneted that it was a close and desperate struggle for our guns two of which they actually had hold of at one time. I have seen hard fighting before and been badly smashed up, but I never saw a battery taken from the field and its guns saved in so bad a state as the Old Second came off that day."[12]

—◦—

When Charles O. Hunt, a lieutenant with the 5th Maine Battery, reached Gettysburg that morning, it must have felt a little bit like coming home. Hunt was from Gorham, near Portland, and had been a senior at Bowdoin College when the war broke out. Many of his classmates enlisted immediately, but Hunt wanted to complete his studies. After graduation, he decided to spend some time with his sister Mary while he contemplated his options. Mary had married Thomas Carson, a bank cashier from Pennsylvania, and she moved with him to Gettysburg—right in the center of town on York Street. Hunt stayed with her from September until the end of 1861 and became very familiar with the town and the surrounding countryside. He climbed the Round Tops, rode across the as-yet-uncapitalized wheat field, and collected hickory nuts on Culp's Hill. By the end of his stay he had decided to join the army and enlisted in the 5th Maine Battery. His brother Henry joined the battery, too. On two occasions during the war when he had fallen ill, Hunt had convalesced at his sister's house. Now, as his battery made its way through Pennsylvania, he joked that if he were to get hit, he hoped it would happen in Gettysburg, because he knew people there would take good care of him. Hunt learned to be careful what you wished for.

Following the death of George Leppien, Capt. Greenlief Stevens had taken command of the battery. He had also aroused the ire of some of his officers by failing to mention Leppien in his official report. Stevens, one of his men complained, "is a thoroughly selfish man." After Chancellorsville, the battery had been reassigned to the I Corps, and on July 1 Stevens and his men were bouncing and clattering up the Emmitsburg Road toward Gettysburg with the rest of the corps. By the time they reached a position just north of the Lutheran Seminary buildings, enemy troops were already visible moving forward from McPherson Ridge to the west. Union infantry were lying on the ground in front of the battery. Stevens had his guns fire over their heads with case shot, but switched to canister once the friendly infantry had moved behind them. The guns belched out a growing pall of smoke until the clouds became so thick Hunt could no longer see the field in front of him. He walked down by the seminary buildings to get out of the haze. "I remember very well the sound of the bullets on the brick house, reminding me of a shower of hail on the roof," he said. He then reentered the smoke cloud and returned to his guns. He wasn't there long before he felt a stabbing pain in his thigh, as though someone had struck him sharply with a cane. He looked down and saw a hole through the pistol holster on his belt. A shot had pierced the holster and gone into his thigh, carrying a piece of his pistol's ramrod into the wound with it. It didn't feel like any bones were broken, but Hunt knew the wound was too serious for him to continue fighting. He reported to Stevens and asked if he could go to his sister's house.[13]

Stevens gave his permission. Hunt needed assistance to get on a horse, but once mounted he set off for York Street. Confederate shells fell around him, "and the ride was anything but a pleasant one," he recalled. When he reached his sister's house, he found that she and her family had taken shelter in the Bank of Gettysburg's vault in the adjoining building after a spent shell had smashed through an attic window and landed in the front hall. There were 19 people and two dogs hiding in the vault. Some of the men carried a mattress to the cellar for Hunt to lie on, and the frightened assemblage prepared to wait out the battle as best they could.[14]

———

The 16th Maine's journey north toward Gettysburg began on June 12, when it broke camp outside Falmouth. That first day had been a tough march in heat and dust, and the parched soldiers had been forced to drink from muddy puddles alongside the roads. They logged 20 miles that first day, 12 the next, and 25 on the third. Still they marched, to Manassas Junction, and then Centreville, which made Small think back to First Bull Run, when he had been with the 3rd Maine. "It seemed two centuries past," he said. On June 17 Gabriel Paul took command of the brigade. Paul was from St. Louis, and his grandfather had been an officer under Napoleon. He was a West Point graduate (class of 1834) who had fought the Seminoles in Florida and served bravely in Mexico. "He was a man of distinguished appearance," Small noted. "He had a noticeably wide head and large eyes and a foreign look that was doubtless an inheritance from his French forebears." The division commander was John Robinson, a no-nonsense regular from New York with long, flowing facial hair. Small said Robinson "was rather fierce in appearance and manner. In a much bearded army, he was the hairiest general I ever saw."[15]

Onward the brigade marched. On June 25 the soldiers crossed the Potomac at Edwards Ferry. Three days later they heard the news that George Gordon Meade had replaced Hooker as army commander. Small would have preferred John Reynolds.

The last couple of marches were brutal. When the 16th Maine finally staggered into Emmitsburg, just short of the Pennsylvania border, on June 29, it had traveled 40 miles over the previous 26 hours. Fortunately for the exhausted men, their march of June 30 was just a short one, and they established a camp just north of Emmitsburg.

On the morning of July 1, a brief rain served to keep down the dust when the 16th Maine began an easy march toward Gettysburg at around eight o'clock. The sound of gunfire ahead provided a jolt of adrenaline as the regiment neared the town. "The heavy cannonading broke upon our ears, and gave elasticity to weary legs, and steps increased to the double-quick as we were met with the intelligence that General

Reynolds was killed, and the First Division desperately fighting double its numbers," said Small. Some men in the regiment thought they could distinguish the sound of Hall's guns. The regiment had a personal interest in that unit, because it included more than 30 men from the 16th who had been detailed to the battery following Antietam.[16]

After passing a peach orchard, division commander Robinson had his command veer to the left and head straight for the Lutheran Seminary. There he had his men throw up whatever fortifications they could contrive, so they used dirt and fence rails to create some protection. The 5th Maine Battery was to their rear. Another of the division's brigades, under Brig. Gen. Henry Baxter, had already moved farther north and was engaging Confederates who had started moving south from Oak Hill.[17]

The 16th Maine was just a shadow of the regiment that had marched out of Portland back in August. When it had left Maine it numbered about 1,000 men, but its toils as the "blanket brigade" and its hard marches since had greatly reduced its numbers. On July 1 the regiment had a mere 275 men.[18]

As the much-reduced regiment waited to go into battle, Capt. Stephen E. Whitehouse of Company K turned to Small. He said he wished he felt as brave as Colonel Tilden appeared to be. Small assured him that the colonel was just as frightened as anyone. When the order to fall in and move forward rang out around 1:00 P.M., Whitehouse turned again to Small. "Good by, Adjutant," he said, "this is my last fight."[19]

The regiment moved forward from the seminary, crossed the Chambersburg Pike and a portion of the unfinished railroad cut, and halted at a fence. Almost immediately it began exchanging fire with enemy soldiers some 200 yards away. Men fell, starting with Cpl. James P. Yeaton of the color guard. Capt. William H. Waldron of Company I was reminding his men to aim low when a bullet hit him in the neck. He supported himself against a tree, one hand over the wound, blood gushing between his fingers. When Lt. George Bisbee saw Waldron, he thought the jugular vein must have been severed. He ran over and helped the wounded man to the ground behind the tree. He wet a handkerchief with water from his canteen, and pressed it against Waldron's neck. "Then I heard the Colonel give the order to charge, and I told the Captain I must leave him, which I did."[20]

Color bearer Sgt. Wilbur F. Mower jumped over the fence, and the regiment followed with a cheer, driving the oncoming Rebels back into some woods. The Maine soldiers found a new position behind a stone wall on Oak Ridge. Said Small, "I remember the trees in the heat, and the bullets whistling over us, and the stone wall bristling with muskets, and the line of our men, sweating and grimy, firing and loading and firing again, and here a man suddenly lying still, and there another rising all bloody and cursing and starting for the surgeon." Tilden was the only officer in the regiment on horseback, and Rebel bullets soon killed his mount, sending him tumbling to the ground.[21]

At some point during the fighting, Lt. Isaac Thompson noticed that a civilian had joined the regiment and was firing at the enemy from the rear. This new arrival was not destined to pass into legend like John Burns, the old citizen-soldier of Gettysburg who had fought earlier that day with the Iron Brigade. Small watched Thompson approach the stranger and say something to him. Then Thompson knocked the man to the ground, yanked him back up by the collar, and dispatched him to the rear with some sharp kicks.

Lt. George A Deering of Company F became so excited he sheathed his sword and grabbed a musket to fire away at the enemy. He forgot to remove the rammer from the barrel after loading, and the rod went whirling through the air. "The peculiar swishing noise made by the rammer, as it hurried through the wood was laughable to the boys, and must have been a holy terror to the rebels," said Small.[22]

Baxter's brigade ran out of ammunition and retired. Gabriel Paul had gone down with a truly terrible wound, the bullet passing behind his right eye and out of his left, leaving him permanently blinded. His replacements in brigade command, Colonels Samuel H. Leonard and Adrian Root, had both been wounded. That left the 11th Pennsylvania's Col. Richard Coulter in command of the brigade. Things were spiraling out of control.

━◆━

Francis Barlow and Otis Howard emerged from the streets of Gettysburg into the broad fields that stretched out to the north of town. Howard left Barlow and rode off to the left in search of Doubleday. Barlow halted his two brigades alongside the Harrisburg Road, which ran to the northeast and across Rock Creek. Off in the distance, Jubal Early's skirmishers were already moving south down the road. Ames ordered four companies of the 17th Connecticut under Maj. Allen C. Brady to move forward, cross the bridge over Rock Creek, and stop at the buildings of the Benner farm. Once there they began fighting "briskly" with Confederate skirmishers.[23]

Barlow had the rest of Ames's brigade take up a position to the right of the Harrisburg Road, and he put von Gilsa's men to the left. Nearby was a small complex of buildings that composed the county almshouse, one of the few landmarks on the largely flat plain. The heights of Oak Hill, already occupied by the first arrivals of Robert Rodes's Confederate division, were ahead and to the far left. A ridge extended from Oak Hill off to the left. This was Oak Ridge, where the I Corps had its left. As Barlow looked out over the area he was responsible for defending, he must have been struck by the lack of terrain features he could use to better anchor his position. The only distinguishing landmark was a slight rise to the left (west) of the road and about a quarter mile ahead of the almshouse, just south of Rock Creek. Locals knew it as Blocher's Knoll, after the farmer who owned the land. It certainly didn't dominate the topography, but Barlow must have decided it was all he had. Without waiting for orders from corps commander Schurz, he decided to secure the knoll. Von Gilsa advanced first and placed his men on the rise, along with Bayard Wilkeson's Battery G, 4th U.S. Artillery. For the time being, Barlow held Ames back as a reserve.

The decision, which Howard later characterized as a "bold advance," may have reflected Barlow's aggressive personality, but it was not tactically wise. By moving forward and stretching to the right, Barlow broke contact with Wladimir Krzyzanowski's brigade on his left and placed his own division in an exposed and precarious position. As Harry W. Pfanz noted in his study of the first day's fighting, "He had blundered, and in doing so he had ensured the defeat of the corps that he so despised."[24]

After leaving Barlow, Howard met briefly with Wadsworth and Doubleday before returning to his headquarters on Cemetery Hill. There he received word that Ewell's Confederate corps was arriving from the north. Fearing the Rebels would strike the XI Corps' unprotected right, he sent orders to Schurz to stop his advance, except for skirmishers sent forward to help the I Corps. Around 2:00 Howard rode forward from Cemetery Hill to consult again with Doubleday near the seminary. Howard returned to his headquarters on Cemetery Hill right around the time that Ewell's men began pressing the right of the XI Corps. While this flank attack was not a surprise, its result was little better for the XI Corps than Jackson's had been at Chancellorsville.

The initial blow came when John B. Gordon's brigade of Early's division slammed into von Gilsa from the northeast, while George Doles's brigade swung to the right to strike them from the west. Von Gilsa's brigade began to crumble under Gordon's onslaught and Ames received orders to push his brigade forward. The 17th Connecticut—minus Brady's detachment—was on the right, with the 25th Ohio next in line, the 107th Ohio on the left, and the 75th Ohio remaining behind as a reserve. Some of von Gilsa's men, outnumbered and outflanked, began to retreat, sowing more chaos and confusion into an already unsteady situation. Ames's brigade began showing signs of wavering.

Lt. Col. Douglas Fowler commanded the 17th Connecticut. On the march to Gettysburg earlier that day, either Barlow or Ames—both of them strict disciplinarians—had ordered Fowler placed under arrest because one of his men, despite orders, had dropped out of ranks to get some water. General Schurz, who considered the breach to be "a mere unimportant peccadillo," had him released. Now Fowler was advancing with his men, mounted. "Dodge the big ones, boys," he told his soldiers as shell and shot began to fall around them. Fowler was unable to dodge the shell that decapitated him, spraying the men around him with his blood and brains.[25]

Ames had Col. Andrew L. Harris and the 75th Ohio fix bayonets and move forward in an attempt to steady the line. "Our situation was perilous in the extreme," Harris recalled. Men fell left and right and lay dead or bleeding in the grass. Moving forward became impossible, but Harris hesitated to retreat without orders from Ames. Finally, with a quarter of his command dead or dying, he decided the choice had been taken out of his hands, and he had his regiment turn around and head back toward town.

As the 75th Ohio began its retreat, Harris received orders to take command of the brigade. Barlow had been badly wounded and was feared dead, so Ames, who had barely time to get a feel for commanding a brigade, now took over the division. Peter Young, an officer in the 107th Ohio, later wrote admiringly that "such imperturbably coolness as Gen. Ames displayed in the trying hours of the first day under a most galling fire, I but seldom saw in my army experience; he has the highest admiration and regard of all under his command who ever fought under his guidance."[26]

According to Howard's estimate, it was around 3:20 when the Rebels began pressing their attacks against the two Union corps. Doubleday and Schurz both sent requests for support, but there was little Howard could do. Doubleday's adjutant, E. P. Halsted, said when he reached Cemetery Hill around 4:00 with Doubleday's plea for reinforcements, he found Howard looking like "the picture of despair." Halstead directed Howard's attention to Rebels off to the north who were threatening to overwhelm the I Corps. "Those are nothing but rail fences, Sir!" Howard snapped peevishly. "I beg your pardon, General," said Halstead, "if you will take my glass you will see something besides rail fences." Howard had an aide take a look. "General, those are long lines of the enemy," the aide said. Howard told Halstead to find Buford and see if he could lend any assistance.[27]

Howard did not want to send his entire reserve force from Cemetery Hill, but he did release three regiments from Charles R. Coster's brigade of Steinwehr's division to provide support for the XI Corps in case it had to retreat. Howard also sent an aide with an order to Doubleday to fall back to Cemetery Hill if he could not hold his position. Doubleday later said he received no such order. The situation on both fronts continued to deteriorate. By 4:10 Howard realized the Union forces had no chance of holding their lines. He sent orders to both Schurz and Doubleday to fall back, but to dispute the ground all the way.

The reinforcements from Coster's brigade were too little, too late. In an article he wrote for the *Atlantic Monthly* in 1876, Howard admitted that the XI Corps broke and retreated first. "Soon the division of the eleventh corps nearest Doubleday was flying to the shelter of the town, widening the gap there; and the enemy in line pressed rapidly through the interval," he wrote. "Of course Robinson and Wadsworth had to give way."[28]

Like a dam with a gap torn through it, the rest of the Union line began to fall apart, with both corps falling back through Gettysburg and getting tangled up in the streets of town. Schimmelfennig found himself trapped by pursuing Rebels and had to clamber over a wall and hide in a tiny backyard for the remainder of the battle.

Brady and his advanced detachment of the 17th Connecticut received orders to rejoin their regiment. They found a chaotic scene when they reached Gettysburg, with the victorious Confederates already beginning to fill the streets. Brady and his New Englanders contested the Rebel advance as best they could, stopping to fire before falling back again, but it was like fighting an incoming tide. "They poured in from every street in overwhelming numbers, which broke our ranks," Brady reported. The detachment finally rejoined what remained of its regiment on Cemetery Hill.[29]

Greenlief Stevens and the 5th Maine Battery added to the chaos in Gettysburg on the retreat from Seminary Ridge. As the battery rumbled through the streets at a trot, a wheel fell off one of the carriages and the axle began dragging along the road. Stevens jumped off his horse and improvised a repair by using gunner's pinchers—a plier-like tool—as a linchpin to secure the wheel. Then the battery continued up Baltimore Street to Cemetery Hill. It eventually took a new position on a small rise between Cemetery and Culp's Hills, today known as Stevens' Knoll.[30]

When the XI Corps fell back, the 16th Maine and its brigade of Robinson's division, on the far right of the I Corps, found its flank exposed, with large bodies of the enemy approaching from the front and on the sides. Sometime around 4:00, division commander Robinson rode up to Colonel Tilden.

George Bisbee was in the color company standing next to the colonel when Robinson arrived. Bisbee heard the general tell Tilden to have his men about-face and advance to attack the oncoming enemy. Tilden and

Robinson then had a short conversation. Tilden explained that the enemy was moving on his front and both his flanks, and that his regiment was already badly cut up. Bisbee said that Robinson stood up in his stirrups and "in a loud voice and some energetic words" ended the conversation by ordering, "Colonel Tilden, take that position and hold it as long as there is a single man left." Others remembered Robinson's telling Tilden to hold the position "at any cost."

"All right, General, we'll do the best we can," Tilden said. Robinson wheeled and spurred his horse, which jumped over the stone wall and carried the general toward Gettysburg.

Tilden turned back to his men. "You know what that means," he said.[31]

"Yes, the regiment knew what it meant," remembered Frank Wiggin, then a sergeant in Company H. "It meant death or capture, and every man realized it perfectly." Robinson was going to withdraw his division, and he wanted the 16th Maine to serve as a last-ditch defense to buy time for the rest of his men. Wiggin compared the situation to a pair of shears, with the two blades closing in on the I Corps, and the 16th Maine sent to the pivot point to keep the blades from snapping closed.[32]

"About-face, fix bayonets, charge," Tilden ordered, and his men moved forward on their doomed, but vital, mission. Somehow, fewer than 275 men had to hold back several thousand of the enemy so the rest of their division could escape to fight another day. "We were sacrificed to steady the retreat," Small said. It was an impossible position. The Maine men blazed away. Soldiers fell on both sides. The enemy was so close, Small could hear a Confederate officer shouting orders to his men. Then he saw the officer fall on his face to the ground. The increasing pressure forced the 16th Maine back to the railroad cut.[33]

The 16th Maine's last, desperate stand did not last long—probably no more than 20 minutes. As the Rebels pushed closer on two sides and the survivors realized they were most likely going to die or be captured, thoughts turned to the regimental flags. Flags were more than pieces of fabric. On the battlefield, the banners played an important role by indicating where specific units were fighting. Commanders could use flags as rallying points for their troops. They also held weighty symbolic significance. They were, in a sense, a representation of the regiment itself. As

Harry Pfanz wrote in his study of Gettysburg's first day, "Like the standards of the Roman legions, they embodied the souls and honor of their regiments." Many regiments received their banners from local citizens, who had them specially made and presented them at solemn ceremonies. Regiments added the names of the battles in which they participated to their flags. The role of color bearer was considered a post of honor, and soldiers died defiantly waving their flags in the faces of enemy soldiers. Capturing an enemy unit's flag was considered a great triumph—losing your own was shameful.[34]

Now 16th Maine risked losing theirs. "We looked at our colors, and our faces burned," wrote Small. "We must not surrender those symbols of our pride and our faith." One Rebel got close enough to make a grab at a flag, but the men closed in around it. Capt. S. Clifford Belcher, a Bowdoin graduate who had just started practicing law in Belfast when he joined the 16th Maine, received the approval of the other officers and ordered the staffs broken, the flags torn to shreds, and the pieces distributed to the men in the regiment. The soldiers hid them away beneath their shirts or in their pockets. "These fragments were carried through Southern prisons and finally home to Maine, where they are still treasured as precious relics more than a quarter century after Gettysburg," Small noted in 1889.[35]

Officers also considered it shameful to give up a sword. So when a Rebel soldier pointed his musket at Tilden and demanded, "Throw down that sword or I will blow your brains out," the colonel stabbed his sword into the ground and snapped off the blade at the hilt.[36]

As he was being led away as a prisoner, Lewis Bisbee came across the body of an officer lying on his face, his coat ripped all the way up the back, his Bible and keys lying atop the body. Bisbee rolled him over and recognized Captain Whitehouse, a "ghastly wound" in his throat. His prophecy had come true. Bisbee passed another soldier sitting with his back to a tree and stopped to ask where he was wounded. The man said nothing, only lifted his shirt to show Bisbee his entrails protruding from a horrible gash. "He was left to die alone."[37]

Some of the men decided to make a break for freedom, so they slipped away and made their way down the railway cut toward Cemetery

Hill, visible on the far side of town. Once all the men who managed to escape had gathered with the rest of the shattered remnants of the I and XI Corps on Cemetery Hill, Small counted 35 men, including himself. The regiment had started the battle with 275.

It had been a bad day for the Army of the Potomac. Reynolds was dead, and the I and IX Corps had been driven from the field with great loss. Some have criticized Howard for blindly following Reynolds's lead and leaving the I Corps in an exposed position, while sending the XI Corps to a line that was equally exposed and difficult to defend. It would have been better had Howard pulled back the I Corps and concentrated his forces. Howard denied that it would have been possible to pull the I Corps back at that time and said things would have gone even worse had he done so. "The repulse of the Oak Ridge line would surely have fallen upon the new line at the cemetery, for the enemy's numbers present were at least two to one," he said. As for the weakness of the XI Corps, Howard argued that if he had not advanced the corps, weak as it was, Early would have had a clear shot at the army's right flank—and Howard had learned all too well about the vulnerability of an army's flank. Better to have even a weak force to delay Early. "A well organized skirmish-line is better than nothing," Howard maintained.[38]

One thing Howard indisputably did right was selecting Cemetery Hill as the spot to post his reserve. And no one could dispute his personal bravery. An Ohio soldier recalled seeing the general on Cemetery Hill encouraging the retreating troops to form a defensive line. Even as enemy bullets from town whistled past him, Howard grabbed the Ohio regiment's flag, placed it under the stump of his right arm, and carried it forward to show the troops where to go. "The whole brigade saw the incident and came forward with a cheer," the soldier recalled.[39]

As the survivors from the I and XI Corps extricated themselves from the streets of Gettysburg and moved south to Cemetery Hill, many were encouraged to see that Winfield Scott Hancock had arrived. Abner Small said Hancock's "imperious and defiant bearing heartened us all." Meade had dispatched him from Taneytown to personally take control of affairs.

He knew Hancock well, trusted him, and had had the opportunity to talk in depth with Hancock that day about the unfolding situation.[40]

Col. Orland Smith was on Cemetery Hill when Hancock arrived. Smith commanded the Second Brigade, Second Division of the XI Corps, and originally hailed from Lewiston, Maine, before he relocated to Ohio in 1852. After Coster's departure, Smith's brigade was the only infantry left from the reserve that Howard had posted on Cemetery Hill. Hancock rode up, praised the men and Smith's dispositions, and then called for the brigade commander. "My corps is on the way, but will not be here in time," he told Smith. "This position should be held at all hazards. Now, Colonel, can you hold it?"

"I think I can," Smith replied.[41]

Otis Howard was not so gratified by Hancock's presence. It felt like a reproach. Howard outranked Hancock and he did not feel he should have to take orders from a junior officer. E. P. Halstead, Doubleday's adjutant, remembered returning to Cemetery Hill after a fruitless search for Buford just as Hancock, "that brilliant, dashing soldier," arrived. Hancock rode up to Howard and told him Meade had sent him to take control of things on the field. Howard "woke up a little and replied that he was senior," Halstead recounted. Hancock said he had his orders from Meade in his pocket. Howard said he didn't doubt that, but added, "You can give no orders while I am here." Hancock knew very well that Meade's orders said he could, but the two men avoided a confrontation. According to Howard's account, he told Hancock to take care of things on the left of the Baltimore Pike, and he would take care of the right. "After a few friendly words between us," said Howard, "Hancock did as I suggested." One must wonder how friendly those words really were. Howard found Hancock's arrival so upsetting he felt compelled to send a message to Meade. Hancock's orders, he wrote, "mortified and disgraced me. Please inform me frankly if you disapprove of my conduct to-day, that I may know what to do."[42]

It appears that Howard attempted to deflect some blame from his corps when he described the situation to Hancock, for when Hancock sent a message back to Meade about the state of affairs he added, "Howard says that Doubleday's command gave way." That sentence may have helped persuade Meade to replace Doubleday with John Newton at the head of the I Corps.

Howard's bruised feelings notwithstanding, Meade's decision to send Hancock turned out to be a wise one. Hancock possessed an air of authority and confidence that the diffident and sometimes self-doubting Otis Howard lacked. One Maine soldier felt that even if Hancock had been wearing civilian clothing, "his order would have been obeyed anywhere, for he had the appearance of a man born to command."[43]

The seniority question would have been a moot point had Henry Slocum, the commander of the XII Corps, responded to the messages Howard had sent him and arrived to take command at Gettysburg. Slocum outranked both Howard and Hancock. Howard knew the XII Corps was nearby—that morning Slocum had moved his corps up the Baltimore Pike to Two Taverns, about five miles away—and he had sent messages to Slocum, asking him to push his men forward. Finally, Howard sent his brother Charles, who found the XII Corps commander a mile or two south of the battlefield. "We had hoped that Slocum would come up to assist in the retreat as he was but two miles away," Charles said later, "but he was too willing to demonstrate the fitness of his name Slow come—in saying he would not assume the responsibility of that day's fighting & of those two corps." By the time Slocum did reach Cemetery Hill, the fighting was over for the day.[44]

It had not been a good day for Adelbert Ames. The division he inherited from Barlow had suffered a casualty rate of nearly 60 percent. When he reported to Howard on Cemetery Hill, Ames said, "I have no division; it is all cut to pieces." Replied Howard, "Do what you can, Ames, to gather the fragments and extend the line to the right." Howard said Ames "succeeded better than he had feared."[45]

Ames was also infuriated by what he considered cowardly behavior by the colonel of the 107th Ohio, Seraphim Meyer. Born in Alsace in 1815, Meyer had moved to the United States in 1828 and became an attorney. He answered Lincoln's 1862 call for troops by raising the 107th Ohio and serving as its colonel. All three of his sons also joined regiments from Ohio.

As might be expected of an attorney with no previous military experience, Meyer was a somewhat eccentric soldier. He was a terrible equestrian, and often seemed to lean forward and grasp his horse's neck in order to remain mounted. He nearly screamed when he gave orders, which were often unintelligible. Some soldiers laughed at him, but Meyer appeared brave enough. At Chancellorsville, he had been shot through the wrist and captured, and he had only recently been paroled and returned to the regiment. As a result, Ames was not familiar with the colonel's peculiarities, and he did not like what he saw. He thought Meyer did a poor job executing orders, and when he saw the foreign-born colonel crouching over his horse's neck while under fire, Ames thought he was dodging the shells and "reproved him at the time for his apparently cowardly conduct." He thought Meyer "was not at all cool" and found his orders "not given in an intelligible manner." When Ames assumed command of Barlow's division, he passed Meyer over and handed the brigade to Harris of the 75th Ohio. Meyer confronted Ames on Cemetery Hill. "Mr. Meyer, so long as I have a Sergeant left to command the Second Brigade your services will not be required," Ames told him. "Your place is in the rear." (Ames had Meyer arrested on July 5, but the resulting court-martial acquitted him of all charges. He resigned from the army in February 1864.)[46]

Ames's own official report of the day's fight is relatively terse. He devoted fewer than 200 words to the events of July 1. Among them: "My brigade was ordered to a number of different positions, and finally it formed in rear of some woods, near a small stream some half a mile from town. From this position we were driven, the men of the First Brigade of this division running through lines of the regiments of my brigade (the Second), and thereby creating considerable confusion."[47]

At the end of that trying day, Ames found space in the cemetery gatehouse and went to sleep. He shared the room with Charles Wainwright, who handled the artillery for the I Corps. Wainwright took time to observe the young Maine general over the next few days. "I found him the best kind of man to be associated with, cool and clear in his own judgment, gentlemanly, and without the smallest desire to interfere," said Wainwright. "We consulted together, but during the whole time we were here he never once attempted to presume on his superior rank. Ames is a gentleman; and a strange thing in the army, I did not hear him utter an oath of any kind during the three days!"[48]

Fairly or not, the soldiers of the XI Corps had done little on July 1 to salvage their reputation. "The eleventh Corps, whatever may have been said of it, was entirely unreliable and quite unmanageable," said Lt. Col. Charles H. Morgan, Hancock's chief of staff, in a typical assessment. "General Howard was himself apparently despondent and his brother, Major Howard could not restrain his mortification at the behavior of his corps."[49]

There were mitigating circumstances. They had been outnumbered by the Confederates and were attacked from two directions. And many soldiers of the XI Corps had fought well. A soldier of the 61st Georgia, who had been part of the force that drove Barlow's division from Blocher's Knoll, said the XI Corps soldiers had initially "stood firm," and when they did retreat they did it "in fine order, shooting at us as they retreated. They were harder to drive than we had ever known them before."[50]

Historians of the battle tend to feel that the XI Corps was unjustly criticized. "Despite its defeat, the rank and file of the 11th Corps had fought with courage and frequently with tenacity," wrote historian D. Scott Hartwig. "Many were the men and officers who distinguished themselves in the fight." Among them was Adelbert Ames. "But theirs had been a hopeless mission from the start, and even the stoutest courage could not have staved off the defeat that ultimately enveloped them."[51]

———

Shortly after Charles Hunt reached his sister's house on York Street, the Union forces fell back through the town to Cemetery Hill, and the Confederates moved in to occupy Gettysburg. As the situation stabilized and the town grew quieter, the people in the bank vault screwed up their courage and ventured out. Hunt watched through a crack in a door as two Rebel soldiers entered his sister's house and raided the pantry. "I did not care to remonstrate," he said. He went to bed in the front room of his sister's house, and a doctor arrived and treated his wound. Probing with his fingers, the doctor recovered not only the bullet, but also the piece from Hunt's Colt revolver. As the doctor worked, two Confederate officers arrived. Hunt's sister met them on top of the front steps. They asked if there were any Union soldiers in the house, and she confessed that her brother was there, but wounded. They asked to see him. "They were very courteous and expressed regret for my hurt," Hunt recalled. "One of them said to the other, 'Had we not better parole him?' To which the reply was, 'We can do that some other time. There will be plenty of time.' From which I judged that they thought they had come to stay."

As the Confederates were leaving, one of them turned to Hunt's sister. "Take good care of your brother and don't let him fight us any more," he said. Recalled Hunt, "Mary replied that she would take good care of me but she could not promise as to the rest of it."[52]

Late in the afternoon of July 1, as the I and XI Corps were making their futile attempts to hold back the Confederates outside Gettysburg, John Sedgwick and the army's VI Corps had reached Manchester, Maryland, about 20 miles from Meade's headquarters at Taneytown and 36 miles from the growing battle. Sedgwick sent Thomas Hyde over to the new commander's headquarters to receive orders and intelligence. Hyde left Manchester a little reluctantly—some officers were arranging to hold a ball with some of the local women and Hyde had been looking forward to attending. But duty was duty, and he set off with a member of Meade's staff to find the new commander of the army. It was dark by the time he arrived. Along the way he ran into Hancock, who had left Gettysburg to report to Meade in person once Henry Slocum finally reached Cemetery Hill. Hancock told Hyde about the death of Reynolds and the day's fighting. At Meade's headquarters, Seth Williams, the Augusta native who was serving as the new commander's adjutant general, ushered Hyde into Meade's tent. Hyde recalled finding Meade standing by a map-covered table with several of his generals. (Hyde's memory failed him, though, when he said those generals included Howard, Sickles, Slocum, and Sykes, none of whom were at Taneytown then.) "General Meade's solemn bearing impressed me very much, and I felt some awe at the circumstances in which I was placed, being little more than a boy in age," Hyde recalled years later. When he left Taneytown around midnight with orders for Sedgwick, Hyde felt as if he "had something to do with the fate of the nation."

The young major experienced a tense ride through the night as he searched for Sedgwick and the VI Corps. Jeb Stuart's cavalry had passed through the region, and several times Hyde hid in the woods when he heard approaching horsemen, thinking they might be Rebels. Around three in the morning he peered out from a hiding place behind a tree and saw, to his great relief, the familiar sight of Sedgwick's trademark straw hat, with the general beneath it and long lines of marching soldiers trailing along behind. Sedgwick would have continued on to Taneytown had Hyde not delivered Meade's orders to march directly to Gettysburg. In his own small way, Hyde thought he helped win the battle. The march to Taneytown would have added miles to what was already going to be a brutal march, and the detour would have made it unlikely that the VI Corps could have reached the battlefield in time to support the fighting on July 2. "We all like to think ourselves of some use, and such were my youthful speculations," Hyde wrote. "General Sedgwick, though unusually stern and quiet, gave me a kind word, and we turned the head of the column to make a cross-cut of a few miles to the Baltimore Pike. Then began one of the hardest marches we ever knew—thirty-six miles in dust and unusual heat; but the men pressed on with vigor and courage through it all, feeling themselves on Northern soil again and feeling that we were expected to decide the victory."[53]

General Meade made his own late-night journey to Gettysburg, riding through the bright moonlight along the Taneytown Road. He reached the gatehouse on Cemetery Hill sometime around midnight. The lights from hundreds of campfires kindled by enemy soldiers flickered in the distance. Howard rode out to meet the army commander with some trepidation, worried that he would be rebuked for his decisions that day. He asked Meade if he had any reason for not approving the actions he had taken. Meade assured him he was not interested in placing blame on anyone. Howard took that as the closest to praise he would get. He told

Meade he thought the army's current position was strong, now that the XII and III Corps had arrived. "I am confident we can hold this position," Howard said.

Slocum was there, too, and he seconded Howard's opinion. "It is good for defense," he said.

Dan Sickles had ridden up, and added his view. "It is a good place to fight from, general!"

"I am glad to hear you say so, gentlemen," Meade said, "for it is too late to leave it."[54]

Otis Howard snatched a few hours of sleep on the ground near the cemetery gatehouse, along with Sickles and Slocum. Before the generals bedded down for the night, Elizabeth Thorn, the wife of the cemetery caretaker, served them bread and coffee. Mrs. Thorn was six months pregnant and her husband was away fighting for the Union. "Those refreshments have never been forgotten," Howard said years later. After the generals had eaten, Thorn asked Howard if he thought she should leave the gatehouse. Howard pondered the question for a moment and then turned to the other generals, "Comrades, I say stay." He told Thorn that if she packed up her best things he would send some men to bring them to the cellar for protection. "I guess you call all *best,*" he said, smiling. Thorn was not charmed. "Some I call better than others," she replied.[55]

John Chase, who had fought so valiantly with the 5th Maine Battery at Chancellorsville, had never been particularly religious when he had been growing up. That changed at Gettysburg. He finally saw the light when he heard a chaplain preaching to the men on the night of July 1. Chase went behind his cannon, knelt on the ground, and said his first prayer. When he stood up, Chase said, "I was a very different boy than I was when I knelt down. I felt light as a bird; all the darkness and doubts had disappeared, and I was rejoicing in God's holy light." Chase's newfound faith would soon undergo a severe test.[56]

Elected as Maine's governor in 1860, Israel Washburn doubted the seceding Southern states would resort to war. He was overly optimistic. LIBRARY OF CONGRESS

Abraham Lincoln's Maine-born vice president, Hannibal Hamlin, told a friend that war was coming, "as sure as the sun will rise tomorrow." LIBRARY OF CONGRESS

Maine Adjutant General John Hodsdon proved to be a capable administrator, adept at handling the huge bureaucratic task of getting the state's soldiers into the field. MAINE STATE ARCHIVES

Thomas Hyde was studying in Chicago when Abraham Lincoln was elected president. Hyde later joined the 7th Maine and served on the staff of VI Corps commander John Sedgwick. MAINE STATE ARCHIVES

Maine-born Owen Lovejoy became an ardent abolitionist and "the greatest stump orator I ever heard," according to Thomas Hyde. LIBRARY OF CONGRESS

After leading the 2nd Maine, Nathaniel Jackson became colonel of the 5th regiment. The soldiers in his new command nearly mutinied when they heard the news. LIBRARY OF CONGRESS

Oliver Otis Howard's religious devotion led some to call him "The Christian General." His men called him "Old Prayer Book." LIBRARY OF CONGRESS

Charles Howard served under his brother during the war. "We always move on in perfect harmony," Otis Howard said. Both men were wounded at the Battle of Seven Pines. LIBRARY OF CONGRESS

Abner Small wrote unvarnished accounts of his war experiences with the 3rd and the 16th Maine regiments. Unlike much of the 16th Maine, he managed to avoid being captured at Gettysburg. MAINE STATE ARCHIVES

Hiram Berry became an exemplary soldier with the Army of the Potomac, although his experiences during McClellan's Peninsula Campaign nearly broke his health. LIBRARY OF CONGRESS

Elijah Walker Col. 4th Me. Vols.

Elijah Walker was Hiram Berry's business partner in Rockland, and he followed Berry into the army. He commanded the 4th Maine at Gettysburg and was wounded defending Devil's Den. MAINE STATE ARCHIVES

Samuel Heintzelman was Otis Howard's first division commander. One soldier said of Heintzelman, "Ugly as his pictures are, they flatter him." LIBRARY OF CONGRESS

Irvin McDowell wanted a little time to test the machinery of his army. He did not get it, and the result was the disastrous Battle of First Bull Run. LIBRARY OF CONGRESS

Although born in Massachusetts, Erasmus Keyes had attended West Point as a cadet from Maine. The National Guard base in Augusta is named after him. LIBRARY OF CONGRESS

After Adlebert Ames was assigned to command the 20th Maine, he earned a reputation as a strict disciplinarian. He was determined to whip his regiment into shape. LIBRARY OF CONGRESS

Abraham Lincoln grew tired of him, but George Brinton McClellan commanded the loyalty of his men. One Maine soldier said his regiment "would follow him to the death." LIBRARY OF CONGRESS

The son of a Maine senator, Samuel Fessenden had experienced some adventure in "Bleeding Kansas" before the war. He was killed at Second Bull Run. MAINE STATE ARCHIVES

Selden Connor spent an uneventful time in a Vermont regiment before becoming lieutenant colonel of the 7th Maine. After the war he became governor of Maine. LIBRARY OF CONGRESS

Although not well-respected as a soldier, Hiram Berdan made an impact on the war with his sharpshooter regiments, which included riflemen from Maine. LIBRARY OF CONGRESS

Edwin Sumner was known as "Old Bull." He was a brave soldier but was also promoted beyond his capabilities, as Otis Howard learned at Antietam. LIBRARY OF CONGRESS

2209. Gen. Phil. Kearney. Photograph taken in 1862.
[FOR DESCRIPTION OF THIS VIEW SEE THE OTHER SIDE OF THIS CARD.]

Philip Kearny lost his left arm fighting in Mexico, but he learned to grasp his reins in his teeth and wield his sword with his right hand. LIBRARY OF CONGRESS

Joseph Hooker liked to fight—and to connive against his superior officers. "He is unmistakably a great man," noted one Maine soldier. LIBRARY OF CONGRESS

Winfield Scott Hancock had a natural air of command and a reputation as a fluent swearer. His arrival at Gettysburg on July 1 to take charge left Otis Howard feeling "mortified and disgraced." LIBRARY OF CONGRESS

Brig Gen Hiram Burnham

Hiram Burnham was an experienced lumberman. His men called him "The Grizzly." At the Battle of Chancellorsville, Burnham led the "Light Division" that captured Marye's Heights. LIBRARY OF CONGRESS

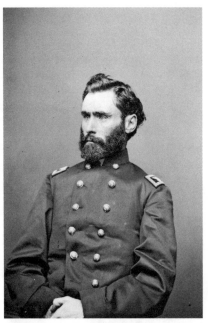

On the Peninsula, Colonel Charles Roberts of the 2nd Maine noted that "we could not cross the Chickahominy without making a stand." The stand came at the Battle of Gaines' Mill. LIBRARY OF CONGRESS

Probably the most famous soldier from Maine, Joshua Lawrence Chamberlain had never led his regiment in battle until the 20th Maine found itself on the south slope of Little Round Top on July 2, 1863. LIBRARY OF CONGRESS

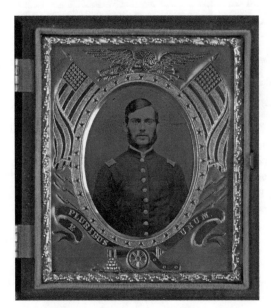

Thomas Chamberlain was the youngest Chamberlain brother; he also served in the 20th Maine. LIBRARY OF CONGRESS

A lawyer in Rockland when he enlisted, Samuel Keene kept a meticulous journal while serving in the 20th Maine. He often complained of feeling "blue" and longed for home. MAINE STATE ARCHIVES

Bowdoin graduate Ellis Spear was a teacher in Wiscasset when he joined the 20th Maine in 1862. At first he bristled over Adelbert Ames's treatment of his soldiers. MAINE STATE ARCHIVES

George Bisbee was living in Dixfield when he joined the 16th Maine. He was wounded at Fredericksburg and taken prisoner at Gettysburg. MAINE STATE ARCHIVES

A no-nonsense regular, Edwin Mason took command of the 7th Maine. He and Thomas Hyde clashed after Antietam, with Mason believing the young major exceeded his authority. LIBRARY OF CONGRESS

Charles Tilden, the colonel of the 16th Maine "could be both brave and gentle, severe yet just," according to one of his men. He was captured at Gettysburg. MAINE STATE ARCHIVES

John C. Caldwell was born in Vermont but was teaching in East Machias, Maine, when war broke out. Hancock sent Caldwell's II Corps brigade to support the fighting in the Wheatfield. LIBRARY OF CONGRESS

Philippe de Régis Dénis de Keredern de Trobriand was a cultured Frenchman who commanded the 17th Maine's brigade at Gettysburg. Some of his men called him "Froggy." LIBRARY OF CONGRESS

A farm boy from Topsham, Holman Melcher was teaching school when he joined the 20th Maine. "I dread the scenes of another bloody field," he wrote to his brother after Fredericksburg. MAINE STATE ARCHIVES

Charles Mattocks joined the 17th Maine as a first lieutenant. One soldier thought he was "very pompous and had yards and yards of superfluous red tape about him." MAINE STATE ARCHIVES

When Ambrose Burnside received command of the Army of the Potomac, he told Otis Howard it was not "a fit subject for congratulation." LIBRARY OF CONGRESS

David Bell Birney commanded the 17th Maine's division at Gettysburg and took over the III Corps after Daniel Sickles was wounded. LIBRARY OF CONGRESS

Major Henry Cunningham of the 19th Maine fought to get promotions for both himself and his son, Edward, leading to some turmoil within the regiment. MAINE STATE ARCHIVES

Born in Standish, VI Corps division commander Albion Howe was "not a commander under whom one would desire very ardently to serve," said one soldier. LIBRARY OF CONGRESS

Francis Heath commanded the 19th Maine at Gettysburg. His brother William had been killed at Gaines' Mill. LIBRARY OF CONGRESS

After Daniel Sickles took command of the III Corps, one of his Maine soldiers said he was "every inch a soldier and looks like a game cock." LIBRARY OF CONGRESS

Carl Schurz had hoped to head the XI Corps but instead commanded a division under Otis Howard. He tried to warn Howard about the danger of a flank attack at Chancellorsville. LIBRARY OF CONGRESS

As commander of the VI Corps, John Sedgwick earned the respect of his subordinates, who called him "Uncle John." He was considered capable and dependable, but cautious. LIBRARY OF CONGRESS

Francis C. Barlow became Adelbert Ames's division commander in the XI Corps. The two shared an appreciation for strict discipline and a dislike for the Germans in their commands. LIBRARY OF CONGRESS

Calvin Douty hailed from Dover, Maine. At the age of 48 he was not in a hurry to join the army, but he ended up in command of the 1st Maine Cavalry. MAINE STATE ARCHIVES

Strong Vincent commanded the 20th Maine's brigade and took personal responsibility to take his men to defend Little Round Top at Gettysburg on July 2. LIBRARY OF CONGRESS

At Gettysburg, Walter Morrill was captain of the 20th Maine's Co. B. His men gave the Rebels a rude surprise near the end of the fighting for Little Round Top. MAINE STATE ARCHIVES

John Reynolds was killed on the first day at Gettysburg, leaving Otis Howard the senior Union commander on the field. LIBRARY OF CONGRESS

Lt. Col. James A. Hall.
1st Regt. Me. Mtd Arty.

Captain James Hall came from Damariscotta. He said his 2nd Maine Battery "fought like the d____ never better" on the first day at Gettysburg. MAINE STATE ARCHIVES

A division commander in the I Corps, John C. Robinson "was the hairiest general I ever saw," said one of his Maine soldiers. LIBRARY OF CONGRESS

Moses B. Lakeman was the son of Hallowell's mayor and he commanded the 3rd Maine at Gettysburg. David Birney extolled Lakeman as "a gallant officer" with "great decision of character." MAINE STATE ARCHIVES

Seaman-turned-artilleryman Freeman McGilvery cobbled together an artillery line late on July 2 at Gettysburg and helped save the Union position on Cemetery Ridge. MAINE STATE ARCHIVES

Edwin B. Dow expected to assume command of the 6th Maine Battery, but Freeman McGilvery fought to block his promotion. Dow threatened to press charges against McGilvery. MAINE STATE ARCHIVES

CHAPTER 12

The 17th Maine Finds a Wall

Our flag was pierced by thirty-two bullets and two pieces of shell, and its staff was shot off, but Sergt. Henry O. Ripley, its bearer, did not allow the color to touch the ground, nor did he receive a scratch, though all the others of the color guard were killed or wounded.
—Elijah Walker, 4th Maine

Otis Howard was up before dawn on July 2 to accompany Meade on a reconnaissance of the battlefield. Henry Hunt, the army's artillery chief, and Capt. William Paine also rode along with Meade. The rising sun was reddening the eastern sky, promising a hot day ahead. Occasional artillery fire or the crack of a skirmisher's musket broke the morning silence. As the officers rode though the slumbering army, Captain Paine sketched the landscape to make maps for the corps commanders. They went to the left of the Union line, riding south down Cemetery Ridge. Then they went back to the highest point in the cemetery so Meade could study the surrounding terrain through his field glasses. Confederate artillery opened a cannonade on the Union lines from Blocher's Knoll. Union guns returned the fire. The sleeping armies were stirring, preparing for another day of bloodletting. Howard sent an aide over to the cemetery gatehouse to tell Elizabeth Thorn to vacate her home and get out of harm's way.

The landscape Meade studied revealed the battlefield's split personality. The fields to the north of town, where the I and XI Corps had struggled the day before, were largely smooth and featureless with the exception of a few hills and rises and the gash of the railroad cut. If anything, the wide fields between Cemetery and Seminary Ridges were even more featureless, broken only by the Emmitsburg Road and various farm fences. Things were quite different south of town, where the land presented a wilder landscape of tumbled boulders, swampy morasses, rugged outcrops, and rock-studded fields. Maine troops would not see action on the steep, rocky slopes of Culp's Hill, although a New Englander, Rhode Island's George Sears Greene, would play a vital role in saving this important position for the Union. Farther south, the dominating features were the two Round Tops, the pair of rocky hills that rose at the southern terminus of Cemetery Ridge. The smaller hill was to the north. It was known by many names—Granite Spur, Sugar Loaf Hill, and High Knob among them—but history remembers it only as Little Round Top. Its eastern slope was wooded, but the western side had been stripped of trees, revealing a craggy face strewn with rocks and boulders of all shapes and sizes. Any troops assaulting from the west would face a difficult climb, with the huge rocks making it nearly impossible to retain any kind of organized line.

Little Round Top descended on its south side into a little wooded valley. Beyond lay Big Round Top. It was also strewn with rocks, some of them as big as houses. Big Round Top was thickly wooded, so despite its greater height, it offered comparatively little tactical advantage to any occupying forces. A sluggish waterway called Plum Run meandered through a swampy bottomland along the eastern base of the Round Tops. This region had yet to gain its new names—the Valley of Death and the Slaughter Pen.

One of the most striking features of the landscape was Devil's Den, which lay just to the west of Plum Run. Huge boulders lay in a jumbled mass, one on top of another, like playthings left behind by the Titans. Why or even when it became known as Devil's Den remains unknown; one story says it got the name from a huge black snake, big enough to swallow a dog, that lived somewhere within the warren of boulders and sometimes emerged to bask on the sun-warmed rocks.[1]

Stretching away to the north from the rocks was a spur of land called Houck's Ridge, which pointed in the direction of the soon-to-be capitalized wheat field. Off to the west, uneven fields broken up by more rocks and boulders stretched off in the direction of Seminary Ridge. Various woods, orchards, and farms dotted this sometimes wild-looking landscape, soon to be the scene of almost unimaginable blood and carnage.

The remnants of the 10th Maine—which contained the 1st Maine within its regimental DNA—reached Gettysburg with Henry Slocum and the XII Corps. Not a single one of its soldiers fired a gun during the battle, although several of them contributed to the fight by wielding notebooks.

The two-year men of the 10th Maine had been mustered out in April, but some 240 or so still had time left on their enlistments. There were not enough for a regiment, so—amid much protest and grumbling—they were placed into three companies and designated as the 10th Maine Battalion and assigned as the provost guard for the XII Corps. Its men served as guards, clerks, and orderlies—the kind of mundane tasks that kept the machinery of an army in motion, but rarely received mention in official reports. When the corps was on the march, the 10th Maine Battalion took up the rear, behind even the wagons with the hospital supplies. When the corps set up camp, the battalion pitched their tents near Slocum's headquarters. "A detail into this guard would ordinarily be considered desirable by a soldier in search of adventure and a free and easy life," noted regimental historian John Mead Gould.[2]

In command was Capt. John D. Beardsley, who had joined Company D of the 10th Maine back in 1861. Many of the company's soldiers were hardy lumbermen from Aroostook County, but there was also a contingent of British soldiers from New Brunswick. Beardsley was a bit of both. He had worked as a lumberman, but he had gained military experience in the provincial militia in New Brunswick. He was also handy with a broadsword. One of his men remembered that he "had a sabre as long as a scythe." Beardsley had been captured at Cedar Mountain, but was exchanged.[3]

July 1 found the battalion at Littlestown, about 10 miles from Gettysburg. The night before, Beardsley had received about 50 Confederate prisoners who had been captured near York; in the morning he took the rebel officers to a hotel in town and got them breakfast. Once corps commander Henry Slocum finally reached Gettysburg later that day, he established his headquarters at Powers Hill, south of town on the Baltimore Pike, and the 10th Maine Battalion established a line across the pike and went to work gathering up skulkers and stragglers. That night, 30 men were dispatched to escort Confederate prisoners away from the battlefield, which required an all-night march.

Late in the morning on July 2, Slocum asked for six volunteers from the battalion for "dangerous duty." They were told to leave their guns behind but take notebooks and advance as far as the Confederate lines, taking notes about the local farms, houses, and springs. If captured, their cover story was to be that they were searching for provisions. The volunteers ventured around the right of the Union line on Culp's Hill, hiking through woods and sometimes climbing trees to get a better view. Four of them were approaching one house when Sgt. James F. Tarr spied Rebels lurking on the other side. He pretended not to see them, and casually warned his men to get ready to run. At a signal they all broke for the woods as rifle fire erupted behind them.[4]

The members of the 10th Maine Battalion "never claimed more than they performed at Gettysburg or anywhere else," said regimental historian John Mead Gould. "They simply did what they were ordered to do," and they did it "promptly and well."[5]

⁓

The 4th Maine reached Gettysburg after dark on July 1, at the end of what brigade commander Hobart Ward described as "a forced march over horrible roads," and camped for the night. The regiment got little chance for rest, though, before it received orders to push forward and establish a picket line just west of the Emmitsburg Road. From this exposed position in the predawn hours of July 2, Col. Elijah Walker could hear the enemy moving on his front. When dawn broke, Rebel skirmishers opened fire on his men. Walker sent back messages to headquarters

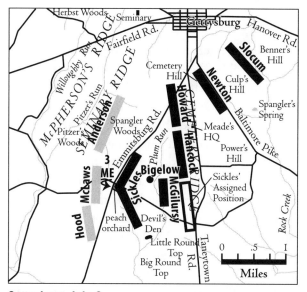

Gettysburg, July 2

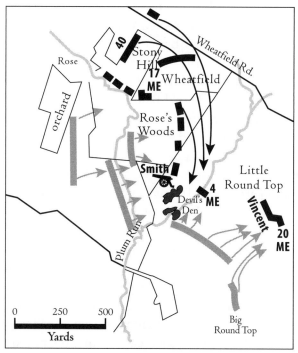

Gettysburg, July 2, The Union Left

saying he had enemy soldiers in front of him, but the answer he received said that was not possible. The enemy had fallen back from that position.[6]

Walker probably felt that was typical of what he could expect from his superiors. He had little respect for his division commander, David Bell Birney, "a sarcastic Philadelphia lawyer" who he felt was as "brave as a lion, when in a safe place, but in danger he wilted." He didn't much like Gov. Abner Coburn, either, feeling that Coburn "yielded to the influence of political demagogues back home, and commissioned men who were the reverse of worthy and desirable." If some of those unworthy men questioned the reports of soldiers who knew what they were talking about, it probably didn't surprise Walker much.[7]

Someone must have paid attention to Walker's report, though, for around nine, Gen. Hiram Berdan, making a rare appearance on a battlefield, arrived with 250 men from the 1st United States Sharpshooters. Berdan had received orders from Birney to drive the Rebels on the other side of the Emmitsburg Road out of a patch of woods owned by a farmer named Samuel Pitzer, and he wanted Walker's men to help. Walker, not one to hide his opinions, told Berdan he did not think that was such a good idea. He believed his superiors had underestimated the number of the enemy he was facing. "I convinced him it was foolish for us to make an advance," Walker said. He told Berdan it would be smarter to attempt a flank attack rather than a frontal one. Berdan agreed with Walker—or at least that's what Walker said—and he departed to report to Birney.[8]

The task that Walker had deflected fell instead to another regiment from the Pine Tree State: the 3rd Maine, under Col. Moses Lakeman, which was also part of Ward's brigade. Sometime around eleven Lakeman received orders to support about 100 of Berdan's sharpshooters who were going to move across the Emmitsburg Road and check out Pitzer's Woods. The sharpshooters took the advance, with the Maine soldiers trailing. As Berdan's men approached farm buildings near the Emmitsburg Road, they encountered a local boy who warned them that Confederate soldiers lay waiting "in rows" in the woods. Some of the sharpshooters told the lad he was talking nonsense and continued forward.

The sharpshooters realized soon enough that the boy knew what he was talking about when they spotted men wearing butternut and gray moving through the trees. They were Alabamians of Cadmus Wilcox's brigade. The sharpshooters opened fire, and the 3rd Maine came running up at double-quick in support. The Union soldiers drove back the Rebel skirmishers, but could see three lines of Rebel infantry advancing beyond the trees. "We felt that the life of the Nation was at stake, and every man in the ranks was conscious of personal responsibility," said one man. When the two sides were about 300 yards apart they commenced firing. The Maine soldiers were not pleased to realize that the sharpshooters had pretty much monopolized the trees to shelter behind.[9]

Cpl. Jonathan Newcomb Jr. of the 3rd Maine's Company A had moved about a hundred yards into the woods when the regiment received orders to deploy as skirmishers. The firing soon became general. Newcomb said he saw General Berdan on a big white horse gallop along the line between the 3rd Maine and the sharpshooters as the bullets flew all around. "After the work began and as I stood in my place, loading and firing, I looked to my right and the only man I could see was John Little," Newcomb recalled. "His face was as white as a sheet of paper. I supposed he had his mortal wound then." Newcomb managed to squeeze behind a tree next to a sharpshooter, and watched as a Rebel regiment advanced his way. When Newcomb jumped out from behind the tree, he found a dozen enemy rifles aimed his way. Newcomb dove to the ground and the bullets flew over him. The sharpshooter was not so lucky, and he fell with a badly wounded knee.

After a short but intense fight of 20 or 25 minutes, the Union troops withdrew. The 3rd Maine had suffered 48 casualties, most of them prisoners. One of them was Newcomb. Taken to a Rebel hospital, he helped nurse the wounded sharpshooter and a mortally wounded private from Company I. The dying private asked Newcomb to write to his wife and say he died happy, "and to keep the promise she made before he enlisted," whatever that might have been. Newcomb ended up a prisoner on Belle Isle in Richmond.[10]

Sgt. Hannibal Johnson was also taken prisoner. Johnson had been 19 and working in a dry goods store in Hallowell when the news of Fort Sumter jolted him with a "thrill of outraged patriotism." Even though he weighed a mere 112 pounds, Johnson was determined to enlist. The state, however, was equally determined that he wouldn't. His brother, Capt. Gorham S. Johnson, was recruiting a company for the 3rd Maine, but he turned Hannibal down flat, saying he wasn't physically fit to be a soldier. But Johnson possessed that streak of cussedness typical of a Maine Yankee. He applied next to Capt. Henry G. Staples of Company B, who also said no. Johnson then wrote Adj. Gen. John Hodsdon. While not encouraging, Hodsdon grudgingly approved Hannibal's recruitment as a private in Company B. By the time of Gettysburg, he had been promoted to sergeant.[11]

Johnson was retreating from Pitzer's Woods with his regiment when one of the men in his company, Nathan Call, fell with a bullet to the hip. He called to Johnson for help. Johnson and another soldier from the company, John Jones, seated Call on a musket and had him wrap his arms around their shoulders so they could hoist him up on their improvised litter. It appeared they were going to escape, until Jones fell with a bullet to the head. Johnson realized he could not get Call to safety alone, but before he could take his own chances some Alabamians surrounded him and sent him back as a prisoner.[12]

The survivors of the 3rd Maine moved back across the Emmitsburg Road to rejoin their brigade, but then they received orders to retrace their steps until they reached a peach orchard on a bit of high ground east of the road. The little orchard, the fruit still green on the trees, was about 300 yards by 150 yards in expanse. Its owner was farmer Joseph Sherfy, whose house and barn stood on the other side of the Emmitsburg Road. The orchard's western edge lay along the road, with the Millerstown (Wheatfield) Road bordering it on the north.

Dan Sickles had been eyeing Sherfy's peach orchard with considerable interest. He did not like the position Meade had assigned his III Corps. Sickles was supposed to form to the left of the II Corps on the line where Cemetery Ridge largely loses its ridge-like qualities and descends to a low point before rising again to the northern slope of Little Round Top. Sherfy's peach orchard offered a bit of high ground to his front. It was also an open space that would provide a good place for artillery and prevent the Rebels from springing any surprises as they had done at Chancellorsville. Sickles seemed haunted by the ghosts of the battle from two months earlier. When he looked out from Cemetery Ridge and saw the peach orchard, he probably thought about what happened when the Confederates occupied Hazel Grove and used its high ground as an artillery platform from which to shell the Army of the Potomac. Berdan's report about the encounter in Pitzer's Woods only reinforced Sickles's concerns that the Rebels were about to fall on his left and capture the high ground on his front.

The III Corps commander decided his assigned line along Cemetery Ridge was no place to fight a battle. Without permission from Meade, he decided to move his two divisions forward, break contact with the II Corps on his right, and occupy the ground to his front. His men began to move to their new positions sometime around two o'clock. On his right, Hancock and John Gibbon of the II Corps watched with astonishment. "We could not conceive what it meant, as we had heard of no orders for an advance and did not understand the meaning of making this break in our line," Gibbon said. In Sickles's new position, Andrew Humphreys' division took the III Corps' right along the Emmitsburg Road and down to Sherfy's peach orchard, and David Birney's division stretched from the peach orchard, across the wheat field, and into the tumbled boulders of Devil's Den to the southeast.[13]

Sickles's move remains controversial today. The advance not only broke the integrity of Meade's line—the fishhook-shaped defense that ran from Culp's Hill, around Cemetery Hill, and down Cemetery Ridge to the Round Tops—it also put the III Corps in an exposed and extended position that would be difficult if not impossible to hold. At Sherfy's peach orchard, where the soldiers of the 3rd Maine waited out the afternoon, Sickles's line formed an angle—a salient—where it changed direction from roughly parallel with the Emmitsburg Road to stretch southeast in the direction of Devil's Den. The III Corps was now roughly in the shape of a V, with the peach orchard at the point. In a sense, Sickles's advance was like Barlow's move from the day before, but on a much larger scale. Before the day was out, many Maine soldiers would be dead or wounded in consequence.

Ironically, the soldiers in Pitzer's Woods who so alarmed Dan Sickles were not part of the force that Lee had sent to fall on the Union left.

Wilcox's Alabamians belonged to A. P. Hill's III Corps, and the initial attack on July 2 was the responsibility of James Longstreet's I Corps. As is the case with Sickles, Longstreet's actions on July 2 remain a controversial topic among Gettysburg historians. Justly or not, critics charge him with moving slowly and grudgingly after Lee disregarded his advice to move from Gettysburg in a big flanking maneuver and place the Southern army between Meade and Washington. Even if sulkiness was not a factor, Longstreet's attack was delayed when it was discovered that his troops could be observed by the flag-waving Union signal officers on Little Round Top. That would spoil the surprise Lee planned to spring on Meade. Longstreet had to stop, backtrack, and take an alternate route. As a result, it was approaching 4:00 P.M. before he had his two divisions in place to pounce on what he hoped was the Army of the Potomac's unsuspecting left.

John Bell Hood's division would open the attack, with Evander Law's brigade of Alabama regiments on the right, and Jerome Robertson's Texas brigade—Hood's former command—next to the Alabamians. The brigades of Henry Benning and George Anderson were to the left. Whether by accident or intent, the Confederate offense would unfold *en echelon*, meaning the brigades would advance one by one, like successive waves hitting a beach—the first crashing ashore, followed by the next down the line, and then the next and the next. Such an attack was designed to keep an enemy off-balance and prevent him from sending troops from one part of the line to support another.

Longstreet instructed his division commanders to attack up the Emmitsburg Road. This is what Lee wanted, and Longstreet had not been able to change his mind. It turned out, though, that Lee's plans were based on faulty reconnaissance. In addition, the Rebels hadn't expected to find Sickles's men in the peach orchard. Division commanders Hood and Lafayette McLaws both argued vehemently to shift the attack more to the right toward the Round Tops, but Longstreet insisted he had to follow Lee's orders.

During the advance across the rocky and uneven terrain from the direction of the Emmitsburg Road, Law's brigade began to diverge from its line of battle and veer off to its right. The 4th and 5th Texas from Robertson's brigade, attempting to maintain contact with Law, also headed to the right, while Robertson's other two regiments, the 1st Texas and 3rd Arkansas, continued in the direction of Devil's Den. Law attempted to correct his wandering line by having the two regiments on the right, the 44th and 48th Alabama, halt and march behind the rest of the brigade and reform on its left. In fact, they ended moving so far to the left they went beyond the 4th and 5th Texas and headed for a collision course with the defenders of Devil's Den, including Elijah Walker and the 4th Maine.

When an exploding shell knocked Hood out of the battle with severe wounds, Law took over division command, leading to more confusion for the attackers. But, as Edwin Coddington pointed out in his land-mark study of the Gettysburg campaign, Rebel mistakes weren't the only reason why the attack—"the best three hours' fighting ever done by any troops on any battlefield," in Longstreet's perhaps biased estimation—was thrown into disorder. Coddington also thought that much credit was due to "the fierce resistance by Yankee soldiers." And those Yankees included several regiments from Maine.[14]

The Maine sharpshooters—Company D of the 2nd U.S. Sharp-shooters—had done plenty of marching and a bit of fighting since leaving their camp of instruction in Washington back in March 1862. Their original commander, James Fessenden, had left the company to serve as an aide to Gen. David Hunter, and command fell on Jacob McClure, the former Rockland stonecutter. McClure was in command when Company D fought during John Pope's Second Bull Run campaign and when it served with Hooker's I Corps at Antietam. "We fought continually for four hours," McClure reported about the fight at Sharpsburg, in which the company lost six men. At Fredericksburg, the company served as skirmishers for General Franklin's force south of the town.[15]

After Fredericksburg, the two sharpshooter regiments were offi-cially combined into a brigade under Berdan's command, and assigned to the III Corps' Third Division. At Chancellorsville, they once again pushed forward ahead of the main Union force and found themselves surrounded. "After sharp fighting in the night, we opened communica-tion with General Hooker, and fell back on the morning of the 3d to Chancellorsville," wrote McClure. For the rest of the battle, Company

D dueled with Confederate sharpshooters, and they retreated across the river with the rest of Hooker's army.[16]

By the time of Gettysburg, the nearly 100 men of Company D had been reduced to only 26. War, disease, and even a railroad accident had eliminated the rest. Company D was not part of the 1st United States Sharpshooters, which fought in Pitzer's Woods with the 3rd Maine. Instead, the 2nd regiment received orders on July 2 to take a position near the north end of Little Round Top, with Company D stationed in the Plum Run valley that ran toward Devil's Den. Around 2:00 P.M., the regiment began moving forward toward the Emmitsburg Road, Company D on the right. The men stopped near the stone farmhouse of John Slyder and his family. There they remained, in advance of the rest of the Union forces, resting quietly, until long lines of Confederate infantry appeared on their front, marching steadily in their direction.

The sharpshooters were now armed with the efficient Sharp's carbine, and even though they were greatly outnumbered by the Rebel line that threatened to overwhelm them, the green-clad riflemen poured a destructive fire into the enemy. "Their fire was so severe that one Confederate regiment broke three times before it could advance," said the company's history in *Maine at Gettysburg*. They were merely delaying the inevitable, though, and the sharpshooters were forced to make a fighting retreat toward Devil's Den. There Company D fell in with skirmishers from Elijah Walker's 4th Maine. Some of them were captured there. Other sharpshooter companies from the 2nd regiment continued falling back to Big Round Top, on their way to a rendezvous with Company B of the 20th Maine.[17]

Things had remained calm for 4th Maine as the afternoon wore on. Some of Walker's men captured and killed a heifer from a herd that was grazing in the fields and roasted its meat on sticks over a fire. "We drank our coffee and ate the very rare and thoroughly smoked meat, sprinkling it with a little salt, of which condiment every soldier carried a little in his pocket," Walker remembered.[18]

The regiment had the 124th New York on its right, and four guns of James E. Smith's 4th New York Independent Battery in front. Smith did not have room on the rocky shelf above Devil's Den for all six of his guns, so he placed four there and put his other two in the valley, or "gorge," to his rear. Worried that the Rebels might be able to outflank him from the left, Smith asked Walker to move his regiment to a belt of trees south of Devil's Den and protect that flank. The battery, he said, could handle the front. Walker, independent as always, told Smith he could protect him just fine where he was. "I would not go into that den unless I was obliged to," he said. Smith complained to brigade commander Hobart Ward, and Ward sent a staffer with orders for Walker to do as Smith asked. "I remonstrated with all the power of speech I could command, and only (as I then stated) obeyed because it was a military order," Walker said. "The enemy were near, there was no further time for argument. I must obey and suffer the results, or disobey and take the consequences; I obeyed." The disgruntled colonel moved his regiment to the woods south of Devil's Den in the Plum Run valley. The 4th Maine was now on the left flank of the brigade—in fact, it was the left of the entire Army of the Potomac. Behind them, Little Round Top remained undefended.[19]

It wasn't long before Smith saw Rebel infantry advancing across the stony fields in front of his battery, heading in the direction of the Round Tops. They were men from Texas and Arkansas who belonged to Robertson's brigade. Smith immediately ordered his men to open fire. "I never saw the men do better work," he wrote, noting that every shot found a target. However, the jumbled terrain of the field worked to the enemy's advantage, for the rocks and swales offered shelter for sharpshooters, who began to take a toll on Smith's men and horses. When the enemy infantry reached the end of the field below the rocky shelf that held Smith's four guns, the Union artillerymen could not lower their muzzles enough to reach them. The situation had become critical.[20]

Walker, in the meantime, was grappling with the Alabamians of Law's brigade. The Maine soldiers had repulsed one attack when Walker looked behind him and saw that Rebels had overrun Smith's guns. He had his men fall back about a hundred yards and fix bayonets. "I shall never forget the 'click' that was made by fixing of bayonets, it was as one," he said. Bayonets lowered, the regiment rushed to Smith's aid. They were joined by the 99th Pennsylvania, which had been ordered over from the right to fill the gap opened when the 4th Maine shifted to the left. The Yankees had a "sharp encounter" with the Rebels near the Union guns. It was sharp and it was close—at one point a Rebel soldier yanked Walker's sword from his hand, but the Maine colonel managed to recover it during the melee. Walker was also shot, the bullet almost severing his Achilles tendon and killing his horse.

The Union soldiers pushed the enemy back from Smith's guns, but the 124th New York to the right had been decimated, its colonel and major both dead, and had been forced to retreat. The 4th Maine had to follow suit. "Our flag was pierced by thirty-two bullets and two pieces of shell, and its staff was shot off, but Sgt. Henry O. Ripley, its bearer, did not allow the color to touch the ground, nor did he receive a scratch, though all the others of the color guard were killed or wounded," Walker reported. Capt. Edwin Libby remembered how Ripley defiantly waved the flag at the advancing enemy—but defiance wasn't enough. The soldiers of Ward's brigade on this part of the line were forced to retreat, ceding Devil's Den to the Rebels.[21]

John W. Lokey of the 20th Georgia later recalled an encounter with a wounded sergeant of the 4th Maine somewhere among the boulders of Devil's Den. The Georgia regiment belonged to Henry Benning's brigade, which had followed Robertson's into the maelstrom. Lokey had just clambered up on the rocks to take aim at the Yankees when a bullet went through his right thigh. "I felt as if lightning had struck me," he said. Lokey was attempting to hobble to the rear when he came across a wounded Yankee. The man identified himself as a sergeant in the 4th Maine (historian John Michael Priest identified him as Zuinglas C. Gowan of Company E). Lokey asked for assistance. The Mainer had the Rebel throw his arm around his neck so he could hold him up. The two enemies then stumbled out of harm's way through a storm of bullets that "were striking the trees like hail all around us." They were behind Rebel lines, so the Union soldier knew he would be taken prisoner. "If you and I had this matter to settle, we would soon settle it, wouldn't we," he said. Lokey replied that they would probably come to terms pretty quickly. After the unlikely duo reached a place of relative safety, Confederate soldiers took the Maine man to the rear. "If he is living, I would be glad to hear from him," Lokey wrote years later.[22]

Walker's wound left him unable to walk, so he had two sergeants help him to the rear. He was trying to mount a new horse when General Ward arrived. He asked Walker if he was wounded. "Slightly," Walker replied, "but if I can get on the horse I can ride." Ward looked him over and said he was wounded worse than he thought. Maj. Ebenezer Whitcomb had also been wounded, so Walker turned command over to Capt. Edwin Libby.

Walker abandoned his horse for an ambulance and a bumpy ride to the III Corps hospital. "I lay on the ground, in full view of our Third corps amputating table, congratulating myself that I was not obliged to lose a limb," he said. A surgeon cut off Walker's boot and dressed his wound. Helped onto a horse, he rode to the rear until he grew too faint to continue, and then he found a house and made a bed on a straw sack. Walker reached Baltimore in a cattle car on July 5, and was home in Rockland two days later. "I always have and ever shall regret that I obeyed the order and moved my command into that Den (the Devil's Den) which caused our entire loss of prisoners and most of the other casualties," he said.[23]

— ⁓ —

Farther down the Union line, Régis De Trobriand's brigade of Birney's III Corps division was the next to receive the Confederate hammer blow. The brigade, which included the 17th Maine, had arrived late to the battlefield, having remained behind in Emmitsburg to block mountain passes to the west. Charles B. Merrill was still in command, despite the groundswell of support for Maj. George W. West. The regiment began its march to Gettysburg around five o'clock on the morning of July 2, and the men were disgruntled because they had not been given time to make coffee. Even without caffeine, the Union men summoned enough energy to cheer loudly when they crossed the Mason-Dixon Line into Pennsylvania. After a march of about three hours De Trobriand allowed his weary soldiers a break. Many immediately kindled fires for the all-important task of brewing coffee—only to receive orders to resume the march before they had time to finish. Time was of the essence. As De Trobriand's brigade marched up the Emmitsburg Road south of Gettysburg, enemy bullets started whistling over their heads. Had they arrived 15 minutes later, regimental historian Edwin Houghton wrote, they would have found Confederates blocking their path.

As the soldiers headed north, they passed Gettysburg citizens going in the opposite direction, laden with whatever they could carry. South of town, the regiment made a right turn off the road, passed through Sherfy's peach orchard, and finally found a position near some woods along a rocky ridge. To their south was a 20-acre wheat field. There were woods at the far side, with a low stone wall running along the edge. Soldiers flung themselves onto the ground and fell asleep. The time was about three o'clock.

George W. Whitman of Woodstock, a private in Company F, recalled being worried by sporadic musket fire to the front, until he realized it was from army butchers, who were shooting cattle roaming the fields so they could get fresh meat for the soldiers. "Considerable anxiety was expressed about that beef," recalled Whitman. "Said one of my Company, 'Boys, we'll fight like damnation before we'll give up that beef.'"[24]

Many men were still sleeping sometime around 4:00 when a gun discharged from the peach orchard and jolted them awake. More guns began firing off to the south, where Smith's New York battery was defending Devil's Den. Lt. Charles Verrill of Company C walked to a high point above the wheat field to investigate. Off to the south he could see Union signalmen on the rocky heights of Little Round Top. They were frantically waving their signal flags. Before Verrill could determine much more, orders came for the regiment to move to their left at double-quick.

The 17th Maine rose up and made a dash across the wheat field toward the stone wall at the south end. Already "the bullets were whizzing," Verrill said. A sergeant fell dead. Like the wheat field and the peach orchard, the stone wall, under ordinary circumstances, would have been nothing special. It was "just a common old fashioned, thirty-inch stone fence," Verrill said. On the battlefield, nothing was ordinary. "The stone wall was a breastwork ready made," Verrill said, and the crucible of battle transformed it into "the best stone wall the 17th Maine ever came across in its travels."[25]

The Maine soldiers had barely positioned themselves behind the wall when skirmishers from the 20th Indiana came running back through the woods in front. Following right behind them was a mass of Confederate infantry pushing its way through the trees. They belonged to the 3rd Arkansas, the left-most regiment of Robertson's brigade, and had been bolstered by troops from the 59th Georgia of George T. Anderson's brigade. Sheltered behind the wall, the 17th Maine poured a destructive, semi-enfilading fire into the advancing Rebels, loading and firing as fast as they could. "And didn't we yell!" said Whitman. "Couldn't I yell with a will! As the boy said when he whistled in school, 'It whistled itself.' So I could say while fighting behind this stone wall, 'It yelled itself.' We kept on loading and firing as fast as we cold. Could hear orders, 'Fire low, fire low. Fire right oblique.'"[26]

"There was a dreadful buzzing of bullets and other missiles, highly suggestive of an obituary notice for a goodly number of Johnny Rebs, and we could see them tumbling around right lively," remembered John Haley. The Confederates were thrown "into disorder," and retired. They regrouped and renewed the attack.[27]

Enemy soldiers to the right seemed to threaten the regiment's flank, but the Rebels did not advance, perhaps stymied by the thick undergrowth. The volleys of musketry and the roar of George Winslow's 1st New York Battery B on the rise at the north side of the wheat field combined to make a "fearful din," said Verrill. He was also startled by bullets that came from the rear; given permission to investigate, he found Union soldiers—perhaps from the 110th Pennsylvania—who had taken shelter behind some rocks and were trying to fire over the heads of the 17th Maine. Verrill suggested they take up a position on the threatened right but they declined his offer.[28]

Charles Merrill realized he had to deal with the threat on his right. He protected his flank by bending his line at an angle. The three companies at the end of the line, C, H, and K, wheeled from the regiment's south-facing position until they were lined along a wooden rail fence, facing west. Such a maneuver was difficult to make while under fire, but it was done, though not without loss. Two captains, one lieutenant, and several enlisted men fell mortally wounded by the time the men formed their new line.[29]

"We had scarcely finished this new formation when the dogs of war were let loose again," said Verrill. On the right, the 8th and 9th Georgia pushed forward out from the tangled growth of alder trees that had been hanging them up, while the 11th Georgia approached from in front of the wall. According to Verrill, "never was loading and firing of muzzle-loaders done more rapidly than by the 17th at that time." Charles Mattocks had three men loading muskets for him while he "blazed away" from behind the wall. Two men were shot and killed beside him. Franklin I. Whitmore, a sergeant in Company D, loaded and fired his gun while lying on his back behind the wall. Somehow a Rebel bullet still managed to tear Whitmore's cap. George Whitman fired until his musket became clogged, so he found another one lying on the ground. Its barrel was stuffed full of bullets, evidently by an overexcited soldier, so Whitman picked up a third gun and resumed firing. Despite the storm of lead from the Maine troops, the Rebels pushed forward. A plucky handful nearly planted their flags on the wall before the color bearer broke and ran. Lt. Joseph Perry accepted the surrender of another, and pulled him over the wall.[30]

"It was a horrid place to be in, with bullets flying like hailstones," said Whitman. "But one thing helps us; we are actively engaged. I always feel better when I have something to do. Yes, I could think even in battle; a fearful reminder of the dangerous situation in which we were exposed was in seeing the dead and wounded around us."[31]

John Haley watched De Trobriand ride over, size up the regiment's situation, and order it to fall back. The Maine soldiers, knowing the Rebels would take the stone wall as soon as they left it, refused to budge. But their options were running as low as their ammunition. The regiment beat back another attack from both the front and the right, and the enemy withdrew again. A relative quiet fell across this portion of the wheat field, and the exhausted, powder-blackened men of the 17th Maine exploded into relieved laughter at the sudden respite. "We were simply hilarious," Verrill said. The break proved short lived. Behind them, Winslow's battery was preparing to roll out of the wheat field, and orders came for the 17th Maine to follow. The men knew this meant there had been a break in the line someplace. Two V Corps brigades of James Barnes's division, sent in to support de Trobriand's right, had suddenly pulled back, and Joseph Kershaw's Confederate brigade forced a passage through the resulting gap. By this point the Rebels had also broken through at Devil's Den to the left.[32]

No doubt it was with regret that the 17th Maine abandoned the stone wall that had served them so well, and they made their way back through the trampled and bloody wheat. Their fight was not quite over. Shortly after the regiment pulled back, General Birney rode up with a staff member and ordered the regiment to form into line of battle and move forward. "[T]he boys gave cheers in the old-fashioned Union style and advanced full of the fire of courageous manhood," said Merrill. Birney admired the regiment's enthusiasm, which he found "cheering." (John Haley, for one, did not share Elijah Walker's caustic opinion about their division commander. He thought Birney and Humphreys, who commanded the III Corps' other division, "two of the ablest Gens in the service.")[33]

But now the Rebels were behind the stone wall and they weren't going to give it back without a fight. Haley recalled De Trobriand ordering the regiment to "make a stand." Told they were running out of ammunition, he said, "Then you must hold them with the bayonet."[34]

"The contest was now of a most deadly character, almost hand to hand, and our loss was very severe," reported Merrill. "In the color guard of 10, but 3 escaped uninjured." During the forward movement, a bullet hit adjutant Charles Roberts in the right leg and he fell face-first onto the ground. Merrill cut a strap from his own sword belt and used it as a tourniquet, and then had Roberts placed on a blanket and carried to the rear.[35]

The Maine men knelt on the ground and fired, eyeing their nearly empty cartridge boxes with concern. Messengers had gone off to the rear to request more ammunition. Fortunately, the Confederates appeared satisfied to remain on their side of the wall and engage in some "target practice." Reinforced by elements of the 5th Michigan and the 110th

Pennsylvania, the regiment fought off more determined attacks by Rebels in the woods to the right. Charles Verrill fell with a serious wound in the thigh.

The 17th Maine, its ammunition nearly exhausted, finally withdrew from the field when soldiers from the II Corps division of John Caldwell—the former teacher from East Machias—arrived as reinforcements. The regiment had been fighting in the wheat field for at least two hours. When the exhausted men reached Taneytown Road, they finally found time to make some coffee.[36]

To the right, in Sherfy's peach orchard, the 3rd Maine had settled in for a long, hot afternoon. Although the regiment was part of Hobart Ward's brigade, division commander Birney had ordered it to the orchard to help support the brigade of Brig. Gen. Charles Graham. The regiment was in line of battle behind a fence at the orchard's edge, facing southwest. Fellow New Englanders from the 2nd New Hampshire were on their right and the 141st Pennsylvania on the left. It was not a pleasant spot to spend the day. Not only was the heat growing oppressive, the regiment was also lying between contending batteries and shells exploded overhead, seriously injuring several men. Adding injury to injury, the men in the peach orchard occasionally had to drive off enemy skirmishers who advanced from their right and, in Col. Moses Lakeman's opinion, "seemed very anxious" to move the Union defenders from their position.[37]

Sometime after 4:00 P.M., Lakeman saw Confederates moving toward the Round Tops to his left. The soldiers waiting behind the fence in the peach orchard knew their time would come soon enough.

Lines of the enemy, bayonets glistening in the sun, appeared on their front. These were not just skirmishers. They were the South Carolinians of Joseph Kershaw's brigade. Lakeman sent a messenger to George Randolph, the III Corps' chief of artillery, and Randolph sent a battery to harass the oncoming Southerners. As Lakeman and his men braced for the attack by Kershaw's men, another brigade, Mississippians under William Barksdale, came into view from the right and front of the peach orchard salient. "As the Third Maine turned from Kershaw to meet Barksdale it received a withering fire," Lakeman reported. Hardest hit was Company K, the regiment's color guard, which was just forming into line. Hit by a volley, Company K "literally melted away. Every man of the color-guard was either killed or wounded," said Lakeman. Among the dead was the head of the color guard, Capt. John Keen, who had enlisted as a private when he was a 26-year-old farmer and shoemaker from Leeds, Otis Howard's hometown. Keen was struck by four bullets. (His brother, Calvin, served with the 19th Maine and would be seriously wounded the next day.) Keen's lieutenant, Henry Penniman of Winthrop, also fell with a severe wound in the leg. Another casualty was Maj. Samuel Lee, Otis Howard's cousin. He would later have his arm amputated at the shoulder.[38]

Under such a withering fire, attacked on two sides, Lakeman felt he had no choice but to order a retreat. He did not notice the loss of his national flag until the next morning. "If I had, they would have had me and my little squad or I would have had my flag," he said.[39]

Writing later to Adjutant General Hodsdon back in Maine, Lakeman said, "I am proud to state that the Regiment, though very small, sustained its reputation as one of the best fighting regiments in the army. They were chosen to open the engagement on the left of the line on the 2nd inst. And the heroic daring displayed by them, when confronting ten times their number, is the source of universal admiration by the commanding General, and throughout the entire Corps, for myself, I cannot say too much in their praise."[40]

One man who may or may not have deserved praise was Charles C. Morgan, the captain of Company F. Morgan had a weakness for drink, which seems to have been exacerbated by his experiences in the war. In fact, his drinking may have been why he joined the 3rd Maine in the first place. Born in Liverpool, Morgan had served in the British army before he immigrated to Canada. He eventually made his way to Augusta, where he found work as a printer for a newspaper called the *Maine Farmer*. He married a woman from Skowhegan and began to raise a family. One of his drinking companions was Moses Lakeman, and when Lakeman became the captain of the 3rd Maine's Company I, he suggested that Morgan join the regiment, too. Morgan did, and became the captain of Company F. The company would have preferred to choose one of its own for captain, and its men resented the outsider's appointment. For his part,

Morgan longed to see his wife and young child and grew tired of war's brutality. On May 7, after Chancellorsville, he wrote to his wife, "I have had enough of this wholesale butchery & destruction of human life that I want to see no more."[41]

In the Peach Orchard, Morgan acquired a sword, captured, he said, when he took one of Longstreet's aides prisoner. "It is a small dress sword, but old and worn," he wrote to his wife when he sent it to her. "It is, nevertheless valuable, as he tried hard to put it into my body—but couldn't come [to] it." He told his wife to keep the sword safe. "It has been where thousands of brave men were killed, and where cowards dare not go." There were, however, men from the 3rd Maine who grumbled that Morgan was one of the cowards, and had been drunk and lying face-down on the ground during the fight, with no idea of what was going on around him.[42]

Like so many regiments in the Army of the Potomac, the 20th Maine made a series of exhausting marches as it followed Robert E. Lee toward Pennsylvania. On the morning of June 29 its still-untested colonel, Joshua Chamberlain, began leading his men north from Frederick. Sgt. Charles Proctor of Company H was carrying the regimental flag, but he had managed to acquire enough liquor to get belligerently drunk. He began spouting abuse at some of the officers, who took the flag away from him. Members of the rear guard had to hold Proctor up to keep him on his feet. They finally gave up and left him behind.

Andrew Tozier took Proctor's place as color bearer. Tozier, then only 24, had already led a difficult life. Born into poverty in Monmouth, he had fled to a life at sea to escape an alcoholic and abusive father, and then he joined the 2nd Maine. He was badly wounded and taken prisoner at Gaines' Mill, but returned to the regiment after his parole. Tozier was one of the mutinous men that Chamberlain had to discipline when they were transferred to his regiment. But he was now the senior sergeant, so the honor of carrying the regimental flag fell to him.[43]

When the regiment crossed the Mason-Dixon Line and reached Northern soil, the color guard unfurled its flags and the soldiers gave a hearty three cheers. By 4:00 P.M. on July 1 it had reached Hanover, Pennsylvania, some 40 miles from Frederick.[44]

Lieutenant Colonel Gilmore did not make the march. True to form, Gilmore had reported himself ill and departed for a Baltimore hospital. Acting major Ellis Spear had truly fallen ill, the victim of a "malarial fever," but he remained with the regiment. "I would not think of going to the hospital in such a time as active campaign, with so much at stake," he wrote. Majors got to ride, but Spear could barely remain on his horse. When he dismounted to rest he found it almost impossible to climb back into the saddle. But he hung on, feeling weak, tired, and hungry.[45]

The day before the 20th Maine marched into Hanover, a cavalry battle had raged through the town's streets, pitting Rebel horsemen under Jeb Stuart against the Union cavalry of Judson Kilpatrick. Chamberlain noted "grim relics" of the battle that lay in the fields outside town. The exhausted soldiers of the 20th Maine expected they could rest for a while in Hanover, and they started scrounging wood to build fires, cook a meal, and boil some coffee. But it wasn't long before their officers were ordering them to their feet for yet another march, this time to Gettysburg, 16 miles away.

Chamberlain recalled the intensity that radiated through the regiments, brigades, and divisions of the V Corps as the soldiers in Hanover fell in and prepared to march. The long blue lines began streaming down the road to Gettysburg by six o'clock, with the prospect of an exhausting night ahead. Color bearers insisted on marching with their flags unfurled, even though few could see them once dusk fell. Men cheered as a rumor spread through the ranks that George McClellan was back in command of the army. Some even passed along a story that the ghostly spirit of George Washington had been seen riding ahead of the marching soldiers. Emotions were so charged that night, Chamberlain said he half believed the story himself.[46]

Residents along the route came outside to cheer the Union soldiers and offer them food and water. Girls stood along the road to sing "The Star-Spangled Banner." "We were in a free state, and among friendly people," Chamberlain noted. Brigade commander Strong Vincent was moved by the sight of the American flags he saw in the moonlight. "What death more glorious could any man desire than to die on the soil of old Pennsylvania fighting for that flag?" exclaimed Vincent, himself a Pennsylvanian.[47]

The celebratory, almost carnival atmosphere from the beginning of the march had dissipated by midnight, when the weary soldiers were allowed to grab some sleep a few miles outside Gettysburg. Then they were ordered back to their feet and marched to the vicinity of the previous day's fight. Once they halted, many of the soldiers in the 20th Maine dropped to the ground and immediately fell asleep again.

Morning wore into afternoon and the day remained strangely quiet. "During this time the stillness of death reigned over the hills and valleys of Gettysburg," recalled Elisha Coan, a private in Company D. "For each army was silently getting ready for the death grapple." Men sat around fires making coffee, or stretched out on the ground to write what could be their last letters home. From time to time they were ordered to their feet and shifted here and there, only to be halted at a new spot to wait some more.[48]

Chamberlain suspected they would find themselves fighting on the Union right someplace, perhaps on the wooded rise he saw that he later found out was called Culp's Hill. Instead, when the bugles again stirred the men to their feet, word came to move at double-quick across Baltimore Pike and then south to support the army's beleaguered left. They passed behind the Peach Orchard where the 3rd Maine was fighting, and near the Wheatfield where the 17th Maine had found its wall. Ahead of them the 4th Maine was feeling pressure from the attacking Alabamians at Devil's Den. Ahead and to the left Chamberlain first saw the hill that would remain forever linked to his name. He noted its "rough forbidding face" and the way it was scattered with rocks, boulders, and scraggly trees. Rising even higher to the south he saw another tree-covered hill.

These bits of high ground on the Union left had obvious tactical significance. When he pushed his corps forward, Sickles had left the hills unprotected. During the afternoon of July 2, Meade sent his chief engineer, Gouverneur Warren, to ascertain the situation on the left. Warren ascended Little Round Top and was astonished to discover that it was empty of troops except for some Union signalmen—the same flag-wavers that Charles Verrill of the 17th Maine had spied from the Wheatfield.

Warren realized the danger this presented, and dispatched a messenger to find V Corps commander George Sykes and have him send some men to Little Round Top immediately. The messenger found Sykes, who sent a captain with orders for division commander James Barnes to send a brigade. The captain could not locate Barnes (there were rumors that he was drunk), but he did run into Strong Vincent, at the head of his brigade to the north of Little Round Top.

"Captain, what are your orders?" Vincent asked.

"Where is General Barnes?" the messenger replied.

"What are your orders?" Vincent repeated. "Give me your orders." The messenger pointed at Little Round Top and said Sykes had asked Barnes to send a brigade to that hill.

Vincent didn't hesitate, even though he knew he risked court-martial by taking the matter into his own hands. "I will take the responsibility of taking my brigade there," he said. Vincent directed Col. James Rice of the 44th New York to have the brigade follow him, and then he spurred his horse into motion to ride ahead and reconnoiter the position. With his bugler and color bearer, Oliver Norton, trotting along with him, Vincent rode up a crude road on the north side of Little Round Top. From there he headed south through the woods along the east side of the slope until he reached a rocky spur at the south end.[49]

It had taken Norton some time to warm up to Vincent. Early in the war Vincent had been the adjutant of a three-month regiment from Erie, and when Norton watched the spit-and-polish young officer drill the men and meticulously correct their formations, he thought he was little more than "a dude and an upstart." He now knew better and appreciated the discipline Vincent instilled in his troops. When many of those three-month men reenlisted in the 83rd Pennsylvania, they formed an experienced and well-trained core for the regiment. Vincent served as its lieutenant colonel, and took command when the colonel was killed at Gaines' Mill. Like Chamberlain, Vincent overcame his lack of military experience through diligent study. "What he did not know about tactics and army regulations he learned, and forced the junior officers to learn and practice," said Norton. After Chancellorsville, Vincent was promoted to brigade command.[50]

As the regiment followed in Vincent's path along the east side of Little Round Top, Confederate artillery shells went crashing through the trees above them, showering the soldiers with leaves and branches. Chamberlain was riding alongside brothers Tom and John when a shot from one of Longstreet's batteries exploded nearby. "Boys, I don't like this," Chamberlain said. "Another such shot might make it hard for mother." He ordered Tom to ride to the rear of the regiment and make sure the men were closed up. He dispatched John to help set up an aid station and get it ready for the wounded men who were soon to need it. The three brothers shook hands and said goodbye.[51]

Chamberlain led his men around Little Round Top until they reached the hill's southern slope. Vincent was there waiting. He had left his sword on his saddle and was armed only with his wife's riding crop, and he gestured with it as he positioned his four regiments. Rice pointed out that his 44th New York had bonded in combat with the 83rd Pennsylvania and requested that the two regiments fight side by side. Vincent agreed and ordered the 16th Michigan to the right of his line, and the 20th Maine to the opposite end. The 83rd Pennsylvania formed on the Maine regiment's right, and the 44th New York formed next to the Pennsylvanians, forming a curved line that wrapped around the hill's southern face. The two rightmost regiments faced west in the direction of Devil's Den, while the two on the left looked south into the wooded valley between the Round Tops. "This is the left of the Union line," Vincent told Chamberlain. "You understand. You are to hold this ground at all costs!"

"I did understand—full well," Chamberlain said, "but had more to learn about costs."[52]

Not only did the 20th Maine form the left of the brigade's line, it was now the leftmost regiment of the entire Union army at Gettysburg. Should Chamberlain's regiment fail to defend its position, it would have serious repercussions for the army. Chamberlain was placed in a position of grave responsibility, in command of a regiment he had never yet led in battle.

Worried about the security of his left flank, Chamberlain decided to send out a company to act as skirmishers. He picked Company B, composed of tough men from Piscataquis County. Their commander was Capt. Walter G. Morrill, a long-jawed 22-year-old from the town of Williamsburg. As a young man, Morrill had made a living as a woodsman and then began cutting slate, both difficult ways to earn a living. When the war began he joined a company called the Brownville Rifles, which became Company A of the 6th Maine. By September 1861 he was a sergeant. He joined the new 20th Maine regiment as a second lieutenant and he was promoted to captain and command of Company B in April 1862. Morrill was quiet but steady, and one of his fellow soldiers described him as "the coolest man we had in the regiment in an emergency, and had no superior on the skirmish line." Sgt. William B. Owen said that Morrill was "a *man* in every sense of the word. He will look out for his boys as he calls them now."[53]

Chamberlain said that at some point, as his men found their positions in the line, he was joined by Colonel Rice of the 44th New York. Rice had a reputation for excitability in combat, and his men called him "Old Crazy." ("He is brave enough, but in a fight too excitable to do anything right," said Oliver Norton.) The two colonels walked over to the right, where they could get a view of the fighting west of the Round Tops. Devil's Den, where Elijah Walker and the 4th Maine were fighting, "was a smoking crater," Chamberlain recalled. He could see Rebels charging a battery in the Wheatfield. The dip formed by Plum Run—an area that soldiers would call the Slaughter Pen—was "a whirling maelstrom." Chamberlain found it all to be "a stirring, not to say, appalling sight." The two officers watched the unfolding cataclysm, exchanged meaningful glances, and returned to their respective regiments to await whatever was in store for them.[54]

As the 20th Maine formed its line on the rocky spur, trouble was approaching from the direction of Big Round Top, across the narrow valley to its front. They were men from two Alabama regiments, the 15th under Col. William Oates and the 47th under Lt. Col. Michael Bulger. Both regiments belonged to Evander Law's brigade of Hood's division. Like Chamberlain, Oates had a brother, Lt. John Oates, serving under him.

The 15th Alabama was fated to become the 20th Maine's main adversary for Little Round Top. It was the final chapter in what had already been a difficult day for Oates and his men. They had made a grueling march of 24 miles just to reach the battlefield. During the march to Gettysburg John Oates had fallen sick. His brother the colonel found him lying on the ground and told him that he was in no condition to fight and should remain behind. John Oates vehemently refused and said he would not disgrace his uniform. "These were the last words ever passed between us," William Oates recalled.[55]

After advancing to Plum Run, the Alabama regiment received fire from U.S. Sharpshooters in the woods at the base of Big Round Top, and Oates ordered his men to swing about to their right to deal with this annoyance. The movement turned into an ascent of Big Round Top, with the Alabama soldiers sweating and panting as they made their laborious progress up the steep hill. Making matters worse, Oates had dispatched 22 men with the regiment's canteens to fetch water, and they had been captured before they could return. The Southerners were already tired and terribly thirsty, and now they had to climb a steep hill on a hot July afternoon.

Things were about to get even worse for the men from Alabama. The burly, independent-minded Oates thought it would be a good idea for his men to hold their position on Big Round Top. Evander Law disagreed. One of Law's aides arrived at the top of the hill to prod Oates back into motion and down the hill's north face to attack the smaller hill to the north. Somewhat reluctantly, Oates ordered his tired and thirsty men back to their feet and pointed them down the hill. Once they reached the base of Big Round Top, they started making their way through the woods in the valley toward the rocky spur of Little Round Top, where only a few minutes before the 20th Maine had formed its line and braced for attack.

CHAPTER 13

The 20th Maine Holds the Left

If you would like to know how one feels in battle, first imagine yourself situated amidst a most terrific thunder storm, with a crash of thunder here, & a crash of thunder there; a streak of lightning here & a flash of lightning there; thunder bolts striking all around, smashing a tree here, & sending a rock there; & in the midst of all this, imagine a constant volley of musketry; & you can form something of an idea as to what a battle would sound like.
—ELISHA COAN, 20TH MAINE

The first glimpse Ellis Spear had of the approaching enemy soldiers was their legs, visible below the underbrush as they moved toward Little Round Top through the little valley to the south. It appeared they were going to make their way around the 20th Maine's left flank. Spear went down the line to advise Chamberlain of the danger. He found the colonel observing the situation from atop a large boulder. Spear suggested that Chamberlain bend the left of the line back to "refuse" the flank. Instead of attacking the weak end of the line, the enemy would find themselves making a frontal attack.

Capt. James H. Nichols of Company K maintained *he* was the one who alerted Chamberlain to the threat. In his report, Chamberlain said only that an officer from the center delivered the warning, but he added that he could see the enemy for himself. "Now, as might well be believed of such gentlemen and soldiers, they are all right; no one of them is wrong," Chamberlain said later about such divergent recollections. However he received his information, Chamberlain did order the movement to refuse the flank, and his men shuffled into their new positions until the line made a 90-degree angle. The regiment's line was now so extended the men were in a single rank. "But we were not a moment too soon; the enemy's flanking column having gained their desired direction, burst upon my left, with great demonstration," Chamberlain reported.[1]

Elisha Coan of the color guard remembered standing in a relatively open area on the rocky spur of Little Round Top. In front of him the ground descended into the woods. He waited for the enemy soldiers to show themselves, biting his lip and working up nerve for what was to come. It was a short wait. "Hardly had our line been formed when we heard a yelling in the distance," he said. It was the famous Rebel yell, and "once heard it is never to be forgotten." Coan and the other men braced for the shock. Bullets began whistling past. Some snipped branches from above. One bullet killed the man to Coan's left; another wounded the man to his right; a third bullet grazed his cap. Then, through the trees, he caught quick glimpses of the approaching soldiers. He watched and waited, holding his fire until he had a clear target, "& when at last I could see through the trees, the rebs dodging behind rocks & every available cover, then I knew it was my turn," he wrote to his brother. "Then our line burst into flames, and the crash of musketry became constant." Coan marveled at the fact that he was not killed as he stood in the open on the rocks, loading and firing as fast as he could. "[W]e know not what we are capable of until we are actually brought into circumstances that will test us," he wrote.[2]

The regiment's fight actually began on its right, where the 47th Alabama first hit Little Round Top. Firing began rolling down the line from right to left. On the left, Spear couldn't recall who first opened fire, and thought maybe both sides shot simultaneously. "Then uproar of musketry, the cloud and smell of battle smoke, tense excitement but no shouting but men loading and firing as fast as possible." For the men fighting, the battle would have been a blur of impressions—the sheets of musket fire, faces seen through the haze of smoke, glimpses of the enemy, shouts, commands, disconnected moments of clarity, and then confusion. As

Coan wrote his brother, "If you would like to know how one feels in battle, first imagine yourself situated amidst a most terrific thunder storm, with a crash of thunder here, & a crash of thunder there; a streak of lightning here & a flash of lightning there; thunder bolts striking all around, smashing a tree here, & sending a rock there; & in the midst of all this, imagine a constant volley of musketry; & you can form something of an idea as to what a battle would sound like."[3]

At some point during the struggle, Spear saw Pvt. James A. Knight of Company B lying on the ground. He went to him and asked where he had been hit. "Right through me," Knight answered. It was a mortal wound. Spear saw color sergeant Andrew J. Tozier loading and firing a musket while keeping one arm wrapped around the flagstaff. The only other man Spear could distinctly remember seeing was Pvt. John Kennedy, "limping to the rear."

"I remember these incidents: the rest was uproar & earnest hot work," Spear recalled. "I smelt the hot smoke, the faces of the men were set. How they worked."[4]

George Buck, the sergeant who had been busted to private by the cruel quartermaster Litchfield, lay bleeding on the ground. "They reduced me to the ranks, but I will show them that I am not afraid to die," he said. Someone sent for Chamberlain, who came over and knelt by the dying man. "I was disgraced," Buck whispered. Chamberlain told Buck he was exonerated, and that he was reinstating him as sergeant, wiping away the stain on his reputation. Then George Washington Buck died.[5]

Chamberlain counted four separate attacks, each one threatening to break his line before Round Top's defenders beat it back. "The edge of the fight rolled backward and forward like a wave," Chamberlain said. Spear remembered that at one point early in the fighting, as the line was being pushed back, he and Capt. Joseph Land gripped their swords with both hands and pressed them flat against the backs of the men in line to hold them in place. Through the whirling clouds of smoke, Chamberlain caught a glimpse of Tozier, "defending his sacred trust in the manner of the songs of chivalry." (After the war, William Livermore wrote to Chamberlain to complain that Tozier had not been standing alone. Livermore was part of the color guard, and he had been there, too, he said.)[6]

Worried about a gap that opened in the center by the color guard, Chamberlain sent his brother forward to try to close it up. He worried that he was sending Tom to his death, but he had no choice. In case Tom fell to enemy fire before he could deliver his instructions, Chamberlain dispatched Sgt. Reuel Thomas, his orderly, with the same orders. He also sent a messenger to the 83rd Pennsylvania to see if they could spare any men. They could not, but Col. Orpheus Woodward did what he could to extend his line to the left toward the Maine regiment.[7]

William Oates recalled advancing with his Alabamians up the rocky spur and seeing his men in hand-to-hand combat with the Federals. "There were never harder fighters than the Twentieth Maine men and their gallant Colonel," he said. He saw one Maine soldier reach out and grab the Rebels' flagpole, and a Confederate sergeant respond by driving his bayonet through the Yankee's head. "I witnessed the incident, which impressed me beyond the point of being forgotten." At some point during the fighting, Oates's brother fell mortally wounded; he would die a little more than three weeks later. It was a hard, savage fight. Oates recalled, "The blood stood in puddles in some places on the rocks; the ground was soaked with the blood of as brave men as ever fell on the red field of battle."[8]

What's indisputable is that the 20th Maine finally charged down the sloping spur of Little Round Top and routed the Alabamians. What remains in dispute is how exactly that charge happened. In Chamberlain's reports and recollections, he stated that the regiment had almost come to the end of its ammunition. As the beleaguered Mainers scavenged charges from the cartridge boxes of the dead and wounded, Chamberlain realized they had no chance of withstanding another attack. "Officers came to me, shouting that we were 'annihilated', & men were beginning to face to the rear," he wrote. Adding to his consternation was the sound of musketry that seemed to be coming from farther north up Round Top, which he thought might be an attack from the rear. The situation appeared desperate. "My ammunition was soon exhausted," Chamberlain said. "My men were firing their last shot and getting ready to 'club' their muskets." Vincent had ordered him to defend his position no matter what the cost. Chamberlain intended to obey those orders. "At that crisis, I ordered the bayonet."[9]

For his part, Spear, off to the regiment's left, disputed the idea that ammunition was running low. "I am aware of the report that we were out of ammunition," he recalled. "That was not the case on the left. It has also been reported that the charge was ordered because of that, but of this I have no knowledge. I received no such orders."[10]

Other soldiers in the regiment gave credit for the charge to Holman Melcher, the young man from Topsham. Melcher was in command of Color Company F, and when the Alabamians pushed the Union line back he was distressed to see that some of the Maine dead and wounded now lay between the contending lines, where they were exposed to fire from both sides. Melcher approached Chamberlain and suggested moving the color company forward to cover the wounded. "Col C hesitated for the step would be a hazardous one for the enemy had a strong position behind the rocks 3 rods in front of us," remembered Elisha Coan. "But our line was melting away like ice before the sun, and something must be done soon or all would be lost."[11]

Most likely, Chamberlain had already been contemplating a forward movement himself when Melcher—"brave, warm-hearted Lieutenant Melcher," as Chamberlain described him—requested permission to move his company. "This would be a most hazardous move in itself, and in this desperate moment, we could not break our line," Chamberlain recalled. "But I admired him. With a glance, he understood, I answered, 'Yes, sir, in a moment! I am about to order a charge!'"[12]

Theodore Gerrish, in an account published in the *Portland Advertiser* in 1882, assigned Melcher an even more active role—although Gerrish was in a Baltimore hospital at the time and missed the battle, so one must wonder about his sources. "With a cheer and a flash of his sword that sent an inspiration along the line, full ten paces to the front he sprang—ten paces—more than half the distance between the hostile lines," Gerrish wrote. "'Come on! Come on! Come on boys!' he shouts. The color sergeant and the brave color guard follow, and with one wild yell of anguish wrung from its tortured heart the regiment charged."[13]

In Chamberlain's recollection—in the report he wrote out in 1884 at the request of the War Department to replace his original report, which had gone missing—he didn't make it sound as though he ordered a charge at all. He said the mere order of "bayonets" informed the men what was going to happen. "The word was enough," Chamberlain said. "It ran like fire along the line, from man to man, and rose into a shout, with which they sprang forward upon the enemy, not 30 yards away." One thing Chamberlain definitely did *not* do—the novel *The Killer Angels* notwithstanding—was order his regiment to make a big sweeping movement from left to right, with the left of the regiment swinging like a door to come into alignment with the right. The extended "right wheel" that Chamberlain described in his report was not a calculated move but more of a natural one, as the bent-back left flank rotated forward as it rushed down the hill.[14]

Coan remembered that the regiment hesitated about moving forward because the men did not know if an order to advance had come from Chamberlain. "Then Col. C gave the order 'forward,'" Coan recalled. "This was heard by but a few but it spread along our lines and the regt. with a yell equal to a thousand men sprang forward in a wild mad charge. The result was like magic. The rebel front line, amazing at the sudden movement, thinking we had been reinforced, and which they declare to this day was the case throw down their arms & cry out 'don't fire! we surrender,' the rest fled in wild confusion back to their starting point a mile away, and the battle on Little Round Top was ended, for about that time the fighting ceased along the whole front of the army."[15]

In an account printed in the *Lincoln County News*, Gerrish, too, said that the regiment had hesitated before rushing down the hill. That raised the hackles of Captain Nichols from Company K. Nichols took pen in hand to write a letter to the *Lincoln County News* protesting the implication. "This is an imputation of cowardice which I respectfully deny," he said. Company K did not hesitate, Nichols insisted, and was already moving before hearing any order to charge, "and that with such a rush that the officer who could get in front of them must have been exceedingly alert in his movements." Chamberlain echoed Nichols's sentiments when he addressed his veterans in 1889. "I am sorry to have heard it intimated that any hesitated when that order was given," he said. "That was not so. No man hesitated."[16]

Over on the left of the line, Spear had no inkling of any charge. The first he knew of the movement came when he heard a shout of "forward" and he saw the line of men off to the right begin to move downhill. Spear inclined to the theory that the charge had begun spontaneously in reaction to the color guard's movement. He saw the colors move and the line follow. "Amongst good men like these, it was easy to start, but nothing but the enemy could stop the movement, and in this case the enemy could not, and were swept away by it," he said. For his part, Oates was adamant that there had been no sweeping away by anyone and that he had already ordered a retreat before the Mainers charged.[17]

However it began, there were many stories told about that charge, small moments that snapped into focus amid the smoke, noise, and confusion. Chamberlain told of lunging toward a Confederate officer, who tried to shoot him with his pistol with one hand while offering his sword in surrender with the other. Spear recalled seeing two Rebels rise up from behind a boulder in front of him. He had not strapped on his revolver because his stomach had been hurting him so badly, so Spear waved them to the rear with his sword, and continued down the hill. Nathan Clark nabbed two prisoners from behind a rock he had been shooting at earlier; he found other Rebels dead behind it, possibly victims of his marksmanship.[18]

There were other actors who played a role in the drama late in the action. These were the men of Walter Morrill's Company B, who had marched away to protect the flank before the fighting began, and apparently disappeared into the forest without a trace. But they had not. When Morrill discovered that the 15th Alabama had gotten between his company and the rest of the regiment, he and his men found shelter behind a stone wall off to the left. There he was joined by some of the sharpshooters who had already tormented the Alabamians on their climb up Big Round Top. Even as Oates's men had to deal with the bulk of the 20th Maine wheeling down the hill to their front, Morrill's men stood up from behind their stone wall and poured a volley into the Rebels' left and rear. The result was all that the Maine soldiers could have wished.

The Rebels broke and ran, and for the rest of his life Oates insisted that there had been two Union regiments attacking him from behind. Writing to Spear in 1896, Chamberlain said that Morrill did "good and praiseworthy work," but wondered why he had waited to tangle with the Alabamians until the fight was nearly over.[19]

During the charge, the 20th Maine bagged more than 300 prisoners. William Livermore of the color guard said the captured Alabamians told their captors that "they had never been whipped before and never wanted to meet the 20th Maine again. Our victory seems complete, and while we mourn the loss of our brave comrades that have fallen, we rejoice over the victory." There was indeed cause for mourning. Thirty-eight Mainers were either killed or dying and almost 100 were wounded. Chamberlain received two slight wounds, one a cut on his right foot, from either a shell fragment or a splintered rock, the other a bruise made by bullet hitting his scabbard.[20]

There was more sad news. Strong Vincent was dying. Over on the far right of his line, the 16th Michigan had recoiled when attacked and started to break for the rear. Vincent was attempting to rally them when he was cut down. He would be promoted to brigadier general as his life ebbed away in a farmhouse not far from Little Round Top.

—◆—

Farther north up the Union line, a former Maine sea captain was about to play a pivotal role in the Union defense. Like Adelbert Ames, Freeman McGilvery's destiny seemed to lie at sea. Born on October 29, 1823, in the town of Prospect near the mouth of the Penobscot River, McGilvery, like all four of his brothers, grew up to become a sea captain. He had sailed the bark *J. Merithew* to California for the gold rush in 1849, and had been in command of the ship *Wellfleet* when the war began. He left the oceans for a landlocked role in the army, helping raise the 6th Battery of the Maine Light Artillery and becoming its captain in January 1862. McGilvery, a somewhat cantankerous man with dark hair and a thick mustache that merged into bristling muttonchop whiskers, made the transition to the artillery without difficulty. He demonstrated his command abilities that August at Cedar Run with "skillful and active management" of his guns, according to his division commander. At Second Bull Run, McGilvery's battery fought a stubborn defense against the Confederates, losing two guns but helping slow the Rebels enough to allow Pope's forces to escape.[21]

McGilvery's superiors recognized his abilities, for he received a promotion to major in the artillery reserve (and in the Maine Mounted Artillery). Lt. Edwin Dow replaced him in temporary command of the battery. By the time the Army of the Potomac reached Gettysburg, McGilvery was in command of the 1st Volunteer Brigade of the army's artillery reserve. The reserve was a force of 21 batteries (106 guns) in four brigades. McGilvery's brigade had four batteries: the 5th and 9th Massachusetts, commanded by Charles A. Phillips and John Bigelow, respectively; 15th New York, under Patrick Hart; and Batteries C and F of the Pennsylvania Light Artillery, combined into a single unit under James Thompson.

McGilvery and his batteries left Taneytown at dawn on July 2 for the march to Gettysburg. Arriving around 10:30, the batteries waited in an artillery park to the rear of the III Corps near the Taneytown Road. Sometime around 3:30, McGilvery said, he received orders from Brig. Gen. Robert O. Tyler, commander of the artillery reserve, to send two batteries forward to support the III Corps. He selected his two Massachusetts batteries, Phillips's 5th and Bigelow's 9th. Bigelow's men had yet to experience combat. McGilvery personally placed the batteries along the Millerstown Road near the peach orchard and it wasn't long before the guns were engaged against the advancing Rebels. McGilvery's other batteries arrived later, and he placed them in position. When the Confederates forced the Union defenders out of the Peach Orchard, the batteries were forced to retreat. With most of their horses dead or wounded, Phillips and some of his men had to drag off one gun by hand; Bigelow was able to withdraw "by prolonge," meaning he used tow ropes and the guns' recoil to help move them back. Eventually Bigelow made it as far as the brick Trostle barn, but the Rebels continued to threaten him from the front and right.

Bigelow was just getting ready to limber up and move his guns out of their dangerous position when McGilvery arrived. He had discovered a dangerous gap in the Union line on Cemetery Ridge, created when Cald-well's II Corps division had moved forward to help out in the Wheat-field. "Captain Bigelow, there is not an infantryman back of you along the whole line from which Sickles moved out," McGilvery declared. "You must remain where you are and hold your position at all hazards, and sacrifice your battery, if need be, until at least I can find some batteries to put in position and cover you." McGilvery galloped off to find artillery to plug the hole in the line while Bigelow prepared to give the oncoming Rebels a hot reception.[22]

One of the batteries McGilvery found was his old command, the 6th Maine Battery, now being led by Lt. Edwin Dow. It had the poten-tial to be an awkward encounter. Following his promotion, McGilvery had actively campaigned to deny Dow command of the battery. Dow had threatened to press charges against McGilvery. The whole issue had turned into a storm of accusations, countercharges, and recriminations that eventually involved officers from other Maine batteries and reached all the way to Governor Coburn.

The situation was exacerbated by the limited possibilities for advancement in the artillery. In 1862 the War Department tried to save money by dispensing with field officers—majors or higher—in the artillery. Maj. Gen. Henry Hunt, the chief of Union artillery, pointed out that at Gettysburg he had only one general beneath him—Tyler of the artillery reserve—and only four field officers. McGilvery was one of them. That was for an artillery arm that included 67 batteries and 8,000 men. Ambitious officers like Adelbert Ames understood that the infantry offered a better route to higher ranks.[23]

So perhaps it's no wonder that artillery officers fought tooth and nail to receive the limited promotions available. When McGilvery received word of his promotion to major in the artillery reserve, Dow, the battery's senior lieutenant, expected to replace him as captain. McGilvery wanted to see Lt. William M. Rogers receive the position. He wrote to Coburn and told him that Dow was "frequently intoxicated while on duty." When Dow learned about McGilvery's charges, he wrote his own letter to the governor and he asked men in the battery to sign a statement testifying to his good character.

Some of his men did sign, but several sergeants sent a follow-up letter to Coburn, telling him they did not want the testimonial used to get Dow the promotion. Their support was "merely a friendly act to assist in cleaning up his private character; which they believed had been unjustly assailed." Several other sergeants must have believed McGilvery's charges were justified, for they sent their own letter to Coburn testifying to Dow's public drunkenness, and said that on one occasion when the men were preparing for battle, Dow "came stagering into camp smashing his fists together boasting that he could thrash any man in the Battery."

As this was going on, McGilvery brooded over his own chances for advancement. He was especially distressed to hear rumors that George Leppien of the 5th Maine Battery might get promoted to lieutenant colonel in the artillery reserve. McGilvery wanted that promotion for himself, and he wrote to the governor to tell him why he deserved it. Not only was he older than Leppien, McGilvery complained, he also had "left an independent-lucrative business to serve for a nominal fee." No doubt, he said, Leppien was an excellent officer, "but he's a great deal younger than myself and as I understand is not making any pecuniary sacrifice by rendering service to this country. He certainly cannot claim to have rendered more valuable service than I have."

McGilvery also continued his efforts to deny promotion to Dow. On May 4, 1863, he sent another letter to Coburn, along with a petition signed by 99 men and 2 officers of the 6th Maine Battery, and again recommended Lieutenant Rogers. "I will further add that I shall give if needed my many and very grave reasons why Lieut Dow should not succeed to the command of the battery," he said.

Dow became even more incensed when he learned that McGilvery had taken advantage of his absence from camp to pressure the men into signing the petition. According to Dow, McGilvery had "harangued" the men and told them "that I could not be Captain if I went to hell for it." He said McGilvery had whipped up the battery into a state of near mutiny and that he intended to press charges against him for "Conduct Prejudicial to good order and Military discipline, Conduct unbecoming an Officer and a Gentleman, and Exciting Mutinous Conduct in my Command."

Things had changed by May 31, when McGilvery wrote to the governor again. Now he asked Coburn "to throw aside everything I have said for or against either of the Lieuts of the 6th Mne Battery" and use his own judgment about the promotion. What had happened? Like a whirlpool of resentment and ambition, the turmoil had started to draw in other Maine batteries. Suddenly McGilvery and Dow found it was more useful to work together. Dow had set aside his grievances and approached McGilvery with news that James Hall of the 2nd Maine Battery and Greenlief Stevens of the 5th were plotting to sabotage McGilvery's hopes of becoming lieutenant colonel by securing the promotion for Hall and the rank of major for Stevens. It was, McGilvery told the governor, an "ingenious scheme."[24]

By this point Coburn must have dreaded the arrival of the mail and wondered if some kind of insanity had infected his state's batteries. Fortunately for McGilvery, he received word of his promotion to lieutenant colonel on June 23. Edwin Dow, though, remained a lieutenant.

Such, then, was the state of affairs sometime around 6:30 P.M. on July 2 when McGilvery rode up to Dow. The 6th Maine Battery did not belong to McGilvery's reserve brigade, but McGilvery nonetheless ordered Dow to wheel his guns into position to help repulse the Confederate advance. Bigelow had been doing heroic work, but Barksdale's Rebels were about to overrun his battery, many of the horses had been killed, and there was no infantry behind him to protect Cemetery Ridge. If the Confederates pushed past Bigelow it could easily spell disaster for the Army of the Potomac.

Dow set aside any grievances he might have been nursing and advanced his battery of four 12-pound Napoleons. "We galloped forward, got into position close to the Trostle farmhouse, and went at the rebels," he recalled years later. "In front of us was the Twenty-first Mississippi," Dow wrote. "They put up a stiff fight, but we got the best of them and drove them from the guns." McGilvery, whose horse had been hit eight times, rode over to Bigelow, who had been shot off his mount and was struggling to his feet. "Cease firing, and get back to our lines as best you can," McGilvery ordered. The wounded Bigelow managed to get his surviving soldiers off the field, although they had to leave four guns behind and had lost 45 horses and 28 men. Dow had nothing but admiration for his fellow New Englanders. "What a fight Bigelow had put up—his first one, too!" he said with admiration.[25]

Now it was up to Dow and the rest of the artillery line that McGilvery had cobbled together to check the Rebels. Along with those of the 6th Maine, the guns included those from Battery I of the 5th U.S. Artillery, the 5th Massachusetts, Thompson's Pennsylvania battery, Pettit's 1st New York, and one other battery that McGilvery could not identify. "Major McGilvery had succeeded in placing in position around my battery twenty-one pieces of artillery, all of which, except the Sixth Maine, had been in the fight all the afternoon," said Dow. Advancing across the fields toward them were Barksdale's Mississippi soldiers, who not long before had swept the 3rd Maine out of the Peach Orchard. "In a few minutes Barksdale's men came charging at us, we opened fire, and the shot went smashing into his columns and drove them back to reorganize," Dow recalled. So far, so good. But some of the Union batteries were running low on ammunition. One of them, the 5th U.S. Artillery, had to abandon its guns on the field. "All that was left of the line of artillery formed by McGilvery to stop the Confederate advance toward the Taneytown Road was my Sixth Maine, with its six guns, and two guns from Phillips' Massachusetts Battery," Dow said. "With this we prepared to stem the tide which we knew was coming."

The tide did come, and with a vengeance. Dow said his guns repulsed three distinct charges and that the Rebels got so close he could see the whites of their eyes. One shot blew off part of his horse's head. Dow watched a Rebel officer encourage his men forward. "Come on, boys, come on here and get those guns!" he shouted. Dow's men had other ideas. "We blew him into a thousand pieces," said Dow. "He wasn't 200 yards away when we killed him. I got his sword, by the way."[26]

It had been an intensive 90 minutes of fighting by the time the enemy had been stopped around 7:45. Dow's battery had fired 244 rounds. It had suffered surprisingly light casualties, with only eight men wounded. Dow was finally relieved by Battery K of the 4th U.S. Artillery; before returning to the rear, Dow and his men recovered seven Union guns that had been abandoned during the day's fierce struggles.

McGilvery's artillery received its long-awaited infantry support when a brigade arrived from the II Corps, followed by more reinforcements from the XII Corps who had been rushed over from Culp's Hill. The crisis was over.[27]

McGilvery had performed exceptional service at a time when the Army of the Potomac's fate hung in the balance. His immediate superior, General Tyler, cited McGilvery's "intrepid conduct and excellent judgment" on July 2. Edwin Dow was also effusive in his official report about his former commander and adversary's conduct in the battle. He wrote, "I deem it due to Major McGilvery to say that he was ever present, riding up and down the line in the thickest of the fire, encouraging the men by his words and dashing example, his horse receiving eight wounds, of which he has since died, the gallant major himself receiving only a few scratches."[28]

McGilvery was equally pleased with his performance, and justifiably so. "I have been told my services at Gettysburg were valuable and of course I am willing to believe it," he wrote to the governor after the battle. He now felt he deserved promotion to full colonel.[29]

<hr/>

The Maine regiments of the VI Corps, the 5th, 6th, and 7th Maine, contributed to the Union victory at Gettysburg with their feet more than with their guns. Along with the rest of John Sedgwick's corps, they completed their epic 36-mile march to reach the battlefield just in time to provide much-needed support to the left of the Union line.

Before leaving Virginia in pursuit of Lee's army, Lt. Col. Selden Connor, who was in command of the 7th Maine while its colonel was back in Maine recruiting, had some misgivings about the Union forces and Joseph Hooker. "The army is not very enthusiastic," he wrote to his sister on June 5. "I'm sorry to say. I don't believe they have confidence in their leader." Once the VI Corps started north, though, Connor's mood improved despite brutal marches that had left some men unconscious and even dead from sunstroke. On June 17 he told his sister that his soldiers were "gay as larks," and had been singing a song about the regiment as they made their way through Virginia. It went:

Then clear the track you rebs,
Here comes the Seventh Maine;
Our Colonel is a fighting man
His boys are all the same.

"The Army of the Potomac isn't dead yet," Connor wrote.[30]

After Thomas Hyde located John Sedgwick and gave him Meade's orders to proceed directly to Gettysburg, the VI Corps resumed its tramp up the Baltimore Pike toward the fighting. The soldiers never forgot that long, exhausting march through the night. The 5th Maine led the corps, and Colonel Edwards recalled marching "without rest or food," with many men lacking shoes and socks. Nevertheless, Edwards said, "there was no faltering, no complaining, but all seemed anxious and determined to drive the invader from our soil." The brief halts along the way didn't provide enough time to make coffee, so a bite of hardtack had to suffice. All through the night the men marched, some of them seeming to fall asleep even as they kept moving forward, their feet moving automatically until some obstacle in the road jolted them back to full consciousness. Dawn arrived, and still the men marched. As the sun rose they could hear the faint sounds of battle ahead, probably the fighting for Culp's Hill.[31]

The 5th Maine reached Gettysburg at 3:00 p.m. on July 2 and was given time to eat and rest before orders came to move forward and defend the Union left. With bayonets fixed, the tired and footsore soldiers advanced at double-quick toward the fray, cheering as they ran. "The effect was electrical," Edwards told John Hodsdon, in an account that might have exaggerated his regiment's role. "The whole line advanced as one with such impetuosity, that the enemy's dense columns reeled, broke and finally fled in all directions. The 5th captured quite a number of prisoners, and came out of the action with a loss of but three men slightly wounded." The Maine soldiers of the VI Corps had done little fighting, but they still felt they had made an impact on the battle's outcome. "Our boys felt proud that, at that almost turning point in the fortunes of the day, the arrival of the Sixth Corps, they should lead that noble body of soldiery into action, and thus become the first regiment under fire," wrote Charles Bicknell. "Who could blame them for a little enthusiastic feeling over the matter?"[32]

Throughout the long and bloody afternoon, the Confederate attacks had moved up the Union line—leaving in their wake the dead, dying, and wounded. Little Round Top, Devil's Den, the Wheatfield, the Peach Orchard—all had witnessed fierce struggles, and still the battle hung in the balance. Now, still farther north up Cemetery Ridge, the 19th Maine was about to experience its first battle.

The regiment now belonged to the brigade of Brig. Gen. William Harrow, a Kentuckian who had once traveled the court circuit in Illinois with future president Abraham Lincoln. Harrow had no military experience before the war began, and he replaced Alfred Sully—the general who had praised the 19th Maine when it first smelled powder at Fredericksburg—in June after Sully had refused orders from division head John Gibbon to execute some mutinous soldiers. The regiment left its camp near Fredericksburg on June 15 for the grueling march north. It suffered its first combat fatality 10 days later, when Jeb Stuart's horse artillery lobbed a few projectiles its way outside the crossroads town of Haymarket, Virginia. One of the Rebel shells killed Company G's Israel D. Jones. "In less than ten minutes from the time that Mr. Jones was chatting cheerfully with the man marching at his side, he was buried by the roadside and left to sleep his last sleep," wrote John Day Smith in his regimental history.[33]

The 19th Maine made its longest march of the campaign, 32 miles, on June 29, but was able to spend the next day relaxing and basking in the patriotic sentiment it found in the aptly named Uniontown, Maryland. On the morning of July 1, the regiment was assigned to guard the division's trains during the day's march. Due to some miscommunication, the II Corps didn't begin moving until around nine o'clock. At one point during the march, the soldiers reached a creek that had a single log thrown across it. Knowing it would take forever for the corps to cross if the men all waited to use the log, Gibbon ordered his generals to make sure the men forded the creek. Soldiers from the 1st Minnesota were unwilling to march with wet feet and used the log anyway, and they verbally abused a staff officer who arrived to enforce Gibbon's order. Members of the 19th Maine were among the jeering rowdies, but only the 1st Minnesota received blame, and Gibbon had its commander, William Colvill, placed under arrest.[34]

Rumors of fighting to the north began to move through the ranks, but it wasn't until midafternoon that the soldiers heard the first sounds of the battle raging at Gettysburg. Then, "it became very evident that there was trouble ahead," remembered Capt. Silas Adams. The regiment marched until 9:00 P.M., and then made camp on the Taneytown Road, south of the Round Tops. About 20 men from the 16th Maine shared their campsite that night. Adams remembered them giving "a very dismal account of the battle of the afternoon."[35]

Early the next morning, the regiment rose and made a short march to Cemetery Ridge. There they whiled away the long day. "All was silence in the early morning save the confused tramping of feet, and the rumbling of long trains of ambulances in the distance, as they uncoiled from their posts and moved along with the column," remembered Hallowell native Charles E. Nash. "The thought that some of our number would occupy them, mangled and bleeding, before night, could not be repressed. The certainty was too apparent."[36]

And then the certainty became reality. John P. Lancaster of Company A had just sat down to eat a dinner of pork and hard bread out of his greasy tin plate when a cannonball came plunging out of the sky and severed the leg of a Massachusetts soldier near him. "I did not want any more pork that meal," Lancaster remembered.[37]

In the afternoon the men watched the III Corps advance to its new position far ahead of the Union line. Andrew Humphreys' division was on the corps' right, closest to the II Corps. Humphreys had hardly positioned his men alongside the Emmitsburg Road before Longstreet launched his attack. From their vantage point on Cemetery Ridge, the men of the 19th Maine, waiting in reserve, could see that the III Corps was getting the worst of things. Throughout the afternoon various regiments and brigades were taken out of the line and sent to support other parts of the army. When Hancock sent John Caldwell's men to the Wheatfield from their position south of the 19th Maine, he opened up the gap that McGilvery would defend so skillfully. As the afternoon went on, the 400 or so Maine soldiers began to feel isolated, as though they had been left alone on their portion of the line.

They finally received orders to move ahead to a position in front of Cemetery Ridge. The 1st Minnesota—with Colonel Colvill released from arrest and back with his regiment—was off to the left some 300 yards or so. General Hancock rode up so he could personally place the 19th Maine exactly where he wanted it. He dismounted and strode over to the man on the regiment's far left, George Durgin of Company F. He moved him slightly forward and to the left. "Will you stay here?" Hancock asked Durgin.

"I'll stay here until hell freezes over," Durgin replied. That got a smile from Hancock. He ordered the rest of the regiment to form on Durgin, mounted his horse, and rode off.[38]

Col. Francis Heath told his men he expected them to hold their line "at all hazards," and then had them lie down and wait. They waited and watched as the battle approached them, like a great storm sweeping in their direction. "It was moving our way, and it was very plain to be seen it was to surge over us, and we would soon be caught in the vortex," recalled Silas Adams. The harbingers of the impending whirlwind were the men of Humphreys' division, which had been overwhelmed by the Rebels and was retreating toward Cemetery Ridge. In Adams's words, "they finally crumbled to pieces and came back toward us as a hopeless and disorganized mass."[39]

It was about six o'clock. The reddening sun was lowering in the sky. Heath paced back and forth in front of the regiment, telling his men to lie still and let the men of Humphreys' shattered division pass over them. A general on horseback whom Colonel Heath believed to be Humphreys himself (but probably wasn't) appeared and told Heath to have his men stand up and stop the retreating soldiers. Heath refused, fearing his troops would get swept up in the panic. That response did not satisfy the general. He ordered Heath to the rear. Heath refused to do this as well. "I was placed here by an officer of higher rank for a purpose, and I do not intend to go to the rear," he said. "Let your troops form in the rear and we will take care of the enemy in front." The general decided to take matters into his own hands and rode down Heath's line, ordering the Maine soldiers to their feet. Heath followed, countermanding the general's orders.[40]

Humphreys' men reached the 19th Maine, and they kept going. "On they came like a great billow, rushing with an irresistible force that no troops could check in fight," remembered Adams. "They swept over us, they stepped on or between the men and even tumbled over us, having no regard to dignity or military order, or to pick out reasonable paths to walk in, as their only object seemed to be to get to the rear, out of the reach of their relentless pursuers." Some of the III Corps men promised the Maine soldiers that they would form in the rear; others preached a gospel of doom, said they were beaten, and advised the 19th Maine to follow them. Adams reported that not a single soldier from his regiment in Maine left the ranks.[41]

The Rebels were not far behind the retreating Union soldiers. On they came. Above the roar of battle, John Lancaster remembered the sound of Heath shouting, "Give it to them!" The Maine men fired an explosive volley. Lt. Edgar A. Burpee of Company I told his sister that "we gave the Rebs a few pills that made the heads and stomachs of some of them ache, I bet." The regiment loaded and fired again, but still the Rebels came closer and closer. "Oh, my God, I thought, would they never stop!" said Lancaster. "Their fire was making dreadful havoc in our ranks. Were our bullets punishing them as severely? We could not tell." Capt. Isaac W. Starbird of Company F approached Heath and told him the regiment's left was threatened. Heath investigated, found it was true, and ordered his leftmost companies to refuse the flank in response, much as both the 17th Maine and 20th Maine had done. It was a risky maneuver in the confusion of battle, especially with a regiment that was experiencing combat for the first time: The rest of the regiment might see the companies on the left fall back and interpret it as the beginning of a retreat—or, once the left began falling back, the men might follow their instincts and continue all the way to the rear. "For when one's back is turned the bravest becomes a coward, and the legs evince to an astonishing degree a desire to perform good service," noted Lancaster.[42]

Somehow, amid the din and the confusion, the 19th Maine completed the maneuver and confronted the danger on the left. The Confederates marched closer. One of their color bearers ran in front, defiantly waving his flag at the Maine troops. "Drop that color bearer," Heath ordered, and a Maine private aimed and fired. The Rebel fell to the ground. "Give it to them," Heath said again. "The Confederate regiment melted away in the smoke and was seen no more."[43]

Thick, sulfurous smoke cloaked the action on the field, and Heath received word that the enemy was now on his right and rear. This time he ordered his men to fall back. But once he emerged from the gunpowder haze, Heath saw it had been a false alarm. In fact, the Confederate soldiers on his front appeared to have halted, the 19th Maine's fire having sowed enough death and confusion in their ranks. Heath saw his opportunity. He halted the retreat and had the regiment about-face. With a shout of "Come on, boys!" he led a charge.

Off to the left, Hancock ordered the 1st Minnesota to make its famous charge against terrible odds, but this was the 19th Maine's similar moment of military glory. As Silas Adams remembered it, "the regiment started like a tornado let loose, down across the field at the heels of the enemy, yelling all the time at the top of our voices, until we nearly reached the Emmitsburg road where we halted, capturing many prisoners, two stands of colors, three pieces of artillery and four caissons." The cannon were Union guns of the 3rd U.S. Artillery, which the Rebels had captured during their advance and had been trying to take from the field.

One of Hancock's aides galloped up as the regiment was charging to the Emmitsburg Road. He stopped Heath and asked him where he was going. "We are chasing the 'rebs,'" Heath replied. The aide suggested that he stop before they ended up as prisoners. The men did stop, even though they had been enjoying the chase. Looking behind him, though, Adams was infuriated to see soldiers from the III Corps following in the 19th Maine's wake, picking up Rebel flags the 19th Maine had not stopped to retrieve. Adams, at least, bore a grudge about that for years to come.[44]

The 19th Maine had performed admirably in its first fight, but at great cost. The regiment had suffered 130 men killed or wounded. John D. Smith, then a private in Company F, recalled men sobbing that night as the roll was called and the magnitude of the losses became apparent. The 19th Maine had experienced a bloody baptism of war indeed.[45]

~ ~

As if the 16th Maine hadn't suffered enough on July 1, fate dealt it one more bad hand on July 2. Capt. Daniel Marston of Company C was the ranking officer in the regiment, which was being held in reserve behind Evergreen Cemetery. There the men attempted to rest, their sleep interrupted by the occasional cannon shot or the rattle of musketry somewhere along the line. Later in the day the soldiers could hear growing sounds of battle off to the south, the rumble of cannon gradually increasing in intensity as the sun lowered over Seminary Ridge. It was almost sundown when the 16th Maine received orders to head south to support the line there. The men were marching past the little white farmhouse where General Meade had made his headquarters when an enemy shell came hurtling over Cemetery Ridge and exploded in their midst. Company B's Lt. Fred H. Beecher and seven enlisted men were badly wounded. The stunned survivors resumed their march through the haze. "In line of battle we hurried on through the smoke, over rough ground, into the uproar, just as the rebels were driven back," Small remembered.[46]

~ ~

Longstreet's assault petered out late on July 2, but the day's fighting wasn't over yet. The Confederates still had one more blow to deliver, and this time it came down on the right of the Union line on Cemetery Hill. It landed on Howard's XI Corps, and especially the division that Adelbert Ames now commanded.

The attack was the responsibility of Jubal Early and his division of Richard Ewell's corps. As dusk fell, Harry Hays's Louisiana brigade and Isaac Avery's North Carolinians began quietly filing out of town and into position for an attack. The rolling terrain and gathering darkness allowed them to remain hidden until they were almost ready to make the assault.

Ames's division held the right of the Union position on East Cemetery Hill, in a line that formed a 90-degree angle, or the shape of a reversed number 7. The 107th and 25th Ohio regiments faced roughly to the north at the end of the line—the top bar of the 7—with the 75th Ohio and 17th Connecticut next, facing east. Leopold von Gilsa's brigade was to the right. Posted behind the infantry on East Cemetery Hill were batteries commanded by Michael Wiedrich, Bruce Ricketts, and Gilbert Reynolds. The terrain provided one disadvantage for the artillery: the slope of the hill to the front meant the gunners would not be able to lower the muzzles of their guns enough to cover the area if any enemy soldiers made it that far.

The 5th Maine Battery, off to the left and slightly forward on the knoll where Hancock had posted it the day before, had a much better angle. Lt. Edward Whittier was now in command. Whittier, from Gorham, Maine, had been attending Brown University in Providence when war broke out, so he initially joined a Rhode Island battery before transferring to the 5th Maine. He was thrust into command on the morning of July 2. Captain Stevens had been standing on the earthworks his men had thrown up in front of the battery the night before, peering through an ordnance glass to assess his battery's marksmanship. A bullet, probably fired by a Rebel sharpshooter on the edge of town, passed through both his legs below the knees and embedded in the earthwork. Stevens survived, but he was out of the battle. One of his men dug out the bullet and later gave it to him.[47]

Another of the unit's casualties that day was John Chase, the soldier who had helped save the battery at Chancellorsville and had experienced a religious epiphany the previous night. The battery had been engaged in an artillery duel with the Rebel guns on Benner's Hill to the north when a shell exploded only three or four feet away from Chase. The effect was violent and terrible. The blast tore the clothes from Chase's body, nearly ripped off his right arm, tore out his left eye, and riddled his body with 48 other wounds. It seemed that no one could have survived such horrible injuries, and two men carried what remained of Chase to the rear and placed him on the ground near the rock where he had prayed the night before.[48]

Dusk was beginning to shroud the battlefield when one of the battery sergeants peered into the gloom. "Look! Look at those men!" he shouted, pointing to the left front. Enemy soldiers were filing out from behind the buildings at the town's southern edge. They formed a line of battle in front of farm buildings that belonged to William Culp, a line that extended almost all the way to Rock Creek to the right.[49]

Whittier was prepared. Earlier in the day, he had used an ordnance glass to determine the distance to various landmarks on his front, and he had a few test shots fired to make sure his measurements were accurate. He now ordered his men to load their Napoleons with spherical case shot, the fuses cut to ignite the shells at three seconds. "Fire by battery," he commanded, and his six guns roared. The commander of the adjoining regiment, the 33rd Massachusetts, thought the sudden explosion was like "a volcano had been let loose." Whittier's earlier preparations bore immediate fruit. "The projectiles exploded with perfect accuracy & with visible effect," he reported. The batteries on East Cemetery Hill added their fire to the destructive rain of iron.[50]

As they moved across the fields toward the Union defenders, the soldiers in Avery's brigade had to wheel to the right to maintain their position in line. This was unfortunate for the North Carolinians, for their new approach placed them at a dangerous oblique angle in front of the 5th Maine. Whittier swung his leftmost guns to face the enemy and moved the ones on the right to the rear to give them an unobstructed field of fire. The Napoleons fired to deadly effect, "pouring a most destructive, enfilading, demoralizing, fire into a confused mass of the enemy."[51]

Col. Andrew Harris of the 75th Ohio, now in command of Ames's old brigade, had been astonished to see the gray lines moving forward through the twilight. "We could not have been more surprised if the moving columns had raised up out of the ground amid the waving timothy grass of the meadow," he said. Harris watched intently as the Union batteries opened fire. "But on, still on, they came, moving steadily to the assault, soon the infantry opened fire, but they never faltered," said Harris. "They moved forward as steadily, amid this hail of shot shell and Minnie ball, as though they were on parade far removed from danger." Von Gilsa's brigade broke under the sudden onslaught, and Ames ordered Harris to send the 17th Connecticut into the resulting gap. This movement merely robbed Peter to pay Paul and created another hole in the line, one the Confederates were able to exploit.[52]

Capt. Peter Young of the 107th Ohio saw the Rebels come swarming up, "yelling like demons." The regiment's color bearer waved his flag in the faces of the advancing enemy until he fell dead. Young grabbed the

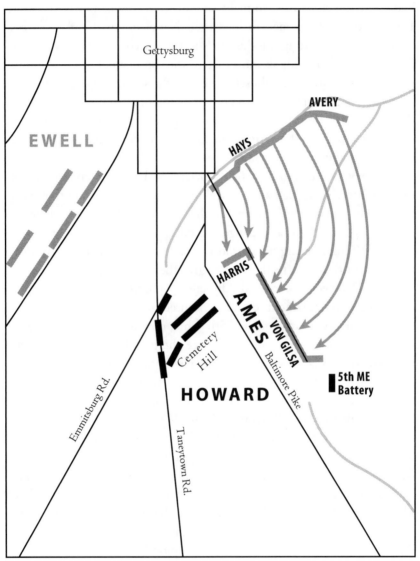

Gettysburg, July 2, Cemetery Hill

flag. Hoping to inspire his men, he brandished his revolver and dashed into the fray. He shot down a Rebel color bearer from the 8th Louisiana and wrestled away "the vile rag" the enemy soldier carried. With the captured flag in one hand and his revolver in the other, Young was turning back toward his men when a bullet hit him in the arm and pierced his lung. He managed to stagger back to his lines.[53]

The Rebels were now among the Union guns. The cannoneers fought back with whatever was handy, including their sponge staffs and rammers. Ricketts saw one of his lieutenants pick up a stone and hurl it at a Rebel, knocking him down. Another artilleryman grabbed the Rebel's gun and was about to brain him with it when Ricketts intervened to save the wounded man.[54]

Fortunately for the Union forces, Hancock realized the danger and dispatched the II Corps brigade of Samuel Carroll from East Cemetery Ridge to help. The reinforcements arrived in time to help check the Rebel attack and throw the enemy back. Carroll, a fiery redhead with thick muttonchop sideburns, was livid that the regiments on Cemetery Hill had been unable to hold their position. The Carroll and Howard families had once shared a cottage at West Point, but that didn't prevent "Old Brick Top" from castigating Howard's command, and "he emptied the vials of his wrath on the devoted heads of the Eleventh Corps officers, high in rank, sparing none of those gathered about him." He wasn't alone in his disdain. Captain Ricketts, whose battery had been in the thick of the Cemetery Hill fight, was scathing in his evaluation of the XI Corps' behavior, saying it had been "cowardly and disgraceful in the extreme."[55]

It appears that Howard shared their opinions. After the attack had been repulsed, Charles Wainwright watched as Howard attempted to get some XI Corps regiments to move forward and capture Rebels who had taken shelter behind a knoll. He could not get a single man to move. "Why don't you have them shot?" Wainwright asked. "I should have to shoot all the way down; they are all alike," Howard replied. Wainwright said at that point he began to believe the stories being told about the XI Corps at Chancellorsville.[56]

Ames was terse about the evening's fight when he wrote his report. It is not difficult to detect some tight-lipped fury between the three short sentences he contributed. "On the evening of the 2d, an attempt was made to carry the position we held, but the enemy was repulsed with loss," Ames wrote. "Colonel Carroll, with a brigade from the Second Corps, rendered timely assistance. The batteries behaved admirably." He pointedly did not mention how his own infantry had behaved. Ames did single out three officers for praise—his assistant adjutant general, Capt. John Marshall Brown; Harris of the 75th Ohio; and Young of the 107th Ohio. It's probably no coincidence that none of them had a German surname.[57]

By the time the Union defenders had pushed the Confederates off Cemetery Hill, the 5th Maine Battery was almost out of ammunition. Its losses were slight—four horses from the leftmost gun had been killed—and Whittier ordered the battery to limber up and move to the rear. As the gun crews prepared to do that, Whittier crept forward in the darkness and ascertained that the Rebels had indeed retreated. The battery moved back to the Baltimore Pike and infantry occupied its position. Whittier reported to Wainwright at the cemetery gatehouse. Once the battery had replenished its ammunition, it moved back and roused the sleepy infantrymen from their entrenchments. Then the battery settled in for a long night. Whittier felt a bit more confident knowing that his limbers were fully stocked.[58]

After the battle, Lieutenant Burpee of the 19th Maine recollected his emotions during the fight. At first, when the Rebels advanced at the heels of Humphreys' men, he had wished he were at home. And then he didn't feel frightened at all. "I felt as if I was safe in God's hands, for unto Him I had committed my all," he wrote his sister. He thought of his family back home, and hoped he would survive the battle. When it came time to stand up and fire, all thoughts of danger vanished. "I felt as secure as though at home. All I wanted was to give the 'Johnnies' fits. I felt almost mad, and could I have got hold of that fellow who carried the flag, I'd have knocked his head off."

For Burpee, the greatest loss was that of his captain, George D. Smith, who had been killed in the fight. Smith had liked to talk about the furlough he was going to take in September and what he planned to do when he got back to Maine. Burpee now had Smith's bloodstained pocket diary in his possession. "Every time I look at it I almost shudder to think it was the life blood of my dear friend."[59]

That night, John Lancaster of the 19th Maine wrapped himself in his blanket on the field where he had fought that day, and tried to fall asleep. Even though he believed the Union army had been victorious he "felt sad, and dreaded the next day." He looked up at the stars and wondered if his mother back in Maine was looking up at them, too. Deciding that she probably was, he rolled over and slept.[60]

CHAPTER 14

The Army of the Potomac Triumphs

Company, regimental and brigade organizations were lost, and we were a great crowd. We would load, run to the front and fire, then others would jump in front of us and fire, and the color bearers, always at the front, would toss their colors up and down to show the enemy that we were not going to give it up, and to encourage us on.
—JOHN P. LANCASTER, 19TH MAINE

On the night of July 2, a courier reached Cemetery Hill with a summons for Otis Howard. The one-armed general climbed onto his horse to make the short ride to George Meade's headquarters. Darkness had fallen and the moon had risen. Howard could see lanterns dotting the battlefield, indicating where ambulance bearers were moving through the carnage to collect the wounded soldiers who still had a chance to survive.

Rowland Howard was helping wounded at the XI Corps hospital at the George Spangler farm, where he quickly learned about "the real and essential character of war." It was far removed from the "pomp and circumstance" that had excited him when he first saw an army on the march, or the patriotic thrill he had felt when he heard the sound of the guns. In the hospital, war showed its true face. It was blood and gore, death and destruction, suffering and horror, and it soon became overwhelming. Rowland was struck by the contrast between the peaceful moon and stars in the night sky and the "ghastly faces of our dead." He was moved by the agonized moans and cries of the dying soldiers who surrounded him. "I said to myself, 'O God, the moon and the stars Thou has made, but not this miserable murder and mangling of men.' It is not like nature: it is anti-natural; it is of the pit."[1]

Otis Howard continued his ride until he reached Meade's headquarters, a little white farmhouse alongside Taneytown Road on the east slope of Cemetery Ridge. That evening Meade had dispatched couriers to find all his corps commanders and request their presence for a meeting. The gathering has since gone down in history as a "council of war," but Meade preferred to call it a "consultation."

One by one, the generals arrived at the building. It belonged to a widow named Lydia Leister, but she had wisely fled the area before the fighting erupted. Frank Haskell, one of John Gibbon's aides, described it as a "shabby little farmhouse." It had only two rooms, a small one in the front and a back bedroom. The generals met in the back room, a tiny, low-ceilinged space that hardly had room for them all. A bed took up one corner. A tiny table in the center of the room held a pail of water for drinking, a tin cup to drink it from, and a sputtering candle stuck with melted tallow to the surface. The generals had a half-dozen rush chairs in which to sit. Gouverneur Warren, who had been slightly wounded in the neck during the fighting, threw himself down on the bed and promptly fell asleep. The rest of the generals discussed the day's events by the flickering light of the candle. Howard was the youngest general there, and Haskell found "nothing marked about him," despite the missing arm. He summed him up as looking like "a very pleasant, affable, well-dressed gentleman." In an account of Gettysburg he wrote to his brother, Haskell made a snide reference to *"the brilliant 11th corps,"* and said it "would have been trusted nowhere but a safe distance from the enemy," but he said that was no fault of Howard's, "for he is a good and brave man."[2]

Meade watched and listened as his generals conversed but said little. Finally his chief of staff, Daniel Butterfield, suggested that the generals put the salient issues on hand to a vote. They all voted to keep the army at Gettysburg, with any necessary corrections in the line. They also voted to remain on the defensive for the time being and wait for Lee to make the next move. The question on how long to wait remained undecided, but it couldn't be for long.

"Such then is the decision," said Meade. The tired generals dispersed to their commands. Howard rode back to the XI Corps and found himself a place to sleep among the silent dead of Evergreen Cemetery, using a grave for a pillow. He fell into a deep slumber.[3]

— ∙ —

With Strong Vincent mortally wounded, his brigade command fell on Colonel Rice of the 44th New York. When Col. Joseph W. Fisher reached Little Round Top with his V Corps brigade, Rice asked him to take some of his men to secure the summit of Big Round Top. Fisher declined. Rice asked Chamberlain if he would do it instead. Chamberlain said he would, even though his men could be excused if they felt they had done enough fighting for one day. "It was then dusk," Chamberlain wrote. "The men were worn out, and heated and thirsty—almost beyond endurance. Many had sunk down and fallen asleep the instant the halt was ordered. But at the command they cheerfully formed their line once more, and the little handful of men went up the hill, scarcely expecting ever to return." He had about 200 soldiers available for the task.[4]

In some ways this night climb was more nerve-racking than the blood and thunder on Little Round Top had been. The regiment had little ammunition and Chamberlain wanted to avoid a firefight that would give away his small numbers, so he had his men move forward with their bayonets attached. The little band crawled and climbed through the darkness. It was "rough scrambling," Chamberlain noted. Ahead they could hear enemy troops crashing through the woods as they fell back. There was a full moon, but its light proved feeble in the dark woods. As the men of the 20th Maine reached the summit, some of the pickets advanced far enough to see the light from enemy campfires flickering through the trees. They fell back, and some of the Rebels pulled themselves away from their fires in pursuit.[5]

"Who goes there?" one of the Mainers shouted.

"4th Texas," came the reply.

"Alright come on, we're 4th Texas," a quick-witted Mainer replied, and the unfortunate Rebels from the Lone Star State emerged from the trees to find themselves facing leveled muskets and a Maine man behind each one. The regiment bagged some 30 prisoners, including Gen. Evander Law's acting assistant adjutant. Ellis Spear remembered how one of the Southerners commented "on the fact that men from the two ends of the country should so meet, in the woods & dark."[6]

Once he reached the summit, Chamberlain sent for reinforcements. Fisher ordered two of his Pennsylvania regiments to climb Big Round Top and provide support on the 20th Maine's right. The Pennsylvanians stumbled and thrashed their way up the dark hill. Alerted by the noise, enemy soldiers fired a volley into the night. Chamberlain said the Pennsylvanians "started like antelopes & went down the way they had come up on, & never stopped till they were behind the line on Little Round Top again." Chamberlain sent a messenger to Rice requesting he send either the 83rd Pennsylvania or the 44th New York for support. He felt he could depend on regiments from his own brigade. Leaving pickets at the summit, he withdrew the rest of the regiment back to level ground until reinforcements arrived from the 83rd Pennsylvania. Then he moved his men back up the steep slope.[7]

There the men of the 20th Maine settled in for a long and uncomfortable night. Overcome by fatigue and illness, Spear fell asleep sitting against a tree. He woke in the middle of the night shaking and shivering with a feverish chill. He found a soldier sleeping on the ground, crawled next to him to share his blanket and body warmth, and fell back asleep.[8]

The 20th Maine had secured Big Round Top without suffering any casualties, but as morning began to brighten the eastern sky, Lt. Arad Linscott decided to grab a musket and see if he could annoy Rebels he heard moving on his front. One of them shot Linscott instead, and the young lieutenant fell with a mortal wound to the thigh. Later that morning the regiment was relieved by the First Brigade and moved back down the mountain. It took up a position somewhere to the left of the center of the Union line on Cemetery Ridge. The men sat down to wait and see what would happen next.[9]

The apparently lifeless body of John Chase, the private from the 5th Maine Battery who had been badly wounded by a shell on July 2, still lay by the rock where he had been placed. His spirit may have ventured elsewhere. Years later, Chase recollected having an out-of-body experience while he lay unconscious on the battlefield. He remembered feeling "perfectly happy" as he looked down on his mangled physical form. "I was taken to a very beautiful place where all was peace and joy," he said. His visit was all too short.[10]

As the sun ascended from behind Cemetery Ridge on July 3, Capt. William Fogler advanced with four companies of the 19th Maine to serve as skirmishers. They moved across the field in front of the Union position toward the Emmitsburg Road and established a line with its right near the Codori farmhouse. Some of the skirmishers occupied the farm buildings. The men had not eaten anything for 24 hours and they had no opportunity to get breakfast or even water. The day was promising to be hot and uncomfortable even for well-nourished soldiers who were not occupying a position dangerously close to the enemy. Fogler and his skirmishers were so exposed they had to lie down in the tall grass to keep from providing targets for enemy sharpshooters. Tired, hot, hungry, and thirsty, they watched and waited as the sun rose higher and the day began to grow warm. Temperatures climbed into the 80s. "The heat in the glaring sun was intolerable, and we had been without food and water since the morning before, and our stomachs were getting to be a little shaky," remembered Silas Adams.[11]

Off to the right of the Union line, at Culp's Hill, a fierce battle erupted in the morning when soldiers of the XII Corps took back the entrenchments Confederates had occupied after the Federals had pulled out and marched south to reinforce the left. The men of the 5th Maine Battery, who had fallen into such an exhausted slumber that even a brief, soaking shower during the night couldn't disturb it, were rudely awakened when Union artillery saluted the dawn with a barrage directed at the Rebels who had taken the XII Corps' positions. The firing continued until ten o'clock or so, as the XII Corps infantry overcame stubborn Confederate resistance and regained their entrenchments. During the struggle, Rebel bullets occasionally zipped past the battery, and Lieutenant Whittier became concerned that an attack on his position might be imminent. He had men get supplies of canister from the ammunition chests he had filled the night before and place them within the entrenchments. Later in the day he considered relocating two of his guns to the higher Culp's Hill, where they would have a better field of fire, but decided that moving them through the woods would have required chopping down too many trees.[12]

After leaving his brothers as they rode on to Little Round Top on July 2, John Chamberlain fell back to the rear, where he listened as the growing swell of battle became "one continuous roar and one mass of smoke." He found Rowland Howard, and the two men shared a bit of hard bread that Chamberlain had with him. Later a local man offered them some nuts he had been saving for his hogs. They accompanied the nuts with a few cherries before Rowland departed for the XI Corps hospital. Chamberlain went to work at the V Corps aid station.

John Chamberlain felt sick on the morning of July 3, but a bit of "paste" a local woman served him and a crust of bread he got from a chaplain had him feeling well enough to work. There was plenty of work to do. The wounded were flooding the V Corps hospital where he volunteered, and he anxiously checked their faces, fearing he would find one of his brothers. He did encounter wounded from the 20th Maine, and he heard plenty of rumors about the fate of its colonel. And he witnessed firsthand the horrors of war. "Men without an eye or nose or leg or arm or with mangled head or body would constantly attract your sympathy, each one looking a little worse than the one before," he said. Dying men gave him messages to pass on to their families. Others begged for water or asked him to find some shelter to protect them from the relentless sun.[13]

Overall, though, the day remained strangely peaceful, considering that two contending armies lay within firing distance of each other. It was the kind of hot summer's day that induced drowsiness and languor, especially for men exhausted by the marching and fighting they had done over the past days and weeks. Flies droned; the grass in the fields between the rival forces swayed in the fitful breezes. More ambitious soldiers used whatever implements they had on hand to dig shallow entrenchments. Others sought out abandoned weapons—the guns of the dead and wounded, or those thrown down by soldiers who had sought shelter in the rear—and began loading them in preparation for what they knew must be coming. From their position near Cemetery Hill, the men of the 16th Maine endured the sun and watched the Union batteries near them wheel their cannons into position, a sign that the silence of that long, hot afternoon was going to be rudely interrupted.

And then, sometime around one o'clock, it was.

For years to come, soldiers who were at Gettysburg attempted to describe the sheer magnitude of the cannonade that erupted on the afternoon of July 3, 1863. When they did, they often reached the limits of language and found it to be nearly indescribable. It started simply enough, when a pair of cannon shots from the Confederate side punctured the lazy afternoon's silence. It was the signal to commence fire— and the Rebel batteries reacted with a vengeance. Cannon after cannon unleashed shot, shell, flame, and thunder. Some 160 Confederate guns took part in the bombardment, and they were soon answered by about 130 on the Union side. Supposedly, the rumble of artillery reached as far away as Pittsburgh and Philadelphia. At Gettysburg, the roar was deafening as well as deadly. "The very earth seemed to tremble as if in the convulsions of a mighty earthquake," said John D. Smith in his history of the 19th Maine. "The earth was thrown up in clouds and the air filled with screeching missiles of death. Upon every side horses were falling and caissons exploding. Animals fled in terror. Horses accustomed to the noises of battle neighed in fright. Shells exploding in the air sent their jagged fragments in all directions. Mothers in neighboring houses, with pale faces and white lips, clasped their little children in their arms in mortal fear. The crash and roar were unearthly. It is impossible to describe the horror and suffering and havoc of this hour."[14]

Abner Small of the 16th Maine also tried to convey his impressions of the bombardment. "For two hours the air was filled with a horrible

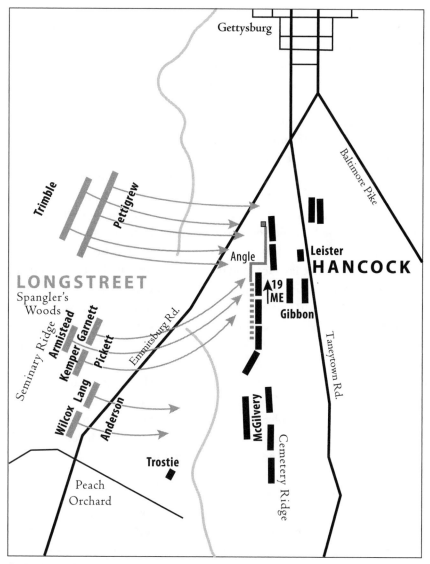

Gettysburg, July 3

concordance of sounds—a roar, echoing the passions of hell loosed among men," he wrote. "Men cover the ground in fragments, and are buried in detail beneath the iron hail. Guns are dismounted, and rest their metallic weight upon quivering flesh. Caissons explode, and wheels and boxes strew the ground in every direction. Horses by the score are blown down by the terrible hurricane, and lie shrieking in agony almost human in its expression. One battery in our immediate front lost forty horses in twenty minutes."[15]

"In the world's history there has been nothing like it before, and there has been nothing like it since," wrote Francis Wiggin, also of the 16th Maine. "It was like the continuous roll of the heaviest thunder that ever shook the earth, so continuous that during the whole time there was not a single instance of rest or silence."[16]

Under such an artillery hell there was little to do but hug the ground and hope that the horrible bombardment ended before a shell found you. John Lancaster of the 19th Maine remembered that he and the other men of the regiment lay face-down on the ground as the Rebel guns in front sent shells hurtling their way and Union guns roared from behind. "It seemed as though, had a knitting needle stood on end it would have been shot off a dozen times in so many minutes, and yet we had nothing to do but lay there and reflect upon the contingencies of being sent into eternity the next minute," Lancaster said.[17]

According to Silas Adams of the 19th Maine, forward with the skirmish line near the Codori farm, "The crashings and explosions seemed more like a volcanic upheaval of nature, trying to reform the face of the earth, than anything that could be produced by man's ingenuity. Every man in our lines protected himself the best he could, behind such protection as nature afforded and his own genius and labor could devise."[18]

Cpl. Wilbur Clifford of the 19th Maine was in the Codori barn when the cannonade began. "You can have no idea of the scene," he wrote his father later. "It seemed as through the air was full of Devils such an unearthly noise and shell bursting all around us ploughing up the ground and some times come crashing tho the old barn that was rocking as tho there was an earth quake under it."[19]

Clifford's regimental commander, Francis Heath, was more laconic when he wrote to Selden Connor years later about his experiences at Gettysburg. "All we had to do while undergoing the shelling was to chew tobacco, watch the caissons explode and wonder if the next shot would hit you," Heath wrote. "On the whole it was not a happy time."[20]

The cannons created noise, concussion, and a hail of lead, but also smoke. As the artillery barrage continued, the battlefield became cloaked in a thick man-made fog that reeked of sulphur and burned eyes and lungs. It wasn't long before the Union troops on Cemetery Ridge could no longer see the enemy lines opposite them, even though it was a bright, sunny day.[21]

Otis Howard witnessed the terrible onslaught from his position in the cemetery. "Shells burst in the air, in the ground to the right and left, killing horses, exploding caissons, overturning tombstones, and smashing fences," he wrote. "There was no place of safety. In one regiment 27 were killed and wounded by one shell, and yet the regiments of this corps did not move excepting when ordered." Despite the onslaught of enemy artillery, Howard was more worried about being hit from the debris—the "strippings"—from the shells the Union guns were launching behind him. He had his staff build a barricade out of cracker boxes and he sat with his back to it on the slope of Cemetery Hill while the guns roared behind him.

When Howard saw Thomas Osborn, the head of the corps' artillery, talking with Henry Hunt, the army's chief of artillery, he joined them. So did Carl Schurz. Osborn suggested having the artillery cease fire as a way to lull the Confederates into a false impression that the Union batteries were spent. Howard and Hunt agreed it was a good idea. Osborn later became miffed that Hunt took credit for the suggestion. "This moment was in fact the turning point in the battle in our favor, and Hunt made the most of it for himself," he complained.[22]

At some point Col. Richard Coulter, the I Corps brigade commander for whom Abner Small served as adjutant, noticed that the color bearer in charge of his brigade flag had disappeared. Coulter flew into a rage. "Where in hell is my flag?" he demanded. "Where do you suppose that cowardly son of a bitch has skedaddled to?" He dispatched Small in one direction to find the missing soldier and he went off to search in another. Coulter found the man lying behind a stone wall with the folded-up flag. The colonel got the frightened soldier to his feet, unfolded the flag, and placed the staff in the man's hands. Just then a shell exploded nearby. It killed a horse, showered both men with dirt, and knocked the flag down. Coulter calmly picked up the banner, planted the staff in the newly formed crater, and told the soldier to hold the flag there. "If I can't get you killed in ten minutes, by God, I'll post you right up among the batteries!" he yelled. As he rode past Small, Coulter assured the adjutant that it was unlikely that two shells would land in the same spot. The man should be safe enough. Coulter spurred his horse and rode off down his line. A few minutes later a sharpshooter shot him through the shoulder.[23]

Farther to the left, Thomas Hyde had been busy fulfilling his responsibilities as a member of John Sedgwick's staff by riding around the battlefield and gathering information for the commander of the VI Corps. On Little Round Top, he saw Meade and Warren arrive to take a look across the battlefield. He enjoyed a Spartan lunch of hardtack with coffee, and had just settled behind a large boulder to rest when the world erupted. "The open ground behind our lines was being torn up in every direction by the shells," he recalled. "Occasionally a caisson exploded, riderless horses were dashing about, and a throng of wounded were streaming to the rear." Hyde endured the barrage from behind his boulder. At its height he was shocked to see a man with a long beard and glasses and wearing a long duster staggering drunkenly towards him across the open country. Hyde recognized him as a sutler's clerk. The man came closer through the fusillade. A shell nearly hit him but the clerk continued on, unfazed. He stumbled up to Hyde and put a hand to his ear. "Listen to the mockingbird," he bellowed, and then he staggered on. "With the providential good fortune of drunken men, he had crossed for some distance in safety over ground upon which it seemed impossible for any living thing to remain a minute," said Hyde, still amazed by the incident years later.[24]

Freeman McGilvery had been busy since completing his hot work the previous evening. Henry Hunt gave him responsibility for more guns, and McGilvery placed them in a long line in preparation for the fight. He now counted 39 guns under his command, including the four 12-pounders of Dow's 6th Maine Battery. He had the artillery crews throw up some crude earthworks to provide protection from enemy shells. After the cannonade erupted, he followed Hunt's orders and told his batteries to hold their fire until they heard otherwise.

Despite its sound and fury, the enemy cannonade failed to impress McGilvery, who said the fire was "very rapid and inaccurate, with most of the projectiles passing from 20 to 100 feet over our lines." This was true of the Rebel cannonade in general. Much of the fire overshot the Union lines and exploded on the far side of Cemetery Ridge. This was good news for the men on the front lines, but not so much for those in the rear. Meade's headquarters was on the back side of the ridge and thus in the danger zone. It began to get riddled by shells, and Meade was forced to move down to Powers Hill to escape the enemy fire.[25]

Captain Charles Phillips, who commanded the 5th Massachusetts Battery in McGilvery's artillery line, also remained unimpressed by the Confederate barrage. "Viewed as a display of fireworks, the Rebel practice was entirely successful, but as a military demonstration it was the biggest humbug of the season," he said.[26]

Whether he stole the idea or not, Henry Hunt did believe it would be a good idea for the Union guns to restrain their fire. Not only would they preserve ammunition for the infantry attack that would inevitably follow the bombardment, it would also give the Rebels a false sense of their artillery's effectiveness. Winfield Scott Hancock, on the other hand, just wanted the guns to keep firing, believing it would help the soldiers' morale to hear the thunder of their own artillery. By following Hunt's orders, McGilvery found himself stuck between two strong-willed generals. "About one-half hour after the commencement, some general commanding the infantry line ordered three of the batteries to return the fire," McGilvery wrote in his official report, his disdain for the unnamed officer, most likely Hancock, clearly evident. (According to one account, McGilvery responded to Hancock by telling him to "go to hell.") McGilvery merely did the minimum required. "After the discharge of a few rounds, I ordered the fire to cease and the men to be covered," he said. When Hancock rode over and personally ordered the 5th Massachusetts

Battery to begin firing, Charles Phillips dutifully obeyed. McGilvery rode over and ordered them to stop. The same thing happened with the 15th New York Battery. Not until the artillery duel had lasted for 90 minutes or so did McGilvery order his men to begin carefully targeting individual enemy batteries and put them out of commission. He was satisfied when he saw the fire from his guns force several enemy batteries to limber up and head for the rear.[27]

—— ⚬ ——

Recollections of the length of the cannonade vary. Some say it lasted for two hours. Others say 90 minutes. The sheer intensity of the man-made thunder seemed to have warped time for some observers. But at some point the firing of the guns began to slow and the unimaginable noise began to diminish, until at last silence once again descended over the smoke-covered battlefield. "It now had become a perfect stillness, almost like a quiet Sabbath morning," remembered Silas Adams.[28]

During the bombardment, Charles O. Hunt of the 5th Maine Battery lay on a mattress in his sister's dining room—which he felt was the safest place to be—and listened to the roar of the guns, which shook the brick house to its foundation. "As the town lay, in a sense, between the two fires, the uproar seemed more terrible to us than it would if we had been on either line," Hunt remembered. "The earth literally shook." After a time, the terrible, unnatural roar gradually died out, and a pregnant silence settled over the town. The house's inhabitants were filled with a great anxiety as to its meaning.[29]

The cannonade had just been the opening act of Robert E. Lee's plan. Now it was time for the main event. From their positions on Cemetery Ridge or Little Round Top, Union soldiers watched with a sense of awe as Confederates by the thousands began to file out of the woods along Seminary Ridge; thousands more rose up from the grass in the fields where they had lain during the barrage. From their forward position near the Codori farm buildings, the skirmishers of the 19th Maine had a ringside seat. They saw the Rebels form as though they were on a parade ground, flags unfurled, lines straight, weapons shouldered. One soldier said the deployment was "a magnificent spectacle" and looked "like the opening of a vast fan." Clearly the battle was entering its final act. "We knew then that a decisive moment was coming; and we felt that we were equal to it," remembered one officer.[30]

Three divisions would take part in Lee's assault. Maj. Gen. George Pickett's three brigades were on the Confederate right. To his left was the division under James Pettigrew, who had taken over from the wounded Henry Heth. Dorsey Pender was also wounded, so Isaac Trimble commanded his division, deploying behind Pettigrew's men. All told there were approximately 13,000 Rebels participating in the charge. They had to march across some 1,400 yards of fields—more than three-quarters of a mile—before they reached Cemetery Ridge. The defenders there remained hunkered down behind the stone walls and any crude entrenchments they had thrown up, where they waited for the killing to begin.

Many soldiers found the Rebel advance to be something of a relief after the nerve-rattling, mind-numbing tumult of the artillery barrage. "It requires less nerve to face the enemy man to man, in open field, than to lie down supinely while he hurls his missiles," noted George Nash of the 19th Maine.[31]

From his position in the grass near the Emmitsburg Road, where he had been baking in the sun and concentrating on his hunger and thirst, Silas Adams watched enemy skirmishers move ahead of the main force and begin dismantling rail fences that would have slowed the advance. The impressively arrayed lines of the enemy were ready to move, and the Maine skirmishers watched with intense interest. "Then they came on in magnificent order and in most perfect military precision which seemed to control their whole movement," remembered Adams. As the enemy came closer, Adams and his fellow skirmishers decided it was time to stir from the sheltering grass and get out of the way. Adams tried to stand, but his legs had fallen asleep during the long wait and were completely numb. It took him a few anxious minutes to kick some life back into his limbs before he could lurch to his feet and begin to stumble back toward his own lines. The Maine men occasionally turned around to fire a parting shot or two. The advancing Rebels did not return the fire. More worrisome was the fire from Union soldiers who thought the returning skirmishers were Rebels.[32]

John Lancaster was with the rest of the 19th Maine on Cemetery Ridge, watching the Rebel infantry move steadily forward in neat lines. Years later, he put things into perspective for an audience in his native state by saying the number of Rebels the Union defenders faced was double the entire population of Bath, Maine. They looked like an irresistible wave about to crash down on the Army of the Potomac.[33]

Back in town, Charles Hunt listened anxiously to the sounds of battle and tried to interpret their meaning. Shortly after the artillery died into silence he heard the ripping crash of muskets, and Hunt knew the fighting had shifted to the infantry. "The most trying feature of our situation was our ignorance of how the battle was going," he said. "I could generally know that our guns were still in position by noting the explosion of shell, but beyond that we could learn nothing. During the whole period of the battle we were oppressed with the most intense anxiety."[34]

As the fighting headed for its climax on Cemetery Ridge, another battle took place behind the Union lines, a clash of the Union and Confederate cavalries that had been contending with each other ever since Brandy Station. "It can be safely said that on no other field did Union cavalry whether on foot or in the saddle, do more effective and brilliant fighting than on this," said division commander David McMurtrie Gregg. The 1st Maine Cavalry, which had fought many pitched engagements as it followed Lee's army north, could take little of the credit for this battle, though. They were little more than spectators.[35]

Some Maine cavalrymen did play small but sometimes vital roles during the three days of battle as orderlies, riding about and delivering messages. It could be very hazardous duty: Pvt. Edward Cunningham of Co. L was killed on July 3 while attached to Abner Doubleday's staff. The 1st Maine's captain, John P. Carson, served as an orderly for John Reynolds and was reportedly at the general's side on July 1 when Reynolds was killed. Sgt. Ebenezer Johnson also served as an orderly for the I Corps. One of his fellow soldiers remembered him as a "marked character, made so by the fact that he was equally at home in leading a prayer meeting or a charge upon the enemy." At Gettysburg he did such sterling service that both Colonel Coulter and General Robinson singled him out for praise. Robinson said Johnson's "chevrons should be exchanged for the epaulette. When we make officers of such men, the soldier receives his true reward and the service great benefit."[36]

After the rolling engagements with Jeb Stuart's cavalry in Virginia, the Maine horsemen had headed north with the Army of the Potomac. Although the journey was relatively uneventful, it was not easy. "The long march had been a terrible one," remembered one participant. "The intense heat had at times been almost unendurable, the dust almost impenetrable." Horses, too tired to move, fell out of the column along the road. Men trudged along the dusty roads on foot, filthy and exhausted, leading their equally spent mounts. Men whose horses had died lugged their own saddles and bridles.

James R. Shehan of Company I, a Biddeford native, derived one benefit from the difficult journey. Riding through the town of Westminster, Maryland, he spied an American flag being waved from a window in one of the houses. This show of patriotism south of the Mason-Dixon Line impressed Shehan so strongly that he later visited the town and sought out the home's owner—and married his daughter.[37]

Gregg's brigade finally reached the vicinity of Gettysburg very early in the morning of July 2. The Maine cavalrymen participated in a little skirmishing that afternoon—nothing even close to the scale of the slaughter on the other side of Cemetery Ridge—and that night were ordered over to the Baltimore Pike to take a position near the artillery reserve. The next morning they returned to the right of the Union line, but weren't sent in to the fight against Stuart and his cavalry until the fighting was nearly over.[38]

They arrived at the tail end of a sharp cavalry battle. Stuart arrived on the field first with about 3,000 men, emerging from the woods near a farm owned by the Rummel family. From that position in the rear of the Union army he threatened the Baltimore Pike, a vital lifeline for Meade's forces. Gregg's Union cavalry, about 3,250 men, including Michigan troopers under George Armstrong Custer, rode forward to confront the Rebels. The two sides attacked and counterattacked, fighting dismounted and behind fences and farm buildings. There were classic cavalry charges, too, with mounted men chopping at each other with sabers. Horses whinnied, men fell, artillery roared. "So sudden and violent was the collision that many of the horses were turned end over end and crushed their riders beneath them," recalled one of the battle's participants. Custer, who was supposed to be with his own division under Judson Kilpatrick but had chosen to remain where the action was, led his command into the fight with a cry of "Come on, you wolverines!" During the melee, the Union cavalry forced the Rebels away from the farm buildings and into the woods beyond. Late in the fight, Colonel Smith and his Maine cavalry received orders to form a line in an orchard on the left of the division, where their presence alone was enough to halt a Rebel advance.

"About three o'clock Friday the enemy attempted to turn our right and a smart cavalry fight took place," William B. Baker, a sergeant in the 1st Maine Cavalry's Co. D, informed his parents. "Our Regt. was in reserve till about four when the enemy made an attempt to take our battery. The 5th Michigan broke badly and scattered all over the fields but as the rebs advanced our guns opened with grape and quick it was I assure you. When we went up in front and to the right of our battery the rebs sent shell over us quite briskly. Lieut. Hall of Co. H was knocked form his horse by the force of one as it passed near him. He was not much hurt. We expected to charge but did not."[39]

Stuart realized he had been checked and moved his troopers back into the woods. Baltimore Pike was safe. This part of the battle was over.

On the other side of the battlefield, the Rebel lines continued their inexorable advance. Initially it appeared that Pickett's division, on the right of the Confederate formation, was on a collision course with the II Corps brigades of William Harrow and Norman Hall. After crossing the Emmitsburg Road, though, Pickett's men began shifting to the left. This placed them on a heading that took them in the direction of Alexander Webb's II Corps brigade. Webb's men—the Philadelphia Brigade—held a line on Cemetery Ridge near a prominent clump of trees. A stone wall ran south to north from the trees before bending at a 90-degree angle to the east and then making another 90-degree angle to continue off to the north. That first bend in the wall would soon gain the name of the "Bloody Angle." Hall's brigade was on Webb's left, continuing the line south from the other side of the trees. Harrow's brigade was next in the line. Harrow's force included the 19th Maine, the only Maine regiment to materially participate in the repulse of Pickett's charge.

As Pickett's division made its course correction to the left, it exposed its flank to the 19th Maine, on the far right of Harrow's brigade. The Maine soldiers held their fire until the Confederates were within range. Pvt. John Day Smith found the sight of the long lines of Rebels to be "inspiring." "There was a coolness, an air of discipline and a precision of movement that called forth from the Union soldiers a spontaneous expression of admiration," he said. Nonetheless, the Federals were eager to kill these soldiers they so admired.[40]

Before they had to withstand musket fire, the Confederates first had to march through an artillery hell. Henry Hunt's directions to his guns to hold their fire no longer applied once the Rebel infantry began moving. The Federal artillery batteries erupted back into life with a vengeance and began to rip great holes in the orderly lines of butternut and gray that were moving remorselessly across the fields toward Cemetery Ridge. First they used solid shot and percussion shells. "The artillerymen endeavored to roll the solid shot through the ranks and explode the percussion shells in front of the lines," explained Thomas Osborn, who said they could see up to a dozen men being taken out with a single shot. As the Rebels came closer, the Union batteries could use timed shells—"the killing and wounding was proportionately more severe," said Osborn. Once the enemy were even closer, the Union guns switched to shotgun-like canister.[41]

"The execution of the fire must have been terrible, as it was over a level plain, and the effect was plain to see," reported McGilvery, whose guns were to the south of the Rebel assault, giving them an oblique fire into the Rebel ranks. "In a few minutes, instead of a well-ordered line of battle, there were broken and confused masses, and fugitives fleeing in every direction."[42]

Edwin Dow of the 6th Maine Battery didn't recall the same amount of chaos that McGilvery did, despite the slaughter. "I tell you the gaps we made were simply terrible," he said. "But they closed up their lines, and closed them up and closed them up till they got to within a hundred yards of our position and then, with one hundred guns pouring lead into them, they closed for the last time and rushed us at the double quick." When the Confederates came close enough to the Union lines, Dow's and McGilvery's other batteries ceased fire so as to not hit their own troops. Despite the havoc sowed by the Union cannon and muskets, the Rebel lines still looked so imposing that Dow felt anxious for the Union defenders.[43]

Many of those defenders shared Dow's anxiety as the Confederate troops reached the Emmitsburg Road, crossed it, and continued on. Alexander Webb, only 28 years old, was very new to brigade command. He had received his promotion only three days before the battle began, as the army was marching north toward Pennsylvania. He didn't know his men, and they didn't know him. Now he watched the enemy advancing "in splendid order" directly at his command. These Rebels were the men in a brigade under Lewis Armistead, who was leading them with his black hat stuck on the point of his sword. Closer and closer they came, even as Union guns continued to take an increasingly heavy toll. The approaching Rebels proved too much for the 71st Pennsylvania of Webb's brigade, which broke for the rear, opening up a dangerous gap in the Union line. John Lancaster of the 19th Maine compared it to the way the end of a piece of birch bark curls back when it is thrown into a fire. Despite the blistering musketry, a small band of Rebels led by Armistead made their way up to the stone fence, stepped over it at the Angle, and crossed into the Union lines. "When they were over the fence the Army of the Potomac was nearer being whipped than it was at any time of the battle," Webb said. He began frantically to get men to move forward to the wall and drive the Rebels back.[44]

Webb's division commander, John Gibbon, was also seeking reinforcements to steady the Union line. As the Rebel attack neared its climax, Gibbon found himself behind the 19th Maine. He tried to get the regiment to change front and move to its right to help Webb's beleaguered men. Unable to prompt the Maine soldiers to move, he trotted out in front of them to offer more encouragement. It was not a particularly good place to be, as Gibbon realized when the 19th Maine opened fire at the advancing Rebels. "I got to the rear as soon as possible," Gibbon recalled somewhat sheepishly. He moved down the line, and then returned to the 19th Maine. As he renewed his efforts to move them over to assist Webb, a bullet struck him in the shoulder, taking him out of the battle.[45]

In the meantime, McGilvery received another chance to hurt the enemy when the Rebel brigades of Brig. Gen. Cadmus Wilcox and Col. David Lang began an ill-advised movement forward to support Pickett's division. They started their advance directly in front of McGilvery's guns, and the Union artillerymen did not neglect the opportunity. One of the officers in Lang's brigade said the advance was "the hottest work I ever saw. My men falling all around me with brains blown out, arms off and wounded in every description." Realizing the futility of the attack, the Confederates retreated.[46]

Back on Cemetery Ridge, Gibbon's aide Frank Haskell did what he could to get the regiments of Norman Hall's brigade—between the 19th Maine and a copse of trees—moving to help Webb. Dashing about on horseback, Haskell next gathered regiments from Harrow's brigade—the 19th Maine, 15th Massachusetts, 82nd New York, and what remained of the 1st Minnesota—and hurried them at double-quick to the crisis point. "It was a wild charge, with little regard for ranks or files," noted the account in *Maine at Gettysburg*. "Volleys were given and received at close quarters. In their anxiety to reach the foe, men thrust their rifles over the shoulders, under the arms and between the legs, of those in the front ranks of the melee."[47]

As Colonel Heath urged his men over to pitch in at the Angle, he found it impossible to keep them in any kind of order. "Everyone wanted to be first there and we went up more like a mob than a disciplined force," he said. A shell fragment struck Heath during this last impetuous charge and he went down and out of the fight. Lieutenant Colonel Cunningham assumed command for the final act in the battle.[48]

Webb ordered the regiment down to the wall. The Maine men pressed in toward the copse of trees with the other soldiers from Harrow's and Hall's brigades. It was less a military maneuver than an excited mass of men with weapons, all of whom wanted to get their licks in while they had the chance. "We were all loading and firing and yelling and pushing towards the gap now filled with the exultant Rebels," remembered John Lancaster. "Company, regimental and brigade organizations were lost, and we were a great crowd. We would load, run to the front and fire, then others would jump in front of us and fire, and the color bearers, always at the front, would toss their colors up and down to show the enemy that we were not going to give it up, and to encourage us on." Lancaster found many abandoned weapons on the ground that he could use. Other soldiers were fighting hand to hand and a few, at least, were simply hurling stones at the Confederates. "And so we kept on and on—then suddenly I found myself rushing with all our crowed upon the enemy with an impetuosity that was irresistible, and the day was ours," he recalled. [49]

The Confederate tide had peaked at the Angle; the last remnants of the seemingly irresistible wave of soldiers that marched from Seminary Ridge shattered and broke. Those attackers who could manage it turned around and started to make their way back to their own lines, a journey that Union fire made nearly as dangerous as the advance. Those unwilling to risk being shot while retreating surrendered instead. The dead and wounded lay where they fell. Armistead was one of them, having fallen mortally wounded on the ground near one of the Union guns that had done so much damage to his men. Frank Haskell stood and watched the defeated enemy soldiers streaming back toward Seminary Ridge. He looked around him and noted the many soldiers—"the thick dead of Maine, and Minnesota, and Michigan, and Massachusetts, and the Empire and Keystone States"—who had given their lives for the country. He thought it was "the saddest sight of many of such a field."[50]

—◆—

The 17th Maine spent the day of July 3 waiting and watching as the battle unfolded in front of Cemetery Ridge. John Haley saw brigade commander de Trobriand pacing up and down alongside his troops, providing "a stream of jokes and repartee in true French style and spirit. Being done in his broken English, made it doubly humorous." He watched Hancock ride up and down the line, looking cool and confident. Haley and his fellow soldiers saw the Rebel infantry begin their advance and watched with a mix of fascination and horror as the Union guns began to tear bloody holes through them, knocking men down by the score. The enemy's parade-ground precision quickly deteriorated into chaos and confusion. By the time de Trobriand's brigade received orders to move toward the crisis point and throw its weight behind the defenders, the Confederate tide had begun to recede across the fields.[51]

Just after the wave had crested, the remnants of the 16th Maine moved up from the rear, through the cemetery and up to Cemetery Ridge. Abner Small was struck by a "strange and terrible" sound, "a vast mournful roar" that came from the hundreds of soldiers engaged in the struggle. Once over the ridge he saw the ground covered with the dead and dying and watched Confederates raise their hands in surrender while others retreated. All he could feel was pity.[52]

Charles Clark of the 6th Maine, one of the VI Corps regiments, watched the climax of Gettysburg from a seat on Little Round Top. When he saw the Rebels falling back toward Seminary Ridge, their once straight and intimidating lines now broken and confused, he knew the battle was over "and that a glorious Union triumph had been achieved." Later, moving in the rear with his regiment, Clark recognized a horse tied to an ambulance. It belonged to Winfield Scott Hancock, who had been the 6th Maine's brigade commander back at Williamsburg in 1862. Like Gibbon, Hancock had been wounded at the climax of the battle, when a bullet had passed through his saddle and into his thigh, taking a nail with it. The men rushed over to see what had happened to their much-loved old commander. They found Hancock inside the ambulance, looking pale and faint. The soldiers gave a cheer when they saw he was still alive, and Hancock rallied. "The old fire came into his eyes, and he said affectionately, 'Why, this is my old Sixth Maine,'" said Clark. "The meeting and greeting were long remembered on both sides."[53]

The 19th Maine's John Lancaster found that once the mad rush of battle subsided it was replaced by a gnawing hunger. On Cemetery Ridge he found a young Rebel who was nearing his end, left behind to die as the Rebels retreated. As his life faded, the young Confederate breathed a last prayer for his wife and child. Lancaster waited until the man was dead, and then ransacked his haversack and found some biscuit and honey to satisfy his appetite.[54]

That night the men of the 17th Maine moved forward across the fields to serve as pickets. They encountered scenes of horror. The stench from the already decomposing bodies was overwhelming, and the wounded men who still lay where they fell cried out for assistance. "The carnage here was of the most revolting nature, and cannot be described accurately," said Haley. "Men's heads torn off, and split open. Men split from the top of their head to their extremities, as a butcher splits an ox. Others had legs and arms, and parts of the trunk gone, and the bowels protruding, and were killed in almost every conceivable manner. This seems more horrible than it was in reality, for many of them could not have had one single instant of consciousness after they were hit, and never knew what struck them. This is merciful to them." Haley was shocked when he discovered that one wounded North Carolina soldier was a 14-year-old boy.[55]

"May Satan, or the evil for which that name stands, get the ones who are doing this devilish work," Haley wrote.[56]

The battle of Gettysburg was over. It was, and remained, the bloodiest fight of the Civil War. Robert E. Lee's army had reached the field with 72,000 men. After three days of sometimes savage and brutal combat, 4,708 of them were dead, 12,693 were wounded, and 5,380 were reported captured or missing. The Army of the Potomac had 94,000 men for the battle. Of those, 3,155 were dead, 14,530 were wounded, and 5,369 were missing or captured.

In the days and weeks to come, families and friends back in Maine—from Kittery to Calais, Vinalhaven to Presque Isle—waited anxiously to hear about loved ones in the army. Some received good news; some bad; some never heard anything at all. The curved arcs of grave markers set into the ground at Gettysburg National Cemetery include 104 from the state of Maine. Among them is one for John L. Little of the 3rd Maine, who had written to his father in October 1861 to say he regretted enlisting; he had been killed in the fight for Pitzer's Woods on July 2. Pvt. Edward Cunningham of the 1st Maine Cavalry is there, too. He is buried with items found on his body—$3.95 in cash, a comb, and some postage stamps. First Sgt. Charles Steele of the 20th Maine, "Great-hearted Charley Steele of Co. H., beloved by all the regiment," as regimental historian Howard Prince remembered him, lies beneath the Gettysburg soil as well. Shot in the breast defending Little Round Top, Steele staggered up to his captain, Joseph Land, and said, "I am going, Captain," and then fell dead.[57]

Capt. George D. Smith of the 19th Maine is another of the dead at Gettysburg. Smith, from Rockland, was one of those soldiers who sensed impending doom as he moved north toward Pennsylvania. On June 29 he told Edwin Burpee, "I think we are on the eve of a terrible battle and I feel that I shall be killed or wounded." He was wounded on July 2 and died in the predawn hours the next day. He was buried with a "gold plate, with artificial tooth."[58]

These are only a few of the soldiers buried here.

Eleven of the markers simply read "unknown." One of them is for a soldier in the 20th Maine who was buried with a letter he carried, signed by someone named Anna Grove. Was she a sister, a wife, a mother? Was she waiting back home in Maine, wondering what had happened to the man she wrote to? It's safe to assume that for each unknown buried here there was at least one person back in Maine tormented by the unanswered questions of what had happened to the soldier who had marched off to war and never returned.

Gettysburg had been a great victory, but it had come at great cost. The Maine soldiers who had fought there could justifiably take credit for the important roles they had played in the battle. They had not, however, ended the war. No one had done that. It had been going on for just over two years, and Maine soldiers had already fallen on battlefields in Virginia and Maryland. They had died in front of Richmond, in the Slaughter Pen of Fredericksburg, in the tangled Wilderness, in Shenandoah Valley, on South Mountain, and on the bloody killing fields of Antietam. The cost had already been astronomical, but almost two more years of war still remained to be fought. Maine soldiers would be in the thick of it until the end.

CHAPTER 15

Aftermath

These exaggerations and the paper and soap-bubble reputations blown out in the last fifty years have grown more and more burdensome to me, and I am more and more impressed with the duty which we owe to posterity and the country at large to tell the truth, however unpleasant it may be to some. Unjust claims made by one are an injury to others and robbery.

—ELLIS SPEAR, 20TH MAINE

For the captured men of the 16th Maine, the second and third days of the battle were perhaps even more suspenseful and tense than they were for the soldiers still in the fight. Taken behind the lines by their captors on July 1, all the Maine prisoners could do was attempt to decipher what was happening on the battlefield by the sounds of the guns. The fact that the heaviest firing on the second and third days seemed to come from the same area gave them hope that the Union army was holding its own. Of even more immediate concern, though, was hunger. The men had received nothing to eat since being captured, and by July 3 they were ravenous. Some Rebels finally tossed them bags of captured flour, but nothing to mix it with or means to cook it. One resourceful Yankee fetched water from a nearby brook and added it to the flour on top of a rubber-lined blanket. The prisoners tossed the resulting substance onto flat rocks they heated in a fire. "It tasted good to those of us who had not had a morsel to eat for two days," said George Bisbee.

On July 3, Bisbee said, he saw Gen. George Pickett ride by before he led his division on the attack that Lee hoped would break the Union center. Like the soldiers on both sides, Bisbee endured the terrible cannonade that preceded the attack, and then he listened to the sound of musketry as the two infantries clashed. All he could see of the battle was smoke rising off in the distance. The suspense was excruciating. Then Pickett's soldiers came stumbling back out of the smoke, "bloody, wounded, straggling, and in short all cut up and with hardly any resemblance to the brave men who so boldly went out a short time before." Bisbee's guards told him that Pickett returned to his tent and sobbed over the deaths of his soldiers.[1]

Charles Augustus Garcelon of Lewiston joined the 16th Maine before he had turned 20 and became second lieutenant in Company I. He was the son of Alonzo Garcelon, Maine's surgeon general during the war, and also the nephew of Charles Waldron, the captain who had suffered the bloody neck wound on July 1. Garcelon and Waldron were both taken prisoner, and on July 4 Garcelon wrote a letter to his aunt to ease the anxiety she would feel when she heard her husband was wounded. "Don't worry about Uncle I think he will get along quite well," Garcelon told her. The ball, he said, had entered the neck and made a small puncture in the windpipe—but both the doctors and Garcelon felt the wound was not terribly serious. (It was serious enough to get Waldron discharged from the army, but he lived until 1881.) Young Garcelon had seen enough of war, however. "It seems this wicked war has gone far enough to stop," he wrote. "Both sides are tired of it." Garcelon had no doubt that there were some men who wanted to see the war continue as long as they could profit from it.[2]

On the night of July 4, as rain poured down, the captured members of the 16th Maine and the rest of the Union prisoners were placed in the rear of the Southern army to begin a weary march south. "While we rejoiced over the defeat of Lee's army and the success of the Union troops it was a sad march for us prisoners," Bisbee said.[3]

The 17th Maine was still dealing with the dead and wounded on July 4 when the heavens opened with a torrential rain. Many soldiers believed

that heavy artillery fire triggered rainstorms. In this case, the unprecedented barrage on July 3 brought equally heavy precipitation. John Haley
and other men from the regiment hastened to move some wounded soldiers who had been placed near a little stream and were threatened with
drowning when the brook became a torrent.[4]

In town, the situation appeared uncertain. Charles Hunt's sister,
Mary, sent out her servant on an errand, and when the woman returned
she told the inhabitants of the house that the Rebels had disappeared
from Gettysburg. "The good news was soon confirmed and the strain of
the anxious three days gave way to rejoicing," Hunt recalled. "Before long
our cavalry came in and occupied the streets, and they were followed by
infantry, and we knew that the battle of Gettysburg had been won."

The rejoicing was short-lived, for frightening rumors began sweeping through town. The Rebels, it was said, had left artillery on Seminary
Ridge and planned to use it to destroy Gettysburg before they departed.
For some citizens, this was the last straw. They grabbed whatever valu-
ables they could carry and fled. Mary fretted about what to do with her
wounded brother. Hunt thought he would be perfectly safe in the cellar,
but his sister was desperate to get him out of Gettysburg before Confederate cannon reduced it to rubble. The next-door neighbor owned a
wheelbarrow and volunteered it to transport Hunt to safety. "I protested
against such an undignified exit and persuaded them to postpone the
start till there was some certain evidence that the enemy would carry
out their supposed threat," Hunt said. "It is needless to add that the
wheel-barrow was not called into requisition."

Later that day Hunt wrote a letter to his mother back in Maine.
"Here I am lying on my back in Mary's back parlor making myself as
comfortable as possible," he told her. He said his wound was not serious
and he expected to be back on his feet in a couple of weeks and ready to
return to Maine to recuperate. "And then, dear Mother, I expect soon to
give you a good solid hug in our own old house in Gorham. Won't that
be worth getting wounded for." He was also pleased to think he might be
home for Bowdoin's commencement. "I think I am the luckiest dog that
ever lived. To think that I should have been wounded here! I have managed to get here every time that anything has been the matter with me."[5]

Joshua Chamberlain and the 20th Maine did not participate in the battle on July 3. From their position they were relatively protected from the Confederate cannonade, although Ellis Spear recalled that "the air in front was full of bursting shells, and the uproar was immense." The men couldn't even see the repulse of Pickett's charge and had to interpret the battle based on the gunfire and cheers they could hear. That night Spear shared a salvaged blanket with Capt. Atherton Clark, but their sleep was interrupted by a sudden downpour. They pulled on their wet boots and spent the rest of the night sitting on a stone wall.[6]

The men did little on the "Glorious Fourth" but watch, wait, and endure the tremendous rainstorm that resumed in the afternoon. Chamberlain found time to write a letter to his wife. "The 20th has immortalized itself," he wrote. "We had the post of honor in the severe fight of the 2d, on the extreme left where the enemy made a fierce attempt to turn the flank. My Regt was the extreme left & was attacked by a <u>whole Brigade."</u> He was justifiably proud of the role he and his regiment had played, and it showed in the letter, in which he briefly described the defense of Little Round Top, the final charge, and the way the 20th Maine had secured Big Round Top. "I am receiving all sorts of praise, but bear it meekly," Chamberlain added.[7]

On the morning of July 5, the regiment formed into line of battle and moved forward through fields strewn with the detritus of war—dead soldiers, muskets, haversacks, horses. The bodies were swollen, their faces black through decomposition. The air was filled with "a sickening odor." In a barn that had burned down during the fighting, the 20th found the partially consumed bodies of men who had died there. Spear was struck by the image of a dead Confederate—probably an officer, based on his fine boots—whose head and shoulders were charred ruins. Lingering over it all was the smell of death and rot. The men buried some of the bodies, and they ate a dinner of hardtack, "for to horrors men may become accustomed, but not to hunger," said Spear.[8]

By a house near an orchard, Nathan Clark was surprised by the incongruous sight of two big piles of bread, which he estimated must have weighed 500 pounds altogether. He assumed the Rebels had forced local women to bake the loaves for them, but had not been able to take them along on the retreat. Clark also noted the burned barn that contained the scorched bodies. One dead Rebel officer had all his clothes burned off, but the Union soldiers found a wallet that contained a letter and a gold ring. The regiment didn't tarry long before returning to its lines. That night it left Gettysburg and began a march into Maryland.[9]

Late in the day on July 4, the 19th Maine and other regiments received orders. Each regiment was to provide a detail to bury the men they had helped kill and collect the weapons and other equipment that had been abandoned on the battlefield.

The work started early the next morning. Soldiers dug ditches—20 feet long, 6 feet wide, and up to 6 feet deep—and began filling them with the bloated and discolored corpses of the dead Confederates. It was horrible work, and the stench from the decomposing bodies was terrible. "One need be buried to forget such dreadful sights," recollected John P. Lawrence. Once the ditches were crammed with bodies, the soldiers filled them with dirt. When the dead could be identified, the burial details added a crude marker with the name and regiment. If not, "Unknown" would have to suffice. At 5:00 P.M., the 19th Maine left the Gettysburg battlefield and began marching south on the Baltimore Pike on a roundabout pursuit of Lee's retreating army.[10]

Benny Worth of the 16th Maine's Co. E, the 15-year-old who had been so proud of his head wound at Fredericksburg, had been captured on July 1. He was determined he wouldn't be taken south with the rest of the prisoners. On July 3, realizing the Rebels were going to lose the battle, Worth snuck into a Confederate field hospital, found some bloody bandages, and wrapped them around one of his ankles. The Confederates took him for a wounded soldier and left him behind when they began their retreat. He returned to the regiment on July 4. Also returning to the regiment on that dismal, rainy day was Maj. Arch D. Leavitt, who had been away sick. As the ranking officer, he assumed command of the pale shadow of the unit he had left behind.[11]

The VI Corps, which included the 5th, 6th, and 7th Maine regiments, had not seen a lot of fighting at Gettysburg, although its mere presence on the field had been a plus for the Union cause. "By making long and rapid marches our corps arrived just in time to turn the battle of Gettysburg in our favor," Lt. Col. Selden Connor of the 7th Maine reported to his father. "We were not heavily engaged," he admitted, but skirmishing cost the regiment six wounded, three of them mortally—"more than the rest of the brigade together." On July 5, Connor's regiment moved out with some cavalry and an artillery battery to follow the retreating Rebels west to the town of Fairfield and get a sense of the situation there. Sedgwick recommended to Meade against pursuing the Rebels through the mountains and passes beyond, so the army commander decided to move his army south through Frederick and then west across South Mountain to reach Lee's army that way. While the rest of the army moved south, the 7th Maine formed part of the force under brigade commander Thomas Neill that shadowed the retreating enemy through the mountains to the town of Waynesboro.[12]

The rest of the VI Corps set out on a march that was, in its own way, as brutal as the one it had made to Gettysburg. On the way north, the soldiers had to cope with heat and sun; now they had to struggle against rain and mud. The march across South Mountain on the night of July 8 was as tough a march as the men had ever made. The rain came down in torrents, the night was pitch black, and the soldiers had to stumble and crawl up a narrow trail so the artillery and wagons could use the main road. "Up—up—up—the path seemed to have no end," wrote Charles Bicknell in his regimental history of the 5th Maine. Wet and exhausted soldiers began dropping out and falling to the ground. "To say that there was no growling, and various expressions indicating anger and irritability upon the part of most everybody, would be to state an absolute untruth, and to record an absolute impossibility," Bicknell wrote. By the time the diehards reached the summit around 1:00 A.M., all they could do was collapse on the ground and fall into a deep sleep that even the drenching rain couldn't interrupt.[13]

By July 12 the Army of the Potomac had Lee's army bottled up in the town of Williamsport, Maryland, with the Rebels' backs against the surging Potomac River. That night General Meade had another one of his consultations with his corps commanders. He said he intended to attack Lee in the morning. This time the majority of his generals recommended reconnoitering the enemy's position first. Of his infantry commanders, only James Wadsworth, who had taken command of the I Corps, and Otis Howard favored an attack. Warren and Pleasonton concurred. The next day, Howard and Vice President Hamlin ascended a church belfry in the town of Funkstown, where they could see the left of the Confederate position. Howard believed the Rebels would retreat without a fight. When the army finally pushed forward the next morning, it turned out that Howard was correct: Lee and most of his army had already crossed the river—some on a hastily built pontoon bridge south of town, and some by fording the river. Lee would live to fight another day.[14]

"To say that the army was mad and disgusted is putting it very mildly," said Sgt. Silas Adams of the 19th Maine. "We felt that through incompetency on our side, Lee had been permitted to escape. Every man then knew that we must travel over the old ground again and that our great victory at Gettysburg was in a great measure lost. So far since the organization of the Army of the Potomac, incompetency had been one of the most conspicuous features in its management. The ten days immediately following Gettysburg did not vary the custom."[15]

Edwin Houghton was not quite as harsh when he wrote his history of the 17th Maine, judging only that "to err is human, to forgive, divine." The regiment had made long, wet marches from Gettysburg to Frederick, across South Mountain, and over to a spot near the old Antietam battlefield. Inspired by the news from the west of Ulysses S. Grant's capture of Vicksburg, Mississippi, the men seemed "eager for a fight" on July 12 and waited anxiously for orders to advance. None came, and the 17th Maine and the rest of the III Corps, now under the command of William French, remained where they were, soaked through by the steady rains, until around noon on July 14. Moving toward Williamsport, they passed through the Rebels' abandoned entrenchments and learned that the enemy had escaped across the river.[16]

John Haley of the 17th Maine was not at all pleased. "And I do but represent the prevailing opinion in this army when I assert most positively, that it was a bitter pill for us to swallow, that Lee was not destroyed here, or his army driven, a fugitive mass, into the Potomac river," he said.[17]

The turn of events was especially dispiriting to George Bisbee and his fellow Union prisoners, who had expected the cavalry to come riding to the rescue. "We were wet to the skin and without hardly any food, but this did not trouble us but little as we were constantly expecting the approach of the Union army," wrote Bisbee. Instead of being rescued, the captives were forced to tramp across the hastily constructed pontoon bridge over to the Virginia side of the Potomac to begin a long march that led to Richmond's Libby Prison.[18]

⌐◦⌐

On July 4 a burial party lifted up the apparently lifeless body of John Chase and placed it in the back of a wagon for burial. Chase moaned. As he regained consciousness, his first words were, "Did we win the battle?" He was taken to a field hospital at the Isaac Lightner barn on the Baltimore Pike, where he lingered for three more days. No one believed he had a chance to survive. Then he was moved to the Lutheran Seminary, where his wounds became infected. The medical personnel put him in a tent outside to die. A soldier from the 8th Virginia, considered another lost cause, was placed in the tent with him. The two men clasped hands, seeking comfort and hoping for survival, but the Rebel soldier died during the night.

Chaplain J. O. Sloan, who was ministering to the wounded for the United States Christian Commission, said that seeing Chase was "one of the worst scenes that ever came under my observation." Even though the doctors said Chase could live for no more than a day or two, the chaplain decided to do what he could for the badly wounded man. Twice a day he applied poultices of "pulverized charcoal and flax seed" and tended to him. Whether it was the poultices, an act of God, or Chase's own will, the wounded soldier defied the odds and was eventually moved to a hospital in Philadelphia, and then home to Maine. He was discharged from the army on November 25, 1863.

After the war, Chase married and had six children. He served as a messenger in the Maine House of Representatives, and became an inventor, with 47 patents to his name. His first was for a hoopskirt with an attached bustle; his last was for a flying machine. Said one newspaper account, "According to Capt. Chase the Wright brothers will have to look to their laurels, for he is more than confident that his ship will sail the balmy air in the near future and will turn all the somersaults that will be required of a faithful flying bird of the mechanical type." Chase was living in Florida when he died in 1914.[19]

One of the people who cared for Chase was Sarah Sampson. She had continued her work with the sick and wounded even after her husband had resigned his commission with the 3rd Maine. In October 1862 she had returned to Washington, where she established a base at the home of Mr. and Mrs. George Hall, formerly of Vassalboro, and began working for the Maine Soldiers' Relief Association of Washington. She visited hospitals, collected the names of Maine patients, and provided them with supplies from the association. A former soldier from the 7th Maine served as her driver. She traveled to Falmouth in February 1863 to arrange for the transfer of wounded Maine soldiers back home. Hiram Berry helped with her transportation. After Chancellorsville, Otis Howard, who owed her a debt of gratitude, provided assistance so she could visit hospitals around Falmouth. She arranged to ship dead soldiers home, and wrote letters for the wounded.

When she reached Gettysburg not long after the battle Sampson brought with her something that doctors had told her was especially good for the wounded—fresh eggs. She combined them with brandy and milk to create an eggnog that she found to be a "most agreeable and nourishing drink for the patients." She started her work in the III Corps hospital, where she tended to soldiers from the 3rd, 4th, and 17th Maine regiments, but soon expanded her range to find wounded from other corps as well. She and other women used donated spirit lamps to heat chocolate and tea for their patients, made fly screens, barbered and washed the wounded, and, perhaps more important than anything, provided friendly faces from home. When Chase heard she was in town he sent for her so he could see "some one from Maine." "We give him and others the goodies we have brought along, take items to write his mother at Togus Springs, and leave with the promise to come again soon," Sampson said. She left Gettysburg on August 15, after the separate corps hospitals had been closed and consolidated into one general facility. "We had seen some of our patients improve under our care; but had received from many the farewell words for their friends, which we invariably promptly forwarded," she said. "We did what we could, but 'twas little to what we would."[20]

Sarah Sampson, like many other women from Maine, continued tending to soldiers from her home state throughout the war. In 1864 she and Harriet Eaton and Ruth Mayhew had a tent at City Point, where General Grant had established his headquarters. "So sterling was the reputation of Maine's relief workers at the Point that soldiers brought in from the Petersburg trenches claimed to be from Maine (even if they were not), the high-quality care and liberal dispersion of quilts simply too good to pass up," noted Jane E. Schulz in her introduction to Eaton's diaries. Sampson returned to Bath after the war was over, and she was buried in Arlington National Cemetery when she died in 1907.[21]

Col. Charles Tilden of the 16th Maine spent seven months in Richmond's Libby Prison, a former tobacco warehouse turned into a miserably uncomfortable place of confinement. On February 9, 1864, he escaped through a 59-yard tunnel that prisoners had dug from the "rat hell" in the basement to a vacant lot outside. Tilden was one of 109 Union officers who emerged from the tunnel, and one of 59 who made his way out of the Confederacy to the Union lines. He returned to his regiment in triumph on March 28, 1864. Tilden arrived by train from Culpeper and was escorted to a parade ground, mounted on a beautiful black stallion that the regiment acquired for him. When the assembled soldiers went to present arms, the colonel doffed his cap. "Shoulder-arms! Order-arms!" shouted Lt. Col. Augustus Farnham. "And now, boys, three times three for Charley Tilden!" The men cheered, the band played, and as soon as the soldiers were dismissed they flocked around their colonel. That night the officers of the brigade attended a special dinner. While rain and the wind raged outside the tent, inside they dined on oysters, "tea with genuine milk," turkey, ham, pies, fruits, and other delicacies, and they toasted Charles Tilden. The next morning, the enlisted men presented Tilden with the stallion he had ridden the day before.

Tilden led the 16th Maine through Ulysses S. Grant's Overland Campaign but he was captured a second time on August 18, 1864—and once again he escaped. This time he remained with his regiment all the way to Lee's surrender at Appomattox Court House. "For four years I have fought, endured and suffered for this consummation, and now I am satisfied," he told his officers. He returned to Castine and moved to Hallowell in 1879 to become secretary of the Hallowell Granite Company. In 1867 Tilden was breveted a brigadier general in the volunteers. Fifty years after the battle of Gettysburg, on July 1, 1913, he and 46 other survivors of the regiment returned to the spot where the 16th Maine had made its stand. He died in Hallowell on March 12, 1914, and was buried in Castine.[22]

Prisoner George Bisbee did not participate in the escape with Tilden because his arm, shattered and almost amputated at Fredericksburg, still gave him too much trouble. "Although sick in the hospital I remember staying up that night and looking out of the window with tears in my eyes and seeing our boys come out from the vacant lot where the end of the tunnel was and take the sidewalk and start for freedom," he wrote. Bisbee moved from prison to prison until he ended up in Columbia, South Carolina, at a bleak place with no tents or shelter. The captives called it Camp Sorghum after the molasses that became a staple of their meals there. Bisbee and his cousin, who was also with the 16th Maine, attempted an escape in December 1864. They were captured after they had gone about a hundred miles. Shortly afterwards he was paroled and transferred to Union authorities. He returned to his regiment on April 5, 1865, just in time to reach Appomattox for Lee's surrender. It was the happiest moment of his life. "I felt that I had been repaid amply for all these hardships and that in a humble way I had performed my duty to the government."[23]

Charles O. Hunt recovered from his Gettysburg wound and returned to the 5th Maine Battery, but he was captured outside Petersburg in 1864. He didn't have much better luck than Bisbee when he attempted to escape from Camp Sorghum with Charles Mattocks of the 17th Maine and Julius Litchfield of the 4th Maine. Taking advantage of the guards' laxity in allowing men to forage unsupervised for firewood in a nearby woods, the three men left the camp on November 3 and set their sights on Knoxville, Tennessee, in Union-held territory about 200 miles away. They had a crude map of the region, and E. A. Burpee of the 19th Maine had loaned them a compass. Their journey was fraught with danger and required swimming across a river, traveling at night, and finding concealed places in the woods to sleep during the day. They would not have made it if it weren't for local slaves, who supplied them with food and shelter. "We never met one who showed any disposition to betray us to the whites," said Hunt. On November 8, Election Day back home, the three men held their own election and voted unanimously for Abraham Lincoln. After two more weeks of travel, with the men achingly close to Tennessee, their luck ran out and they were captured and sent to a prison in Danville, Virginia. On the way, they heard the news that William T. Sherman had captured Atlanta and was on his way to the sea.

After the war, Hunt studied medicine and became the superintendent of Portland's Maine General Hospital, a position he held until just before his death in 1909.[24]

Thomas Hyde was still on John Sedgwick's staff when the Army of the Potomac embarked on the Overland Campaign in the spring of 1864. In one particularly horrifying incident during the battle of the Wilderness, Hyde was knocked off his feet by the head of a man who had been decapitated by a cannonball. Hyde was uninjured, "but was not much use as a staff officer for fully fifteen minutes." On the morning of May 9, he had been talking with Sedgwick outside Spotsylvania Court House when the general went to talk to some artillerymen. Hyde heard someone cry, "The general!" and ran over to find out that a Rebel sharpshooter had shot Sedgwick through the face as the general was admonishing some soldiers for trying to dodge the bullets. "They couldn't hit an elephant at that distance," he said. They were his last words. Hyde found the general lying on the ground, blood trickling from a hole below his eye. "Gradually it dawned upon us that the great leader, the cherished friend, he that had been more than a father to us all, would no more lead the Greek Cross of the 6th corps in the very front of battle; that his noble heart was stilled at last!" wrote Hyde, who remained on the staff of Sedgwick's successor, Horatio Wright.[25]

In July, when Confederate general Jubal Early threatened Washington, DC, Hyde received temporary command of his old regiment, the 7th Maine, during the resulting campaign in the Shenandoah Valley, and he led a brigade starting that fall. When Lee surrendered, Hyde was serving as military governor in Danville, Virginia, and he ended the war as a brevet brigadier general. When the VI Corps marched through Washington to celebrate the war's end, Joshua Chamberlain noted "the young general, Tom Hyde, favorite in all the army; prince of staff-officers, gallant commander, alert of sense, level of head, sweet of soul." Back in Maine he married his wartime sweetheart, Annie Haydon; the couple named their first son John Sedgwick. Hyde became a very successful businessman and parlayed his purchase of a small foundry in Bath into Bath Iron Works, still a major shipbuilding concern today. He published his memoirs, *Following the Greek Cross, or Memories of the Sixth Army Corps,* in 1894. Thomas Hyde died on November 14, 1899.[26]

⌁

Selden Connor left the 7th Maine in December 1863 to become colonel of the 19th Maine following Francis Heath's resignation. "The soldiers of the regiment expected great things from him, and they were not disappointed," wrote John Day Smith in his history. "His dignified bearing, his constant solicitude for the welfare of his soldiers, and his coolness and bravery in action won their confidence and esteem, which he always retained." Connor was temporarily promoted to brigade command but returned to the regiment when the army was reorganized and Alexander Webb assigned to the brigade.[27]

Connor did not remain in command of his regiment for very long. On May 6, 1864, the second day of the battle of the Wilderness, he was shot in the thigh as the 19th Maine defended against a surprise flank attack by James Longstreet's corps. Some of his men bundled him into a blanket and took him to the rear. The bullet had shattered the thigh, and the wound removed Connor from the fighting for the rest of the war. He was promoted to brigadier general in June 1864 and left the army in April 1866. He was elected governor of Maine as a Republican in 1875 and served for three terms. Selden Connor died in 1917 and was buried in Augusta.[28]

William C. Morgan, the 3rd Maine captain who said he had captured a sword belonging to one of Longstreet's aides at the Peach Orchard, received a promotion to major on December 3, 1863. He continued to drink heavily. Pvt. Charles Maxwell of Company F was particularly vocal about his dislike of Morgan, and a letter he wrote home about it was published anonymously in the *Skowhegan Clarion*. "He is a common drunkard, and the worst of any of the regiment's officers," wrote Maxwell. "For courage he has very little unless he is full of liquor." Morgan learned that Maxwell was the letter's author and had him court-martialed. "When Private Maxwell's court-martial convened, in mid-April 1864, the evidence was so presented that, in effect, Maj. William Morgan was placed on trial," wrote historian Wiley Sword. Col. Moses Lakeman and Maj. Gen. David Birney supported Morgan, but many other men testified to his drunkenness and the court-martial acquitted Maxwell of all but one minor charge and returned him to duty. Despite this public humiliation, Morgan remained with the regiment. He was wounded in the arm in the Wilderness, and mortally wounded by a bullet through the breast at the North Anna River on May 23, 1864.[29]

In August 1864 Freeman McGilvery received appointment as the artillery chief for the X Corps, but he did not have long to enjoy his new position. A week later he received a slight wound on a finger of his left hand. When the wound became infected, McGilvery agreed to have the finger amputated. During the procedure on September 2, McGilvery died on the operating table from the anesthesia. There are only two roads at Gettysburg National Military Park named after soldiers with rank below colonel; McGilvery Avenue is one of them.[30]

Edwin Dow received promotion to captain of the 6th Maine Battery in September and remained in command through the Overland Campaign of 1864 until he was discharged in December. William H. Rogers, the man McGilvery had wanted to take over the battery, finally got his chance when he replaced Dow.[31]

John Haley remained with the 17th Maine until the regiment was mustered out on June 10, 1865. "This day Uncle Sam refused to feed or clothe us any longer, so we were thrown on our own resources," he noted. "Pending our release, though, we were put under guard and given mouldy bread and rotten pork which were promptly stamped into the mud." It was not Haley's way to wax sentimental. He returned to Saco and attempted to resume civilian life. He married and had a son and a daughter. He found work as a night watchman, a clerk and freight agent for the railroad, spent 14 years as a bookkeeper for the Saco and Biddeford Gas-Light Company, worked as a reporter for a local paper, and finally spent 28 years as the librarian at Saco's Dyer Library. At some point Haley recorded his war experiences in a series of notebooks, and he later fleshed out those accounts in a narrative of his experiences. By the time he was done he had written 440,000 words, which included two versions of his "journals," and a third volume he called *Old Battlefields Revisited*. He died on April 7, 1921. In 1981 Ruth L. Silliker came across his handwritten works at the Dyer Library and published one version of his journal as *The Rebel Yell & the Yankee Hurrah*. Even almost a century after his death, Haley's voice emerges from his sardonic, self-deprecating, and closely observed account of his years with the Army of the Potomac. His Civil War recollections are still preserved at the Dyer Library.[32]

Abner Small managed to escape capture with the 16th Maine at Gettysburg, but he was not so lucky later in the war. On August 18, 1864, during the fighting for the Weldon Railroad outside Petersburg, Virginia, Small was captured and sent to Libby Prison. He later endured spells in other prisons in Salisbury, North Carolina, and Danville, Virginia. Paroled in February 1865, Small returned to Maine and got married. He rejoined his regiment on April 24, just over two weeks after Lee's surrender. When the 16th Maine marched through Washington for the Grand Review of the Armies in May 1865, Small, now promoted to major, was in temporary command. The regiment reached Augusta on June 10 and presented its colors to the current governor, Samuel Cony. Small felt haunted by sad faces he saw in the welcoming crowds, faces, he thought, of mothers and fathers who had lost children in the war. Small's memoir of his war experience, *The Road to Richmond*, was published posthumously in 1939. "Sometimes I wish I could forget it all," he wrote, "and again I rejoice that it is indelibly stamped into my being, that my sons cannot but inherit along with their father's loyalty, some of the conclusions of a life offered in a cause of making secure, lasting, and forever free, the government under which they are living." Abner Small died on March 12, 1910, in Oakland, Maine, at the age of 73.[33]

＊ ＊ ＊

When the U.S. Congress issued a joint resolution of thanks for the battle of Gettysburg on February 1, 1864, it listed three generals it felt deserved the most credit. Joseph Hooker came first—somewhat surprisingly, considering he had not been at the battle. George Gordon Meade—Hooker's replacement and the man who had commanded the army at Gettysburg—had to be satisfied with being named second. The third general was Oliver Otis Howard. "As I have read the history of that campaign, the man who selected the position where the battle was fought, and who, indeed, fought in on the first day, was General Howard," said Iowa senator James Wilson Grimes, who had added Howard's name to the resolution. Howard felt "glad and proud of this unsought and unexpected testimonial," even though it probably owed more to Republican dislike of General Meade than any great appreciation of Oliver O. Howard.[34]

Congress's thanks notwithstanding, Howard had not managed to restore the XI Corps' reputation at Gettysburg, but his own military reputation improved over the course of the war. In the fall of 1863, the XI and XII Corps were transferred to fight under Hooker in the western theater, where they participated in the relief of Chattanooga. The next spring the XI and XII Corps were merged into the XX Corps, and Howard received command of the IV Corps in the Army of the Cumberland under George H. Thomas. After James McPherson was killed during the battle for Atlanta, William T. Sherman picked Howard to take McPherson's place at the head of the Army of the Tennessee. Howard led the army during Sherman's march to the sea. In the western theater, Howard experienced "little but success and victory," wrote biographer John A. Carpenter. "The principal reason that Howard became a successful commander is that he had learned." Howard would have given some credit to God. He ended the war as a brigadier general in the regular army and rode at Sherman's side during the Grand Review of the Armies in Washington.[35]

After the war Howard was appointed to lead the Freedman's Bureau, which was intended to ease the transition for freed slaves into post–Civil War American society. Buffeted by the political turmoil of Reconstruction and resisted by both Southern whites and President Andrew Johnson, the bureau under Howard had, at best, mixed results. After the bureau was disbanded in 1872 Howard had to undergo congressional investigations over funding. He was ultimately exonerated, but the accusations took their toll. "If I must be crippled & broken—if God has no future use for me why so be it—if He has I will cheerfully, by his help, perform my part," he wrote to his brother Rowland in February 1874.[36]

At the same time he was running the Freedman's Bureau, Howard cofounded and served as president of the university in Washington that bears his name. In 1872 he embarked on a daring expedition into the wilds of Arizona to personally negotiate a treaty with the Apache chief Cochise. In the meantime, his and Lizzie's family continued to grow, with three more children added to the four they already had.

In 1874 Howard received orders to pack up and move to Oregon to take charge of the military Department of the Columbia. It was a largely uneventful posting, until the spring of 1877. Restive warriors of the Nez Perce tribe were resisting U.S. demands that they move onto a reservation. When Nez Perce warriors killed white settlers, Howard pursued the Native Americans as they moved north toward the Canadian border. Not until October 5 did Chief Joseph of the Nez Perce surrender, telling Howard, "From where the sun now stands I will fight no more forever." One fallout from the campaign was the end of Howard's friendship with Gen. Nelson Miles, who had served on Howard's staff early in the Civil War. The two men quibbled over the question of proper credit for the campaign. Miles felt Howard did not properly acknowledge his role; Howard was "heartbroken" to see that Miles did not even mention him in his report.[37]

Howard later served as superintendent of West Point, the position Robert E. Lee had held when Howard was a cadet. Postings in Nebraska, San Francisco, and New York followed before his retirement in 1894. One bit of terrible news arrived in 1898, when Howard learned that his son Guy, who had followed him into the military, died fighting in the Philippines. Howard lived until 1909 and was buried in Burlington, Vermont, where he had been living.[38]

Charles Howard went west with his brother and served on his staff. When Sherman's army was on the brink of capturing Savannah, Georgia, Charles received orders to proceed to Washington, where he received command of the 126th (later the 128th) regiment of the United States Colored Troops. While in Washington he met with President Lincoln to provide a briefing about Sherman's march to the sea. After the war he received a brevet promotion to brigadier general. He worked for his brother's Freedman's Bureau, helping establish schools for freed blacks in the South. In 1867 Charles Howard married Katharine Foster, who had been a pupil of his in Bangor before the war. The couple moved to Chicago when Charles took a job with the American Missionary Society. They raised seven children while Charles later served as a newspaper editor. He died in 1908.[39]

In 1870, Roland Howard left Farmington and served as the minister at various congregations in Illinois, New Jersey, and Massachusetts. He died in 1892 while attending a conference in Rome.

During the Army of the Potomac's pursuit of Lee back in Virginia, Joshua Chamberlain fell ill and had to be briefly hospitalized.

He returned in time to take up new duties as commander of the Third Brigade but then a case of "malarial fever" struck him down again. By the time he returned to the army he had lost his brigade and resumed command of the 20th Maine.

When Grant kicked off his Overland Campaign in May 1864, Chamberlain was in New Jersey on court-martial duty. He rejoined the army too late to experience the terrible fighting in the Wilderness and outside Spotsylvania but returned in time for the bloodshed of Cold Harbor. After that bloody defeat, Gouverneur Warren—now in command of the V Corps—placed Chamberlain in command of the First Brigade of the First Division. On June 12 the Army pulled away from the stalemate after Cold Harbor and made a wide swing across country, around Lee's army, across the James River, and toward the vital railroad junction of Petersburg.

Chamberlain's war nearly ended on the afternoon of June 18, 1864, in an attack on an artillery position called Rives Salient outside Petersburg. After crossing a small streambed, Chamberlain was encouraging his soldiers when a bullet struck him, ripping through his body from hip to hip. Chamberlain steadied himself with his sword, not wanting his men to see him fall. Finally he collapsed and was taken to the rear, bleeding profusely. The wound appeared to be a mortal one and Grant even authorized a field promotion to brigadier general. Skillful work by doctors managed to save Chamberlain, although the wound would torment him for the rest of his life. He remained determined, though, to see the end of the war. "I owe the Country three years of service," he wrote to his parents in February. "It is a time when every man should stand by his guns. And I am not scared or hurt enough yet to be willing to face to the rear, when other men are marching to the front." He was back in command of the First Brigade of Charles Griffin's division in the V Corps in time for the final campaign against the Army of Northern Virginia.[40]

Dawn on April 9, 1865, found Chamberlain and his men about six miles from Appomattox Station, just west of the little town of Appomattox Court House. A cavalryman arrived to waken Chamberlain with a message from cavalry commander Philip Sheridan. "If you can possibly push your infantry up here tonight, we will have great results in the morning," read Sheridan's message. The night had passed; the morning had already arrived.

Chamberlain had his bugler rouse his exhausted men and, fortified by "a tin plate of nondescript food and a dipper of miscalled coffee," he led his men on toward Appomattox Station. They reached it by sunrise as the sound of distant guns indicated the Confederates were attacking Sheridan's line. Chamberlain was moving his men toward the fighting when a cavalryman galloped up. "Sir, General Sheridan wishes you to break off from this column and come to his support," he said. "The rebel infantry is pressing him hard. Our men are falling back. Don't wait for orders through the regular channels, but act on this at once."

Chamberlain did as he was told.

From atop a crest he saw Lee's army around the courthouse. A Confederate horseman approached from the distance. He carried a white flag and requested a cessation of hostilities for the proposed surrender. Chamberlain watched as Robert E. Lee rode through the lines. Then he saw Grant. "Slouched hat without cord; common soldier's blouse, unbuttoned, on which, however, the four stars; high boots, mud-splashed to the top; trousers tucked inside; no sword, but the sword-hand deep in the pocket; sitting his saddle with the ease of a born master, taking no notice of anything, all his faculties gathered into intense thought and mighty calm."[41]

That night Griffin called Chamberlain to his headquarters and told him he had been assigned to oversee the formal surrender. As Chamberlain described the scene years later, he saw Confederate general John B. Gordon approach, and ordered his men snap to attention to carry arms—"the marching salute," as Chamberlain called it. "Gordon at the head of the column, riding with heavy spirit and downcast face, catches the sound of shifting arms, looks up, and, taking the meaning, wheels superbly, making with himself and his horse one uplifted figure, with profound salutation as he drops the point of his sword to his boot toe; then facing to his own command, gives word for his successive brigades to pass us with the same position of the manual—honor answering honor."[42]

Chamberlain returned to Maine, where, boosted by his war record, he served four one-year terms as the state's governor and became president of Bowdoin College. For a time, Chamberlain employed Andrew Tozier, the color bearer on Little Round Top, in his household in Brunswick and he also recommended Tozier for the Medal of Honor in recognition of his actions at Gettysburg. Tozier received the medal in 1898, five years after Chamberlain did.

Chamberlain's brothers died before he did. John died of consumption, like brother Horace had, in 1867. Tom married John's widow three years later. Tom, who was appointed lieutenant colonel of the 20th Maine in June 1865, may never have come to terms with his experiences in the war, for he had become an alcoholic by the time of his death in 1896. Their oldest brother lived on until 1914, and until his death he remained in great demand as an orator, especially for veterans groups. Along the way he sometimes related events more as he felt they should be than as they actually happened. When he embellished the details of his war experiences he sometimes burnished his own reputation.

That aspect of Chamberlain's character came to bother Ellis Spear. Spear had ended the war as a brevet brigadier general, but he left the service to work in the U.S. Patent Office, rising to the position of commissioner in 1876. Two years later he started his own patent office in Washington. When Spear's first wife died in 1874 he married the widow of Samuel Keene, his comrade from the 20th Maine. Keene had been shot by a sharpshooter outside Petersburg on June 22, 1864, and he died in Spear's arms. Spear said Keene's last words were, "Write to my wife. It is all well. I die for my country."[43]

As he grew older, Spear grew increasingly disenchanted with the deference Chamberlain received as Maine's most celebrated war hero. Spear was so irritated by Chamberlain's account of Fredericksburg in *Cosmopolitan* that he wrote a sarcastic commentary on the article, which he found "misleading, and unjust." (In Chamberlain's defense, it's not known how much the Hearst editors changed his manuscript.) On December 21, 1912, Spear typed out a letter to Adelbert Ames to share his irritation about the article. "So many things in it are stated which I do not remember and so many contrary to my remembrance that I am left in wonder," Spear said. "Perhaps this story may have been intended for pure fiction."[44]

In a letter from May 1, 1913, Spear wrote to Ames and disparaged "the class of those who, since the war, have been industriously blowing their own trumpets, and ingeniously weaving stories the fabric of which is fiction, with here and there a thread of fact.

"These exaggerations and the paper and soap-bubble reputations blown out in the last fifty years have grown more and more burdensome to me, and I am more and more impressed with the duty which we owe to posterity and the country at large to tell the truth, however unpleasant it may be to some," Spear said. "Unjust claims made by one are an injury to others and robbery."

Spear was writing to Ames on the eve of the 50th anniversary of the battle of Gettysburg. He said he would probably attend the 20th Maine's reunion there, even though it would mean hearing the old stories he had heard time and time again. "It will remind me doubtless of the story of a guest of mine whom I entertained at my summer home in Maine some ten years ago, and whom I took out deep sea fishing," said Spear. "He was a landsman, but by some accident caught a little codfish. The fish was about a foot long when caught, but the last time I heard the story he was as long as a piano."[45]

Ellis Spear died on April 3, 1918.

On July 3, 1863, Adelbert Ames dashed off a note to Chamberlain after hearing about the fight on Little Round Top. "I am very proud of the 20th Regt. and its present Colonel," he wrote. "I did want to be with you and see your splendid conduct in the field." Perhaps Ames was thinking about his own disappointments at Gettysburg when he added, "The pleasure I felt at the intelligence of your conduct yesterday is some recompense for all that I have suffered."[46]

In a letter written home that August, Ames recounted how he was reunited with his old regiment. He was riding with Gouverneur Warren when the men they were passing began shouting and waving their hats. Ames thought they were cheering Warren, but the engineer corrected him. They were cheering Ames. "I soon found it was the 20th," he wrote. "They gave me three times three. They will do anything for me." He also mentioned that the regiment's officers had chipped in to buy him a sword, sash, and belt. "The sword is very elegant. It has some fine carbuncles on the hilt—It was made to order, and all cost some two hundred dollars." All that strict discipline had paid off.[47]

After Gettysburg, Ames rose to command a division. For his role in the capture of Fort Fisher in North Carolina, he received a brevet promotion to major general in the volunteers and brigadier general in the regular army.

Ames had proven himself in battle, but he ran into difficulties when he entered politics. After the war he moved to Mississippi and served as the state's provisional governor and then as a senator. In 1870, with Mississippi readmitted to the Union, he became the state's official governor and found himself embroiled in contentious Reconstruction politics. Ames was a Republican who fought to protect the rights of the newly freed slaves. This did not sit well with the state's conservative Democrats. When they regained power in 1876, the Democrats began proceedings to impeach Ames, mainly on charges that he had abused his powers by dismissing various state officials. There was also a charge that Ames had illegally armed a militia to quell anti-Reconstruction forces. Perhaps most damning in the eyes of Ames's opponents was that the militia had been "composed of colored men." Ames, the indictment claimed, intended "to create a disturbance, and plunge the country into a war of races, with all its attendant horrors." Notably absent was any mention of the war of terror that reactionary forces had already unleashed on African Americans in Mississippi.[48]

Ames was an honest man—even his enemies had to concede that—but he realized he would not prevail against the forces aligned against him. So he brokered a deal. If the Democrats dropped all charges against him, he would resign. And he did.

Ames went on to live a long, productive life. He happened to be conducting business in Northfield, Minnesota, when the James-Younger Gang raided the town in 1876, and he helped citizens fend off the attack. He fought in Cuba during the Spanish-American War. He became oil tycoon John D. Rockefeller's regular golf partner and played 36 holes a day into his 90s, until his old Bull Run wound began giving him too much trouble. "In appearance, this blue-eyed old soldier has lost but little of the 'straight as a ram rod' condition he received at West Point," read a *Boston Globe Magazine* profile of 91-year-old Ames. When he died in 1933 at the age of 97, Ames was the oldest surviving Civil War general (non-brevet).[49]

He also happened to be author George Plimpton's great-grandfather. Plimpton once wrote about a visit he made to the White House when John F. Kennedy was president. Kennedy took him aside to ask if he could do something about the letters Plimpton's grandmother kept writing to him. The grandmother was Blanche Ames, Adelbert's daughter. She had been incensed by a passage about her father in young Senator Kennedy's *Profiles in Courage*. Kennedy had written that as governor of Mississippi, Ames's "administration was sustained and nourished by Federal bayonets." Blanche wanted Senator Kennedy to rewrite that passage for subsequent editions. Kennedy self-deprecatingly told her he doubted there would be any more editions. But there were, and Blanche Ames continued to write letters. Kennedy asked Plimpton if he could do something to stop the correspondence—"it was cutting into the work of government," the president said.

Plimpton remembered, as a small boy, sitting in his grandfather's lap, looking into his eyes, and thinking that this old man had witnessed Pickett's Charge at Gettysburg. He had done that—and so much more.[50]

Notes

Introduction

1. *Maine at Gettysburg*, v.
2. Ibid., 545.
3. Dedication of the 20th Maine Monuments, text available online here: http://www .gdg.org/Research/People/Chamberlain/20ded.html.
4. Chamberlain's address in *Maine at Gettysburg*, 546–59.
5. *OR*, Series 1, Vol. 27, Part 1, 604.
6. Spear, *National Tribune*, June 12, 1913; Spear to Ames, May 31, 1913, Smith College.
7. Dedication of the 20th Maine Monuments.
8. *Bangor Daily News*, October 17, 2015. http://bangordailynews.com/2015/10/17/news/ bangor/nasa-scientist-from-maine-names-mars-rock-after-war-hero-chamberlain/.
9. *Maine at Gettysburg*, 577.
10. Beard, "Gettysburg's Forgotten Hero"; United States War Department, *Official Records* (henceforth *OR*), Series I, Vol. 27, Part 1, 898.
11. *Reunions of the Nineteenth Maine*, 11.
12. *Maine at Gettysburg*, 560.
13. Whitman and True, *Maine in the War*, 23.
14. Small, *The Sixteenth Maine*, 97.
15. Stanley and Hall, *Eastern Maine and the Rebellion*, 83–85; for Elliott, see http:// www.maine.gov/tools/whatsnew/index.php?topic=arcsesq&id=118605&v=article; Beattie, Cole, and Waugh, *A Distant War*, 127–39.
16. Cleaveland, *History of Bowdoin College*, 8; Judd, Churchill, and Easton, *Maine*, 194; Thompson, *Civil War to the Bloody End*, 4.
17. Cleaveland, 667; Calhoun, *Small College*, 173–74, 185, n. 63. Cleaveland says MacArthur was killed near Richmond in June 1862.
18. Whitman and True, 204; Cleaveland, 679.
19. *Maine at Gettysburg*, 558.

Chapter 1: Maine Goes to War

1. http://www.maine.gov/tools/whatsnew/index.php?topic=arcsesq&id=118389&v =article.
2. Description from Hunt, *Israel, Elihu and Cadwallader Washburn*, 7; vote from 3.

3. Hunt, *Israel, Elihu and Cadwallader Washburn,* 86.
4. Hamlin, *Life and Times of Hannibal Hamlin,* 406.
5. Hazelton, Gary W. "The Chicago Convention of 1860 and the Man It Nominated," in *War Papers Read Before the Commandery of the State of Wisconsin, Military Order of the Loyal Legion of the United States* (Milwaukee: Burdick and Allen, 1914), 4:268.
6. Hyde, *Following the Greek Cross,* 3.
7. http://www.maine.gov/tools/whatsnew/index.php?topic=arcsesq&id=118381&v =article.
8. Thomas Hyde to Annie Hayden, November 24, 1860; copy of letter in the Hyde papers, Bowdoin College.
9. Hamlin, 84–85 and 347, and Hatfield, *Vice Presidents of the United States,* 203–9.
10. For Scammon, see http://www.lawpracticeofabrahamlincoln.org/reference/html%20 files%20for%20biographies/Bio_1150.html; Hyde, *Following the Greek Cross,* 4–5.
11. *New York Times,* July 9, 1860. http://www.nytimes.com/1860/07/09/news/the -chicago-zouaves-our-military-companies-to-look-after-their-laurels.html.
12. http://www.maine.gov/tools/whatsnew/index.php?topic=arcsesq&id=118400&v =article; Stanley and Hall, 382–83.
13. http://www.maine.gov/tools/whatsnew/index.php?topic=arcsesq&id=118389&v =article.
14. Bangs, *Military History of Waterville,* 6.
15. Maine Adjutant General, *Annual Report 1863,* 138.
16. http://www.maine.gov/tools/whatsnew/index.php?topic=arcsesq&id=124020&v= article; http://www.maine.gov/tools/whatsnew/index.php?topic=arcsesq&id=110143&v =article.
17. Stanley and Hall, 31.
18. http://www.maine.gov/tools/whatsnew/index.php?topic=arcsesq&id=123505&v =article.
19. Clark, "Campaigning with the Sixth Maine," 3–6.
20. Census records are here: https://www2.census.gov/library/publications/decennial/ 1860/population/1860a-17.pdf; Gould and Jordan, *History of the First,* 40.
21. Stout, *Upon the Altar of the Nation,* 12; Gilmore, *Civil War Memories,* 16.
22. Gould, *Journals,* 1, 5; Gould and Jordan, 24.
23. Whitman and True, *Maine in the War,* 28, 31.
24. Gould and Jordan, 34.
25. *New York Times,* June 3, 1861; Whitman and True, 28.
26. http://www.maine.gov/tools/whatsnew/index.php?topic=arcsesq&id=146645&v =article.
27. Whitman and True, 33.
28. Stanley and Hall, 21 and 26.
29. Ibid., 362.
30. Ibid., 54–55.
31. Whitman and True, 39.
32. Howard, *Autobiography,* 12–13.
33. Ibid., 18–19.

34. Ibid., 51–52; *Newark Sunday Call*, February 6, 1910.
35. Howard, *Autobiography*, 114.
36. Ibid., 81.
37. Ibid., 128, 165.
38. Ibid., 103.
39. Ibid., 107.
40. Ibid., 114.
41. Ibid., 114–15.
42. Small, *Road to Richmond*, 9.
43. Howard to his mother, March 23, 1862, Bowdoin College.
44. Howard, *Autobiography*, 122.

CHAPTER 2: MAINE SPILLS BLOOD

1. http://www.bowdoin.edu/about/history/index.shtml.
2. Walker, *The Old Soldier*, 6.
3. Ibid., 8; Stanley and Hall, 209.
4. Gould, *Major-General Hiram G. Berry*, 49.
5. Rollins letters, AHC.
6. Howard to Lizzie, undated letter, Bowdoin College (filed in December 1861).
7. Howard, *Autobiography*, 132.
8. Small, *Road to Richmond*, 12
9. Small to Luther and Lucilla Emerson, July 7, 1861, MHS.
10. Rollins letters, AHC.
11. Small, *Sixteenth Maine*, 19; Clark, 11.
12. Howard, *Autobiography*, 133.
13. Whitman and True, 60; Rollins letters, AHC.
14. Wainwright, *Diary of Battle*, 38; Howard, *Autobiography*, 142.
15. Davis, *Battle at Bull Run*, 10.
16. Longacre, *Early Morning*, 92.
17. Jones, *Generals in Blue and Gray*, Vol. I, 50.
18. Higgins letter, MSA.
19. Rollins letters, AHC.
20. Bicknell, *History of the Fifth*, 23.
21. Howard to Lizzie, July 18, 1861, Bowdoin College; Howard, *Autobiography*, 149; Small, *Road to Richmond*, 18.
22. *OR*, Series I, Vol. 2, 311.
23. Gould, *Major-General Hiram G. Berry,* 58–59.
24. Sherman, *Memoirs*, 168.
25. Howard, *Autobiography*, 152; Walker, 10.
26. Howard, *Autobiography*, 154.
27. *OR*, Series I, Vol. 2, 350. The National Guard's Camp Keyes in Augusta is named after him.
28. Lawrence's letter is in Stanley and Hall, 72–78.
29. Ibid., 80.

30. *OR*, Series I, Vol. 2, 353 and 355.

31. Longacre, 398.

32. Ames, *Adelbert*, 59–60.

33. *OR*, Series I, Vol. II, 394.

34. Rollins letters, AHC; Bicknell, 28; Stanley and Hall, 82; Howard, *Autobiography*, 158.

35. Rollins letters, AHC.

36. Howard, *Autobiography*, 158.

37. Gould, *Major-General Hiram G. Berry*, 63–64.

38. Small, *Road to Richmond*, 22; McIntyre, *Alonzo Palmer Stinson*, 22; Howard, *Autobiography*, 159.

39. Rollins letters, AHC.

40. Howard, *Autobiography*, 160; Bicknell, 31.

41. Small, *Road to Richmond*, 23.

42. Howard, *Autobiography*, 160–61.

43. Gould, *Major-General Hiram G. Berry*, 65; *OR*, Vol. 2, 420; Gould, *Major-General Hiram G. Berry*, 67.

44. See http://www.maine.gov/tools/whatsnew/index.php?topic=arcsesq&id=123755&v=article.

45. http://www.maine.gov/tools/whatsnew/index.php?topic=arcsesq&id=262171&v=article.

46. https://www.mainememory.net/media/pdf/34140.pdf.

47. Stanley and Hall, 82.

48. Ibid., 87–88.

49. Rollins letters, AHC.

Chapter 3: McClellan Makes His Move

1. Sneden, *Eye of the Storm*, 16.

2. McClellan, *Civil War Papers*, 59.

3. Ibid., 70; Warner, *Generals in Blue*, 245.

4. Ames, *Adelbert*, 71.

5. Rowland to Otis, August 17, 1861, Bowdoin College.

6. Letters from Mrs. Haskell, August 18 and September 1, 1861, and Howard's response, August 24, Bowdoin College.

7. Howard to Lizzie, September 23, 1861, Bowdoin College.

8. Howard to Lizzie, October 31, 1861; Howard, *Autobiography*, 170–71.

9. Small to Emersons, July 30, 1861, MHS.

10. Gould, *Major-General Hiram G. Berry*, 72; Walker in the *Rockland Tribune*, May 6, 1893 (reprinted in *Old Soldier*).

11. Dawson letter in U.S. pension files, AHC; Rollins letters, AHC.

12. Bicknell, 56–57.

13. Little to his father, October 11, 1861, AHC.

14. http://www.maine.gov/tools/whatsnew/index.php?topic=arcsesq&id=118790&v=article.

15. French letters on the Maine Memory Network.
16. Rollins letters, AHC.
17. Ames, *Chronicles*, 4, 5.
18. Gould, *Major-General Hiram G. Berry*, 102.
19. Ibid., 108.
20. Ibid., 158; Maine Adjutant General, *Annual Report 1862*, 141.
21. Hyde, *Following the Greek Cross*, 56.
22. Samuel Fessenden MS, Bowdoin College; Jellison, *Fessenden of Maine*, 92.
23. Hyde, *Following the Greek Cross*, 12.
24. Packard, *Bowdoin in the War*, 8.
25. Connor, Selden, "The Boys of 1861," 324; letter to his brother, April 16, 1861, Brown University.
26. Connor, "The Boys of 1861," and Connor correspondence, Brown University.
27. Connor, "The Boys of 1861," 17 and 14.
28. Bilby, *Civil War Firearms*, 105; Sword, *Sharpshooter*, 8; http://www.maine.gov/tools/whatsnew/index.php?topic=arcsesq&id=403378&v=article.
29. See http://www.maine.gov/tools/whatsnew/index.php?topic=arcsesq&id=403396&v=article.
30. Connor letters, October 26 and 31, 1861, Brown University.
31. Hyde, *Following the Greek Cross*, 36.
32. March, day not indicated, 1862, Connor letters.
33. Hyde, *Following the Greek Cross*, 38, 40.
34. Ibid., 42.
35. Sears, *Gates of Richmond*, 71; Howard to his mother, March 23, 1862, Bowdoin College; Howard, *Autobiography*, 210.
36. George Redlon to his father, April 13, 1862, MHS.
37. Gould, *Major-General Hiram G. Berry*, 114.
38. Redlon letter, April 13, 1862, MHS.

CHAPTER 4: HOWARD LOSES HIS ARM

1. Hyde, *Following the Greek Cross*, 45, 46.
2. Kearny, *Letters from the Peninsula*, 25.
3. Connor to his father, April 22, 1862, Brown University.
4. Howard, *Autobiography*, 218–19; Connor to his sister, May 14, 1862, Brown University.
5. *OR*, Series I, Vol. 11, Part 1, 465.
6. Ibid.
7. De Peyster, *Personal and Military History*, 281.
8. *OR*, Series I, Vol. 11, 459.
9. Ibid., 505.
10. Gould, *Major-General Hiram G. Berry*, 126 and 129.
11. Smith, *History of the Nineteenth*, 77.
12. *OR*, Series I, Vol. 11, Part 1, 550.
13. Ibid., 550–51.

14. Hyde, *Following the Greek Cross*, 51; Connor to his mother, May 8, Brown University.
15. Clark, 18.
16. Connor to his sister, May 14, 1862, Brown University.
17. Hyde, *Civil War Letters*, 5.
18. Howard to Lizzie, May 7, Bowdoin College.
19. Gould, *Major-General Hiram G. Berry*, 157–58.
20. Howard, *Autobiography*, 240–41.
21. The account of Howard's wounding and amputation from Howard, *Autobiography*, 246–52. Sarah Sampson's account from Maine Adjutant General, *Annual Report 1864 and 1865*, 110.
22. Gould, *Major-General Hiram G. Berry*, 170–71, 173–74.
23. "Virginia Creeper" from De Peyster, 312; Bicknell 99.
24. *OR*, Series I, Vol. 11, Part 1, 296.
25. Johnson and Buel, *Battles and Leaders*, II, 337.
26. Bicknell, 100–101.
27. *OR*, Series I, Vol. 11, Part 2, 448; Bicknell, 103.
28. Bicknell, 104.
29. Gould, *Major-General Hiram G. Berry*, 171–72.
30. Hyde, *Following the Greek Cross*, 71.
31. Bicknell, 109; Hyde, *Following the Greek Cross*, 72.
32. Bicknell, 113, 110, 112.
33. Maine Adjutant General, *Annual Report 1862*, 122–23.
34. Bicknell, 115.
35. Ames, *Chronicles*, 12; *OR*, Series I, Vol. 11, Part 2, 259.
36. *OR*, Series I, Vol. 11, Part 2, 253.
37. Sam Washburn to Elihu, undated; McClellan was on board the *Galena* on June 30 and July 1. From the collections of the Washburn Norlands Living History Center, available online via the Maine Memory Network, https://www.mainememory.net/artifact/100582.
38. Maine Adjutant General, *Annual Report 1864 and 1865*, 110–11; Whitman and True, 63; http://www.maine.gov/tools/whatsnew/index.php?topic=arcsesq&id=147045&v=article.
39. Connor to his father, July 6, 1862, Brown University.
40. Ames to Washburn, July 11, 1862, Civil War Regimental Correspondence, Maine State Archives.

CHAPTER 5: AMES GETS A REGIMENT

1. *Reunions of the Nineteenth Maine*, 6. A note in the files at GNMP identifies the author as Lancaster. Joseph P. Spaulding, who was a captain in the 19th Maine at Gettysburg, read the account at a regimental reunion and said it was "written by a member of the regiment." Unless he was being coy, Spaulding was not the author. The author's father addresses the narrator as "John," which would also seem to rule out Spaulding. Lawrence and Spaulding were both from Richmond.

2. Whitman and True, 7.

3. *Maine at Gettysburg*, 273.

4. Keene file, GNMP.

5. Spear, *Recollections,* 6.

6. Ibid., 8–9.

7. Longacre, 27.

8. Trulock, *In the Hands of Providence*, 42.

9. Quoted in Nesbitt, *Blood and Fire*, 9–11.

10. Calhoun, *Small College*, 169.

11. Smyth reference in letter from Chamberlain to Fanny, October 26, 1862, LOC; letter in Civil War Regimental Correspondence, MSA.

12. Chamberlain to Eugene Hale, August 15, 1862, MSA.

13. Small, *Road to Richmond*, 36.

14. Bisbee, 114.

15. Small, *Road to Richmond*, 41–42.

16. McClellan, 368, 369.

17. OR, Series I, Vol. 12, Part 2, 172.

18. More about Beal here: http://www.norwayhistoricalsociety.org/GeorgeLBeal.php.

19. For "Old Pills," see Horace Porter, *Campaigning with Grant* (New York: Century Company, 1907; reprint, Old Saybrook, CT: Konecky and Konecky, 1992), 248; *OR* Series I, Vol. 12, Part 2, 151.

20. Gould and Jordan, 174–75.

21. Ibid., 178; Gould, *Journals,* 171.

22. http://www.maine.gov/tools/whatsnew/index.php?topic=arcsesq&id=147260&v =article.

23. Gould and Jordan, 180.

24. McClellan, 254.

25. OR, Series I, Vol. 12, Part 2, 426.

26. Walker, *Old Soldier*, 36.

27. Warner, 193–94; Cudworth, *History of the First Regiment*, 273.

28. OR, Series I, Vol. 12, Part 2, 427.

29. *Kennebec Journal*, June 5, 1863, Bowdoin College.

30. *Maine at Gettysburg*, 29.

31. Howard, *Autobiography*, 255.

32. Howard to Lizzie, August 21 and 28, Bowdoin College.

33. Howard, *Autobiography*, 269.

34. Small, *Sixteenth Maine*, 26; Small, *Road to Richmond*, 43.

35. Johnson and Buel, *Battles and Leaders*, II, 550.

CHAPTER 6: THE 7TH MAINE MAKES A CHARGE

1. Maine at Gettysburg, 273; Melcher, *Flash of His Sword*, vi and 2; discharge papers, MHS.

2. Gerrish, *Army Life*, 13.

3. Ibid., 17–18.

4. Spear, *Recollections*, 11; Nathan S. Clark diary, Maine State Archives.

5. Spear, *Recollections*, 293.

6. Bicknell, 133.

7. Ibid., 137.

8. Ibid., 139; Franklin's report quoted in Johnson and Buel, *Battles and Leaders*, II, 593.

9. Bicknell, 140–41.

10. Gerrish 27; Melcher, 4.

11. Gerrish, 29.

12. Gould and Jordan, 241–42; Gould, *Journals*, 186.

13. Gould and Jordan, 235.

14. Ibid., 236–37.

15. Description from Gould and Jordan, 235–43.

16. Howard, *Autobiography*, 296–97; Banes, *Philadelphia Brigade,* 112–14.

17. Hyde, *Civil War Letters*, 45.

18. *OR*, Series 1, Vol. 19, Part 1, 413; Hyde, *Civil War Letters*, 51.

19. Hyde's account is in Hyde, *Following the Greek Cross*, 99–105.

20. *OR*, Series I, Vol. 19, Part 1, 409–10.

21. Bicknell, 150.

22. Gould, *Journals,* 198.

23. Ibid., 254.

24. Long, *Hard Times*, 6.

25. Bailey, September 23, 1862, copy in the files of GNMP; Chamberlain to Fanny, September 29, 1862, transcript at PHS.

26. Chamberlain to Fanny, October 26, 1862, LOC.

27. Pullen, *Twentieth Maine*, 36.

28. Gerrish, 45.

29. Long, 10.

CHAPTER 7: THE 19TH MAINE SMELLS POWDER

1. Small, *Road to Richmond*, 47.

2. Military Order of the Loyal Legion of the United States, "Charles W. Tilden"; Small, *Road to Richmond*, 40.

3. Small, *Sixteenth Maine*, 37.

4. http://www.maine.gov/tools/whatsnew/index.php?topic=arcsesq&id=125805&v =article.

5. Small, *Sixteenth Maine*, 51.

6. Ibid., 37–38.

7. Ibid., 59.

8. Gould, *Major-General Hiram G. Berry*, 196.

9. Ibid., 197–98.

10. Ibid., 207.

11. *Maine at Gettysburg*, 224.

12. Warner, *Generals in Blue*, 122; O'Brien, "Hold Them with the Bayonet"; Extract from the transcript of a MS written by a private in Co. I (possibly John Haley), GNMP; Haley journal transcripts, 167.

13. De Trobriand, *Four Years*, 328–29.
14. Haley, *Rebel Yell*, 12–13, 25.
15. Ibid., 13.
16. Ibid., 23.
17. Mattocks, *Unspoiled Heart*, xiv and xxi.
18. Haley, *Rebel Yell*, 33.
19. Ibid., 39.
20. Chamberlain to Fanny, November 3, 1862, LOC (transcribed in Nesbitt); Chamberlain to Fanny, November 22, 1862, original at NCWM (transcribed in Chamberlain, *Life in Letters*).
21. Howard, *Autobiography*, 311; Calhoun, 179.
22. Howard to Charles, November 9, 1862; Howard to Lizzie, November 9, 1862, Bowdoin College.
23. Bicknell, 159; Haley, *Rebel Yell*, 50.
24. Houghton, *Campaigns of the Seventeenth Maine*, 15; Larry letter, AHC, Carlisle.
25. Bailey to his sister, November 28, 1862, GNMP.
26. Smith, *History of the Nineteenth*, 26; *Reunions of the Nineteenth Maine*, 7–8.
27. *OR*, Series I, Vol. 21, 371.
28. *Reunions of the Nineteenth Maine*, 72. The author is not named in *Reunions*, but John Day Smith identifies him as Nash in his regimental history. Nash wrote a series of reports for his hometown newspaper, the *Hallowell Gazette* (Smith, *History of the Nineteenth*, 10).
29. Small, *Sixteenth Maine*, 58.
30. Haley, *Rebel Yell*, 57.
31. Small, *Sixteenth Maine*, 73.
32. Small, *Road to Richmond*, 63, 65.
33. Hopkins's account in Small, *Sixteenth Maine*, 70–75; 79.
34. Small, *Sixteenth Maine*, 80.
35. Bisbee, 116; Small, *Sixteenth Maine*, 69 and *Road to Richmond*, 70.
36. Small, *Sixteenth Maine*, 81.
37. Tilden's report in *OR*, Series I, Vol. 21, 490; Bisbee, 116; Small, *Sixteenth Maine*, 237 and 67.
38. Bisbee, 116–18.
39. Birney from Civil War Regimental Correspondence, MSA.
40. *OR*, Series I, Vol. 21, 368–70.
41. Gould, *Major-General Hiram G. Berry*, 220.
42. Ibid., 219; Haley, *Rebel Yell*, 59.
43. Lovell letter, copy at AHC.
44. Haley, *Rebel Yell*, 60.
45. Gould, *Major-General Hiram G. Berry*, 222, 226.
46. Howard to Lizzie, December 13, 1862, Bowdoin College.
47. Smith, *History of the Nineteenth*, 28.
48. Howard, *Autobiography*, 327; Smith, *History of the Nineteenth*, 30.
49. Johnson and Buel, *Battles and Leaders*, III, 113.
50. Howard, *Autobiography*, 343.

51. *OR*, Vol. 21, 270; *Reunions of the Nineteenth Maine*, 8.
52. Howard, *Autobiography*, 346.
53. Chamberlain to Fanny, December 17, 1862, in *Life in Letters*, 178; Chamberlain, "*Bayonet!,*" 5.
54. Chamberlain, *Life in Letters*, 179.
55. Gerrish, 77; Chamberlain, *Life in Letters*, 180.
56. Chamberlain, *Life in Letters*, 180.
57. *OR*, Series I, Vol. 21, 412.
58. Chamberlain, "*Bayonet!,*" 11–12.
59. Gould, *Major-General Hiram G. Berry*, 223.
60. Haley, *Rebel Yell*, 63.
61. Rollins letters, AHC.
62. Small, *Sixteenth Maine*, 90.
63. Melcher to his brother, January 17, 1862, Bowdoin College.

CHAPTER 8: HOOKER TAKES COMMAND

1. http://www.maine.gov/tools/whatsnew/index.php?topic=arcsesq&id=318040&v=article.
2. *Reunions of the Nineteenth Maine*, 9.
3. Freland N. Holman letters, AHC.
4. Ford, *Cycle of Adams Letters*, 161; Charles Howard in a note added to Otis's letter to their mother, January 25; Howard to Lizzie, January 27, 1863.
5. Smith, *History of the Nineteenth*, 39.
6. Bicknell, 201–2.
7. Copy of letter in Lenfest file, Pejepscot Historical Society.
8. Charles Howard to his mother, February 19, 1863, Bowdoin College.
9. Transcriptions of Wood letters at GNMP; Gould, *Journals*, 259.
10. Melcher to his brother, February 11, 1863, Bowdoin College.
11. Warner, 239; De Trobriand, 312–13.
12. Connor to his father, March 25, 1863, Brown University.
13. Clifford transcripts at GNMP; Cunningham's letters in Civil War Regimental Correspondence, MSA.
14. Account from letters in Civil War Regimental Correspondence, MSA.
15. Smith, *History of the Nineteenth*, 41.
16. Civil War Regimental Correspondence, MSA.
17. Howard to Lizzie, January 1 and 4, 1863, Bowdoin College; *New York Times*, January 16, 1863.
18. Howard to Lizzie, January 14, 1863.
19. Jeannie Grey to Howard, December 9, 1861; Howard to Lizzie, March 9, 18, and 28, 1863. Charles Howard did not marry until 1867, to a woman who had been a pupil of his in Bangor before the war.
20. Haley, *Rebel Yell*, 66; Gould, *Major-General Hiram G. Berry*, 227 and 230–34.
21. Gould, *Major-General Hiram G. Berry*, 230–34 and 242–43.
22. Ibid., 230 and 231.

23. Ford, *Cycle of Adams Letters*, 38.
24. Haley, *Rebel Yell*, 102.
25. Howard to Lizzie, January 27, 1863, Bowdoin College.
26. Valuska and Keller, *Damn Dutch*, 39.
27. Schurz, *Reminiscences*, II, 405.
28. Howard, *Autobiography*, 349.
29. Blackstone to his father, January 7, 1863, MSA.
30. Hyde, *Following the Greek Cross*, 172–73.
31. Nesbitt, 52.
32. Ames, 98; Berry to Hamlin, November 24, 1862, original in Ames papers, Smith College.
33. Ames, *Chronicles*, 16.
34. Letter in Civil War Regimental Correspondence, MSA.
35. Fogg letter, February 26, 1863, in Regimental Correspondence, MSA. In *The Birth Place of Souls*, the published diaries of Harriet Eaton, another Maine woman who nursed soldiers, editor Jane E. Schulz says Eaton actually penned the letter, but apparently did not sign it, being unwilling to get pulled into the controversy (Eaton, 37). In her diaries, Eaton called Litchfield "a great rascal." "Are our sons to be under the tyranny of such an awful man?" she asked (110–11).
36. Gerrish, 69.
37. Donald, *Lincoln*, 433–34; Haley, *Rebel Yell*, 75; Gould, *Journals*, 265.
38. Hunt to his mother, April 12, 1863, Bowdoin College.

CHAPTER 9: HOWARD GETS FLANKED

1. Warner, *Generals in Blue*, 237.
2. Howard, *Autobiography*, 353.
3. Summarized from Williams, *Abner Coburn*.
4. Small, *Road to Richmond*, 83.
5. Haley, *Rebel Yell*, 76.
6. Howard, *Autobiography*, 349.
7. Warner, 123; Schurz, II, 405; *OR*, Vol. 25, Part 1, 413.
8. Gould, *Major-General Hiram G. Berry*, 258.
9. Howard, *Autobiography*, 365; Sears, *Chancellorsville*, 246; *OR*, Series 1, Vol. 25, Part 2, 360–61.
10. Schurz, II, 416.
11. Ibid., 416.
12. Ibid., 418; Howard, *Autobiography*, 368.
13. Keifer, *153rd PA*, 171.
14. Dodge, *Campaign of Chancellorsville*, 94.
15. Johnson and Buel, *Battles and Leaders*, III, 198; Howard, *Autobiography*, 370–71; *San Francisco Chronicle*, May 23, 1872.
16. Howard to Lizzie, May 9, 1863, Bowdoin College; *Battles and Leaders*, III, 191.
17. Howard, *Autobiography*, 374–75.
18. Gould, *Major-General Hiram G. Berry*, 270.

19. Ibid., 261.

20. Ibid., 262, 263.

21. Mattocks, 13; Haley, *Rebel Yell,* 80.

22. Gould, *Major-General Hiram G. Berry,* 264.

23. Ibid., 266–67, 295, 268; Rusling, *Men and Things,* 303; Gould, *Major-General Hiram G. Berry,* 271.

24. Mattocks, 19.

25. Blackstone's service record, NARA.

26. Beyer and Keydel, *Deeds of Valor,* 157–59; *Maine at Gettysburg,* 109; *OR,* Vol. 25, Part 1, 310.

27. From a reprint of a speech Chase gave at the United Veterans of the Blue and the Gray, February 27, 1906, originally published in the *St. Petersburg* (FL) *Independent,* March 31, 1906. In the collections at GNMP.

28. Edwards to Hodsdon, May 9, 1863, Civil War Regimental Correspondence, MSA.

29. Bicknell, 216.

30. Account from Bicknell, 217–20.

31. Connor to his father, May 10, 1863, Brown University.

32. Edwards to Hodsdon, MSA; *Battles and Leaders,* III, 227.

33. Hyde, *Following the Greek Cross,* 125.

34. Ibid., 127.

35. Stanley and Hall, 338; Warner, *Generals in Blue,* 55; Mundy, *No Rich Men's Sons,* 19.

36. Mundy, 30, 48–49.

37. Hyde, *Following the Greek Cross,* 126; Sears, Chancellorsville, 355.

38. Clark, 33; Cushing, "Charge of the Light Division," 339–40; Whitman and True, 153; figures from *Maine at Gettysburg,* 416; Hyde, *Following the Greek Cross,* 128.

39. Connor to his father, May 10, 1863, Brown University.

40. Connor to his father, May 10, 1863, Brown University; Hyde, *Following the Greek Cross,* 130–31. In his book, Hyde said he was the one who predicted the attack by five o'clock, but since Connor's letter was written less than a week later, I will trust his recollection.

41. Clark, 35–37.

42. *Report of the Joint Committee on the Conduct of the War,* Part 1 (Washington, DC: Government Printing Office, 1865), 135; also Dodge, 226.

43. Houghton, 65–66; Haley, *Rebel Yell,* 85.

44. Bisbee, 118.

45. Small, *Sixteenth Maine,* 104–5.

46. Bisbee, 119.

47. Mattocks, 27.

48. Gould, *Major-General Hiram G. Berry,* 271–83; Whitman and True, 220.

49. Howard to Lizzie, May 9, 1863, Bowdoin College.

CHAPTER 10: THE ARMY MOVES NORTH

1. *OR,* Series I, Vol. 25, Part 1, 171.

2. *San Francisco Chronicle,* May 23, 1872.

3. *OR*, Series I, Vol. 25, Part 1, 631.

4. Howard to Lizzie, May 10, May 12, and May 31, 1863, Bowdoin College.

5. Howard to Rowland, May 16, 1863.

6. Howard to Lizzie, May 31, 1863, Bowdoin College.

7. Dodge, 252.

8. http://www.maine.gov/tools/whatsnew/index.php?topic=arcsesq&id=116181&v =article.

9. http://www.maine.gov/tools/whatsnew/index.php?topic=arcsesq&id=186628&v =article.

10. Tobie, *History of the First Maine Cavalry*, 451–52.

11. Merrill, *Campaigns of the First Maine*, 121.

12. Unpublished William Gardiner memoir, copy in AHC.

13. Tobie, 20, 21, 25; Stanley and Hall, 248; Gardiner memoir, AHC.

14. Tobie, 36.

15. Gardiner memoir, AHC.

16. http://www.maine.gov/tools/whatsnew/index.php?topic=arcsesq&id=403445&v =article.

17. Ford, "Charge of the First Maine Cavalry," 273; Martin, *Kill-Cavalry*, 193; Coddington, *Gettysburg Campaign*, 220; Martin, 12.

18. *Maine at Gettysburg*, 491–92; Tobie, 143, 144; Merrill, 101.

19. Ford, "Charge of the First Maine Cavalry," 274.

20. Tobie, 149.

21. Merrill, 109.

22. Tobie, 150; *OR*, Series I, Vol. 27, Part 1, 986.

23. Ford, "Charge of the First Maine Cavalry," 278.

24. Merrill, 112–13; Tobie, 151; casualty figures from Ford, "Charge of the First Maine Cavalry," 284.

25. Tobie, 155.

26. *OR*, Series I, Vol. 27, Part 1, 1043.

27. *OR*, Vol. 27, Part 1, 1046.

28. Schurz, III, 7–8.

29. Barlow, "*Fear*," xvii, 133, 130, 138; Howard to Lizzie, July 20, 1863, Bowdoin College.

30. Whitman and True, 168; Spear, *Recollections*, 307.

31. Spear, *Recollections*, 306–8.

32. Nesbitt, 60, 62.

33. Chamberlain, "*Bayonet!*," 24.

34. Ford, "Charge of the First Maine Cavalry," 282; Tobie, 162.

35. http://www.maine.gov/tools/whatsnew/index.php?topic=arcsesq&id=140102&v =article.

36. Tobie, 165–67.

37. Spear, *Recollections*, 310.

38. Melcher, 34; Spear, *Recollections*, 310.

39. *OR*, Vol. 27, Part 1, 614; Melcher, 34; Nathan S. Clark diary, MSA.

40. Tobie, 171–72; *Maine at Gettysburg*, 484.
41. Gardiner memoir, AHC.
42. Hoisington, *Christian Commission*, 82. Chamberlain's diary is in the collections of the Pejepscot Historical Society but is transcribed in Hoisington.
43. Ibid., 89–90.
44. Jordan, *Red Diamond Regiment*, 4.
45. Civil War Regimental Correspondence, MSA.
46. Haley journal transcripts, 21; *Rebel Yell*, 21, 22.
47. Haley, *Rebel Yell,* 93; Houghton, 73.
48. Mattocks, 39; Haley journal transcripts, 78.
49. Haley, *Rebel Yell,* 96.
50. Houghton, 77.
51. Mattocks, 43–44.
52. Haley, *Rebel Yell,* 98.
53. Howard, *Autobiography*, 396.
54. Weld, *War Diary*, 230; *OR*, Vol. XVII, Part 1, 707.
55. Houghton, 84.
56. Haley, *Rebel Yell,* 99.
57. Mattocks, 46.
58. Howard, "First Day at Gettysburg," 241.
59. Howard, *Autobiography*, 404.

Chapter 11: The 16th Maine Gets Sacrificed

1. *Maine at Gettysburg*, 23.
2. Tagg, *Generals*, 18–19; Warner, *Generals In Blue*, 110; Dawes, *Service with the Sixth*, 130, 20, 26.
3. Hall's accounts in Ladd and Ladd, *Bachelder Papers*, I: 24 and 385–89.
4. Howard, "At Gettysburg."
5. Howard, *Autobiography*, 410.
6. Ibid., 411.
7. Small, *Sixteenth Maine*, 131–32.
8. Alleman and Skelly, *Battle of Gettysburg*, 75; Howard, "Campaign and Battle," 54.
9. Howard, *Autobiography*, 412–14; Alleman and Skelly, 75–76.
10. Howard, "Campaign and Battle," 56.
11. Ladd and Ladd, II: 891; *OR*, Vol. 27, Part 1, 359; Ladd and Ladd, I: 387.
12. Hall's account in Ladd and Ladd, I, 385–89 and *OR*, Vol. 27, Part 1, 359–60; Hall to Hodsdon, http://www.maine.gov/tools/whatsnew/index.php?topic=arcsesq&id=403905&v=article.
13. Twitchell to Hodsdon, June 29, 1863, MSA; Hunt's account from his papers, Bowdoin College.
14. Hunt's account from his papers, Bowdoin College.
15. Warner, 363; Small, *Road to Richmond*, 94–97, 80.
16. Small, *Sixteenth Maine*, 116; *Maine at Gettysburg*, 30.
17. Small, *Sixteenth Maine*, 116.
18. *Maine at Gettysburg*, 38.

19. Small, *Sixteenth Maine*, 116–77.
20. Copy of Bisbee's account at GNMP.
21. Small, *Road to Richmond*, 99–100.
22. Small, *Sixteenth Maine*, 119.
23. *OR*, I, Vol. 27, Part 1, 717.
24. Pfanz, *First Day*, 231.
25. Schurz, III, 6; Pfanz, *First Day*, 235.
26. Harris in Ladd and Ladd, II, 742–49; Young in Barlow, "*Fear*," 159.
27. Halstead, "First Day," 6.
28. Howard, "Campaign and the Battle," 58; *OR*, Series I, Vol. 27, Part 1, 366.
29. *OR*, Series I, Vol. 27, Part 1, 718.
30. *Maine at Gettysburg*, 86.
31. Bisbee, 122.
32. Wiggin, "Sixteenth Maine," 158.
33. Small, *Road to Richmond*, 101.
34. Pfanz, *First Day*, 360.
35. Small, *Sixteenth Maine*, 231
36. *Maine at Gettysburg*, 44; Wiggin, 159.
37. Bisbee, GNMP.
38. Howard, "Campaign and Battle," 55.
39. Osborn, *Trials and Triumphs*, 98.
40. Small, *Road to Richmond*, 102.
41. Tagg, 134; Osborn, *Trials and Triumphs*, 97.
42. Halstead, 6; Howard, *Autobiography*, 418; *OR*, Vol. XXVII, Part 1, 697.
43. Smith, *History of the Nineteenth*, 77.
44. Charles Howard to Major Whittelsey, July 9, 1863, Bowdoin College.
45. Howard, "Campaign and Battle," 58.
46. Information about Meyer from Baumgartner, *Buckeye Blood*, 19–20, 45, 47, 67.
47. *OR*, Series I, Vol. 27, Part 1, 712.
48. Wainwright, *Diary of Battle*, 242.
49. Ladd and Ladd, III: 1351.
50. Hartwig, "11th Army Corps."
51. Ibid.
52. Hunt's journals, Bowdoin College.
53. Hyde, *Following the Greek Cross*, 144.
54. Howard, *Autobiography*, 423.
55. Howard, *Autobiography*, 419; Conklin, *Women at Gettysburg*, 168.
56. From a reprint of a speech Chase gave at the United Veterans of the Blue and the Gray, February 27, 1906, originally published in the *St. Petersburg* (Florida) *Independent*, March 31, 1906, in the collections at GNMP.

CHAPTER 12: THE 17TH MAINE FINDS A WALL

1. Adelman and Smith, *Devil's Den*, 11.
2. *Maine at Gettysburg*, 519.
3. Gould and Jordan, 83–84, 180.

4. *Maine at Gettysburg*, 521–22.

5. Ibid., 527.

6. *OR*, Series I, Vol. 27, Part 1, 493.

7. Walker, *Old Soldier*, 20, 24.

8. Walker's account in Ladd and Ladd, *Bachelder Papers*, II: 1093–96.

9. Stevens, *Berdan's*, 303; *Maine at Gettysburg*, 129.

10. Newcomb, "A Soldier's Story," *First Maine Bugle*.

11. Johnson, *Sword of Honor*, 6–7.

12. Ibid., 11–12.

13. Gibbon, *Personal Recollections*, 136.

14. Coddington, 386.

15. *Maine at Gettysburg*, 358.

16. Ibid., 359.

17. Ibid., 350.

18. Ibid., 181.

19. Smith, *Famous Battery*, 109; Ladd and Ladd, II: 1093–96.

20. Smith, *Famous Battery*, 103.

21. Walker, *Old Soldier*, 56.

22. Lokey, "Wounded at Gettysburg," 400; Priest, "Stand to It," 266.

23. Account from Ladd and Ladd, II: 1093–96; Walker, *Old Soldier*, 55–62.

24. Whitman, *Civil War Memories*, 19.

25. Verrill, "Seventeenth Maine," 263.

26. Whitman, 19.

27. Haley, *Rebel Yell*, 101.

28. Verrill, 265.

29. See O'Brien, "Hold Them with the Bayonet."

30. Verrill, 266; transcription of Whitmore letter at GNMP; Whitman, 20; Mattocks, 50.

31. Whitman, 20.

32. Haley, *Rebel Yell*, 101; Verrill, 276.

33. *OR*, I, Vol. 27, Part 1, 485 and 522; Haley journal transcripts, 148.

34. Haley, *Rebel Yell*, 102.

35. Roberts, "At Gettysburg," 52.

36. Jorgensen, "John Haley's Personal Recollections," 75.

37. *OR*, Series I, Vol. 27, Part 1, 508.

38. Howard, *Autobiography*, 443.

39. *OR*, Series I, Vol. 25, 508; http://www.maine.gov/tools/whatsnew/index.php?topic=arcsesq&id=248332&v=article.

40. http://www.maine.gov/tools/whatsnew/index.php?topic=arcsesq&id=186535&v=article.

41. William C. Morgan file in 3rd Maine folder, GNMP.

42. Sword, "Capt. William C. Morgan."

43. Nathaniel Clark diary; http://www.mainestatemuseum.org/resource/d/42983/alphabeticalbios.pdf.

44. Livermore diary, reprinted in Melcher, 76.

45. See Chamberlain's letter to Abner Coburn; Spear, *Recollections*, 310–11; http://www.maine.gov/tools/whatsnew/index.php?topic=arcsesq&id=145532&v=article.

46. Chamberlain, *"Bayonet!,"* 18.

47. Ibid. 18; Norton, *Army Letters*, 281.

48. Unpublished Coan MS, Bowdoin College.

49. Norton, 264.

50. Ibid., 283–84.

51. Chamberlain, *"Bayonet!,"* 22.

52. Ibid., 23.

53. Chamberlain, *Grand Old Man*, 310–11; Dedication of the Twentieth Maine Monuments, http://www.gdg.org/Research/People/Chamberlain/20ded.html; Vickery, "Walter Morrill," 133–34.

54. Norton, 165; Chamberlain, *"Bayonet!,"* 25.

55. Oates, *War Between the Union and the Confederacy*, 226.

CHAPTER 13: THE 20TH MAINE HOLDS THE LEFT

1. "Dedication of the 20th Maine Monuments; *OR*, Series I, Vol. 27, Part 1, 623.

2. Coan to his brother, August 5, 1863, Bowdoin College.

3. Spear, *Recollections*, 34; Coan, August 5, 1863, Bowdoin College.

4. Spear, *Recollections*, 314.

5. Clark diary, 16.

6. Chamberlain's report is in *OR*, Series I, Vol. 27, Part 1, 622–26; Spear, *Recollections*, 314; Chamberlain, *"Bayonet!,"* 29; copy of Livermore letter at GNMP.

7. Chamberlain, *"Bayonet!,"* 29.

8. Oates, 219, 220.

9. Chamberlain's reports quoted in Nesbitt, 81, 91.

10. Spear, *Recollections*, 35–36.

11. Coan MS, Bowdoin College.

12. Chamberlain, *"Bayonet!,"* 32–33.

13. Gerrish, 110.

14. This report is quoted in Nesbitt, 91.

15. Coan MS, Bowdoin College.

16. Reprinted in Melcher, 72; Chamberlain in "Dedication."

17. Spear, *Recollections*, 36.

18. Chamberlain, *"Bayonet!,"* 33; Spear, *Recollections*, 35; Clark diary.

19. Chamberlain, *Grand Old Man*, 155. In the same letter, Chamberlain added, "The 'whole truth' is sometimes quite different in its bearings from what is called truth. But to make a part truth displace the whole is not in accordance with old-fashioned ethics."

20. *Maine at Gettysburg*, 261.

21. McGilvery background from Matthews, *American Merchant Ships*, 368–69; *OR*, Series 1, Vol. 12, Part 2, 159.

22. Baker, *History of the Ninth Mass. Battery*, 60–61.

23. Cole, *Civil War Artillery*, 20.

24. Quotes from 6th Maine Battery letters from Civil War Regimental Correspondence, MSA; copies in collections of GNMP.
25. Dow's account from *New York Times*, June 29, 1913; Priest, 390; Baker, 62; Sears, *Gettysburg*, 310.
26. Dow's account from *New York Times*, June 29, 1913.
27. *Maine at Gettysburg*, 328.
28. *OR*, Series 1, Vol. 27, Part 1, 898.
29. McGilvery to Coburn, July 11, 1863, MSA.
30. Connor to his sister, June 5 and June 17, 1863, Brown University.
31. Edwards to Hodsdon, August 3, 1863, MSA.
32. Edwards to Hodsdon, August 3, 1863, MSA; Bicknell, 242.
33. Tagg, 47; Smith, *History of the Nineteenth*, 58.
34. Tagg, 47; Smith, *History of the Nineteenth*, 61.
35. Adams, 251.
36. *Reunions of the Nineteenth Maine*, 74.
37. Transcript of letter at GNMP. Also in *Reunions of the Nineteenth Maine*, 10.
38. Smith, *History of the Nineteenth*, 70.
39. Adams, 252.
40. *Maine at Gettysburg*, 292.
41. Adams, 253–54.
42. *Reunions of the Nineteenth Maine*, 11; *Maine at Gettysburg*, 293; Sword, "Edgar A. Burpee," 54.
43. *Maine at Gettysburg*, 293; Lancaster transcript, GNMP.
44. Adams, 257.
45. Smith, *History of the Nineteenth*, 73.
46. Small, *Road to Richmond*, 103; *Maine at Gettysburg*, 48.
47. http://www.maine.gov/tools/whatsnew/index.php?topic=arcsesq&id=265080&v=article; Whittier letter in files of GNMP.
48. From a reprint of a speech Chase gave at the United Veterans of the Blue and the Gray, February 27, 1906, originally published in the *St. Petersburg Independent*, March 31, 1906; in the collections at GNMP.
49. *Maine at Gettysburg*, 94.
50. Whittier, "The Left Attack," 87; Maine at Gettysburg, 95; http://www.maine.gov/tools/whatsnew/index.php?topic=arcsesq&id=265080&v=article.
51. Whittier, 88.
52. Ladd and Ladd, *Bachelder Papers*, I: 745–46.
53. Ladd and Ladd, I: 310–12.
54. Ibid., 238.
55. Whittier, 92; Howard, *Autobiography*, 101; Ladd and Ladd, I: 236.
56. Wainwright, *Diary of Battle*, 247.
57. *OR*, Vol. 27, Part 1, 713.
58. *Maine at Gettysburg*, 98.
59. Sword, "Burpee," 54.
60. *Reunions of the Nineteenth Maine*, 12.

Chapter 14: The Army of the Potomac Triumphs

1. Rowland Howard, "At Gettysburg."
2. Haskell, *Battle of Gettysburg*, 15, 68–69, 149.
3. Johnson and Buel, *Battles and Leaders*, III: 314; O. Howard, *Autobiography*, 433.
4. Chamberlain's report is available here: http://permanent.access.gpo.gov/lps68440/chamberlain.pdf.
5. *Maine at Gettysburg*, 260.
6. Spear, *Recollections*, 37; Priest, 444.
7. Ladd and Ladd, *Bachelder Papers*, II: 992–93.
8. Spear, *Recollections*, 38.
9. Dedication of the 20th Maine Monuments.
10. From a reprint of a speech Chase gave at the United Veterans of the Blue and the Gray, February 27, 1906, originally published in the *St. Petersburg Independent*, March 31, 1906, in the collections at GNMP.
11. Smith, *History of the Nineteenth*, 79; Adams, 259.
12. *Maine at Gettysburg*, 99.
13. Hoisington, 92–93.
14. Artillery numbers from Adkin, *Gettysburg Companion*; Smith, *History of the Nineteenth*, 80.
15. Small, *Sixteenth Maine*, 122–23.
16. Wiggin, "Sixteenth Maine," 163.
17. *Reunions of the Nineteenth Maine*, 12.
18. Adams, 259–60.
19. Clifford to his father, August 15, 1863, copy at GNMP.
20. Heath to Connor, August 25, 1889, http://www.maine.gov/tools/whatsnew/index.php?topic=arcsesq&id=186465&v=article.
21. Hess, *Pickett's Charge*, 128.
22. *OR*, Vol. 27, Part 1, 706; Howard, *Autobiography*, 437; Osborn, *Eleventh Corps Artillery*, 39–40.
23. Small, *Road to Richmond*, 105–6 and *Sixteenth Maine*, 123–24.
24. Hyde, *Following the Greek Cross*, 153–54.
25. *OR*, Series I, Vol. 27, Part 1, 883–84.
26. Quoted in Rollins, *Pickett's Charge!*, 124.
27. Rollins, 124 and 231; *OR*, Vol. 27, Part 1, 883–84; Gottfried, *Artillery*, 197.
28. Adams, 260.
29. Hunt recollections, Bowdoin College.
30. *Maine at Gettysburg*, 296.
31. *Reunions of the Nineteenth Maine*, 75.
32. Adams, 260–61.
33. *Reunions of the Nineteenth Maine*, 13.
34. Hunt papers, Bowdoin College.
35. Tobie, 179.
36. *National Transcript*, April 14, 1910, quoted in Sauers, *Fighting Them Over*, 71–72; Tobie, 217; *OR* Series I, Vol. 27, Part 1, 291.

37. First Maine Cavalry Association, "Twelfth Annual Reunion of the First Maine Cavalry," *First Maine Bugle*, July 1890, 38.

38. Brooke-Rawle, "Gregg's Cavalry Fight on the Right Flank at Gettysburg," *First Maine Bugle*, April 1891, 25.

39. Transcription of letter from William B. Baker, from the William B. Baker Papers (3506) of the Southern Historical Collection, GNMP.

40. Smith, *History of the Nineteenth*, 81.

41. Osborn, *Eleventh Corps Artillery*, 42.

42. *OR*, Vol. 27, Part 1, 884.

43. "How One Brave Battery," *NY Times*, June 29, 1913.

44. Ladd and Ladd, I: 18–19; *Reunions of the Nineteenth Maine*, 13.

45. Hess, 276–77; Gibbon, 152.

46. Quoted in Hess, 298.

47. *Maine at Gettysburg*, 297.

48. Adams, 262.

49. *Reunions of the Nineteenth Maine*, 13.

50. Haskell, 67.

51. Haley journal transcripts, 167.

52. Small, *Road to Richmond*, 107.

53. Clark, 43–44.

54. *Reunions of the Nineteenth Maine*, 14.

55. Haley journal transcripts, 178.

56. Haley journal transcripts, "July 3rd."

57. Commonwealth of PA, *Revised Report*, 134; Dedication of the 20th Maine Monuments; Gerrish, 109.

58. Smith, *Nineteenth Maine*, 63; *Revised Report*, 134.

CHAPTER 15: AFTERMATH

1. Bisbee, 123–24.

2. Garcelon to his aunt, July 4, 1863, in Edmund S. Muskie Archives and Special Collections Library, Bates College, Lewiston, Maine, and also online here: https://www.mainememory.net/artifact/66024.

3. Bisbee, 125.

4. Haley, *Rebel Yell*, 107.

5. Hunt papers, Bowdoin College.

6. Spear, *Recollections*, 38–39.

7. Original letter in the Chamberlain papers, Library of Congress. Also quoted in Nesbitt, 79.

8. Spear, *Recollections*, 40–41, 318.

9. Clark diary.

10. Smith, *Nineteenth Maine*, 91, 93; *Reunions*, 14.

11. Small, *Sixteenth Maine*, 126–27.

12. Connor to his father, July 11, 1863, Brown University.

13. Bicknell, 248–49.

14. Howard, *Autobiography*, 445.

15. Smith, *Nineteenth Maine*, 95.

16. Houghton, 112, 110.

17. Haley journal transcripts, 199.

18. Bisbee, 125.

19. Undated newspaper clipping (perhaps 1909) in Chase's pension records, NARA.

20. Maine Adjutant General, *Annual Report 1864–1865*, 114–20.

21. Eaton, 19; "Sarah Sampson: Caring for Soldiers, Orphans," https://www.maine memory.net/sitebuilder/site/854/page/1264/display.

22. Smith, Steven Trent, "The Great Libby Prison Breakout"; Military Order of the Loyal Legion of the United States. "Companion Charles W. Tilden."

23. Bisbee, 133–49.

24. Hunt's account from "Our Escape from Camp Sorghum."

25. Hyde, *Following the Greek Cross*, 185, 193.

26. Chamberlain, *"Bayonet!,"* 182.

27. Smith, *Nineteenth Maine*, 130.

28. Warner, *Generals in Blue*, 88–89.

29. Sword, "Capt. William C. Morgan."

30. Newton, 201–2.

31. *Maine at Gettysburg*, 345.

32. Haley, *Rebel Yell*, 283; summary from Haley, 12–16.

33. Small, *Road to Richmond*, xiii, xxx.

34. Howard, "Campaign and Battle of Gettysburg," 70; Lash, "Congressional Resolution."

35. Carpenter, *Sword and Olive Branch*, 73.

36. Carpenter, 230.

37. Ibid., 262–63.

38. Howard's later life summarized from Carpenter.

39. Charles Howard's later life summarized from Howard, *We Are in His Hands*.

40. Nesbitt, 149.

41. Chamberlain, *Passing of the Armies*, 168.

42. Ibid., 178.

43. Notes in the 20th Maine file, GNMP.

44. Spear and Spear, *The 20th Maine at Fredericksburg*, 50; Spear to Ames, December 21, 1912, Smith College.

45. Letter in the Ames collection, Smith College.

46. Quoted in Desjardin, *Stand Firm*, 91.

47. Typescript in Ames Papers, Smith College.

48. Testimony in State of Mississippi, *Impeachment of Adelbert Ames*, 5.

49. *Boston Globe Magazine*, sometime in 1926, in collections at Smith College.

50. Plimpton, George. "A Clean, Well Lighted Place." *New York Review of Books*, December 18, 1980. Available online here: http://www.nybooks.com/articles/1980/12/18/a–clean–well–lighted–place/.

BIBLIOGRAPHY

PAPERS AND COLLECTIONS

Army Heritage Center, Carlisle, PA (AHC).

Dyer Library, Saco, ME.

George J. Mitchell Department of Special Collections & Archives. Bowdoin College, Brunswick, ME.

Gettysburg National Military Park, Gettysburg, PA (GNMP).

Hay Library, Brown University, Providence, RI.

Library of Congress, Washington, DC (LOC).

Maine Historical Society, Portland, ME (MHS).

Maine State Archives, Augusta, ME (MSA).

National Archives and Records Administration, Washington, DC (NARA).

Pejepscot Historical Society, Brunswick, ME.

Raymond H. Fogler Library Special Collections. University of Maine at Orono.

Sophia Smith Collection. Smith College, Northampton, MA.

ARTICLES

Beard, Rick. "Gettysburg's Forgotten Hero." *Civil War Times*, August 2015.

Brake, Robert L. "How One Brave Battery Saved the Union Left." *New York Times*, June 29, 1913.

Brooke-Rawle, William. "Gregg's Cavalry Fight on the Right Flank at Gettysburg," *First Maine Bugle*, April 1891, 25.

Callihan, David L. "A Cool Clear Headed Old Sailor: Freeman McGilvery at Gettysburg." *The Gettysburg Magazine*, no. 31.

First Maine Cavalry Association, "Twelfth Annual Reunion of the First Maine Cavalry," *First Maine Bugle*, July 1890, 38.

Hartwig, D. Scott. "The 11th Army Corps on July 1, 1863: 'The Unlucky 11th.'" *The Gettysburg Magazine*, no. 1. Available online at http://www.gdg.org/Research/OOB/Union/July1-3/11thidx.html.

Henig, Gerald S., ed. "'Give My Love to All': The Civil War Letters of George S. Rollins." *Civil War Times Illustrated*, November 1972.

Howard, Oliver O. "Campaign and Battle of Gettysburg." *Atlantic Monthly*, July 1876.

Jordan, Brian Matthews. "The Unfortunate Colonel." *Civil War Monitor*, Winter 2016.

Jorgensen, Jay. "John Haley's Personal Recollections of the Battle of the Wheatfield." *The Gettysburg Magazine*, no. 27.

Lash, Gary O. "The Congressional Resolution of Thanks for the Federal Victory at Gettysburg." *The Gettysburg Magazine*, no. 12.

Lokey, J. W. "Wounded at Gettysburg." *Confederate Veteran*, vol. 22, 1914, p. 400.

Newcomb, Jonathan, Jr. "A Soldier's Story of Personal Experience at the Battle of Gettysburg." *The Maine Bugle*, April 1896.

New York Times. "An Appeal from an Officer of the Army to the Country." January 16, 1863.

O'Brien, Kevin E. "Hold Them with the Bayonet: De Trobriand's Brigade Defends the Wheatfield." *The Gettysburg Magazine*, no. 21.

O'Neill, Robert F. "Aldie, Middleburg, and Upperville." *The Gettysburg Magazine*, no. 43.

Plimpton, George. "A Clean, Well Lighted Place." *New York Review of Books*, December 18, 1980. Available online at http://www.nybooks.com/articles/1980/12/18/a-clean-well-lighted-place/.

Smith, Steven Trent. "The Great Libby Prison Breakout." *Civil War Times*, August 2010.

Spear, Ellis. "The Left at Gettysburg." *The National Tribune*, June 12, 1913.

Sword, Wiley. "Capt. William C. Morgan, 3rd Maine Infantry: Hero or Scoundrel at the Peach Orchard." *The Gettysburg Magazine*, no. 25.

———. "First Lt. Edgar A. Burpee, 19th Maine Infantry Vividly Describes the Repulse of Perry's (Lang's) Florida Brigade on July 2." *The Gettysburg Magazine*, no. 44, January 2011.

Wuthman, Walter. "NASA Scientist from Maine Names Mars Rock after War Hero Chamberlain." *Bangor Daily News*, October 17, 2015, http://bangordailynews.com/2015/10/17/news/bangor/nasa-scientist-from-maine-names-mars-rock-after-war-hero-chamberlain/.

WEBSITES

Maine Memory Network
https://www.mainememory.net/
Maine State Archives
http://www.maine.gov/sos/arc/
Norway Historical Society
http://www.norwayhistoricalsociety.org/GeorgeLBeal.php

BOOKS AND PUBLICATIONS

Adams, Charles. *Charles Francis Adams, 1835–1915: An Autobiography*. Boston: Houghton Mifflin Co., 1916.

Adams, Silas. "The Nineteenth Maine at Gettysburg," in *War Papers Read Before the Commandery of the State of Maine, Military Order of the Loyal Legion of the United States*, edited by the Military Order of the Loyal Legion of the United States, 4:250–63. Portland, ME: Lefavor-Tower Company, 1915.

Adelman, Garry, and Timothy H. Smith. *Devil's Den: A History and Guide*. Gettysburg, PA: Thomas Publications, 1997.

Adkin, Mark. *The Gettysburg Companion: The Complete Guide to America's Most Famous Battle*. Mechanicsburg, PA: Stackpole Books, 2008.

Alleman, Matilda "Tillie" Pierce, and Daniel Skelly. *The Battle of Gettysburg as Seen by Two Teens: The Stories of Tillie Pierce and Daniel Skelly*. Edited by Frank Meredith. Schoharie, NY: Savannah Books, 2010.

Ames, Blanche. *Adelbert Ames: 1835–1933, General, Senator, Governor; The Story of His Life and Times and His Integrity as a Soldier and Statesman in the Service of the United States of America throughout the Civil War and in Mississippi in the years of Reconstruction*. New York: Argosty-Antiquarian, 1964.

———. *Chronicles from the Nineteenth Century: Family Letters of Blanche Butler and Adelbert Ames, Married July 21st, 1870*. Two volumes. Privately issued, 1957.

Baker, Levi Wood. *History of the Ninth Mass. Battery: Recruited July, 1862; Mustered in Aug. 10, 1862; Mustered Out June 9, 1865, at the Close of the Rebellion*. South Framingham, MA: Lakeview Press, 1888.

Banes, Charles H. *History of the Philadelphia Brigade, Sixty-ninth, Seventy-first, Seventy-second, and One hundred and sixth Pennsylvania Volunteers*. Philadelphia: J. B. Lippincott and Company, 1876.

Bangs, Isaac S. *Military History of Waterville, Maine*. Augusta, ME: Kennebec Journal, 1902.

Barlow, Francis C. *"Fear Was Not in Him": The Civil War Letters of Major General Francis C. Barlow, U.S.A.* Edited by Christina G. Samito. New York: Fordham University Press, 2004.

Baumgartner, Richard A. *Buckeye Blood: Ohio at Gettysburg*. Huntington, WV: Blue Acorn Press, 2003.

Beattie, Donald W., Rodney M. Cole, and Charles G. Waugh, eds. *A Distant War Comes Home: Maine in the Civil War Era*. Camden, ME: Down East Books, 1996.

Beyer, W. F., and O. F. Keydel. *Deeds of Valor: How America's Civil War Heroes Won the Congressional Medal of Honor*. New York: Smithmark Publishers, 2000.

Bicknell, George W. *History of the Fifth Regiment Maine Volunteers, Comprising Brief Descriptions of its Marches, Engagements, and General Services from the Date of its Muster In, June 24, 1861, to the Time of its Muster Out, July 27, 1864*. Portland, ME: Hall L. Davis, 1871.

Bilby, Joseph G. *Civil War Firearms: Their Historical Background, Tactical Use and Modern Collecting and Shooting*. Conshohocken, PA: Combined Books, 1996.

Bisbee, George D. "Three Years a Volunteer Soldier in the Civil War, Antietam to Appomattox." In *War Papers Read Before the Commandery of the State of Maine, Military Order of the Loyal Legion of the United States*, edited by the Military Order of the Loyal Legion of the United States, 4:114–49. Portland, ME: Lefavor-Tower Company, 1915.

Block, Eugene. *Above the Civil War: The Story of Thaddeus Lowe, Balloonist, Inventor, Railway Builder*. Berkeley, CA: Howell-North Books, 1966.

Calhoun, Charles C. *A Small College in Maine: Two Hundred Years of Bowdoin*. Brunswick, ME: Bowdoin College, 1993.

Carpenter, John A. *Sword and Olive Branch: Oliver Otis Howard*. Pittsburgh, PA: University of Pittsburgh Press, 1968.

Chamberlain, Joshua Lawrence. *"Bayonet! Forward" My Civil War Reminiscences*. Gettysburg, PA: Stan Clark Military Books, 1994.

———. *The Grand Old Man of Maine: Selected Letters of Joshua Lawrence Chamberlain, 1865–1914*. Edited by Jeremiah E. Goulka. Chapel Hill: University of North Carolina Press, 2004.

———. *Joshua L. Chamberlain A Life in Letters*. Edited by Thomas Desjardin. Long Island City, NY: Osprey Publishing, 2012.

———. *The Passing of the Armies*. 1915. Reprint, New York: Barnes & Noble Books, 2004.

Clark, Charles Amory. "Campaigning with the Sixth Maine: A Paper Read Before the Iowa Commandery Military Order of the Loyal Legion of the United States." Des Moines, IA: Kenyon Press, 1897.

Cleaveland, Nehemiah. *History of Bowdoin College, with Biographical Sketches of its Graduates*. Boston: James Ripley Osgood & Co., 1882.

Coddington, Edward. *The Gettysburg Campaign: A Study in Command*. New York: Charles Scribner's Sons, 1968.

Cole, Philip M. *Civil War Artillery at Gettysburg: Organization, Equipment, Ammunition, and Tactics*. Cambridge, MA: Da Capo Press, 2002.

Commonwealth of Pennsylvania. *Revised Report of the Select Committee Relative to the Soldiers' National Cemetery, Together with the Accompanying Documents, as Reported to the House of Representatives of the Commonwealth of Pennsylvania*. Harrisburg, PA: Singerly, Myers, State Printers, 1865.

Conklin, Eileen F. *Women at Gettysburg, 1863*. Gettysburg, PA: Thomas Publications, 1993.

Connor, Selden. "The Boys of 1861." In *War Papers Read Before the Commandery of the State of Maine, Military Order of the Loyal Legion of the United States*, edited by the Military Order of the Loyal Legion of the United States, 1: 322-43. Portland, ME: Lefavor-Tower Company, 1915.

Cudworth, Warren Handel. *History of the First Regiment (Massachusetts Infantry), from the 25th of May, 1861, to the 25th of May, 1864; Including Brief References to the Operations of the Army of the Potomac*. Boston: Walker, Fuller & Co., 1866.

Cushing, Wainwright. "Charge of the Light Division at Marye's Heights, May 3, 1863." In *War Papers. Read Before the Commandery of the State of Maine, Military Order of the Loyal Legion of the United States, Published by the Commandery*, edited by the Military Order of the Loyal Legion of the United States, 3:334–50. Portland, ME: LeFavor-Tower Company, 1908.

Dalton, Pete, and Cyndi Dalton. *Into the Valley of Death: The Story of the 4th Maine Volunteer Infantry at the Battle of Gettysburg, July 2, 1863*. Union, ME: Union Publishing Co., 1994.

Dalton, Peter B. *With Our Faces to the Foe: A History of the 4th Maine Infantry in the War of the Rebellion.* Union, ME: Union Publishing Co., 1998.

Davis, William C. *Battle at Bull Run: A History of the First Major Campaign of the Civil War.* Baton Rouge: Louisiana State University Press, 1977.

Dawes, Rufus. *Service with the Sixth Wisconsin Volunteers.* Marietta, OH: K. R. Aldeman & Sons, 1890.

Dedication of the 20th Maine Monuments at Gettysburg, Oct. 3, 1889. With Report of Annual Reunion, *Oct. 2d, 1889.* Waldoboro, ME: News Steam Job Print, 1891.

Desjardin, Thomas A. *Stand Firm Ye Boys from Maine: The 20th Maine and the Gettysburg Campaign.* New York: Oxford University Press, 1995.

De Peyster, John Watts. *Personal and Military History of Philip Kearny, Major-General United States Volunteers.* Elizabeth, NJ: Palmer & Co., 1870.

———. *These Honored Dead: How the Story of Gettysburg Shaped American Memory.* Cambridge, MA: Da Capo Press, 2003.

Desmond, Jerry. *Turning the Tide at Gettysburg: How Maine Saved the Union.* Lanham, MD: Down East Books, 2014.

De Trobriand, Regis. *Four Years with the Army of the Potomac.* Boston: Ticknor and Company, 1889.

Dodge, Theodore Ayrault. *The Campaign of Chancellorsville.* Boston: James R. Osgood and Company, 1881.

Donald, David Herbert. *Lincoln.* New York: Simon & Schuster, 1995.

Dreese, Michael A. *Torn Families: Death and Kinship at the Battle of Gettysburg.* Jefferson, NC: McFarland, 2007.

Eaton, Harriet. *This Birth Place of Souls: The Civil War Nursing Diary of Harriet Eaton.* Edited by Jane E. Schulz. New York: Oxford University Press, 2011.

Faust, Patricia L., ed. *Historical Times Illustrated Encyclopedia of the Civil War.* New York: Harper & Row, 1986. Reprint, 1991.

Ford, Charles W. "Charge of the First Maine Cavalry at Brandy Station." In *War Papers Read Before the Commandery of the State of Maine, Military Order of the Loyal Legion of the United States,* edited by the Military Order of the Loyal Legion of the United States, 2:268–89. Portland, ME: Lefavor-Tower Company, 1915.

Ford, Worthington Chauncey. *A Cycle of Adams Letters, 1861–1865.* Vol. 2. Boston: Houghton Mifflin Co., 1920.

Gerrish, Theodore. *Army Life: A Private's Reminiscences of the Civil War.* Portland, ME: Hoyt, Fogg & Donham, 1882.

Gibbon, John. *Personal Recollections of the Civil War.* New York, G. P Putnam's Sons, 1928.

Gilmore, Pascal Pearl. *Civil War Memories.* Bangor, ME: Publisher unknown, 1928.

Gottfried, Bradley M. *The Artillery of Gettysburg.* Nashville, TN: Cumberland House, 2008.

———. *Brigades of Gettysburg.* New York: Skyhorse Publishing, 2002.

Gould, Edward K. *Major-General Hiram G. Berry: His Career as a Contractor, Bank President, Politician, and Major-general of Volunteers in the Civil War, Together with His War Correspondence, Embracing the Period from Bull Run to Chancellorsville.* Rockland, ME: Courier-Gazette, 1899.

Gould, John Mead. *The Civil War Journals of John Meade Gould, 1861–1866.* Edited by William B. Jordan. Baltimore: Butternut and Blue, 1997.

———. *Joseph K. F. Mansfield, Brigadier General of the U.S. Army: A Narrative of Events Connected with his Mortal Wounding at Antietam, Sharpsburg, Maryland, September 17, 1862.* Portland, ME: Stephen Berry, Printer, 1895.

Gould, John Mead, and Leonard G. Jordan. *History of the First—Tenth—Twenty-ninth Maine Regiment: In Service of the United States from May 3, 1861, to June 21, 1866.* Portland, ME: Stephen Berry, 1871.

Haley, John W. *The Rebel Yell and the Yankee Hurrah: The Civil War Journal of a Maine Volunteer.* Edited by Ruth L. Stiller. Camden, ME: Down East Books, 1985.

Halstead, E.P. "The First Day of the Battle of Gettysburg." In *War Papers: Being Papers Read before the Commandery of the District of Columbia Military Order of the Loyal Legion of the United States,* edited by the Military Order of the Loyal Legion of the United States, I: 1–10. Wilmington, NC: Broadfoot Publishing Co., 1993.

Hamlin, Charles Eugene. *The Life and Times of Hannibal Hamlin.* Cambridge, MA: Riverside Press, 1899.

Haskell, Frank A. *The Battle of Gettysburg.* 2nd ed. Madison: Wisconsin History Commission, 1910.

Hatfield, Mark O., et. al. *Vice Presidents of the United States, 1789–1993.* Edited by Wendy Wolff. Washington, DC: U.S. Government Printing Office, 1997.

Hazelton, Gary W. "The Chicago Convention of 1860 and the Man It Nominated," in *War Papers Read Before the Commandery of the State of Wisconsin, Military Order of the Loyal Legion of the United States.* Milwaukee: Burdick and Allen, 1914.

Hebert, Walter H. *Fighting Joe Hooker.* Lincoln: University of Nebraska Press, 1999.

Hennessy, John J. *Return to Bull Run: The Campaign and Battle of Second Manassas.* New York: Simon & Schuster, 1993.

Hess, Earl J. *Pickett's Charge: The Last Attack at Gettysburg.* Chapel Hill: University of North Carolina Press, 2001.

Hoisington, Daniel J. *Gettysburg and the Christian Commission.* Roseville, MN: Edinborough Press, 2002.

Houghton, Edwin B. *The Campaigns of the Seventeenth Maine.* Portland, ME: Short & Loring, 1866.

Howard, Charles H. "The First Day at Gettysburg." In *Military Essays and Recollections: Papers Read Before the Commandery of the State of Illinois, Military Order of the Loyal Legion of the United States,* 4: 238-64. Wilmington, NC: Broadfoot Publishing Co., 1992.

———. *We Are in His Hands Whether We Live or Die.* Edited by David K. Thomson. Knoxville, TN: The University of Tennessee Press, 2013.

Howard, Oliver Otis. *Autobiography of Oliver Otis Howard, Major General, United States Army.* Vol. 1. New York: The Baker & Taylor Company, 1907.

Howard, Rowland B. "At Gettysburg." Boston: The American Peace Society, 1887.

Hunt, Charles O. "Our Escape from Camp Sorghum." In *War Papers Read Before the Commandery of the State of Maine, Military Order of the Loyal Legion of the United States*, edited by the Military Order of the Loyal Legion of the United States, 1:85–128. Portland, ME: Lefavor-Tower Company, 1915.

Hunt, Gaillard, ed. *Israel, Elihu and Cadwallader Washburn: A Chapter of American Biography*. New York: Da Capo Press, 1969. First published 1925 by MacMillan (New York).

Hunt, H. Draper. *Hannibal Hamlin of Maine, Lincoln's First Vice-President*. Syracuse, NY: Syracuse University Press, 1969.

Hyde, Thomas W. *Civil War Letters of General Thomas W. Hyde*. Privately printed, 1933.

———. *Following the Greek Cross; or, Memories of the Sixth Army Corps*. Boston: Houghton, Mifflin, 1894.

Jellison, Charles A. *Fessenden of Maine: Civil War Senator*. Syracuse, NY: Syracuse University Press, 1962.

Johnson, Hannibal Augustus. *The Sword of Honor: A Story of the Civil War by Lieut. H. A. Johnson, Third Maine, Regt, N.V.M.* Worcester, MA: Blanchard Press, 1906.

Johnson, Robert Underwood, and Clarence Clough Buel. *Battles and Leaders of the Civil War: Being for the Most Part Contributions by Union and Confederate Officers*. New York: Century Company, 1887–1888; reprint, Secaucus, NJ: Castle Books, n.d.),

Jones, Wilmer L. *Generals in Blue and Gray. Vol. 1, Lincoln's Generals*. Mechanicsburg, PA: Stackpole Books, 2006.

Jordan, William B., Jr. *Red Diamond Regiment: The 17th Maine Infantry, 1862–1865*. Shippensburg, PA: White Mane Publishing, 1996.

Jorgensen, Jay. *Gettysburg's Bloody Wheatfield*. Shippensburg, PA: White Mane Books, 2002.

Judd, Richard W., Edwin A. Churchill, and Joel W. Eastman, eds. *Maine: The Pine Tree State from Prehistory to the Present*. Orono: University of Maine Press, 1995.

Kearny, Philip. *Letters from the Peninsula: The Civil War Letters of General Philip Kearny*. Edited by William B. Styple. Kearny, NJ: Bell Grove Publishing Co., 1988.

Kiefer, William R., and Newton Heston Mack. *History of the One Hundred and Fifty-third Regiment Pennsylvania Volunteers Infantry: Which was Recruited in Northampton County, Pa., 1862-1863*. Easton, PA: Chemical Publishing Company, 1909.

Kirshner, Ralph. *The Class of 1861: Custer, Ames, and Their Classmates after West Point*. Carbondale: Southern Illinois University Press, 1998.

Ladd, David L., and Audrey J. Ladd, eds. *The Bachelder Papers: Gettysburg in Their Own Words*. 3 vols. Dayton: Morningside Press, 1994–1995.

Long, Hezekiah. *Hard Times, Hard Bread, and Harder Coffee: Hezekiah Long, Company F, 20th Maine Infantry*. Edited by Richardson's Civil War Round Table. Northport, ME: Richardson's Civil War Round Table, 2008.

Longacre, Edward G. *The Early Morning of War: Bull Run, 1861*. Norman: University of Oklahoma Press, 2014.

———. *Joshua Chamberlain: The Soldier and the Man*. Conshohocken, PA: Combined Publishing, 1999.

Maine Adjutant General. *Annual Report of the Adjutant General of the State of Maine for the Year Ending December 31, 1862.* Augusta, ME: Stevens & Sayward, 1863.

Maine Gettysburg Commission. *Maine at Gettysburg.* Portland, ME: The Lakeside Press, 1898.

Mangol, Edward. *Owen Lovejoy, Abolitionist in Congress.* New Brunswick, NJ: Rutgers University Press, 1967.

Martin, Samuel J. *Kill-Cavalry: The Life of Union General Hugh Judson Kilpatrick.* Mechanicsburg, PA: Stackpole Books, 2000.

Matthews, Frederick C. *American Merchant Ships, 1850–1900, Volume 1.* New York: Dover Publications, 2012.

Mattocks, Charles. *"Unspoiled Heart": The Journal of Charles Mattocks of the 17th Maine.* Edited by Philip N. Racine. Knoxville: The University of Tennessee Press, 1994.

McClellan, George B. *The Civil War Papers of George B. McClellan: Selected Correspondence, 1860–1865.* Edited by Stephen W. Sears. New York: Ticknor and Fields, 1989.

McIntyre, Philp Willis, ed. *Alonzo Palmer Stinson: The First Portland Soldier Who Fell in Battle During the Civil War.* Portland, ME: Lefavor-Tower Co., 1909.

Melcher, Holman S. *With a Flash of his Sword: The Writings of Major Holman S. Melcher, 20th Maine Infantry.* Edited by William B. Styple. Kearny, NJ: Belle Grove Publishing Co., 1994.

Merrill, Samuel H. *The Campaigns of the First Maine and First District of Columbia Cavalry.* Portland, ME: Bailey & Noyes, 1866.

Military Order of the Loyal Legion of the United States. "Companion Charles W. Tilden." Portland, ME: Commandery of the State of Maine, 1914.

Mississippi, State of. *The Testimony in the Impeachment of Adelbert Ames, as Governor of Mississippi.* Jackson, MS: Power & Barksdale, state printers, 1877.

Mundy, James H. *No Rich Men's Sons: The Sixth Maine Volunteer Infantry.* Cape Elizabeth, ME: Harp Publications, 1994.

Nesbitt, Mark. *Through Blood and Fire: Selected Civil War Papers of Major General Joshua Chamberlain.* Mechanicsburg, PA: Stackpole Books, 1996.

Newton, George W. *Silent Sentinels: A Reference Guide to the Artillery at Gettysburg.* New York: Savas Beatie, 2005.

Nineteenth Maine Regiment Association. *Reunions of the Nineteenth Maine Regiment Association, at Portland, Bath, Belfast, Augusta and Richmond.* Augusta, ME: Sprague, Owen & Nash, 1878.

Norton, Oliver W. *Army Letters, 1861–1865: Being Extracts from Private Letters to Relatives and Friends from a Soldier in the Field During the Late Civil War, with an Appendix Containing Copies of Some Official Documents, Papers and Addresses of Later Date.* Chicago: O. L. Deming, 1903.

———. *The Attack and Defense of Little Round Top, Gettysburg, July 6, 1863.* New York: Neal Publishing Company, 1913.

Oates, William Calvin. *The War Between the Union and the Confederacy.* New York: Neale Publishing Co., 1905.

Osborn, Hartwell. *Trials and Triumphs: The Record of the Fifty-fifth Ohio Volunteers Infantry.* Chicago: A. C. McClurg & Co., 1904.

Osborn, Thomas Ward. *The Eleventh Corps Artillery at Gettysburg.* Edited by Herb S. Crumb. Hamilton, NY: Edmonston Publishing, 1991.

Packard, Alpheus S. *Bowdoin in the War.* Brunswick, ME: Bowdoin College, 1867.

Pfanz, Harry W. *Gettysburg—Culp's Hill and Cemetery Hill.* Chapel Hill: University of North Carolina Press, 1993.

———. *Gettysburg—The First Day.* Chapel Hill: University of North Carolina Press, 2001.

———. *Gettysburg—The Second Day.* Chapel Hill: University of North Carolina Press, 1987.

Priest, John Michael. *"Stand to It and Give Them Hell": Gettysburg as the Soldiers Experienced It from Cemetery Ridge to Little Round Top, July 2, 1863.* El Dorado Hills, CA: Savas Beatie, 2014.

Pullen, John J. *The Twentieth Maine.* 1957. Reprint, Mechanicsburg, PA: Stackpole Books, 2008.

Relaford, Judith. *Glory and Grace: The Civil War Career of the "Christian General," Oliver Otis Howard.* Thesis, University of Oregon, 1983.

Roberts, Charles W. "At Gettysburg in 1863 and 1888." In *War Papers Read Before the Commandery of the State of Maine, Military Order of the Loyal Legion of the United States,* edited by the Military Order of the Loyal Legion of the United States, 1:49–57. Portland, ME: Lefavor-Tower Company, 1915.

Robertson, James I. *Stonewall Jackson: The Man, the Soldier, the Legend.* New York: MacMillan, 1997.

Rockland Courier-Gazette. *Memoirs and Services of Three Generations.* Rockland, ME: Courier-Gazette, 1909.

Rollins, Richard, ed. *Pickett's Charge! Eyewitness Accounts.* Redondo Beach, CA: Rank and File Publications, 1994.

Rusling, James F. *Men and Things I Saw in Civil War Days.* New York, Eaton & Mains, 1899.

Sauers, Richard A., ed. *Fighting Them Over: How the Veterans Remembered Gettysburg in the Pages of the* National Tribune. Baltimore: Butternut and Blue, 1998.

Schurz, Carl. *The Reminiscences of Carl Schurz,* Volumes 2 and 3. London: John Murray, 1909.

Sears, Stephen W. *Chancellorsville.* New York: Houghton Mifflin, 1996.

———. *Controversies and Commanders: Dispatches from the Army of the Potomac.* New York: Houghton Mifflin, 1999.

———. *George B. McClellan: The Young Napoleon.* New York: Ticknor and Fields, 1988.

———. *Gettysburg.* New York: Houghton Mifflin, 2003.

———. *Landscape Turned Red: The Battle of Antietam.* New York: Mariner Books, 1993.

———. *To the Gates of Richmond: The Peninsula Campaign.* New York: Ticknor and Fields, 1992.

Shain, Charles, and Samuella Shain, eds. *The Maine Reader: The Down East Experience from 1614 to the Present.* Jaffrey, NH: David R. Godine, 1997.

Sherman, William Tecumseh. *Memoirs of General William T. Sherman*. New York: Penguin Books, 2000.

Small, Abner R. *The Road to Richmond: The Civil War Memoirs of Abner R. Small of the Sixteenth Maine Volunteers. Together with the Diary which He Kept when He Was a Prisoner of War*. Berkeley: University of California Press, 1939.

———. *The Sixteenth Maine in the War of the Rebellion, 1861–1865*. Portland, ME: B. Thurston & Co., 1886.

Smith, James E. *A Famous Battery and Its Campaigns, 1861–'64*. Washington, DC: W. H. Lowdermilk & Co., 1892.

Smith, John Day. *History of the Nineteenth Regiment of Maine Volunteer Infantry, 1862–1865*. Minneapolis: The Great Western Printing Co., 1909.

Sneden, Robert Knox. *Eye of the Storm: A Civil War Odyssey*. Edited by Charles F. Bryan Jr. New York: The Free Press, 2000.

Spear, Ellis. *The Civil War Recollections of General Ellis Spear*. Edited by Abbott Spear, Andrea C. Hawkes, Marie H. McCosh, Craig L. Symonds, and Michael H. Albert. Orono: University of Maine Press, 1997.

———. "The Story of the Raising and Organization of a Regiment of Volunteers in 1862." Washington, DC: Military Order of the Loyal Legion of the United States, Commandery of the District of Columbia, 1903.

Spear, Ellis, and Abbott Spear. *The 20th Maine at Fredericksburg: The Conflicting Accounts of General Joshua L. Chamberlain and General Ellis Spear*. Union, ME: Union Publishing Co., 1989.

Stanley, R. H., and George O. Hall. *Eastern Maine and the Rebellion*. Bangor, ME: R. H. Stanley & Co., 1887.

Stevens, Charles Augustus. *Berdan's United States Sharpshooters in the Army of the Potomac, 1861–1865*. St. Paul, MN: Price-McGill Co., 1892.

Stout, Harry S. *Upon the Altar of the Nation: A Moral History of the Civil War*. New York: Viking, 2006.

Sword, Wiley. *Sharpshooter: Hiram Berdan, His Famous Sharpshooters and Their Sharps Rifles*. Lincoln, RI: Andrew Mowbray, 1988.

Tagg, Larry. *The Generals of Gettysburg*. Cambridge, MA: Da Capo Press, 2003.

Tanner, Robert G. *Stonewall in the Valley*. Mechanicsburg, PA: Stackpole Books, 1996.

Thompson, Jerry. *Civil War to the Bloody End: The Life & Times of Major General Samuel P. Heintzelman*. College Station: Texas A&M University Press, 2006.

Tobie, Edward P. *History of the First Maine Cavalry, 1861–1865*. Boston: Emery & Hughes, 1887.

Trulock, Alice. *In the Hands of Providence: Joshua Chamberlain and the American Civil War*. Chapel Hill: University of North Carolina Press, 1992.

United States War Department. *The War of the Rebellion: A Compilation of the Official Records of the Union and Confederate Armies*. Washington, DC: Government Printing Office, 1880–1901.

Valuska, David L., and Christian B. Keller. *Damn Dutch: Pennsylvania Germans at Gettysburg*. Mechanicsburg, PA: Stackpole Books, 2004.

Verrill, Charles W. "The Seventeenth Maine at Gettysburg and in the Wilderness." In *War Papers Read Before the Commandery of the State of Maine, Military Order of the Loyal Legion of the United States*, edited by the Military Order of the Loyal Legion of the United States, 1:260–82. Portland, ME: Lefavor-Tower Company, 1915.

Vickery, James B. "Walter G. Morrill: The Fighting Colonel of the Twentieth Maine." In *A Handful of Spice: A Miscellany of Maine Literature and History*, edited by Richard S. Sprague, 127–51. Orono: University of Maine Press, 1968.

Wainwright, Charles S. *Diary of Battle: The Personal Journals of Colonel Charles S. Wainwright*. Edited by Allan Nevins. New York: Harcourt, Brace and World, 1962.

Walker, Elijah. *The Old Soldier: History of the Fourth Maine Regiment in the Civil War*. Articles extracted from the *Rockland Tribune*, 1893.

Wallace, Willard M. *Soul of the Lion: A Biography of General Joshua L. Chamberlain*. Gettysburg, PA: Stan Clark Military Books, 1991.

Warner, Ezra J. *Generals in Blue: Lives of the Union Commanders*. Baton Rouge: Louisiana State University Press, 2006.

Weld, Steven. *War Diary and Letters of Stephen M. Weld*. Cambridge, MA: Riverside Press, 1912.

Wheeler, William. *In Memoriam: Letters of William Wheeler of the Class of 1855, Y. C.* Cambridge, MA: Privately printed by H. O. Houghton and Co., 1875.

Whitman, George W. *Civil War Memories of George W. Whitman*. Edited by Guy Campbell. Norway, ME: Norway Historical Society, 1999.

Whitman, William E. S., and Charles H. True. *Maine in the War for the Union: A History of the Part Borne by Maine Troops in the Suppression of the American Rebellion*. Lewiston, ME: Nelson Dingley Jr. & Co., 1865.

Whittier, Edward N. "The Left Attack (Ewell's) at Gettysburg." In *Civil War Papers Read Before the Commandery of the State of Massachusetts*, edited by the Military Order of the Loyal Legion of the United States, 1:75–108. Boston: Commander of the State of Massachusetts, 1900.

Wiggin, Francis. "Sixteenth Maine Regiment at Gettysburg." In *War Papers Read Before the Commandery of the State of Maine, Military Order of the Loyal Legion of the United States*, edited by the Military Order of the Loyal Legion of the United States, 4:150–70. Portland, Maine: Lefavor-Tower Company, 1915.

Williams, Charles E. *The Life of Abner Coburn*. Bangor, ME: Thomas W. Burr, 1885.

Wittenberg, Eric J. *The Union Cavalry Comes of Age: Hartwood Church to Brandy Station, 1863*. Washington, DC: Brassy's, 2003.

Index